To Des/Stella

Frank Aiken

GW00507519

FRANK AIKEN

In memory of

John William Evans
'Pamp'
(1925-2013)

&

Eamonn Kelly
A loving brother, father and son
(1964-2013)

FRANK AIKEN

NATIONALIST AND INTERNATIONALIST

Editors

Bryce Evans
and
Stephen Kelly

IRISH ACADEMIC PRESS

First published in 2014 by Irish Academic Press

8 Chapel Lane
Sallins
Co. Kildare, Ireland

www.iap.ie

This edition © 2014 Irish Academic Press
Chapters © 2014 Individual Contributors

British Library Cataloguing in Publication Data
An entry can be found on request

ISBN: 978-07165-3239-2 (paper)
ISBN: 978-07165-3238-5 (cloth)
ISBN: 978-07165-3241-5 (pdf)
ISBN: 978-07165-3256-9 (epub)
ISBN: 978-07165-3257-6 (mobi)

Library of Congress Cataloging in Publication Data
An entry can be found on request

Printed in Ireland by
SPRINT-print Ltd

All rights reserved. Without limiting the rights under copyright reserved
alone, no part of this publication may be reproduced, stored in or
introduced into a retrieval system, or transmitted, in any form or by any
means (electronic, mechanical, photocopying, recording or otherwise)
without the prior written permission of both the copyright owner and
the above publisher of this book.

Table of Contents

Acknowledgements

The authors gratefully acknowledge the assistance of the following institutions and individuals:

The Liverpool Hope University Research Funding Committee, in particular the Reverend Professor Kenneth Newport, for financing the Frank Aiken symposium (March 2013), the book's images, and the proofreading and indexing expenses.

Dr Michael Kennedy and Professor Rory Miller, whose original idea this was. In particular, thank you to Michael Kennedy for his support, advice and guidance every step of the way. Thanks also to Frank Aiken Jnr, for his encouragement, invaluable insights and friendship, all those who participated in the Frank Aiken symposium and contributed to this volume either through authorship, interview or informal advice, in particular the Aiken family and Dr Rory O'Hanlon, and to Dr Aoife Breatnach, for the use of her doctoral dissertation on the subject of Aiken's period as Minister for External Affairs.

Thanks also to Professors Nick Rees, Michael Mulqueen and Dr Michael Holmes, Gemma Peers and Sue Harwood, who supported the Aiken symposium and to Eileen O'Neill, for her indexing skills. A special word of thanks to Lisa Hyde of Irish Academic Press for having faith in the project.

Staff at University College Dublin Archives, particularly Mr Séamus Helferty; The National Library of Ireland; The National Archives of Ireland; the National Archives of the United Kingdom; the Public Record Office of Northern Ireland; the Irish Military Archives; the Bodleian Library; The University of Birmingham Archives; Franklin Delano Roosevelt Library; and the Irish Newspaper Archive.

For Marian Carey, Jenny Campbell and members of the Evans and Kelly families, for their love and forbearance.

And finally to our authors – Dr Noel Dorr, Dr Brian Hanley, Lar Joye, Dr Conor Keelan, Dr Michael Kennedy, Dr Robert Lynch, Dr Eoin Magennis, Dr Kate O'Malley, Professor Rory Miller and Dr Helen O'Shea – and the archival institutions who assisted them in their research.

Glossary

AARIR	The American Association for the Recognition of the Irish Republic
AOH	Ancient Order of Hibernians
BO	Bodleian Library, Oxford
CIA	Central Intelligence Agency
COFLA	Cardinal Ó Fiaich Memorial Library and Archive
CJ	Northern Ireland Files
DE	Dáil Éireann, official debates
DFA	Department of Foreign Affairs
DO	Dominions Office
DT	Department of the Taoiseach
ECHR	European Convention on Human Rights
EEC	European Economic Community
EOKA	National Organisation of Cypriot Fighters
FCO	Foreign and Commonwealth Office
FLN	Front de Libération Nationale (Algeria)
GAA	Gaelic Athletic Association
HA	Home Affairs
HO	Home Office
IRA	Irish Republican Army
IRB	Irish Republican Brotherhood
LDF	Local Defence Force (Irish)
LSF	Auxiliary Local Security Force (Irish)
NAI	National Archives of Ireland, Dublin
NATO	North Atlantic Treaty Organisation
NAUK	National Archives of United Kingdom
NLI	National Library of Ireland
NLF	National Liberation Front of Southern Vietnam (Vietcong)
NLS	National Library of Sweden
OAS	Organization of American States
ONUC	Organisation des Nations Unies au Congo

RIC	Royal Irish Constabulary
ROC	Republic of China
RHL	Rhodes House Library, Oxford
PRC	People's Republic of China
PREM	Prime Minister's Office
PRONI	Public Records Office of Northern Ireland
SE	Seanad Éireann, official debates
SHAPE	Supreme Headquarters Allied Powers Europe
UBSC	University of Birmingham Special Collections
UCDA	University College Dublin Archives
UIL	United Irish League
UO	University of Oxford
UN	United Nations
UNA	United Nations Archives
UNRWA	United Nations Relief and Works Agency
WO	War Office

NB. Readers should note that, in general, this study has followed the below rules for capital letters and punctuations. The use of a capital U for Unionists or Unionism denotes organised unionism, i.e. the Ulster Unionist Party; the use of lower case, unionist opinion, etc., refers to those citizens of Northern Ireland who wished to maintain the Union between Great Britain and Northern Ireland. Likewise, a capital N for Nationalists refers to organised nationalism, i.e. the Nationalists Party in Northern Ireland; the use of lower case, nationalist opinion, etc., refers to the nationalist population of Northern Ireland who opposed the partition of Ireland. The use of upper case is used to refer to political/ government positions associated with politicians and civil servants, i.e. the use of upper case is used when referring to 'Taoiseach' and 'Prime Minister'. The use of capitals is also employed to refer to government departments, i.e. 'the Department of the Taoiseach' and 'the Commonwealth and Relations Office'.

List of Contributors

Noel Dorr is a retired Irish diplomat. He served as Ambassador to the UN in New York, Ambassador in London and Secretary General of the Department of Foreign Affairs. He is a Member of the Royal Irish Academy (MRIA). He is the author of two books: *Ireland at the United Nations: Memories of the Early Years* (Institute of Public Administration, Dublin 2010) and *A Small State at the Top Table: Memories of Ireland on the UN Security Council, 1981–82* (IPA, Dublin 2011).

Bryce Evans is Senior Lecturer in History at Liverpool Hope University. A graduate of the University of Warwick (with first-class honours) and University College Dublin (where he was awarded his doctorate), he has taught at Liverpool Hope since 2011. He has published widely on modern Irish economic and political history, including the books *Seán Lemass: Democratic Dictator* (Collins, 2011) and *Ireland during the Second World War: Farewell to Plato's Cave* (Manchester University Press, 2014).

Brian Hanley has lectured in modern Irish history at various academic institutions, including University College Dublin, St Patrick's College Drumcondra, Liverpool University, NUI Maynooth and Queens University Belfast. He is the author of a wealth of articles in both scholarly journals and popular publications. His books include *The IRA 1926–1936* (Four Courts, 2002) and *The IRA: A Documentary History, 1919–2005* (Gill and MacMillan, 2010).

Lar Joye is curator of Military History at the National Museum of Ireland and curator of the award-winning *Soldiers & Chiefs* Exhibition at Collins Barracks and the *History of Ireland in 100 objects* and *1913 Lockout* Exhibitions. He is a graduate of UCD with an MA in Twentieth-Century Irish History, the University of Leicester, where he obtained an MA in Museum Studies, and the Museum Leadership Course at the Getty Leadership Institute at Claremont Graduate University, California.

Conor Keelan holds a Ph.D in Economics from Trinity College Dublin. He has published several journal articles concerning his main research interest: Consumer Demand Analysis. He holds a personal interest in the history of the Fianna Fáil party, having been elected to local politics in 2009, when he succeeded his father Séamus as Fianna Fáil's representative in Dundalk. The third generation of his family to serve on Dundalk Town Council, he was elected chairman of that body in 2010.

Stephen Kelly is a Lecturer in Modern History at Liverpool Hope University. He was awarded his Ph.D from University College Dublin. He has published extensively on modern Irish history and the Blessed John Henry Newman. His most recent publications include the critically acclaimed *Fianna Fáil, Partition and Northern Ireland, 1926–1971* (Irish Academic Press, 2013) and *A Conservative at Heart? The Political and Social Thought of John Henry Newman* (Columba Press, 2012).

Michael Kennedy is the Executive Editor of the Royal Irish Academy's *Documents on Irish Foreign Policy* series, volume IX of which will be published in 2014. For over twenty years he has published on Ireland's military history, international relations and diplomacy, most recently *The Irish Defence Forces: 1940–1949* (with Comdt. (Ret.) Victor Laing (Irish Manuscripts Commission, 2011) and has recently completed a history of the Irish Defence Forces' service in Congo in the early 1960s.

Robert Lynch graduated from the University of Stirling, where he later completed a Ph.D looking at the role of the IRA in opposing the establishment of Northern Ireland, 1920–1922. He has held research fellowships at Trinity College Dublin (IRCHSS), Hertford College Oxford, the Institute of Irish Studies, Queens University Belfast, and Edinburgh University. He is the author of several journal articles and the book *The Northern IRA and the Early Years of Partition* (Irish Academic Press, 2006).

Eoin Magennis works in the area of cross-border business and economic research. He is editor of the journal *Seanchas Ard Mhacha*, and is writing the County Armagh volume in the series *The Irish Revolution, 1912–23*, under the editorship of Mary Ann Lyons and Daithí Ó Corráin. He has written and edited over thirty books, articles and chapters on various eighteenth-century Irish political, social and economic topics, as well as on aspects of cross-border cooperation on the island of Ireland.

Rory Miller is currently a Professor in the Middle East & Mediterranean Studies Programme (MEMS) at King's College London. He is the author or editor of eight books, including *Ireland and the Middle East: Trade, Society and Peace* (Irish Academic Press, 2008) and, most recently, *Britain, Palestine and Empire: The Mandate Years* (Ashgate, 2010) and *Inglorious Disarray: Europe, Israel and the Palestinians since 1967* (Hurst, 2011). Apart from scholarly works he has published extensively in policy publications and the international media, and is co-editor of the Palgrave Macmillan book series on the Political Economy of the Middle East.

Kate O'Malley is the Assistant Editor of the Royal Irish Academy's Documents on Irish Foreign Policy series. She is a graduate and Research Associate of the Centre for Contemporary Irish History, Trinity College, Dublin. She is the author of *Ireland, India and Empire: Indo-Irish Radical Connections, 1919–64* (Manchester University Press, 2008) and has written extensively on Indo-Irish relations. Her research interests include Irish diplomatic and political history, twentieth century Indian history, British imperial and Commonwealth history, decolonisation as well as intelligence and transnational history.

Helen O'Shea was awarded her Ph.D in history from the University of Edinburgh in 2010. Her research interests focus on comparative decolonisation, the British colonial legal service and modern Irish history in transnational and comparative contexts. Geographical areas of particular interest include Kenya, Malaya, Cyprus, Algeria and Ireland. She is author of the forthcoming *Ireland and the End of the British Empire: The Republic and Its Role in the Cyprus Emergency* (I.B.Tauris, 2014).

List of Plates

1. Aiken and his mother, in a Keogh Brothers portrait, 1901.

2. Aiken with a donkey foal on his shoulders, Inishere, Aran Islands, late 1920s.

3. Aiken with cigarette in mouth, beside windmill, c. 1937.

4. Air Corps shot of the Aiken home, Sandyford, Dublin, 1932.

5. Aiken and Maud outside the National Library of Ireland, Dublin, c. 1932.

6. Aiken and Maud posing with bows and arrows, c.1932.

7. Aiken, the family, and their dog on a child's scooter, c. 1939.

8. Aiken, dozing off while reading, c.1940.

9. Frank and Maud on their wedding day, October 1934.

10. Aiken on the hustings, Dundalk, c. June 1943.

11. Aiken at a potato alcohol factory in Cooley, Co Louth, c. 1946.

12. Aiken and Éamon de Valera beside a concrete hut, c.1944.

13. Group portrait of Éamon de Valera and Frank Aiken, wearing garlands, standing with Martin Higgins by their aeroplane at John Rogers Airport, Honolulu, 25 April 1948.

14. Frank Aiken at Dublin airport before leaving to go to the UN General Assembly in New York, pictured with DFA officials Conor Cruise O'Brien, Counsellor, Political Section, Con Cremin, Secretary, Hugh McCann, Assistant Secretary, 1958.

15. Signing the nuclear non-proliferation treaty in Moscow, 1 July 1968.

16. Aiken, George Colley and Con Cremin at the UN, 1967.

17. Aiken looks on at Winston Churchill and Éamon de Valera, Downing Street, c.1955.

18. Aiken, Seán Lemass and John Foster Dulles, US Secretary of State, at the Lincoln Monument, Washington DC, c.1962.

Preface

FRANK AIKEN JNR

This is a story that has been waiting a long time to be told. Perhaps it is only now, without fear of inciting young men to violence, that the long boy-to-man chronicle of a South Armagh native, Frank Aiken, can be outlined. His is not the only story from among those young, nationally-minded Irish men and women, but his 'extraordinary journey' – in Harold O'Sullivan's memorable phrase[1] – is now beginning to be written.

My father, Frank Aiken, was born the youngest of seven on 13 February 1898. He lost his father when he was two years old and was orphaned at fifteen. The eldest, Jimmy (b.1884), became a doctor and left County Armagh while his brother was very young. Only three of his five sisters, May, Madge and Nano, survived to adulthood. By 1911, at thirteen years old, he ran the family farm; at sixteen joined the Irish Volunteers; and soon became secretary of the Bessbrook flax-milling cooperative. His nephew, Feidhlimidh Magennis, his nearest sister Nano's son, reminded us regularly of his school nickname – 'corrlá' or 'odd day'. We can understand why.

It seems timely that the instigators of and the contributors to this book have seen his wide-ranging political career to be of interest. It was of course extraordinary (in any period) that in 1925, at twenty-seven years old, Frank Aiken had already been a schoolboy, a farmer, an Irish Volunteer, a soldier, fought two wars, had been twice jailed, had been to America and had been, in 1923, elected to Dáil Éireann. Not only had he been Chief of Staff of the IRA, but he also signed the ceasefire order that brought the Irish Civil War to an end. And yet his career was only just about to start. He was, to quote Liam C. Skinner, something of a 'politician by accident'.[2]

***

It is only now, in the third generation since the many dreadful events of the 1920s, that a new curiosity has arisen at the reticence (necessarily accepted by his nearest family) of my father's generation. There are similar examples of this reticence, the most recent described by Kieran Glennon in his book on his grandfather, Tom Glennon of the Third Northern Division IRA.[3] Other stories are now emerging, many describing sadness and loss, not only for Frank Aiken and his family. The Aiken home was burned down, along with other houses in Camlough, in retaliation for an attack on the local Royal Irish Constabulary barracks in December 1920. His closest sister, Nano, later spent twenty-one months in Armagh jail, interned without charge.

Frank Aiken's Fourth Northern Division of the IRA was the last, in August 1922, to 'take sides' in the Civil War and become 'Irregulars'. He signed the ceasefire order to end the Irish Civil War on 23 May 1923 at the age of twenty-five. My father's words to us as children that 'dreadful things happen in war and worse in Civil War' have never lost their meaning. He encouraged us to look forward in the interests of the country, and not backwards – except to study history and learn from mistakes rather than repeating them. My brother Loclann and I wish that our sister Aedamar (24/07/38 to 13/02/91) were here to help write this preface, as she was the eldest and the intellectual leader of us children.

The reticence can also be seen in a story from one morning in June 1969, when my father's secretary of long standing, Roisín Ennis, entered his office in the Department of External Affairs. He was about to depart as minister, having occupied the post since 1957. It was unusually warm in the room for that time of day. 'Roisín, I had a great bonfire this morning', was my father's remark. She saw ashes in the open fire-grate, where papers had been burnt. After his death, later in 1983, Máire O'Kelly, Éamon de Valera's long-time secretary, rang to enquire about a white canvas bag of papers. I remembered the bag. When I saw it, it was empty. It is possible that some of Éamon de Valera's Civil War papers were also burned.

My father's resistance to writing memoirs was based on his view that to do so 'would only bring the whole thing up again, and it would be my views against those of others'. He had had enough of conflict. He had little regard for politicians who 'spent half the day working and the other half making notes for their book'. Was he a historian's worst nightmare? In retirement he would not engage with a journalist to tell his side of the events of those early times. The later, ministerial events were already well recorded. My father would regularly talk about these and any other subject at length and with enthusiasm. There was frequently humour attached to descriptions of his endeavours and his patents. It was said that he tried to design a gun that would shoot around corners. He clearly had strong survival instincts for his men and himself. He also had a sense of humour and he laughed a lot.

Subsequent to his death in May 1983, Aedamar, Loclann and I opened his two private filing cabinets. These cabinets had returned to Sandyford during the inter-party governments of 1948 to 1951, and 1954 to 1957, returning finally in 1969, at the end of a thirty-one-year ministerial career. His files remained undisturbed and in order until collected by UCD Archives, where they remain on loan. Interestingly, in one of the filing cabinets there were thirteen pistols, with ammunition (now housed in the Aiken Barracks, Dundalk). They were to have armed the Cabinet (and Vivion de Valera) as Fianna Fáil took office on 9 March 1932. We, his children, were unaware of his arranging of this 'arming' event, and were surprised to see the guns and boxes of ammunition, some of which were unopened.

Our dad was a man who hated violence, having experienced it and practised it. He would speak little of either. He never engendered feelings of anger in us against his opponents of the past. We were aware of some personal misgivings about a few by listening to conversations with other colleagues and friends, such as Paddy Smith, Malachy Quinn, Todd Andrews and Aodhagan O'Rahilly, who may have shared a whiskey with him on occasion. We had never heard of the 'Altnaveigh Massacre' by the Fourth Northern IRA until Toby Harnden's book was published in 2000.[4] These views were neither our business, nor our burdens. That said, he had a fascination with history, read avidly and encouraged our reading.

**

After 1923, my father found that he could not return safely to his native County Armagh. His 'bolthole' in Dublin was Dr James Ryan's house in Greystones, Co Wicklow, where he first met the lively musician Maud Davin. They were each too busy with their very different careers to then form any sort of relationship, but they each remembered where they first met. The Aikens sold the Carrickbracken farm and other properties in Camlough. From his share, Frank purchased land in Sandyford, County Dublin, and built a wooden house – like he had seen in the USA – with the lofted garage first, so he could put the tent away and have somewhere drier for Peter Boyle and other helpers to stay. He resumed farming in the later 1920s.

Maud Davin and he married in October 1934, each aged thirty-six. She had to give up her job as the first female Principal of the Dublin Municipal School of Music. From then, apart from the 'Affairs of State', his interests were his family, his farming projects (Paddy Smith bought and sold his cattle) and his inventions. The inventions were many and varied. There was always one under consideration – and they are another, longer, story.

***

Others will comment on aspects of Frank Aiken's political life. However, we believe that for him some highlights were the professionalism of the army in 1932 when becoming 'subject' to previous opponents in the Civil War; the recovery of the ports in the aftermath of the Anglo-Irish Agreement of 1938; the development of the bogs; the wider use of the Irish language; and the entire period at the United Nations from 1957 to 1969, even with its disappointments.

His own personal highlight seems to have been making the first signature on the Non-Proliferation of Nuclear Arms Treaty in Moscow in 1968, perhaps because of its global importance. His pride in this was something he explained to Nollaig McCarthy in a quite rare radio interview. Conor Cruise O'Brien somewhere describes it as his 'monument', one that can, in political terms, be viewed simultaneously from east and west. It makes the world a smaller place.

Political disappointments (after the hated Civil War) included the misunderstanding – or non-acceptance – of Irish neutrality during the Second World War and the unprofessional behaviour of the US Minister to Ireland, David Gray.[5] Interestingly, in 1941 my father tolerated being shown around American military and other installations while Roosevelt made up his mind about meeting him. 'The Americans', my father recounted with us, 'can be very polite while their President is being rude'. The assassination of American President John F. Kennedy in 1963 shocked and saddened my father greatly. There is a really friendly and appreciative letter from Jackie Kennedy in his papers.

The annexation of Tibet by China was the major disappointment of his tenure in External Affairs. He believed that Tibet had come to China like a forgotten trunk in the attic of a house sale, and that it was never Chinese. He admired the organisational skills and focus of Genghis Khan without expressing any admiration of that Khan's operational methods. The management of the vast territories creating the Mongolian Khanate also fascinated him. Successions of the Mongolian dynasties through Kublai Khan, Genghis's grandson, controlled most of China by the fourteenth century and extended the Khan dynasty to Tibet. On the withering of the Khan dynasty, the injustice of the Chinese annexing an area called Tibet in 1957 was clear to him. In my father's mind, Tibet was always autonomous from China and the many Chinese dynasties.

Censorship during the Second World War was bitterly opposed by those with pens and typewriters, maybe understandably so, as their livelihoods were made more difficult. Editors were thus compromised in having to accept the national view as seen by the elected government. A media prejudice seems to have then developed against my father for his interpretations of censorship and his reticence, which never really went away. We remember, in particular, his disdain for the attitude of Mr R.M. Smyllie, long-time editor of *The Irish Times*.

***

Having accepted in February 1973 his fifteenth nomination to represent County Louth in the Dáil, Frank Aiken challenged Fianna Fáil leader Jack Lynch to resist the ratification of election candidates whom he deemed unsuitable to represent the party. My father was particularly perturbed by Lynch's decision to ratify Charles J. Haughey (the other was Joseph Lenehan of Mayo). He informed Lynch that if Haughey were ratified he would refuse to contest the 1973 general election, and publicise his reasons for doing so. Lynch panicked, and asked several senior Fianna Fáil members to ask my father to change his mind. He refused to budge. President de Valera also tried to persuade his old colleague and friend, whom he wished to be the next president, to reconsider. Consequently, after much arm-twisting, my father decided not to make public his dissatisfaction concerning Haughey's ratification. Instead, in the unconvincing words of Jack Lynch, my father's retirement from active politics was attributed to 'health grounds'. How mistaken the Fianna Fáil Party was. In our view, Mr Lynch was weak, as he had been in 1970 on the arms importation issue, of which there were long-term and national-level consequences. In the aftermath of the debacle my father never participated again in the Fianna Fáil organisation, of which he was a founder.

On his death, with Garret FitzGerald as Taoiseach and a State funeral already advised, our sister Aedamar quickly requested George Colley to deliver a graveside oration in Camlough – to which he graciously agreed. Until that time, as was the tradition within Fianna Fáil, the serving party leader would customarily deliver the graveside eulogy. My family, however, was resolute that Charles J. Haughey should be refused this honour. Mr Haughey, in retribution, behaved disgracefully at the removal of my father's remains from the mortuary at St Vincent's Hospital, indirectly seeking a 'historic photo' (in an *Irish Independent* photographer's phrase) with a family member standing beside the open coffin. Mr Haughey said in the mortuary to that member that there had been 'a misunderstanding'. In this, he was correct.

***

Finally, we are glad that a gap in the history of the formation of the Irish state, the northern perspective, is also filled out in this book. The misunderstandings of events surrounding the 'Northern Rising', as explained in RTÉ's 2006 documentary, *Frank Aiken: Gunman and Statesman*, saddened us Aikens at the time. We were happy to read in Kieran Glennon's account that Patrick Casey's statement on those events, as O/C of the Newry Brigade, was ill-informed.[6] The ill-considered 'Northern Rising' was only partly called off by an apparently dysfunctional GHQ team of Michael Collins, Richard Mulcahy and Eoin O'Duffy on 19 May 1922. No wonder Frank Aiken did not wish to revisit, through his papers, these events and the terrible consequences for their colleagues of the Second and Third Northern Divisions in this tragic adventure. Through the event of the 'Northern Rising' my father may have developed diminished respect for Collins, Mulcahy and O'Duffy. There may have been other reasons. He told me that he thought Collins might not have made a good politician, but he had admired him.

Lastly, the Aiken family would like to thank Doctors Bryce Evans and Stephen Kelly of Liverpool Hope University, the several contributors and Lisa Hyde of Irish Academic Press for undertaking to assemble and publish this collection of insights into aspects of Frank Aiken's life.

Frank Aiken Jnr
November 2013

Notes

1   Recorded in *Frank Aiken: From Gunman to Statesman* (Mint Productions Hidden History documentary for RTÉ Television, 2006).
2   Liam C. Skinner, *Politicians by Accident* (Dublin: Metropolitan, 1946).
3   Kieran Glennon, *From Pogrom to Civil War: Tom Glennon and the Belfast IRA* (Dublin: Mercier Press, 2013).
4   Toby Harnden, *Bandit Country: The IRA and South Armagh* (London: Hodder, 2000).
5   This is best described in Aengus Nolan, *Joseph Walshe: Irish Foreign Policy, 1922–1946* (Dublin: Mercier Press, 2008), chapters 5–7.
6   Glennon, *From Pogrom to Civil War*, 115 to 127.

Introduction

Frank Aiken: Nationalist

BRYCE EVANS

Man of Property

According to a recently published global history of guerrilla warfare, there have been a total of 443 uprisings since the outbreak of the American Revolution in the late eighteenth century. Of these, just 25 per cent have been successful.[1] While we might quibble over the author's mathematics, one point remains clear: wars of the weak most often end in failure. For Irish nationalists of Aiken's generation, subsequently to become the heroes of the independence struggle, the opening odds were overwhelmingly against a successful revolution.[2]

It is therefore remarkable that Frank Aiken (1898–1983), who occupied a senior role in the national uprising, not only survived it but, after opposing the newly independent state, went on to enjoy a lengthy career as part of its executive. As a revolutionary, Aiken played an active political role in major events spanning from Éamon de Valera's by-election victory in Clare in 1917 to the ceasefire of the Irish Civil War, which he ordered in May 1923. Until now, though, Aiken was the most significant politician of the Irish revolutionary generation not to have a biography devoted to him.[3]

He thus remains something of a shadowy figure and, in certain circles, a deeply unpopular one. Clearly, in post-Peace Process Ireland, Frank Aiken's reputation remains controversial. Damagingly, his impressive fighting record is tainted by accusations of sectarian murder. In Irish State broadcaster RTÉ's 2006 'Hidden History' documentary *Frank Aiken: Gunman and Statesman*, killings in a small Presbyterian community in Altnaveigh, a village which straddles counties Down and Armagh, featured most prominently.[4] One version of the documentary was later posted online with Aiken contemptuously dubbed the 'Butcher of Altnaveigh'.[5]

But the poverty of Aiken's reputation is also a consequence of trends in Irish history-writing, which, for a generation or so, pedalled a tasty but

3

simplistic dichotomy whereby figures associated with modern, liberal, free trade Ireland were lauded as progressive; figures associated with rustic, backward, Gaelic Ireland dismissed as twee.[6] Viewed as an acolyte of de Valera, Aiken was invariably placed in the latter category. Many of these sideswipes were composed before the Aiken papers were opened at University College Dublin Archives at the turn of the century and the Irish Military Service Pensions and Bureau of Military History records were made public. Such accounts were therefore published before a comprehensive picture of the man based on full documentary evidence emerged.

The very fact that Aiken was born and brought up in what would become Northern Ireland provides the outline sketch for the anti-partitionist dinosaur of caricature. He suffered the destruction of his family home by Crown forces in 1920 and, finding himself practically exiled within his own country, remained deeply attached to his Ulster heritage. Aiken's northern identity was not the only marker of difference from the majority of his political colleagues. In contrast to many of the Irish revolutionary generation, Aiken's upbringing was a comfortable one. Born in 1898, he came from a sturdy Catholic nationalist farming family in County Armagh, one of the seven children of James and Mary Aiken, five of whom survived into adulthood.[7] In the 1911 census of Ireland, his mother Mary's name appears as a property owner on over twenty properties in the area.[8] His father James was a strong farmer, himself a substantial property owner, and involved in local government.

Aiken, then, was a product of the politically respectable agrarian middle class of late-Victorian Ireland. This heritage jarred with that of his Dublin-born contemporary and self-styled 'man of no property' Todd Andrews, who claimed that Aiken's 'easy' farming background ensured that he was out of touch with the common man's daily grind.[9] One notable corollary of Aiken's farm upbringing was his mature agro-scientific understanding, something later demonstrated in his passionate advocacy of turf as a means of meeting the fuel demands of the young state. This talent would find its outlet in the inventive, and occasionally zany, scientific inventions of his imagination, the workings of which he would sketch out on paper and, when in power, occasionally present to the Cabinet.

In popular memory, Aiken may be firmly associated with the Irish Ireland of de Valera, yet in his early life there are to be found glimpses of a figure distinct from many of his republican comrades. This son of the big farm failed to fulfil some central cultural nationalist staples: the family was of Scottish Protestant planter extraction, his Gaelic footballing skills were 'terrible', his hurling 'worse', and his Irish – notwithstanding his dedication to the language – never strong.[10]

This was despite his immersion in Sinn Féin politics and the honing of his anti-imperialist political instincts while still a precocious teenager.

All the King's Horses

Aiken may have been a poor practitioner when it came to Gaelic games, but, tellingly, he was a keen boxer. His early life is explored in more detail in Eoin Magennis's chapter, but it is clear that from a young age he was physically imposing. Having suffered the early loss of his father, by his adolescent years he had already established himself as a leader of men, and would oversee the drilling of Irish Volunteers on property owned by his parents. Born in the centenary year of the 1798 rebellion, Aiken, like other members of his generation, carried the inheritance of Patrick Pearse's 1916 rally to arms upon his broad shoulders. Although he did not take part in the 1916 Easter Rising, being 'completely out of touch' with the men who organised the event, he reportedly purchased military equipment 'so as to be ready to join the fight if required'.[11]

In the aftermath of the Rising, the young Aiken changed the 'patron saint' of his Sinn Féin club in Camlough from Eoin MacNeill, the Volunteer leader who had issued the countermand, to that of hunger-striker Thomas Ashe, who was martyred in 1917. He also, provocatively, hoisted the tricolour opposite the Royal Irish Constabulary (RIC) barracks in the town.[12] These actions were telling of the shift in the broader national mood towards radicalism. Aiken's first significant political action came soon afterwards, with his employment as an outrider for Kerry republican Austin Stack during the 1917 Clare by-election. During his time in Clare he stayed with de Valera, beginning a lifelong friendship between the two men – a relationship that has been described as 'almost symbiotic'.[13] The young Aiken subsequently threw himself into nationalist politics, and was elected secretary of the South Armagh Sinn Féin organisation later that year.[14] But democratic politics were soon overtaken by the welter of revolutionary violence spreading across Ireland in 1918–1919. In 1918, Aiken was arrested for illegal drilling and sentenced to a month's imprisonment in Belfast. His comrades protested against the conviction by smashing up the courthouse in Newry after his trial.[15]

It was not long before Aiken was organising daring, if initially unsuccessful, Irish Republican Army (IRA) raids in South Armagh and South Down. A raid on Ballyedmond Castle in May 1919 was described by his battalion adjutant John McCoy as 'a bit of a fiasco'. McCoy similarly described how the attempted capture of the police barracks in Newtownhamilton in February 1920 failed after Aiken (disguised as a British Army officer) was refused admission after attempting to call the policemen's bluff by politely knocking on the door. A repeat raid on

Newtownhamilton in May 1920 faltered at first after Aiken, who was supposed to signal the attack by blowing a whistle, lost it, and instead had to try to whistle with his fingers.[16]

With experience, his command record soon improved. He supervised the destruction of Newry customs house in April 1920, and in December 1920 he commanded a model raid on the police station in his home town. He had by this point already embarked on a romantic yet gruelling life on the run at the head of a flying column, moving from safe house to safe house, carrying out sporadic raids for arms, and entirely reliant on the generosity of the local population. In early 1921 he led numerous successful ambushes including those at Carrickbracken and Cregganduff, County Armagh.[17]

By March 1921, Aiken, every inch the IRA 'big man', had risen to commandant of the IRA's Fourth Northern Division.[18] A few months later, his reputation was bolstered by his responsibility for a brutally efficient piece of derring-do: the derailment of the train carrying the cavalry regiment that had escorted King George V at the opening of the Northern Ireland parliament in June 1921. Aiken prepared meticulously for this outrage, overseeing the laying of mines beside the line and personally removing bolts from the track, boiling, greasing, and then replacing them.[19] The ambush was laid at a steep incline in the vicinity of Ayallogue Bridge, not far from Adavoyle train station, County Armagh, and nearby telegraph wires were cut.[20] The resulting carnage resembled a scene from a childhood war game: the train careered off the tracks, horses and soldiers flung out of the carriages and scattered wantonly around. The carriages were, according to reports, 'reduced almost to matchwood', their contents 'smashed to atoms'. An estimated forty horses, two British soldiers and a railway lineman were killed. As usual, there was a civilian cost as well: under duress, dozens of local men were ordered to clean up the mess and bury the horses.[21]

By the Anglo-Irish truce of July 1921, the national struggle in Aiken's area of operations had already descended into a series of tit-for-tat killings. He remained a full-time IRA officer and political activist during the cessation in hostilities. In September 1921, he put his name to a petition against the partition of the country submitted to de Valera. It described his native Armagh as a historically integral part of Ireland; 'the burial place of Brian Boru', 'the home of Cúchullain', 'the ecclesiastical capital of the motherland' as well as being 'preponderatingly [sic] Nationalist' in its political demographics.[22] For Aiken, who later subscribed to the scholarly journal *Irish Historical Studies*,[23] the partition of Ireland would leave a deep historical scar. The Anglo-Irish Treaty, which delivered this, 'was wrong', Aiken claimed, 'and if it were allowed to come into operation it would be an obstacle instead of an aid to independence'. He opposed the Treaty not merely because of partition, but because he distrusted 'the type of men who would work it'.[24]

And yet he showed restraint after the Irish republican parliament Dáil Éireann endorsed the Anglo-Irish Treaty, and with it partition and allegiance to the British monarch, in January 1922. With conflict looming over the terms of the Treaty, Aiken assumed a neutrality he would later apply to the highest reaches of foreign policy. In a list drawn up in March 1922, Aiken was the only senior IRA officer described as 'non-partisan'.[25] His earnest efforts to avert civil war were reflected in his role in the negotiation of the ill-fated electoral pact between chairman of the provisional government of the Free State, Michael Collins, and Aiken's political guru, de Valera, in May 1922. Aiken was primarily opposed to what he perceived to be a new sectarian entity, Northern Ireland, and was determined to avoid fratricidal war amongst nationalists opposing it. A series of attacks against the northern state were covertly sanctioned by Collins, and action took place in several counties. Aiken's division, however, and somewhat oddly, took no major part in this offensive.

'A child could see the justice of our cause', Aiken said of the War of Independence, 'and England was left without the slightest excuse for her oppression'.[26] But opposing the Saxon foe was one thing, the emerging internecine strife quite another, and Aiken's name would soon become tainted by the actions of his IRA Fourth Northern Division. Responding to the gang rape of a heavily pregnant local Catholic woman by a group of Ulster Special Constables, Aiken's men carried out a notorious reprisal massacre in the town of Altnaveigh, which lies on the Down/Armagh border, on 17 June 1922. Several innocent members of a small Presbyterian community were shot dead in cold blood. In Ulster unionist historical memory, 'the Butcher of Altnaveigh' was born. Notably, the action at Altnaveigh was omitted from the division's roll of engagements – a roll of honour of sorts – later submitted as evidence to the Military Service Pensions Board established by the Irish Free State to compensate veterans.[27]

Meanwhile, Aiken was struggling to maintain his neutrality in the civil conflict. It is clear that he was trying to remain wedded to an uncomfortable middle ground between Free State Minister for Defence Richard Mulcahy and IRA Commandants Liam Lynch and Rory O'Connor.[28] He attempted to stall the slide towards war by urging republican colleagues to hold tight, hoping that a more thoroughgoing republicanism would emerge from the redrafting of the Free State constitution.[29] But his eventual refusal to endorse the provisional government in Dublin led to his arrest and imprisonment in Dundalk jail in July 1922, while he was still attempting to maintain unity against 'the second plantation of Ulster by England'.[30] Aiken had been in Dublin for talks with Richard Mulcahy and, shortly after returning to Dundalk from this 'peace mission', he and 300 of his men were seized by Free State troops at the barrack headquarters of the Fourth Northern Division.[31] He had refused Mulcahy's demand that his troops respect the authority of the Free State, which involved adhering to the hated oath of allegiance to the British Crown.[32]

The irrepressible Aiken was not in custody for long. After IRA comrades led by acting Divisional Commanding Officer, John McCoy, blew a hole in Dundalk jail wall, he led a mass escape of over 100 prisoners. At a hastily convened meeting on that evening, 27 July 1922, Aiken and his men decided to abandon their previously 'neutral' stance, giving their Free State opponents forty-eight hours' notice that their previous attitude of trusting in God and keeping their powder dry, as Aiken put it, had changed.[33] A fortnight later, he masterminded a meticulously planned midnight raid on the evening of 13 August 1922, when his men recaptured Dundalk and its military barracks.[34] This was, as Aiken would later point out to the Military Pensions Board, the first military action in the Civil War undertaken by the 4th Northern Division.[35] A participant recalled Aiken's bravery in leading the advance on the barracks, firing on Free State troops shielded by a Lancia car.[36] Todd Andrews – a man whose memoirs rarely contain a good word for anyone – called the recapture of Dundalk the most 'spectacularly efficient' operation of the IRA during the entire Civil War.[37]

The famous republican writer Ernie O'Malley met Aiken shortly after this escapade, with the IRA preparing to assault Dundalk once more. 'Aiken puffed slowly at his pipe', wrote O'Malley, 'his quiet brown eyes glanced over operations maps; he held up a finger to emphasise points'. O'Malley noted the devotion of his officers to Aiken, but also the atmosphere of democratic discussion that he fostered. Later, O'Malley was impressed by his brazenness in obtaining food and shelter at a border farmhouse by pretending to be a Free State officer. 'We're Staters', Aiken calmly and duplicitously announced, 'as he tapped the knocker'.[38]

The success of the Dundalk raid notwithstanding, Aiken remained a hunted man. Disaffected by the Civil War, his division did not play a leading role in the conflict, and he declined an invitation to join the IRA executive until de Valera formed a republican government in late 1922. As Robert Lynch notes in his chapter, Aiken and his men were caught in a 'curious limbo' by the Civil War. Whereas previously they could retreat to safety over the border, they now found themselves unwelcome in both states. The authorities in both territories were now conducting a manhunt against Aiken and the members of his dwindling column. Rather hysterical RUC reports claimed that this lonely bogeyman was spotted disguised as a beggar walking the streets of Armagh city and as an old woman at a border crossing.

A Farewell to Arms

In early April 1923, O'Malley complained that he 'had hopes of Aiken's area keeping "the ball rolling" with somewhat more energy'.[39] Later that month, Aiken was elected as successor to Liam Lynch as IRA Chief of Staff by the Army Executive. As Lynch's brother recalled, Aiken had helped to carry the dying IRA leader across the Knockmealdown Mountains in County Tipperary 'under intense fire, until he ordered them to leave him down'.[40] Wearied by war, 'pragmatic and downbeat' as Alvin Jackson puts it, Aiken brought his swashbuckling exploits to an end and secured his place in history when he gave the order 'to dump arms' in May 1923. The warrior had become the peacemaker. It speaks of Aiken's standing as a man of the gun that this order to the IRA to suspend operations was obeyed up and down the country.

Still on the run, Aiken later topped the poll as the Sinn Féin abstentionist candidate in Louth at the general election of August 1923, a seat he held until his retirement from politics fifty years later. As Brian Hanley notes in his chapter, he still maintained a senior role in the IRA: supporting republican hunger strikes, setting about establishing a foreign reserve of IRA volunteers that sought to maintain membership amongst emigrants and, seeing the Free State Army Mutiny of 1924 as a falling out amongst two reactionary camps, counselling against any attempt by the IRA to capitalise upon it. O'Malley wrote to Mollie Childers, the widow of prominent Civil War casualty Erskine Childers, in late 1923, describing Aiken quite simply as 'our best man'. In 1924, he was still to be found in IRA safe houses, dividing his time between reading Aristotle and practising shooting by riddling bath mats with air rifle pellets.[41]

By autumn 1925, however, his fellow high-ranking IRA officers were suspicious that Aiken was contemplating dumping Sinn Féin's policy of abstention from the Irish Free State parliament established under the Treaty. Aiken, of course, eventually endorsed Éamon de Valera's decision to jettison abstentionism and joined his new political party, Fianna Fáil. But it is significant that when the IRA broke with de Valera's new political direction in November 1925, Aiken was re-elected as a member of the Army Executive despite aligning with Dev. His colleague Seán Lemass, then 'Minister for Defence' in de Valera's shadowy republican government, was not. Aiken had proposed bringing the IRA under the civil control of the unpopular Lemass, a suggestion Aiken's fellow Ulsterman Peadar O'Donnell rejected.[42] Yet Aiken was still, it seems, trusted by the IRA Army Council.

As a founding member of the Fianna Fáil party in 1926, Aiken was coming to embrace constitutional politics, even if he was still denouncing Ireland's 'two unlawful governments', and threatening violence 'if a war is forced on us'.[43] A Fianna Fáil government, he promised in June 1926, would 'abolish' the oath of allegiance to the British Crown. 'We are Republicans', he exclaimed, 'our objective is to set up a Republican Government which will control the Country without any interference from England'.[44] In an open letter to the people of Louth during the same period, he urged 'every Irishman, no matter what his past political creed or mistakes may have been, to join Fianna Fáil, and to work openly and energetically to rid our country once and for all of foreign domination …'.[45]

Aiken also used his standing within the IRA to canvass support for de Valera's new party in a trip across the United states in 1926, meeting with former colleagues who had since emigrated. It was said that Aiken never forgot an old republican comrade.[46] But this trip to the USA, like his return journey to America in 1928 alongside Ernie O'Malley, was all about raising funds. Back home, Aiken sincerely believed that a new republican movement could address the question of 'how to clear away the impediments that obstruct the flow of national sentiment and not allow it to be dammed up until it bursts forth in another Easter week'. With a certain scepticism typical of interwar European politics, he was lending his influence to what he and his contemporaries conceived of as a national *movement* rather than a conventional political party. Fianna Fáil would 'use the powers possessed by the Free State so-called parliament', but they would never subscribe to it.[47]

Soon, though, Fianna Fáil was forced to adhere to the Free State constitution. This followed the State's clampdown after the assassination of Vice President of the Executive Council and Minister for Justice and External Affairs, Kevin O'Higgins, by IRA renegades in 1927. Biting the bullet, Aiken, along with fellow party whips Seán Lemass and Gerald Boland, was among the first from the republican party to enter the Dáil and, in so doing, sign the oath of allegiance to King George V.[48] Aiken finally left the IRA that year, but did not shed his recalcitrant attitude. Shortly after Fianna Fáil's entry to the Dáil, Aiken was ordered out of the house by the Speaker. Aiming a cheap shot in populist Catholicism in the direction of the government, he had falsely claimed that Patrick McGilligan, Minister for Industry and Commerce and External Affairs, had refused to send for a priest as his colleague O'Higgins lay dying. 'The statement I made that Mr McGilligan had refused to go for the priest was untrue and I regret very much having made it' read his humble public apology in the next day's newspapers.[49] Situated on his party's 'left wing' by police intelligence reports of the time, Aiken was still secretly, yet unsuccessfully, trying to bring the IRA under Fianna Fáil's aegis.

In 1928, he returned to America to raise funds for the *Irish Press* newspaper. While there, he was impressed by the way of life of the native American warrior and, signalling this affinity, bought himself a set of bow and arrows.[50] Travelling had also aggravated a yearning for the rural life of his native Armagh and, on returning to Dublin, Aiken left his Dublin digs and bought a dairy farm at Sandyford, County Dublin. The move was financed by the sale of several properties belonging to Aiken in counties Down and Armagh.[51] The *Irish Independent* duly composed an eligible bachelor piece, reporting that Aiken, 'the best looking man in the Dail', had 'camped out nearby and directed operations' while the house was being constructed. The house was 'exceedingly up to date, with central heating', but 'the handsome deputy remains an unrepentant bachelor'.[52]

Unbeknownst to journalists, Aiken's time as a bachelor was gradually coming to an end. He was often a guest at the Greystones residence of fellow republican activist Jim Ryan. It was there that Aiken met the music student Maud Davin, his future wife. Maud Aiken is remembered as a wiry, strong little woman, a feminist who, despite the height disparity when alongside her 6'2" husband, 'had the running' of him. The young Maud had missed the revolutionary years in Ireland, studying at the Royal Academy of Music in London between 1917 and 1922.[53] She returned to Dublin in time to see Michael Collins, the most high-profile casualty of the Civil War, lying dead in St Vincent's Hospital.[54]

Maud enjoyed the music and merriment of the arts scene, partying late, playing cards and gambling on horses.[55] In her diary of 1925 she recalled meeting Aiken for the first time. They 'chatted all the time'. On their next meeting, Maud recalled Jim Ryan and Aiken picking her up in Ryan's car. Her friends had just told the effervescent Maud that she was 'hard to live with', and she was so upset that she could not bring herself to practise her beloved violin. Aiken provided a shoulder to cry on, and she described him as 'really nice' with 'charming ways'. Later that year she went to see him sit for his portrait.[56] Maud had other suitors, Aiken was abroad for long periods, and both had their careers and so, unusually for the time, they did not marry until 1934. Aiken proposed to her on a trip to Kindelstown, County Wicklow. Maud subsequently wrote in her diary that she was 'gloriously happy'. After marrying they settled down together at the Three Rock Dairy and had three children: a girl, Aedamar, and two boys, Proinsias and Loclann.

The Reins of Power

When Fianna Fáil entered government in April 1932, de Valera made Aiken Minister of Defence. This was seen by contemporary commentators as a shrewd move on de Valera's behalf, calculated to test the loyalty of the army, while at the same time mollifying radical republicans. Indeed, Aiken's appointment to the defence portfolio, as Lar Joye explains in his chapter, represented a 'vital link between the hard-line republicans' within Fianna Fáil and de Valera.[57]

Famously, Aiken was dispatched to Arbour Hill Prison to hold talks with the IRA leaders still languishing there. The republican prisoners were released the next day. But as Brian Hanley asserts in his chapter, once he had made the break from the IRA, Fianna Fáil was categorically the senior partner in the republican effort for Aiken. Symbolising this fact, in March 1932, newspapers carried photographs of him taking the salute at a march past of the Free State Army in College Green, Dublin.[58] Shortly thereafter, Aiken publicly signalled his recognition of the Irish Defence Forces he had opposed so recently by laying a wreath at the annual Theobald Wolfe Tone commemoration at Bodenstown. To the outrage of former republican comrades, the wreath was laid on behalf of the Free State Army.[59]

His enduring links with the IRA were instrumental in reconciling some former republicans to the Fianna Fáil government, and in 1932 he introduced pensions for former IRA and Cumann na mBan volunteers.[60] The following year, however, his plans for a new army volunteer reserve came up against the opposition of the IRA's Army Council.[61] Clearly, an influential rump of republican opinion remained unreconciled to his political departure. Exacerbating these tensions with former comrades, in 1935 he was involved in a nasty spat with Tom Barry, the War of Independence hero from County Cork whose swashbuckling memoir *Guerrilla Days in Ireland* (1949) would become a classic of its genre. Aiken, taking a dislike to what he saw as Barry's grandstanding, questioned his fighting record in the Civil War. Barry, in turn, accused Aiken of 'malicious innuendo', avoiding 'the scene of all fighting' during the Civil War, and flirting with the Free State.[62] This bitterness would play out again when Aiken, in his ministerial capacity, came to review Barry's application for a military service pension.[63] The republican 'big men' were still scrapping over ownership of the glorious past.

During his early years in government, Aiken offered his unconditional support for de Valera's self-imposed mission to tear apart the 1921 Anglo-Irish Treaty. Privately, Aiken noted that the Fianna Fáil government was determined to dismantle the treaty systematically 'at any cost'.[64] Its first measure focused on the removal of article seventeen of the 1921 constitution, which made the oath of allegiance obligatory on the members entering Dáil Éireann. Coinciding with this new Bill was de Valera's decision to retain the land annuities, hitherto handed over to the British government under consecutive land acts of the late nineteenth and early twentieth century.

While her husband was making bold political steps, Maud proved a strong and supportive partner for Aiken, continuously pushing him to further his political career.[65] His career duly blossomed in the 1930s with successive ministerial appointments. As a Cabinet minister, Aiken supported the expansion of semi-state companies in the 1930s and, using his farming knowledge, enthusiastically championed state-driven turf development, favouring a cooperative system of credit to support such development.[66] Bolstering his 'man of action' image, he became a patron of amateur gliding and amateur boxing. As 'the most enthusiastic of amateur inventors', as a contemporary dubbed him, he devised many schemes of scientific innovation, some hare-brained and some brilliant. His polymathic belief that he could turn his hand to anything was, according to his eldest son, 'infuriating' and 'maddening' at times. He was particularly interested in alternative energy sources, and areas to which Aiken applied his inimitable brand of scientific enquiry and innovation included steam power, wind turbines, seat belts, solar energy and hurricanes.[67]

Applying this hands-on approach to his ministerial responsibilities, for six months in 1936 Aiken was Minister for Lands and Fisheries as well as Minister for Defence. Next to the conservatism of the preceding Cumann na nGaedheal administrations, Aiken and his Fianna Fáil colleagues brought a greater sense of social conscience amid the deprivation of the Great Depression. 'We are outraged by the sight of children with bare feet living in tenements', he once declared.[68] Likewise, he attempted to get left-leaning republicans on side by claiming that alliance with Fianna Fáil was the only way to guarantee social justice for the 'labourers and working farmers'.[69] In the late 1930s, he backed the state's provision of family allowances.[70] As Minister for Defence, Aiken also oversaw many applications for the military service pension. While he contested parts of former British soldier Tom Barry's claim, he overcame substantial political opposition to secure pensions for members of the Connaught Rangers who mutinied as British soldiers in 1920 upon hearing of atrocities in Ireland.[71]

Our subject retained a revolutionary dislike and distrust of Westminster, although family members insist that it was anti-establishmentarianism, rather than Anglophobia, which underlay such actions as the infamous snubbing of the Westminster-appointed Governor-General James McNeill at the French legation in Dublin in 1932.[72] Privately, Aiken boastfully exclaimed that his government wished to 'put him [McNeill] in his place'.[73] Neither did Aiken seek to make peace with former enemies from across the Civil War divide in the Fine Gael party. His passionate dislike of men such as Eoin O'Duffy, James Dillon and Ernest Blythe is well documented, although he did not prevent his children from maintaining friendships with the children of those 'from the other side'.[74]

Although to a great extent a social conservative, Aiken suffered excommunication from the Catholic Church during the Irish Civil War, and insisted on drawing a distinction between God and religion.[75] It is also notable that he submitted nine A4 pages of changes to de Valera's 1937 constitution at the drafting stage.[76] But, like many republicans who had undergone excommunication during the Civil War, Aiken pursued a rapid rapprochement with the Church once political power beckoned and he and Maud were received in private audience by Pope Pius XI on their honeymoon.[77] 'Some people are afraid that the new constitution will do away with the rights of women', he told a Mayo crowd in 1937, before reminding them that Fianna Fáil had 'taken care of the widows and orphans'.[78] But while Aiken helped to craft the much maligned paternalism of his party in government, Maud was pursuing her own career in music. This was highly unusual for the time, and Aiken competed for column inches with his wife, who went on to head the Royal Irish Academy of Music.

In a letter written from prison in 1921, Jim Ryan had advised the young Maud to curb her extravagant expenditure on musical instruments in case she ever fell in love with a man who was 'wanting in capital'.[79] Aiken was certainly not wanting in capital, yet neither was Maud dependent on him. Whereas her husband was caricatured as an unreconstructed son of the soil – 'the iron man with the wooden head', as a popular jibe put it – Maud delighted Dublin's polite society. In 1936 her viola solo at the Dublin Philharmonic, as part of Mozart's *Duo Concertante*, was described as 'masterly' by the sharp-tongued arts correspondent of *The Irish Times*.[80] As a Dublin society figure, she occasionally indulged people from her social circle who were seeking political favours. These people knew that Maud was a direct and reliable route to the forbidding Aiken.[81]

Consistent with his 'iron man' image, Aiken was no liberal. With the coming of the Second World War ('the Emergency') in 1939, he would do much to sully his reputation by overseeing a fastidiously neutral censorship regime. His actions constituted 'an ignorant, excessive and grotesque infringement of civil liberties' according to historian Dermot Keogh.[82] Infamously, Aiken's obstinate articulation of Irish neutrality before US President Franklin Delano Roosevelt in 1941 prompted FDR to fly into a rage during which he pulled the tablecloth from the Oval Office table, sending cutlery flying around the room. Back home, Ireland's newspaper editors were similarly exasperated by the minister's truculence. Amid a straitened supply situation, question marks arose over whether his quasi-authoritarianism was masking patronage. Indeed, Maud used her husband's standing to flout stringent Emergency restrictions on private motoring.

Geopolitically, Aiken knew that acquiescing to Anglo-American attempts to get Ireland to compromise neutrality would have improved the supply situation in the country, which was truly desperate by 1941 thanks to the British economic squeeze. Aiken the inventor experienced the frustration of Emergency shortages first-hand, blaming the contraction in supplies for consumer complaints about one of his many inventions, the patented 'Aiken Red Top' turf-burning stove.[83] He was, though, determined to use Emergency censorship to protect what he judged to be the common good, whether to prevent panic buying or to quell sympathy for martyred dissident republicans. Armed with this righteous moral imperative, he wielded his powers with an omnipotent swagger.

In his survey of Ireland during the war years, Brian Girvin rolls out the well-worn juxtaposition between Aiken the ideologue (whom he describes as 'blunt, uncompromising') and Lemass the pragmatist ('a subtle mind open to nuance').[84] The fact remains that, against the 'terrific and all-prevailing force of modern warfare', as Aiken himself put it, his rather draconian approach was, at times, simultaneously the most pragmatic one.[85] A lifelong reader of poetry, Aiken also possessed an under-documented and, at times, lyrical wit. With the lifting of censorship in 1945, he drily invited his antagonist 'Bertie' Smyllie (editor of *The Irish Times*) to an end-of-censorship dinner in Dublin Castle with the words 'Dinner Jacket optional. Rapier de rigueur. Dagger verboten'.

Post-War Activity

Despite having been frozen out of de Valera's vanguard Cabinet committee on economic planning during the Emergency, Aiken served as Minister for Finance between 1945 and 1948. In his chapter, Conor Keelan explores the extent to which Aiken's cooperative agrarianism clashed with the conservative deflationary orthodoxy of the department. Aiken had requested the finance portfolio from de Valera and, according to Ronan Fanning, proved to be a 'dogged and inquisitive' minister.[86] His tenure at the Department of Finance coincided with the ministry's growing concern for the need to reduce state expenditure. There were flashes of a redistributive ethic in Aiken's attitude to social credit and banking. In particular, he believed that the state ought to pump money into the national economy on a social credit basis, a view associated with the economic ideas of Major C.H. Douglas, which were popular in the 1920s and 1930s.[87]

Todd Andrews remarked that Aiken's technical knowledge of the sector ensured that his colleagues at Finance 'developed a great respect for him', while 'the banks developed a great mistrust of him – a situation greatly to his credit'.[88]

Resisting Aiken's instruction that they facilitate cheap credit, a delegation of bankers once asked Aiken: 'Minister, how can we possibly lend money to you at half a per cent and pay our depositors two and a half per cent?' Aiken responded tartly: 'You don't have to pay two and a half per cent for it. You can create money at the stroke of a pen. You get it for nothing'.[89]

Irrespective of his radical distaste for Department of Finance orthodoxy, Aiken and the party were booted out of government by the Irish electorate in 1948 amidst popular resentment at the rise in the cost of living in post-war Ireland and Fianna Fáil's failure to deal with the poverty that was its result. Following an economic downturn in late 1947, Aiken's tough supplementary budget was widely cited as a reason for the party's defeat.[90] Fianna Fáil's general election defeat came as a shock to Aiken. Senior Fianna Fáil politician Gerald Boland recalled that Fianna Fáil ministers, including Aiken, had 'all loved power' and were bitterly disappointed to be relegated to opposition.[91]

Freed from ministerial duties for the first time in sixteen years, Aiken devoted much time to a new commercial interest – apple pressing – and travelled to France and Germany to source equipment.[92] Apart from entrepreneurial engagements during his time in opposition from 1948 to 1951, he also turned his attention towards Fianna Fáil's anticipated worldwide anti-partition campaign. Working alongside de Valera, Aiken travelled throughout the world propagating the 'evils' and 'crime' of a divided Ireland.[93]

Aiken's eldest son, Frank Jnr, writes in the preface to this book that when Fianna Fáil was removed from office in 1948, Aiken cleared his office at Leinster House. He brought back to his family home in Sandyford three filing cabinets full of papers and ephemera, which were kept under lock and key. As his family discovered, on his death in 1983, one filing cabinet also contained thirteen handguns and several packs of ammunition: the fabled guns rumoured to have been bulging out of Fianna Fáil TDs' pockets when they took their places in Dáil Éireann as the governing party in 1932.[94] As his fellow Cabinet colleague Seán MacEntee remarked, 'Frank never left anything to chance'.[95] Back in 1933 Aiken had cautioned colleagues that Eoin O'Duffy, leader of the fascistic Blueshirt movement, was planning a putsch in Dublin. Twenty years on, with Fianna Fáil now in opposition, he continued to keep watch on paramilitary elements in Irish society, even complaining about the firing of shots at funerals by members of the 'so-called IRA'.[96]

But just as the anticipated coup against Fianna Fáil did not take place in 1932, so Aiken's obduracy against Anglo-American hegemony was, at times, overly theatrical. He had done much in the war years to secure a prickly reputation; one that was merely enhanced due to his involvement with Fianna Fáil's worldwide anti-partition campaign from 1948 to 1951. Pub rumours might have had it that Aiken, given half a chance, would order a border incursion of Northern Ireland,[97] but de Valera continued to place his trust him. In 1951, with his party's return to power, he chose Aiken to succeed him as Minister for External Affairs. His career on the international stage as Minister for External Affairs from 1951 to 1954 and 1957 to 1969 is discussed in the second half of this introduction.

Aiken's attitude to partition and Ulster Unionism from 1948 to 1954 is examined in Stephen Kelly's chapter. Aiken steered close to his 'Chief' on the subject of Northern Ireland. Throughout the 1930s and into the early 1950s he routinely demanded a British declaration in support of Irish unity, insisted that Ulster Unionists did not have the right to vote themselves out of a united Ireland, and that a federal agreement between Belfast and Dublin was a workable solution for an end to partition. But while Aiken may have been perceived as the 'the most Anglophobic' senior member of Fianna Fáil, by the mid-1950s he had reluctantly conceded that the party's approach towards Northern Ireland had proved unsuccessful and that a change in direction was needed.

The Long Goodbye

Privately, Aiken was a family man, whose letters to Maud from his frequent trips away from home exhibit affection and humour. Take his description of seasickness on a trip to the Aran Islands with his children in 1946:

> I noticed nurse getting a bit pale and I insisted on her lying down … before long I was holding out the bucket for casualty number one. After nurse had a few shots at the bucket, Lochlann started to compete with her. The bucket was small and the two heads were slightly too big for it. As the two heads bumped about and together … the people who were keeping in the open air 'for their health' joined in … I forbade Aedamar and Proinsias to look and explained the outside noises by saying the folk had terrible coughs.[98]

As this glimpse of the Aikens' domestic arrangements suggests, home life on the Sandyford farm conformed neither to the rustic de Valeran idyll nor to the impoverishment of much of contemporary Dublin. Aiken qualified for the highest possible military service pension of £350 a year, a handsome sum, which came on top of his pay as a minister and TD. After initially applying for a pension in 1936, Aiken withdrew his claim in 1942, settling for a service medal instead. But the overturning of the proportionate reduction in payments to those who were in receipt of other remuneration from the state in 1953, coupled with the loss of his ministerial salary after Fianna Fáil lost power in 1954, prompted him to successfully reapply in 1955.[99] Insurance documents from the post-war period also reveal substantial assets. In addition to his agricultural produce and plant, which, along with household goods, was valued at over £16,000, Aiken owned an oil painting of himself by Seán Keating, valued at £300, and a portrait of Maud by Leo Whelan, valued at £150.[100] He employed a number of people on his house and farm, and a Dublin doctor raised questions about employee safety on the premises after one of his workers was charged by a bull, suffering broken ribs.[101]

Prefiguring Ireland's shift away from economic protectionism, Aiken solicited foreign firms for materials for home improvement. He procured special cloths for cider-making from an American company, and fibreglass and resin for his home-made windmill from English firms.[102] From his *Cruiskeen Lawn* column, Myles na Gopaleen derided Aiken's use of the Irish language as well as his scientific inventions. In a column derisorily titled 'Aiken feet', the writer invited Aiken to his house for 'a run-through in elementary Irish' and to test how well the latest of his inventions – an 'improved' pair of boots – would cope with 'a bout of Irish step-dancing'.[103] With Aiken ruminating over the consequences of allowing the influx of foreign capital into the country as early as 1947,[104] na Gopaleen's jibe about the limitations of homespun design was unintentionally prescient.

Although he loved home life, Aiken's high-profile international role necessitated long absences from Dublin as well as from his parliamentary constituency. He nonetheless polled strongly in Louth, regularly topping the poll by comfortable margins. He received 800 fewer votes in the 1957 election than he had in 1954, but was still able to bring in well over 30,000 votes.[105] With the ageing de Valera increasingly seen as out of touch, Aiken was tipped by many commentators to assume the leadership of Fianna Fáil. Aiken adored de Valera, and was not the first to compare his wiry party leader to George Washington.[106] He also fitted the bill to succeed Dev, noted *The Irish Times*, not only in his 'straight-from-the-shoulder' approach, but in the fact that he was 'by background and preference a farmer'.[107]

Yet it was slick urbanite Seán Lemass who replaced the 'Long Fella' as President of Fianna Fáil and Taoiseach in June 1959. With de Valera moving to the Áras as President, many within the party feared that the unity of his era would be shattered. Sure enough, there were soon signs of open rivalry within the party. In April 1959, with de Valera shortly to leave the Dáil, Maud received an acerbic letter from a supporter of Aiken's colleague Gerald Boland. It complained that Aiken had overlooked Boland for a trip to Strasbourg, warning her that 'you and your set' are 'too puffed up with power'.[108] There was a known coolness between Aiken and his old colleague Boland. Writing in 1962, Boland recalled that Aiken was a 'condescending ... menace'[109] who wanted to be 'as usual the big noise', but really was only 'a selfish show man'.[110]

The rivalry between Lemass and Aiken, two of de Valera's most loyal lieutenants, is renowned, and Aiken's papers contain plenty of frosty exchanges between the two men. Significantly, though, Aiken backed Lemass's major foreign policy strategy as Taoiseach: the orientation of Ireland towards Europe, noting the economic benefits of reciprocal trade with the continent and the improvement of social standards that integration would bring.[111] He found it impossible, however, to overcome his dislike of Lemass's son in law, Charles J. Haughey. Unlike the teetotal Taoiseach, Aiken enjoyed a social drink and, unlike the majority of his contemporaries, he drank wine (and occasionally sherry) rather than beer.[112] But he baulked at the ostentatious wining and dining of builders and speculators in Dublin bars and restaurants undertaken by Haughey and his circle, and worried about the long-term effects of the political ascent of the brash 'CJ'.

Aiken's left-leaning image is bolstered by his disdain for such 'men in the mohair suits', and yet he remained, like Lemass, a social conservative who was anxious about the creeping liberalisation of Irish society. He backed Lemass's attempts to muzzle the journalistic independence of RTÉ, worrying that television images simplified complex political issues.[113] Moreover, he was clearly concerned that the modernisation of the 1960s threatened Anglicisation. He denied that the Catholic Church had had an undue influence on Irish politics during his time in power. Unionist accusations of 'Rome Rule' south of the border were untrue, he claimed in 1972, arguing that it was the medical profession, not the Catholic bishops, who had sunk the Mother and Child scheme.[114]

For a subscriber to de Valera's frugal vision for Irish society, however, Aiken privately accumulated substantial wealth. While it was not quite the swish bachelor pad that the *Irish Independent* imagined, his Sandyford house was inspired by American interior design fashions and the latest building techniques.[115] In the impressive residence, Aiken employed a staff of female domestic workers including a nurse, a general servant and a charwoman, as well as numerous farm and dairy labourers.[116] He owned shares in the *Dundalk Examiner* newspaper, and had substantial property holdings.[117] In the 1960s Aiken invested in concerns owned by transport magnate Aodogan O'Rahilly.[118] A leading member of the new crop of Lemass-era businessmen dismissed as 'lounge lizards ... devoted to the bitch goddess success' by Todd Andrews,[119] O'Rahilly enjoyed Aiken's support in subsequent clashes with the Department of Transport and Power.[120] Although he never flaunted it, then, Aiken's privileged life was by no means antithetical to that of Haughey, although his dogged opposition to him bolsters this impression. When he died in 1984, Aiken left the substantial sum of £149,756.[121]

Nonetheless, when Lemass stepped down as Taoiseach in 1966, Aiken firmly opposed Haughey's leadership campaign, instead proposing George Colley as the new Fianna Fáil leader. Aiken had known another rival candidate, Cork TD Jack Lynch, for over twenty years. When, in 1946, a 29-year-old Lynch first mounted the hustings at Blackpool Bridge, Cork, it was to speak alongside Aiken.[122] Yet he told party members that he was 'firmly convinced that George Colley had something to give the nation'.[123] Colley, the protégé, eventually lost to Lynch, and was to die prematurely in 1983, just months after describing Aiken as 'a man of rock-like integrity and dedication to principle' at his mentor's funeral.[124]

Under Lynch's premiership, an ageing Aiken was reappointed as Tánaiste and Minister for External Affairs. Lemass's resignation, preceded by Seán MacEntee's ministerial retirement in April 1965, now left Aiken as the sole serving member of the first Fianna Fáil Cabinet of 1932 in Lynch's new Cabinet. In July 1969 he nominated Lynch as Taoiseach in the Dáil. Although the septuagenarian Aiken was excluded from Lynch's 1969 Cabinet, he provided redoubtable support for his party leader during the Arms Crisis of 1970, when he instructed Lynch to sack ministers Haughey and Neil Blaney, and expel the two men, along with Kevin Boland and Paudge Brennan, from the Fianna Fáil parliamentary party.[125]

Such was his venom towards Haughey, Aiken privately announced that he would resign rather than fight the 1973 election if Haughey were ratified as a candidate. Aiken even told Lynch that he would write a letter to the newspapers explaining that Haughey was his reason for resigning. Lynch asked de Valera to intervene on his behalf, which he duly did. After the intervention of de Valera and his close friend Joe Farrell, Aiken agreed not to record publicly his reasons for retiring from public life. Thus, on the night of 13 February 1973, Lynch announced that the former Tánaiste and Minister for External Affairs was retiring from politics on 'doctors' orders'. Disillusioned, Aiken never attended another party event.[126]

The following year, 1974, Aiken's only sister, Nano, died. They had formed a close bond during the revolutionary years, when she was in the republican female auxiliary Cumann na mBan. Maud's sudden death in a car crash in 1978 was of enormous personal sadness to Aiken. He had generally enjoyed good health, although he had fallen ill on one of his trips to the United States in 1928; a medical examination then had identified 'bronchial thickening', and he later underwent oesophageal surgery.[127] Now, as he entered his eighties, Alzheimer's disease tightened its grip on him. He became increasingly irritable and, latterly, bewildered. His daughter Aedamar diligently recorded his illness, writing tenderly about the physical and emotional distress it caused him.[128] Aiken died in Dublin in 1983. He was buried with full State honours in his native Camlough, County Armagh.

In recent years, a major revision of the actions of the 'Good Old IRA' has taken place, with revelations of sectarian killings carried out under the banner of Irish republicanism.[129] One interesting personal detail, which adds fuel to the fire of those who lean towards the monstrous image of Aiken, is that medieval Mongol warlord Genghis Khan was his personal hero.[130] Moreover, to some commentators, Aiken's scientific imagination exceeded his political imagination. The more quixotic of Aiken's agrarian innovation schemes certainly lent themselves easily to liberal metropolitan ridicule. For others, the U-turn on some of his early republican principles, coupled with a selective take on exactly when and where republican violence was justified, smacked of hypocrisy, while the wealth and privilege accumulated over his political career signalled pomposity.

He was, at the same time, a much more complex figure than monochrome interpretations allow. One reason for the persistence of his buffoonish image was his disdain for the public relations techniques utilised by today's politicians.[131] On the contrary, it is clear that Aiken was an enterprising, intelligent and well-informed man who retained, to his death, the principled radical tinges of early Sinn Féinism and early de Valerism. As historian Joseph Lee notes, as early as the outbreak of the Civil War in 1922, he had forever lost his 'blood lust'.[132] From then on, politics trumped militancy and, as this book illustrates, his subsequent career would leave an indelible mark, not only on mainstream republicanism in Ireland, but on modern Irish history and, with it, the essence of Irish identity.

Notes

1   Max Boot, *Invisible Armies: An Epic History of Guerrilla Warfare from Ancient Times to the Present* (New York: W. W. Norton, 2013).

2   J.J. Lee, in Cormac O'Malley and Anne Dolan (eds), *No Surrender Here! The Civil War papers of Ernie O'Malley, 1922–1924* (Dublin: Lilliput Press, 2012), 4.

3   Aiken did not even make it into *The Irish Times*' 2008 biographical collection *Great Irish Lives: An Era in Obituaries* (edited by Charles Lysaght). The only recorded published biography on Aiken is Liam C. Skinner's 1946 brief chapter in his book, *Politicians by Accident* (Dublin: Metropolitan, 1946).

4   See *Frank Aiken: From Gunman to Statesman* (Mint Productions Hidden History documentary for RTÉ Television, 2006).

5   For reference to this documentary and reaction to news of the publication of a biography of Aiken, see Bryce Evans, *Frank Aiken: Nationalist and Internationalist*, originally published at www.irishstory.com, 11 Feb. 2013, and republished on www.politics.ie, 11 Feb. 2013.

6   See Bryce Evans, *Seán Lemass: Democratic Dictator* (Cork: Collins Press, 2011), 1–5.

7   For further biographical information on Frank Aiken, see University College Dublin Archives (UCDA), Frank Aiken Papers (P104)/447–448, marked 'from biographical agencies, 1929–1972'.

8   Records accessible at http://www.census.nationalarchives.ie, accessed 10/01/13.

9   Todd Andrews, *Man of No Property: An Autobiography (Volume Two)*, (Dublin: Lilliput Press, 1982), 125.

10 Aiken's Irish was famously derided by James Dillon in Dáil Éireann in 1937. See Dáil Debates (DE), 31 March 1937, Vol. 66, col. 90.

11 Biographical sketch of Aiken, Sept. 1929. UCDA, P104/447.

12 Charles Townshend, *The Republic: the Fight for Irish Independence* (London: Allen Lane, 2013), 22, 32.

13 See Máire Cruise O'Brien, *The Same age as the State* (Dublin: O'Brien Press, 2003), 217.

14 Ronan Fanning, 'Frank Aiken', *Dictionary of Irish Biography* (http://dib.cambridge.org, accessed 18/04/13).

15 Irish Military Archives (MA), Military Pensions Service Collection (MPSC), 34REF16473, John McCoy.

16 MA, MSPC, 34REF16473, John McCoy.

17 MA, MSPC, 34REF59339, Frank Aiken.

18 MA, MSPC, RO/403, 4th Northern Division GHQ.

19 Interview with Frank Aiken junior, 23 March 2013.

20 *The Irish Times*, 25 June 1921.

21 *The Times*, 25 June 1921.

22 *Irish Bulletin*, Vol. 5, No. 79, 20 Sept. 1921. By kind permission of Dr Rory O'Hanlon.

23 Richard English, *Irish Freedom: the History of Nationalism in Ireland* (London: Pan, 2007), 350.

24 Townshend, *The Republic*, 354.

25 Skinner, *Politicians by Accident*, 157–58.

26 Frank Aiken, *A Call to Unity* (Dublin, June, 1926). Copies of this pamphlet are available from the National Library of Ireland (NLI), P2127 and UCDA, P104/1499.

27 MA, MPSC, RO/403, 4th Northern Division GHQ.

28 Aiken to all officers and men, 17 July 1922. UCDA, P104/1247.

29 Townshend, *The Republic*, 399.

30 Townshend, *The Republic*, 433.

31 MA, MPSC, RO/403, 4th Northern Division GHQ.

32 Aiken to Mulcahy, 15 July 1922, UCDA, P104/1246.

33 MA, MPSC, RO/403, 4th Northern Division GHQ.

34 *Dundalk Democrat*, 19 Aug. 1922.

35 MA, MPSC, RO/403, 4th Northern Division GHQ.

36 M. Smyth to Aiken, 9 April 1933. UCDA, P104/1297.

37 Andrews, *Man of No Property*, 37.

38 Ernie O'Malley, *The Singing Flame* (Cork: Mercier Press, 1978), 212–213.

39 O'Malley to Jim Donovan, 7 April 1923, in Richard English and Cormac O'Malley (eds), *Prisoners: The Civil War Letters of Ernie O'Malley* (Dublin: Poolbeg Press, 1991), 35.

40 Seán Lynch to editor, *Irish Independent*, 4 April 1935. UCDA, P104/1304.

41　O'Malley to Childers, 12 November 1923, English and O'Malley eds, *Prisoners: The Civil War Letters of Ernie O'Malley*, 48; Francis Carty, 'Frank Aiken: some personal impressions', *Irish Press*, 8 July 1969.

42　See Evans, *Seán Lemass: Democratic Dictator*, 43–44.

43　Aiken, *A Call to Unity*.

44　Aiken, *A Call to Unity*.

45　Aiken, *A Call to Unity*.

46　Interview with Frank Aiken junior, 23 March 2013.

47　Aiken, *A Call to Unity*.

48　*Irish Independent*, 12 August 1927.

49　*The Irish Times*, 31 March 1927.

50　Cassius Styles – Aiken correspondence, 7 Jan. - 8 Feb. 1929. UCDA, P104/2669.

51　Henry Collins to Frank Aiken, 18 Oct. 1927. UCDA, P104/213.

52　*Irish Independent* clipping, UCDA, P104/26.

53　Helen Andrews, 'Maud Aiken', *Dictionary of Irish Biography* (http://dib.cambridge.org, accessed 18/06/13).

54　Richard Mulcahy to O/C, St Vincent's Hospital, 24 Aug. 1922. UCDA, P104/822.

55　Maud Aiken notebook. UCDA, P104/760 and 762.

56　See Maud Aiken diary. UCDA, P104/762.

57　See Labhras Joye, '"Aiken's slugs": the Reserve of the Irish Army under Fianna Fáil', in Joost Augusteijn (ed.), *Ireland in the 1930s, New Perspectives* (Dublin: Four Courts Press, 1999), 144.

58　*The Irish Times*, 18 March 1932.

59　Donnacha Ó Beacháin, *Destiny of the Soldiers: Fianna Fáil, Irish Republicanism and the IRA, 1926–1973* (Dublin: Gill and MacMillan, 2010), 131.

60　*The Irish Times*, 22 Oct. 1932.

61　*The Irish Times*, 28 June 1933.

62　Tom Barry to editor, *Irish Press*, 3 June 1935. UCDA, P104/1283.

63　MA, MSPC, 34REF57456, Tom Barry.

64　Record of conversation between Aiken, Tom Barry, Seán MacBride and Gilmore, 16 July 1932. UCDA, Moss Twomey Papers (P69)/52 (56).

65　Interview with Aiken family, 23 March 2013.

66　Aiken memorandum on the utilization of peat resources, UCDA, P104/3016.

67　See UCDA, P104 368.

68　Dermot Keogh, *Twentieth Century Ireland: Nation and State* (Dublin: Gill and MacMillan, 1994), 76.

69　Brian Hanley, *The IRA, 1926–1936* (Dublin: Four Courts Press, 2002), 126.

70　J.J. Lee, *Ireland 1912–1985: Politics and Society* (Cambridge: Cambridge University Press, 1989), 283.

71　MA, MSPC, Con.Ran.23 (DP17), James Daly.

72　Interview with Aiken family members, 23 March 2013. Ronan Fanning dubs Aiken Anglophobic in his *Independent Ireland* (Dublin: Helicon, 1983), 141.

73　Record of conversation between Aiken, Tom Barry, Seán MacBride and Gilmore, 16 July 1932. UCDA, P69/52 (56).

74　Interview with Frank Aiken junior, 23 March 2013.

75 Interview with Frank Aiken junior, 23 March 2013.

76 See Evans, *Democratic Dictator*, 97.

77 Fanning, 'Frank Aiken', *Dictionary of Irish Biography* (http://dib.cambridge.org, accessed 18/04/13).

78 *The Irish Times*, 17 May 1937.

79 Ryan to Davin, 6 July 1921. UCDA, P104/821.

80 *The Irish Times*, 2 March 1936.

81 See various letters to Maud Aiken, UCDA, P104/829.

82 Keogh, *Twentieth Century Ireland*, 127.

83 Aiken to Joe Connolly, 31 March 1943. UCDA, P104/271.

84 Brian Girvin, *The Emergency: Neutral Ireland, 1939–45* (London: MacMillan, 2006), 32–33.

85 See Aiken's memorandum on censorship, 23 Jan. 1940, National Archives of Ireland (NAI), Department of the Taoiseach (DT), S11586A.

86 Ronan Fanning, *The Irish Department of Finance, 1922–58* (Institute of Public Administration: Dublin, 1978), 392–393.

87 Fanning, *The Irish Department of Finance, 1922–58*, 392–393.

88 C.S. Andrews, 'The last of the great Sinn Féiners', *Irish Press*, 21 May 1983.

89 Cited in William Kingston, 'What Gladstone Could Teach the EU', *History Ireland* vol. 21, no. 6 (Nov./Dec. 2013), 47.

90 *The Irish Times*, 19 May 1983.

91 See 'Gerald Boland's story' – 11, *Irish Press*, 19 Oct. 1968.

92 Aiken to Hans Kadtenback, 25 Oct. 1950. UCDA, P104/137.

93 See, for example, speech by Aiken. DE, Vol. 112, col. 840, 20 July 1948; and speech by Aiken, Camlough, County Armagh. *Irish Press*, 10 Feb. 1949.

94 Interview with Frank Aiken junior, 23 March 2013. The guns mentioned are today housed in the Aiken Army Barracks museum, Dundalk, County Louth.

95 Interview with Frank Aiken junior, 23 March 2013.

96 Ó Beacháin, *Destiny of the Soldiers*, 176.

97 See for example, Brendan Anderson, *Joe Cahill: a Life in the IRA* (Dublin: O'Brien Press, 2002), 27–30.

98 Aiken to Maud, 1 Aug. 1946. UCDA, P104/817.

99 MA, MSPC, 34REF59339, Frank Aiken.

100 Irish National Insurance Company Policy No. F94926G. UCDA, P104/106.

101 J. F. Neary to Aiken, 5 June 1946. UCDA, P104/106.

102 Aiken to E. I. du Pont de Nemours, 9 Feb. 1953. UCDA, P104/43.

103 *The Irish Times*, 19 June 1958.

104 Memo on foreign capital, 16 Aug. 1947. UCDA, P104/4119.

105 *The Irish Times*, 7 March 1957.

106 Aiken note, 28 Oct. 1947. UCDA, P104/1463.

107 *The Irish Times*, 21 Nov. 1957.

108 E. O'Loughlin to Maud Aiken, 6 April 1959. UCDA, P104/843.

109 Gerald Boland's unpublished memoirs, marked, 6 (x) and 7(x).

110 Gerald Boland's unpublished memoirs, marked, 2 (b) and 12 (a).

111 Aiken speech to the Council of Europe, 8 May 1963. UCDA, P104/5668; Aiken speeches to Fianna Fáil 'Into Europe' meetings, 18 April – 20 May 1972, UCDA, P104/5718.

112 Interview with Aiken family, 23 March 2013.

113 DE, 13 April 1967, Vol. 227, col. 1662.

114 Aiken speech, 2 Dec. 1972. UCDA, P104/1498.

115 See UCDA, P104/20–47.

116 Leslie Dexter to Aiken, 10 Sept. 1930. UCDA, P104/106.

117 P. Weldon to Aiken, 18 Dec. 1942. UCDA, P104/2129.

118 O'Rahilly to Aiken, 19 Sept. 1963. UCDA, P104/2149.

119 Andrews, *Man of No Property*, 122.

120 Aiken memo on Greenore ferry service, 13 March 1963. UCDA, P104/2146.

121 'Frank Aiken', *Oxford Dictionary of National Biography*, entry by Eunan O'Halpin.

122 T. Ryle Dwyer, *Nice fellow: A Biography of Jack Lynch* (Cork: Mercier Press, 2001), 26.

123 Meeting of Fianna Fáil parliamentary party, 9 Nov. 1966. UCDA, P176/448.

124 *Irish Press*, 19 May 1983.

125 See Kelly, *Fianna Fáil, Partition and Northern Ireland, 1926–1971*, 317–322.

126 Typescript copy of an article by Geraldine Kennedy, 'Frank Aiken: the story that was never told', as related by Francis Aiken (Frank Aiken's son), June 1983. UCDA. P104/2341.

127 Howard Ruggle to Aiken, 30 Nov. 1928. UCDA, P104/463.

128 Aedamar Aiken, 'Dada – 1980 – Illness' notebook, UCDA, P104/1206.

129 The chief texts in this revision, both of which focus on the IRA's activities in County Cork, are Peter Hart's *The I.R.A. and Its Enemies: Violence and Community in Cork, 1916–1923* (Oxford: Oxford University Press, 1998) and Gerard Murphy's *The Year of Disappearances: Political Killings in Cork, 1920–1921* (Dublin: Gill and MacMillan, 2010).

130 Interview with Frank Aiken junior, 23 March 2013.

131 Francis Carty, 'Frank Aiken: some personal impressions', *Irish Press*, 19 July 1969.

132 Lee, *Ireland 1912–1985*, 176.

Frank Aiken: Internationalist

STEPHEN KELLY

'Their mortal danger'

Addressing the General Assembly of the United Nations in November 1957, Irish Minister for External Affairs Frank Aiken outlined the 'one sole purpose' of his foreign policy. 'Everything I said', he explained, was to get the nations of the world to recognise 'their mortal danger' and to 'plead with them progressively to eliminate the causes of conflict' in which disputes 'would be settled on a basis of law and justice'.[1] These words encapsulate perfectly Aiken's pursuit of a pacifist, non-aligned and distinctive foreign policy during the course of his political career. His own revolutionary and anti-imperialist background left a lasting imprint upon his political thought, convincing him of the necessity to find peaceful solutions to international problems.

In June 1951, following Fianna Fáil's return to government after three years in opposition, Aiken was appointed Minister for External Affairs. To this day, he remains the longest serving Irish minister to hold the foreign affairs portfolio, retaining the post for seventeen years from 1951 to 1954 and from 1957 to 1969. Under previous Fianna Fáil administrations Éamon de Valera had retained the Department of External Affairs along with the headship of his successive governments from 1932 to 1948. After several years of dwelling in de Valera's long shadow, Aiken was now presented with the opportunity to place his own identity on Irish foreign policy. As Minister for External Affairs, Aiken fashioned a reputation as the steward 'of Ireland's foreign policy',[2] showing 'a remarkable breadth and depth of feeling and an acute understanding of the currents of world politics'.[3]

Aiken's tenure as Minister for External Affairs coincided with profound changes in Irish society. The 1950s was scarred by mass emigration, widespread

27

unemployment, civil unrest and political instability. The 1960s heralded a new sense of optimism. During this decade, inspired by Thomas Kenneth Whitaker's 'First Programme for Economic Expansion' of 1958, Ireland's once lacklustre economy gradually flourished. Ireland – for so long the backwater of Europe – now dared to embrace cultural and societal changes from far beyond her shores. This march towards modernity was encapsulated by American President John F. Kennedy's visit to Ireland in 1963.

Nonetheless, impeded by engrained political conservatism and the dogmatic teachings of the Catholic Church, this transition was a slow and tortuous journey. It is within this context that Aiken's heyday as Minister for External Affairs occurred. A revolutionary conservative – the embodiment of the old-guard traditionalist within Fianna Fáil – Aiken was not immune or indeed ostensibly opposed to the changing nature of Irish society. His seventeen years as Minister for External Affairs in fact reveal a man eager to transform Ireland's reputation on the world stage. Although sometimes couched in a conservative ethos, Aiken was willing to take political risks, and was not afraid to ruffle political feathers, at home and abroad.

Aiken as Minister for External Affairs, 1951–1954

Aiken's 1951 to 1954 term as Minister for External Affairs was characterised by Ireland's inability, arguably unwillingness, to involve itself in world affairs. The shadow of Irish neutrality during the Second World War still blighted bilateral relations with the western powers and, as Aoife Bhreatnach surmises, Irish foreign relations were 'neither innovative nor expansive but cast in the mould of aloof neutrality'.[4] Aiken's strategy towards Irish foreign policy on becoming Minister for External Affairs was to retain Ireland's neutrality, strengthen its military defensive capabilities, protest against the maintenance of partition and seek to improve relations with Ulster Unionism. Addressing the Dáil on 30 January 1952, Aiken recorded that partition and the goal of securing a united Ireland would 'dominate' the Irish government's 'external policy'.[5]

Aiken's first term was quiet, constrained by the state's economic difficulties and lack of opportunities on the international stage. Ireland's non-membership of the United Nations and the North Atlantic Treaty Organisation (NATO) and the government's unwillingness to support the Mutual Security Act of 1951,[6] together with the country's withdrawal from the European Recovery Plan, reinforced a sense of isolation and introspection. During his first term at Iveagh House, Aiken also found himself impeded by de Valera's unwillingness to release full responsibility for foreign relations to the Department of External Affairs.

Frederick Boland, for example, advised the British government to contact de Valera on a regular basis for 'general chats', suggesting that, despite Aiken's brief, the Taoiseach remained at the centre of foreign policy formulation.[7]

Although against any formal military alliance with the western powers, as this would jeopardise Irish neutrality, Aiken was determined to procure military assistance from the American government, believing that civilisation stood on the brink of a third world war. Amid Cold War tensions, he was not alone in predicting impending destruction; Cabinet colleague Seán Lemass also regularly predicted renewed global conflict.[8] In August 1951, Aiken informed General Douglas MacArthur, Adviser on International Affairs to American President General Dwight D. Eisenhower, that Ireland should be given assistance to strengthen its defensive capabilities against possible Soviet attacks. In return for military supplies, Aiken promised MacArthur that Ireland would offer joint military staff talks that would 'enable NATO planners to have knowledge of Ireland's defence plans so that there could be proper military coordination should aggression against Ireland occur'.[9]

In April 1952, Aiken met Eisenhower during an 'informal call' to SHAPE (Supreme Headquarters Allied Powers Europe), where he once again raised the prospect of military assistance for Ireland. The President, however, was little interested in Aiken's appeals for military assistance, recording that the issue was a 'low priority' on the American defence programme.[10] Aiken also notified Eisenhower that, although not an opponent of European unification, he was not overly enthusiastic about the prospect of a federal Europe. He 'expressed the view that while Europe should be more unified politically, it was dangerous to press too rapidly toward total European economic unification since this would result in many serious dislocations'.[11] Throughout Aiken's first term as Minister for External Affairs he continually pleaded with successive American administrations for military supplies for the Irish Defence Forces.[12] This was a depressing period for Aiken, who was gravely worried about the impending outbreak of nuclear war. His anxieties were exasperated by the inadequate state of the Irish Army. In early 1952, for example, the Chief of Staff of the Irish Defence Forces, Major General William S. (Liam) Egan, wrote to Aiken personally, warning of the urgent necessity to modernise the army. 'Most of our weapons', Major General Egan explained, 'are now obsolete or obsolescent'.[13]

Cold War tensions shaped Aiken's rather stiff attitude towards east-west trade. When Eisenhower adopted a fairly liberal approach to such trade, Ireland followed suit. Aiken, however, still had qualms about trade with regimes behind the Iron Curtain. While private individuals could do as they pleased, he prohibited Irish officials from dealing with Eastern European officials.[14] Aiken's attitude was coloured by the Irish state's policy of non-recognition of the German

Democratic Republic (East Germany) and its minimal trade with the Eastern bloc, but also the outspoken anti-Communism of much of the Irish press. In particular, the *Irish Independent* and *The Standard* regularly denounced trade with Eastern regimes on account of the religious persecution of Catholics. Amid this red-baiting atmosphere, Aiken and his Cabinet colleagues took care not to offend Catholic sensibilities.[15]

Apart from Aiken's repeated requests for military assistance from the American government, and his stance on tough east-west trade, his first term was also notable for the emphasis he placed on improving relations with the Ulster Unionist government in Belfast. Except for his outbursts and frustration in 1953 over the Coronation Oath and the official title of Queen Elizabeth II (the first British monarch to specifically use the term 'Northern Ireland' in her title),[16] Aiken's tone was notably conciliatory.[17] The sore-thumb approach of continually stressing the injustice of partition, espoused by Aiken's predecessor Seán MacBride, was a tactic that the Fianna Fáil government believed had run its course. Henceforth, in the words of Aiken in October 1952, his 'policy' was focused on allowing 'the temperature drop to a point at which Partition could be ended on the basis of reason and goodwill'.[18] Guided by a policy of 'persuasion', particularly on issues of cross-border economic cooperation, the Fianna Fáil government attempted to reassure the Northern Ireland government of the 'benefits of an economically and politically unified Ireland'.[19]

Fianna Fáil's defeat at the 1954 election general came as a bitter disappointment to Aiken. In May 1954 a Fine Gael-led coalition, with John A. Costello as Taoiseach, took office. Aiken, thus, found himself out of ministerial office. His first term as Minister for External Affairs had been both short and quiet, characterised by a lack of involvement on the international stage. His second period as Minister for External Affairs was neither short nor quiet.

Aiken as Minister for External Affairs, 1957–1969

In March 1957, Fianna Fáil returned to government and Aiken returned to the external affairs portfolio. Over the next thirteen years, until his forced ministerial retirement in July 1969, Aiken remained at Iveagh House. The period began with a major shift in Ireland's UN policy. Under Aiken's guidance, the Fianna Fáil government was eager for Ireland to end its 'subservient' position under the American administration.[20] Such an approach categorically rejected the pro-western policy pursued by the second inter-party government, under Minister for External Affairs Liam Cosgrave, since Ireland's admittance to the UN at the Tenth General Assembly in December 1955.[21]

Having studied the inter-party government's performance at the UN, Aiken believed that under his authority the Irish delegation should follow a more independent position, and 'not become part of any tied groups, bound by agreements to support one another, no matter what the subject matter up for discussion'.[22] This determination to follow an independent policy had its roots in de Valera's approach to the League of Nations during the 1930s. De Valera often went to great lengths to emphasise the importance of the smaller states playing a positive role in the League, independent of the pressures from larger powers. Twenty years on, his views had changed little, although he remained somewhat sceptical of the UN's role as the moral watchdog of the world. By the mid-1950s he believed that at the UN Ireland should remain 'independent' and avoid becoming too closely aligned to 'hostile blocs'.[23]

It is, therefore, not surprising that from the moment Aiken arrived at the UN General Assembly in September 1957 he advocated Ireland's autonomous, independent and activist approach to foreign policy. As a small nation in an era dominated by Cold War tensions and the threat of nuclear war, Aiken believed that Ireland's mission at the UN was to help to alleviate international hostility, while at the same time carving a distinctive identity in the pursuit of his country's interests. In the words of Conor Cruise O'Brien, Irish policy at the UN was focused towards promoting 'the cause of international peace through the exercise of independent judgement on the issues'.[24]

Michael Kennedy and Joseph Morrison Skelly describe Aiken's period at the UN as a 'Golden Age' of Irish multilateral diplomacy. From 1957 to 1969, they argue, Aiken 'raised the Irish delegation's profile in the General Assembly to new heights'.[25] In particular, writers pinpoint the years from 1957 to 1961 as Aiken's most successful period as Minister for External Affairs, describing him as the 'architect of Irish UN policy'.[26] Ronan Fanning writes that it was Aiken, 'more than any other Minister for External Affairs', who used the UN as 'a platform for Irish affirmations of independence'.[27] Indeed, Ben Tonra notes that Aiken's influence on Irish policy at the UN during this period was 'profound'.[28]

Aiken's public performance at the UN was in stark contrast to his undistinguished first term as Minister for External Affairs from 1951 to 1954. He led the Irish delegation to the UN General Assembly every year from 1957 to 1968, and on several occasion sat on the Security Council during Ireland's one-year term as a member in 1962.[29] He greatly enjoyed his annual sojourns to the UN; he particularly loved New York and the ambience of the UN. For example, between 1957 and 1965 he spent 437 days at the UN, at a cost to the taxpayer of £7,293.[30] Former Taoiseach Seán Lemass allegedly said that the UN was Aiken's 'playpen'.[31] Certainly Aiken dedicated more attention and time to the UN than most other foreign ministers, to a point where he was sometimes to be found wandering its corridors when few other foreign ministers were in New York.

From 1957 to 1960, Aiken moved the outlook of the Irish General Assembly delegation towards an independent stance at the UN. He believed that Ireland, as a small nation, neutral and without colonial and imperialist ambitions, should champion three central principles: self-determination for smaller nations, preventative diplomacy, and a dedication to safeguard and protect the legal and institutional structures of the UN. His willingness to formulate plans for military disengagement and disarmament, to discuss the admission of Communist China to the UN and to support the claims of self-determination for the smaller, newer Member states allowed Aiken to carve out a reputation as a staunch anti-imperialist and a supporter of decolonisation.

The Irish delegation's championing of self-determination was a by-product of an Irish historical consciousness that permeated the Department of External Affairs and Irish public opinion generally.[32] Addressing the General Assembly in October 1960, Aiken passionately argued that Ireland was a sovereign, independent state, yet its people retained 'a historical memory' of the years when it too was dominated by a foreign power.[33] Remembering his own battles against British forces in Ireland, and the continued partition of his country, he advocated Greek-Cypriot self-determination. Besides his support for independence for emerging European counties in the aftermath of the Second World War, such as the South Tyrol,[34] he also championed the right of self-determination for the emerging nation states throughout the continent of Africa, including Algeria, South Rhodesia, French Togoland and Portuguese Goa.

Aiken's personality and previous revolutionary experiences impacted greatly on Ireland's stance at the UN. His guerrilla days during the Irish War for Independence, his position as Commandant of the Fourth Northern Division of the IRA and his brief time as Chief of Staff of the republican anti-Treaty forces during the Irish Civil War left a strong imprint on his political philosophy. Apart from his alleged lifelong Anglophobia,[35] Ireland's crusade for independence from the might of the British Empire left him convinced of the right for small states to gain self-determination. His prominent role in maintaining Irish neutrality in the Fianna Fáil Cabinets during the Second World War also reinforced his feeling of isolation and sense of inequity in Ireland's relationship with both Great Britain and America.

Aiken's revolutionary background thus greatly influenced his independent and activist attitude at the UN. It convinced him of the necessity to find peaceful solutions to international problems rather than turning to violence. As he informed the UN in 1960, Ireland's 'supreme interest' was to 'reduce violence and to extend the principle of peaceful settlement'.[36] An article published in 1958 entitled 'Man of Peace Who Killed Forty' (a reference to Aiken's masterminding of the derailment of a train carrying British troops in Adavoyle, County Armagh, in June 1921), placed his pacifism in the context of his revolutionary past. In Aiken's own words, 'A revolutionary background puts a responsibility on you'.[37] During Aiken's thirteen years of involvement at the UN, this sense of responsibility lay heavy on his shoulders.

As is discussed below, during this period Aiken endorsed several initiatives at the UN in the hope of securing greater world peace and security. These included his 1957 'Disengagement proposals' for Eastern Europe, his Middle Eastern peace plan of 1958 and his novel 'Areas of Law' proposal of 1959. Aiken's most famous contribution at the UN – and his abiding legacy on foreign affairs – was his successful crusade to find an agreement between the United States and the Soviet Union on the non-proliferation of nuclear arms.

During his long stints at the UN, Aiken formed a bond of trust with a small group of influential Irish civil servants. The cunning and ambitious Conor Cruise O'Brien, Counsellor (later Assistant Secretary) in the International Organization Section of the Department of External Affairs, was Aiken's greatest ally; O'Brien spoke of Aiken as a man of 'integrity'.[38] They had first worked together on Aiken's appointment as Minister for External Affairs in 1951,[39] and shared a common outlook on foreign policy. Aiken's relationship with Freddie Boland, Ireland's urbane Permanent Representative (Ambassador) at the UN from 1956 to 1964, was also important for Irish foreign policy. Although they did not always agree with one another, Aiken diligently listened to and respected Boland's views, the latter having a strong input into the 'intellectual basis' of his minister's stance at the UN.[40] Cornelius (Con) Cremin, Secretary of the Department for External Affairs from 1958 to 1963 and Irish Ambassador at the UN from 1964 to 1974, also had an important intellectual input into Irish UN policy. Cremin was close to Aiken; in New York, Aiken would regularly dine with the Cremin family.[41] A stickler for detail and a master of his brief as Secretary of External Affairs, Aiken used Cremin as a middleman between O'Brien and Boland.[42]

The Aiken-Lemass relationship and Irish foreign policy

As Ireland entered the 1960s, Aiken continued to play an active role in Irish foreign affairs until his retirement as Minister for External Affairs in 1969. Initially, Seán Lemass's appointment as Taoiseach in the summer of 1959 had little impact on the direction of Irish foreign policy at the UN; between June 1959 and the early months of 1961 foreign affairs issues were rarely raised by Fianna Fáil at either government or party level.[43] This approach gradually changed during the final months of Lemass's first term as Taoiseach. After April 1961, Lemass's involvement at the UN entered a pivotal stage, wherein the Irish delegation abandoned its overtly activist role in favour of one more sympathetic to its European allies and the American government. This transition away from the de Valera/Aiken independent policy stance to a pro-western policy at the UN is described as heralding the 'unfettered Lemass Era'.[44]

Why the shift in policy by mid-1961? The most obvious answer was Ireland's application to join the European Economic Community (EEC) in July 1961.[45] On becoming Taoiseach, Lemass pinpointed Ireland's successful admittance to the EEC as a central goal of Irish foreign policy. In September 1961, Lemass instructed Con Cremin and T. K. Whitaker to visit the capitals of the six EEC Member states to clarify various aspects of Ireland's EEC application. Lemass also lent a hand on the diplomatic and propaganda mission, taking to the airwaves to affirm the Irish government's commitment to the goal of European political cooperation.[46] Lemass realised that Ireland might have to abandon its independent stance at the UN if the course of European political cooperation so required. In September 1961, for instance, Lemass informed Aiken that, in the interests of retaining Italian goodwill during the EEC negotiations, Ireland should not take an initiative on South Tyrol.[47] This did not mean that the Irish delegation at the UN would have to side automatically with EEC members; rather, Aiken would have to take into account European susceptibilities when deciding on how to vote.

The Aiken–Lemass relationship is also central to understanding Ireland's shift in foreign policy. Many have commented on the poor relationship between Aiken and Lemass. John Horgan notes that Lemass's relationship with Aiken was 'problematic', characterised by a sense of reserve at best.[48] According to Brian Lenihan, Lemass regarded Aiken 'as a fool', and was delighted to see him disappear over the horizon in the direction of the UN for three months every year.[49] Todd Andrews recorded that there was a 'known coolness' between Lemass and Aiken.[50] There is little doubt that there was, indeed, a degree of coldness between them. Personally, Lemass had little time for Aiken, and the feeling was mutual. Michael Lillis, a successful career civil servant and Irish Ambassador to the UN from 1986 to 1988, noted that during his early years in the Irish civil service in the late 1960s he acquired the distinct impression that the Department of External Affairs had an 'aura of unreality', and was indulged by Lemass mainly because of Aiken's 'unquestioned authority as a senior statesman' and due to his close personal relationship with Irish President Éamon de Valera.[51]

Evidentially, Aiken and Lemass saw Ireland's place in the world from different perspectives. Lemass's sights were firmly focused on EEC membership and American foreign investment. Aiken, in contrast, remained preoccupied with Irish involvement at the UN. Tensions, therefore, were bound to arise between the two men. On the subject of Irish foreign policy, Dermot Keogh describes Lemass as 'heterodox' and Aiken as 'doctrinaire'.[52] In particular, Lemass's push for Irish economic development meant the primacy of economic interdependence in relation to his stance on foreign affairs. It found expression in his drive to improve Irish–American relations with a view to attracting American companies to Ireland.[53] Aiken, however, never showed much interest in the economic aspects of international affairs.

Despite their mutual antipathy for one another, it is far too simplistic to say that Aiken and Lemass remained at loggerheads in relation to Irish foreign policy, particularly at the UN. For instance, T.D. Williams states that in relation to foreign policy Aiken and Lemass 'kept out of each other's way and as far as was possible left a free hand to the other'.[54] Such observations are inaccurate. An examination of Aiken's personal papers reveals that both men worked closely with one another on the formulation of Irish policy at the UN.[55] Any personal animosity was suppressed, allowing for an amicable working relationship to develop between Aiken and Lemass. They stayed in close contact during Aiken's lengthy visits to New York, with Lemass regularly speaking to his minister by phone. In fact, although not always agreeing on points of foreign policy, they generally respected one another's point of view. As long as it did not harm Ireland's economic interests, both men concurred on several issues at the UN, such as the importance of the UN as a peace-broker in world affairs, Irish peacekeeping duties abroad and nuclear non-proliferation.

One important point must be stressed, however. Lemass always had the final say on foreign policy, and this included his minister's important UN speeches and votes. Noel Dorr, who had front-line experience of the Aiken–Lemass relationship, acknowledges that the Taoiseach took a 'close interest' in what Ireland was doing at the UN, and 'exercised his authority whenever an issue impinged on his wider European and economic priorities'.[56] Therefore, as Michael Kennedy outlines in his chapter, although Aiken remained the public face of Irish UN policy, by the early 1960s, Lemass took ultimate control.

The perception that Aiken and Lemass differed with one another on Irish foreign policy has gained credence because of the difference between them in relation to Europe and Irish membership of the EEC.[57] Norman Macqueen, for example, argues that 'Europe, and specifically the EEC, seemed to be of little concern' to Aiken.[58] This assessment is reinforced by Patrick Keatinge, who writes that Aiken showed 'a lack of interest' in European affairs.[59] This view is supported by the fact that Lemass, not Aiken, assumed responsibility for Ireland's stance on Europe from the late 1950s onwards. From 1957 to 1959, the question of Ireland's relationship with the proposed free trade area in Europe and with EEC membership remained plainly in the hands of Lemass's Department of Industry and Commerce and not with Aiken's Department of External Affairs. For example, when a motion to establish a committee to discuss Ireland's position vis-a-vis Europe was proposed in July 1957, the government spokesman was Lemass, not Aiken.[60]

However, the well-trodden argument that Aiken simply wished to remain aloof of European affairs is yet another inaccuracy within the historiography. It was not that Aiken was an antagonist to the idea of Ireland joining the EEC, or opposed to European integration. Rather, he was content to allow Lemass take the lead. An examination of Aiken's personal papers reveals that he supported the Fianna Fáil government's commitment to Ireland's application for EEC membership. He routinely raised the matter with his European and international colleagues, explaining that 'Ireland', in his own words, 'had always been in favour of European unity'.[61] Addressing the Dáil in July 1961, he spoke positively of the 'trend towards uniting [Europe] economically and politically'.[62] A further speech by Aiken, delivered in Dáil Éireann in April 1963, best sums up his stance on Ireland and Europe:

> The Taoiseach is and has been, as is right and natural, in charge of major constitutional matters such as joining the EEC. I have no hesitation in saying that inside and outside the Cabinet, I have supported the Taoiseach in his application for membership of EEC. I did so not in the past six or 12 months: I have always been in favour of a European Community in which European countries would combine to run Europe in accordance with the principles of western civilisation and in which they could try to give an example to the rest of the world of how neighbours could live in peace and co-operate to develop their resources, thus helping not only themselves but others in greater need.[63]

As the above quotation demonstrates, by the mid-1960s Aiken offered his unconditional support for Ireland's application for EEC membership, viewing such a measure as the fulfilment of the country's economic and agricultural expansion since the First Programme for Economic Expansion in the late 1950s,[64] and a stepping stone towards securing a united Ireland based on 'harmony and agreement'.[65]

Aiken and the UN, 1957–1969: An overview

One of Aiken's earliest contributions at the UN involved his proposal that the General Assembly declare itself, in principle, in favour of a drawing back of non-national armies and military personnel in Eastern Europe. Aiken's initiative was in response to the Soviet Union's crushing of the Hungarian popular uprising in late 1956. It reflected his determination to carve out Ireland's reputation as an independent player on the world stage, uninhibited by its small status. Addressing the Twelfth Session of Assembly in September 1957, Aiken advocated consideration of a European 'drawback' plan, which envisaged America withdrawing its influence from Greece and Turkey, in exchange for the Soviet Union withdrawing from 'the territories which they occupy in Eastern Europe'.[66] The offer was originally proposed by the leader of the Soviet Union, Nikita Khrushchev, as a solution to the build-up of armed forces in Europe.

In Ireland, although Aiken's wife Maud reported that his speech caused 'great excitement',[67] and de Valera praised it as being 'splendidly received',[68] opposition parties rounded on the minister's proposals.[69] Moreover, William Warnock, Irish Minister in Bonn, Germany, reported the German Foreign Office's distaste for Aiken's 'partial withdrawal' proposal, because it failed to take into consideration the 'outstanding political matters'.[70] Likewise, NATO and the American and British governments showed little interest in Aiken's disengagement strategy, viewing the plan as overly ambitious and simplistic.[71] Despite his detractors, Aiken's motives were sincere and considered, reflecting his determination to use the UN as a forum to negotiate peaceful solutions to Cold War friction.

In the same month that Aiken proposed his 'drawback' initiative, Ireland cast its most controversial vote at the UN: its endorsement of an Indian motion seeking a discussion of the 'The Representation of China' on the UN Assembly's agenda. The motion proposed a debate on whether the Nationalist government in Taiwan (under the exiled leader Chiang Kai-shek) or the Communist government in Peking (under Mao Zedong) should represent China at the UN.[72] The Americans backed the Nationalist government. The Soviets supported Mao. Under the previous inter-party government, Dublin had been counted as a safe vote in blocking the entry of Chinese Communists into the UN. Aiken, however, saw the China vote as a litmus test for the Irish delegation's non-partisan and autonomous identity at the UN. Although he emphasised, in a speech on 23 September 1957, that he had 'no sympathy whatever with the ideology of the Peking Government' – that Ireland despised the 'horror of despotism' – he believed that the Assembly was entitled to have 'a full and open discussion of the question of the representation of China in this Assembly'.[73]

Initial reaction in some quarters to Aiken's decision to support the motion raised questions concerning his judgement. His actions, Noel Dorr remembers, caused a 'seismic tremor'.[74] Some even wrongly accused Aiken of being a Communist sympathiser, whose 'highly dangerous' actions on the China vote were inspired by his 'very anti-American and anti-West' outlook.[75] Writing from Ireland, a concerned spectator, Síle Ní Líonnaín professed that Aiken's actions had 'scandalised Catholic Ireland at home and abroad'.[76] The Americans were furious on learning of Aiken's decision to change Ireland's vote on China. Behind Aiken's back, American Ambassador to the UN, Henry Cabot Lodge, Jr., and John Foster Dulles, American Secretary of State, vigorously campaigned for Ireland to reverse its decision. According to Lodge, Aiken was 'going nuts'.[77] Unbeknown to Aiken, Dulles even asked Cardinal Francis Spellman, Catholic Archbishop of New York, to convince the Irish to alter its vote. His Eminence put a call through to the Irish Consul-General in New York in order to make his views clearly known. 'Tell Aiken', he exclaimed, 'that if he votes for Red China we'll raise the Devil'.[78]

By the turn of the 1960s, in line with Lemass's pro-western postures, Ireland's attitude towards the China issue modified. In July 1959, only one month into his new role as Taoiseach, Lemass wrote to Aiken to warn his colleague of the dangers of permitting the Chinese Communists admittance into the UN.[79] In his chapter, Noel Dorr examines in greater detail Aiken's attitude to the China issue at the UN. Dorr argues that, under the watchful eye of Lemass, Aiken followed a moderate, middle-of-the-way approach to the China vote. Aiken did not wish to antagonise the American administration, but at the same time he was determined to speak out on behalf of the Chinese people, irrespective of their political persuasion.

Aiken's preoccupation, arguably obsession, with the rights of smaller nations for self-determination against imperialist forces was his next noteworthy contribution to Ireland's involvement at the UN. Addressing the UN General Assembly in early October 1960, Aiken eloquently articulated his anti-imperialist philosophy:

We know what imperialism is and what resistance to it involves. We do not hear with indifference the voices of those spokesmen of African and Asian countries who passionately champion the rights to independence of the millions who are still, unfortunately, under foreign rule. On the contrary, those voices strike an answering chord on every Irish heart. More than eighty years ago the then leader of the Irish nation, Charles Stewart Parnell, proclaimed the principle that "the cause of nationality is sacred, in Asia and Africa as in Ireland". That is still a basic principle of our political thinking in Ireland today, as it was with those of my generation who felt impelled to assert in arms the right of our country to self-determination and independence.[80]

The Algeria crisis was Aiken's first major opportunity to demonstrate Ireland's commitment to the principle of self-determination for smaller nations. For over a century, Algeria had been a départment of France; by the mid-1950s, however, the French government worried that Algerian nationalists might mobilize international support for independence at the UN. At this time both Tunisia and Morocco were on the verge of securing independence from the French Republic, partly as a result of UN resolutions. By 1957, the French government's intransigence on the subject of Algerian independence sparked an upsurge of violence in the region. Although the French government introduced the *loi-cadre*, a new legal framework redefining the relationship between France and Algeria, it did not meet the demands of the Algerian independence movement.[81]

In response to the unfolding crisis, Aiken stepped into the debate. On 20 September 1957, he requested that the UN adhere to its own Charter related to the principle of self-determination, and called on the French to recognise 'absolutely and unequivocally ... the right of self-determination to Algeria at the earliest practicable date to be fixed in agreement with' the UN. Furthermore, Aiken called for greater autonomy for Algerian regions within a federal framework and total equality for all its inhabitants. Due to 'Ireland's traditions', he said, he felt compelled to support Algeria's independence from France.[82] Unsurprisingly, Aiken's remarks outraged the French. The French representative left the room to mark his displeasure. Aiken's comments were reportedly 'seen as a slap in the face' by the French.[83] Despite Aiken's outspoken criticism, he always remained conscious of not offending the French in the hope of maintaining good relations with a traditional European ally. On the whole the Irish were successful, managing to facilitate Algerian independence through its UN policy without compromising its relations with France.

In 1962, the Algerian crisis was finally resolved. The Évian Agreement, signed on 18 March, finally opened the way to the proclamation of Algerian independence on 3 July of that year. In October 1962, addressing the UN Security Council, Aiken delivered a speech expressing his satisfaction, both with Algeria becoming a member of the UN and with the manner in which France had overcome the crisis. Describing Algeria's quest for independence as encompassing 'qualities of vision, courage and foresight', he equally praised French President Charles de Gaulle for his 'supreme calibre – a man who ... faced all the difficulties of solving the problem of Algeria with unshakable resolve and unbounded confidence in the destiny of this own country'.[84] Aiken's desire to find a political settlement to the Algerian dispute signalled to the UN and the wider world the Irish government's commitment, in his own words, to 'passionately champion the rights to independence' of small nations. Over the subsequent years, Aiken continued to pursue this policy at the UN with a determination that made him stand out from many of his contemporaries.

In her chapter, Helen O'Shea reveals Aiken's 'relentless antipathy' towards British imperial rule and Irish partition. Based on a forensic examination of departmental government files from the British and Irish national archives, O'Shea explores Aiken's support for Greek-Cypriot self-determination from Britain, using the Cyprus question as a 'useful yardstick' by which to measure attitudes towards raising the partition of Ireland at the UN. Initially, at least, Aiken's arrival at the UN in 1957 raised expectations that partition would be formally raised at the General Assembly. On the advice of Conor Cruise O'Brien, Aiken gave the proposal serious consideration in 1957. However, after much soul-searching and bickering among the Irish delegation, Aiken decided against raising partition at the Thirteenth Session of the General Assembly in 1958.

Although partition was raised by some members of the Irish delegation at the UN in debates in committees on other issues, and indeed on rare occasions by Aiken personally, from time to time in his speeches to the General Assembly,[85] Ireland never raised the issue of partition formally at the UN. The reason for this is that, as Noel Dorr observes, within Irish circles there was a memory of the unsuccessful 'sore-thumb' policy followed at the Council of Europe, where partition had been raised during the early 1950s. The policy achieved almost nothing, and merely irritated other delegates.[86] By early 1962, Aiken had come to the firm conclusion that the raising of partition at the UN was a fruitless exercise that had not given any concrete results.[87] Instead, he preferred to channel his efforts towards direct negotiations with London and Belfast. It was not until 1969, with the outbreak of the Troubles in Northern Ireland, that the government again realistically considered the UN as a forum to voice Irish grievances over partition. Aiken's simultaneous support for Greek-Cypriot self-determination and his opposition to Irish partition was a precarious balancing act. On the one hand, and despite his own nationalistic prejudices, he was against using the forum of the UN as an instrument to bash the anti-partitionist drum and demand a united Ireland. On the other hand, through his speeches on Cyprus he sought to reassure the Irish electorate of the Fianna Fáil government's commitment to ending partition.

Aiken's willingness to involve the Irish delegation in the Tibetan crisis further demonstrated his commitment to the principle of self-determination for smaller nations against aggressive imperialist powers. Kate O'Malley offers an astute examination of Aiken's private and public attitude to the Tibetan crisis. Her chapter, which utilises an assortment of primary sources, convincingly argues that Tibetan demands for self-determination assumed far greater priority for Aiken than his desire to raise the 'China vote' at the UN. The Tibetan crisis struck a chord with Aiken's revolutionary past. His support for the persecuted people of Tibet, a nation recognised for its pacifism, provided a counterpoint to Aiken's own past as a physical-force nationalist.

The crisis in Tibet found its origins in China's long-standing objective of superseding its internationally recognised suzerainty over Tibet with the annexation of the country. China invaded Tibet in the spring of 1950. Tensions were temporary abated in 1951 following the signing of the Sino-Tibetan Agreement. The treaty granted Tibet limited autonomy, with the Dalai Lama's authority remaining intact. However, under the terms of the agreement, China became responsible for Tibet's external affairs and stationed troops in the country. [88] Aiken was drawn directly into the crisis following the Chinese suppression of a Tibetan uprising in 1959. Encouraged by Freddie Boland, Aiken decided to respond to the Tibet crisis. On 11 April 1959, in a speech delivered to his constituents in Dundalk, Aiken issued a statement excoriating the Chinese for their conduct in Tibet. The Chinese actions in Tibet, Aiken stated, were a case of 'cruel injustice being inflicted by a powerful country against a weaker neighbour …'.[89]

Aiken had to wait for several months before he was able to raise his concerns over the Tibet crisis at the UN. Addressing the Assembly on 21 September 1959, he spoke against the 'brutal crushing of Tibetan autonomy'.[90] Throughout late September and early October of that year the Irish, together with the Malaya delegation, repeatedly called for respect for the fundamental rights of the Tibetan people. Between 7 and 21 October alone, Aiken delivered five speeches on Tibet. He was anxious to remind the UN that the Irish delegation did not seek a Cold War debate, but rather they spoke of upholding the Charter, and in particular to defend the rights of smaller nations against larger powers.[91]

The Tibet resolution, adopted by the General Assembly on 21 October 1959 by a margin of forty-five to nine, with twenty-six abstentions, called for the respect of the fundamental rights of the Tibetan people and the restoration of their civil and religious liberties. The Assembly, therefore, registered its disapproval of the Chinese action, but the resolution did not accord international support for Tibetan sovereignty.[92] Despite the limited nature of the resolution (from a political perspective at least), Aiken succeeded in registering international revulsion towards Communist China, thus strengthening the Assembly's mandate of tackling human rights issues. Aiken's endeavours were warmly welcomed from the previously hostile American delegation. Henry Cabot Lodge Jr. 'congratulated the Minister, warmly expressing the view that the whole operation had been splendidly handled from first to last'.[93] The Soviet delegation, on the other hand, reacted bitterly, suggesting that Ireland was being used by the very 'self-same imperialists against whom it had fought so gallantly' in introducing the resolution.[94]

Over the following years, in defiance of Chinese ignorance of the Irish-sponsored Tibet resolution, Aiken continued to raise the plight of the Tibetan people at the UN.[95] Aiken's endeavours won him the admiration of the Dalai Lama and his brother Thondup. In March 1961, the Dalai Lama wrote to Aiken to express his gratitude to 'your Government and your good-self for the great interest that you have taken on the question of Tibet'.[96] In assessing Aiken's stance on the Tibet issue, it ranks as one of his most successful policies at the UN, demonstrating his commitment to anti-colonial and self-determination principles.

Aiken's involvement with the question of South Africa at the UN further emphasised his commitment to the plight of persecuted minorities and his opposition to colonialism in Africa.[97] Broadly speaking, Ireland's position focused on two central issues: apartheid, and the treatment of persons of Indian origin in the Republic of South Africa; in addition to the question of South Africa's defiance of the UN through its continued occupation of the former mandated territory of South-West Africa (present day Namibia).[98]

On the subject of apartheid, Aiken regularly spoke out against the South African government's flagrant violation of the UN Charter. Although eager to stress that he could offer 'no magic wand' to bring apartheid to a speedy conclusion, he was determined to confront 'majorities' who 'cruelly' repressed minority groups.[99] Addressing a gathering at Dublin Airport on his arrival back from the UN General Assembly in November 1959, Aiken expressed his government's view that their South African counterparts 'should give human rights to all colours of their citizens and treat them as human beings'.[100] In March 1960, following the massacre of sixty-nine civilians by the South African police during a demonstration at Sharpeville, he publicly declared that the Irish people were 'deeply shocked' by events in the country.[101] In response, the following month, the Irish government excluded South Africa from its invitation to Dublin to all leaders attending the Commonwealth conference in London.[102]

While remaining a vocal critic of the apartheid regime in South Africa, by the early 1960s Aiken's experience of Africa during the previous ten years convinced him of the need to seek 'gradual reform' rather than immediate improvements, such as demands for 'one man one vote'.[103] This explains Aiken's opposition to imposing sanctions against South Africa. Addressing the Special Political Committee at the Twenty-First Session of the UN in December 1966, Aiken voiced his disagreement with proposals to impose sanctions and boycotts as a means of solving apartheid.[104] This should not suggest, however, that Aiken forgot about the plight of the black suppressed majority in South Africa. In correspondence with Taoiseach, Jack Lynch, in early January 1968, for example, Aiken wrote that 'a few million whites in South Africa cannot forever deny with impunity the rights of the [UN] Charter to the teeming millions of the non-whites in the world'.[105]

On the issue of South-West Africa, the 'Achilles heel of apartheid', as Aiken phrased it, he was again a vocal critic of the South African government.[106] The region had been a German Protectorate from 1890, until it was seized from Germany by South Africa during the First World War. Thereafter, South Africa retained responsibility for South-West Africa. By the 1950s, many activists within and outside the UN, including Aiken, began to argue that South-West Africa should secure self-determination. In his speeches at the UN, Aiken routinely declared his opposition to the South African government's claim over South-West Africa. Addressing the UN General Assembly in October 1966, Aiken focused on the principle that 'mutual respect and friendship' called for the 'rights of man' to be preserved, and that the 'freedom of nations' and the 'rule of law' should be enforced in South-West Africa.[107]

Apart from Aiken's diplomatic involvement with South Africa at the UN, he also offered unwavering military support to the General Assembly during the Congo crisis, The Congo was geographically the largest state in southern and central Africa. Ireland's contribution to UN peacekeeping activities in the region, lasting four years from 1960 to 1964, signalled the country's determination to remain loyal to the principles of internationalism, irrespective of any perceived loyalties to western ideals.[108] Although it was a testing time for Irish foreign policy, in which twenty-six Irish soldiers lost their lives, Aiken never wavered in his unconditional support to the UN, both diplomatically and militarily.

Irish diplomacy was shown in the government's defence of the UN from Soviet criticisms, and militarily by contributing troops to the UN's Peacekeeping Force in the Congo (ONUC or *Organisation des Nations Unies au Congo*). The Congo crisis found its origins in colonial tensions and Cold War paranoia. In the summer of 1960, Congo secured independence from Belgium; Aiken actually visited Leopoldville, the Congolese capital, for its independence celebrations on 30 June 1960. However, street violence and intense rioting broke out across the country, and this was quickly followed by a mutiny amongst Congolese soldiers against their Belgian officers. In response, Belgium ordered additional troops into Congo, with the pretext of wishing to defend Europeans still living in the region. The aggressive action by the Belgian government was deeply resented by the Congolese people, and their President Joseph Kasavubu and Prime Minister Patrice Lumumba opposed their ex-colonial masters' plans. Sensing an opportunity in the height of the unfolding crisis, in July 1960, the leader of the Katanga province, Moise Tshombe, announced the secession and independence of Katanga.

The UN, under its Secretary-General Dag Hammarskjöld, reacted immediately. In July 1960, the Security Council met, and agreed to establish a United Nations Peacekeeping Force in the Congo in order to alleviate the threat of civil war and facilitate the withdrawal of Belgian forces. Hammarskjöld implemented a resolution requesting that a variety of non-aligned countries, from independent African contingents and those European contingents non-aligned with NATO, provide contingents for the UN force. In mid-July, Hammarskjöld appealed to Lemass. Following consultation with his Cabinet, and in particular Aiken, it was agreed that the Irish government would supply a light infantry battalion to the ONUC; in August the government acceded to Hammarskjöld's request for a second battalion.[109] This was a seismic political and indeed historical decision. This was the first time in Ireland's history as an independent state that the country contributed an armed military contingent to a full-scale peacekeeping force.

Despite Soviet protests over the UN's handling of the Congo crisis (against Hammarskjöld's wishes Khrushchev supported the secession of Katanga and even supplied Prime Minister Lumumba with transport plans in an attempt to invade the province) Aiken resolutely defended the institutions of the UN as the moral watchdog of the world, and Hammarskjöld's office of Secretary-General. In a speech to the General Council, in October 1960, Aiken appealed to all delegations to remember that 'if smaller powers are to be effective in building a better world order, they must, at whatever short-term inconvenience to themselves, support the [UN] Charter and the Universal Declaration of Human Rights …'.[110] In the following year, March 1961, Aiken again reiterated his support for the Secretary-General's office and the UN as a collective.[111]

In his chapter, Michael Kennedy explores Aiken's attitude to events in the Congo during the turbulent years of 1960 to 1961, when under intensive Soviet and American political aggression, the UN, as a functional institution, almost imploded. The death of Hammarskjöld in a plane crash in September 1961 only compounded the crisis. Furthermore, Kennedy examines Conor Cruise O'Brien's controversial period as representative of the UN Secretary-General in Katanga, from May 1961 until his 'recall' to the Irish Foreign Service in the winter of that year. O'Brien's effective sacking from his post in Katanga – following immense pressure from the newly appointed Secretary-General of the General Assembly, U Thant – left a bitter taste in O'Brien's mouth. O'Brien was particularly upset because he believed that Aiken had played a part in his dismissal. Rather than returning to the Irish Civil Service, O'Brien resigned from the Department of External Affairs.[112] In assessing Aiken's role in the Congo crisis, Kennedy skilfully argues that the former did not have free reign over Ireland's actions, and had to work with Lemass, and at times 'work to Lemass's orders', particularly where Ireland's stance on the Congo issue had to fit within the wider plan of Ireland's overall international interests.

Aiken's contribution to the thorny issue of the Middle East was a further example of his determination to embroil Ireland in the affairs of the world. In his chapter, Rory Miller makes excellent use of the official records of the UN General Assembly when analysing Aiken's involvement at the UN with the Middle East from 1957 to the Arab–Israeli War of June 1967 (also known as the Six Day War). Despite Aiken's general reservations towards involving himself in the Arab–Israeli dispute, for a brief period during the late 1950s he did seek to find a permanent peace settlement in the Middle East.[113] In August 1958, Aiken presented the UN General Assembly with his Middle Eastern peace plan. Aiken's main focus was to restrict the great power rivalry within this region, holding the strong conviction that the 'acute diplomatic competition' between the great powers for regional hegemony only led to war. He called on the UN to recognise Arab aspirations towards unity in this region. Simultaneously, he also prepared a clause affirming that the 'existence of the State of Israel is also a historic fact'.[114]

As Ireland entered the 1960s, and Lemass consolidated his 'pro-western' stance at the UN, the Irish delegation refrained from entering the Middle Eastern dispute. This detached stance, however, was dramatically altered during the weeks and months both preceding and following the outbreak of the Six Day War in the Middle East in June 1967.[115] Miller explains how Aiken played an important part in formulating the UN's response to the unfolding crisis. Aiken was, as he expressed in his own words, eager to find a 'speedy' solution to the conflict, and the 'signing of a permanent treaty of peace by Israel and the neighbouring States', which would be 'guaranteed' by the UN.[116]

Besides a preoccupation with the plight of emerging nations in Africa, and the crisis in the Middle East, Aiken also found himself involved in one of the most famous and perilous episodes of the Cold War: the Cuban Missile Crisis of October 1962. During this famous month the world stood on the brink of nuclear war as the two superpowers, the United States of America and the Soviet Union, became engaged in a diplomatic and military game of chess. Following reports from the United States Central Intelligence Agency (CIA) that the Soviets were in the process of installing ballistic missiles in Cuba, which had the capacity to fire nuclear warheads, the world held its breath.

Aiken was in New York throughout the ensuing crisis. Addressing the UN Security Council on 24 October 1962, he described the presence of missiles in Cuba as 'upsetting the existing delicate balance of world security'.[117] In his chapter, Noel Dorr recounts in vivid detail Aiken's involvement with this dramatic affair. Coincidentally, at this time, Ireland held a seat on the Security Council, permitting the Irish delegation a front-row seat as events unfolded. Dorr explains how Aiken followed an 'interesting and sensible' approach, as Ireland offered the American delegation its full and unconditional support; this went so far as Lemass granting permission for the searching of Cuba-bound Czechoslovakian planes for munitions during their stopovers at Shannon Airport.[118]

By this point it seemed that all of Aiken's previous foreboding warnings of the genuine threat of nuclear war were about to come true. As the world faced into the abyss, Aiken remained convinced of the need to reduce Cold War tensions, and in particular to secure an agreement among the superpowers to reduce the production of nuclear weapons. It was this steadfast commitment to nuclear disarmament, and his role in successfully securing an agreement at the UN between the Americans and Soviets on this issue, which remains Aiken's abiding legacy and greatest achievement as Minister for External Affairs.

At the Twelfth Session of the General Assembly in September 1957, Aiken first spoke out in favour of general disarmament.[119] The following year the central theme of Aiken's speeches at the UN centred on the non-proliferation of nuclear arms (then referred to as non-dissemination). It was a shrewd move to decide to focus on one particular aspect of disarmament – non-proliferation – rather than becoming consumed by mammoth topics of international proportions. In October 1958, at a gathering of the First Committee's General Disarmament Debate, Aiken proposed a draft motion calling for the establishment of 'an *ad hoc* committee to study the dangers inherent in the further dissemination of nuclear weapons …'.[120] When the vote was taken, Aiken's resolution was rejected out of hand by France, England, America and the Soviet Union. Although disappointed by the rejection of his 1958 resolution, Aiken did not concede defeat, and over the following years the Irish delegation continued to raise the profile of the nuclear non-proliferation issue within the UN's General Assembly. By this time Aiken's ideas concerning the urgency of stopping the spread of nuclear weapons had gained ground, even among previously sceptical countries.

In 1961, Aiken sponsored the so-called 'Irish Resolution': Resolution 1665 (XVI). To Aiken's delight, the resolution was adopted by the UN General Assembly on 4 December 1961: the first such resolution to be adopted concerning the problem of the proliferation of nuclear weapons.[121] The adoption of this resolution by the First Committee, and subsequently the Plenary Session of the UN Assembly in 1961, marked the beginning of a long process of several years of further negotiations, leading to the signing of the Nuclear Non-Proliferation Treaty in 1968. This treaty was agreed by the two superpowers, America and the Soviet Union, though not by France and China. Aiken's contribution was recognised in the Nuclear Non-Proliferation Treaty signing ceremony in Moscow in July 1968. On the invitation of the Soviet government, Aiken's was the first signature on the version signed in Moscow. Although this treaty was the result of bilateral negotiations between the Americans and the Soviets, Aiken's single-mindedness, and committed pursuit of this cause, played a crucial factor in keeping the issue alive.

The ratification of the Nuclear Non-Proliferation Treaty dramatically enhanced Ireland's – and Aiken's – international profile, signifying the country's confidence on the world stage, and helping to free it from negative stereotypes associated with its foreign policy in the aftermath of Irish neutrality during the Second World War. In recent years, Aiken's commitment to non-proliferation of nuclear weapons has been acknowledged by the Irish political class. In June 2012, Tánaiste and Minister for Foreign Affairs and Trade Eamon Gilmore noted in Dáil Éireann that 'it is important that the international community continue with this crucial work, which was launched by Frank Aiken in the late 1950s and which has given Ireland special prominence in the international efforts to eliminate nuclear weapons'. In words that would have no doubt pleased Aiken, Gilmore was at pains to 'assure the House' that non-proliferation of nuclear arms will 'remain a top priority for the government'.[122]

Conclusion

How does one assess Aiken as Minister for External Affairs? Despite the positive aspects of Aiken's legacy on foreign affairs, his contribution to Ireland's international reputation is blemished by examples of his unwillingness to upset the American government and a determination to censor the Irish media. Conor Cruise O'Brien, for example, was disgusted by Aiken's willingness during the 1960s to succumb to Lemass's pro-western sensibilities, accusing the government of being subservient to American influence in its failure to condemn American participation in the war in Vietnam.[123] Aiken's 'silence' on Vietnam is likewise criticised by Ronan Fanning, who describes the minister's inaction as an 'eloquent' example of Ireland's shift during the early 1960s to a more American-oriented, pro-western UN policy.[124] Such criticisms are warranted. The available evidence supports the argument that Aiken refrained from publicly criticising the American leadership for their actions during the Vietnam War, instead calling for a ceasefire and the end of military hostilities.[125]

Aiken's actions in later years in relation to freedom of the press revealed the conservative side to his foreign policy; a conservatism that echoed the censorious Aiken of the Second World War. Firstly, in 1967 he refused permission for an RTÉ news crew to visit Vietnam on the grounds that they would possibly jeopardise the Irish government's quest for American investment in Ireland,[126] and that the despatch of a film crew 'would not be in the best interest of the nation'.[127] Secondly, in the same year, Aiken prevented staff of the RTÉ current affairs programme *Seven Days* from travelling to Nigeria because of fears that if Irish public opinion became too pro-Biafran in the Nigerian Civil War, it might endanger Irish missionaries elsewhere in Nigeria.[128]

Aiken's own personality, which at times lacked warmth, impacted upon how others perceived his ministerial capabilities. His performance as Minister for External Affairs was construed as autocratic, peppered with a determined single-mindedness. He never hesitated to speak his mind or vigorously argue a point of view. His style, as Alvin Jackson notes, was a stubborn mixture of 'cussedness and idealism'.[129] Aiken rarely felt a responsibility, when delivering his reports to the Dáil on the affairs of the Department of External Affairs, to expand on the notes prepared by his civil servants. As Noel Dorr recalls, it was 'simply not his [Aiken's] style to engage in public debate on foreign policy issues'.[130]

Aiken's notorious stubbornness did not meet with universal praise. For many of his opposition colleagues in Dáil Éireann, Aiken's refusal to debate Irish foreign policy revealed the minister's authoritarian style and distain for debate. James Dillon, the leader of the main opposition party Fine Gael, was Aiken's main antagonist. Dillon believed that Aiken was 'inept, vain and stupid'.[131] Addressing the Dáil in July 1959, Dillon sarcastically noted that Aiken's 'cracked obsession' with maintaining an independent stance at the UN was 'foolish'.[132] Speaking in 1963, Dillon declared that Aiken was the 'most incompetent Minister for External Affairs', accusing the minister of making 'a "hames" of our external relations'.[133]

Aiken also faced criticism from within his own Fianna Fáil government. Gerald Boland, minister in consecutive Fianna Fáil Cabinets from 1932 until 1957, said that 'a worse minister for external affairs could not be found'.[134] In January 1961, Minister for Health, Seán MacEntee, ridiculed Aiken's 1960 resolution, which called on 'all governments to make every effort to achieve permanent agreement on the prevention of the dissemination of [nuclear] weapons'. MacEntee described Aiken's proposal as an 'absurdity' that was 'not realistic and is in principle inequitable'.[135]

Despite such criticism, Aiken's contribution to Irish foreign policy at the UN deserves particular commendation. His pursuit of an independent policy at the UN (primarily before 1961), his advocacy of self-determination for small European countries and emerging nation states in Africa, and not least his tireless endeavours to restrict the proliferation of nuclear weapons, are but a few examples of Aiken's influence on Irish foreign policy. Although his first term at Iveagh House was unremarkable, from 1957 to 1969 he carved out a reputation as a 'man of commanding authority, keen intelligence, [and] a reflective turn of mind ...'.[136] Aiken's distinctive approach to UN matters helped Ireland punch above its weight in the General Assembly. Indeed, on learning of Aiken's retirement as Minister for External Affairs in 1969, *The New York Times* wrote that 'it is hard to envisage anyone but Frank Aiken heading Ireland's delegation at the opening of a United Nations General Assembly'.[137]

Notes

1   Speech by Aiken, 28 Nov. 1957. Dáil Éireann (DE), Vol. 164, cols. 1204–1205.

2   Joseph Morrison Skelly, *Irish Diplomacy at the United Nations, 1945–1965, National Interests and the International Order* (Dublin: Irish Academic Press, 1997), 288.

3   *The Irish Times*, 21 May 1983.

4   Aoife Bhreatnach, 'Frank Aiken and the Formulation of Foreign Policy, 1951–1954; 1957–1969' (M.Phil thesis, National University of Ireland, Cork, 1999), 5. To date, Bhreatnach's M.Phil thesis is the only comprehensive study of Frank Aiken's seventeen years as Minister for External Affairs. Please note that Dr Bhreatnach did not have access to the personal papers of Frank Aiken currently held at University College Dublin Archives (UCDA), Frank Aiken Papers (P104). We wish to express our gratitude to Aoife for granting the editors of this book permission to access this unpublished study.

5   Speech by Aiken, 30 Jan. 1952. DE, Vol. 129. col. 48.

6   See, for example, letters and memoranda between Aiken and various American diplomats dealing with Ireland's refusal to partake in the Mutual Security Act. UCDA, P104/5821–5824.

7   See P. Liesching to W. C. Hankinson, 10 Dec. 1951. National Archives of the United Kingdom (NAUK), Dominions Office (DO), 130/112.

8   Aiken expressed his anxieties about a coming third world war within the political context of the Irish Red Scare and the emergence of Clann na Poblachta. His warnings about impending global destruction echoed those of Cabinet colleague Seán Lemass. See Bryce Evans, *Seán Lemass: Democratic Dictator* (Cork: Collins Press, 2011), 162–172.

9   Copy of report of a meeting by Cremin marked 'secret' between Aiken and MacArthur, 30 Aug. 1951. UCDA, P104/5807.

10   Record of meeting between Aiken, General Dwight Eisenhower and Douglas MacArthur, 14 April 1952. UCDA, P104/5834.

11   Record of meeting between Aiken, General Dwight Eisenhower and Douglas MacArthur, April 1952. UCDA, P104/5834. See also Trevor Salmon, *Unneutral Ireland: An Ambivalent and Unique Security Policy* (London: Clarendon, 1989).

12   See, for example, copy of minutes of conversation between Aiken and United States Ambassador to Ireland Francis Matthews, dealing with the question of defence and the supply of arms to Ireland, 11 Oct. 1950. UCDA, P104/5801. See also, Aiken to Francis Matthews, 24 Dec. 1951. UCDA, P104/5819; and copy of a note of an interview between Aiken and Francis Matthews, 13 Feb. 1952. UCDA, P104/5831.

13   Major General L. Egan to Aiken, 22 Feb. 1952. UCDA, P104/5825.

14   See Till Geiger, 'Trading with the Enemy: Ireland, the Cold War and East–West trade, 1945–1955', *Irish Studies in International Affairs*, Vol. 19 (2008), 122–135.

15   See Evans, *Seán Lemass*, 162–172.

16   The full title is: Her Majesty Elizabeth the Second, by the Grace of God of the United Kingdom of Great Britain and Northern Ireland, and of Her other Realms and Territories Queen, Head of the Commonwealth, Defender of the Faith.

17   See Bhreatnach, 'Frank Aiken and the Formulation of Foreign Policy', 11–14.

18   Meeting between Aiken and Lord Salisbury, Leader of the House of Lords, 28 Oct. 1952. UCDA, P104/8037.

19   For further reading on Aiken's attempts to improve relations with the Northern Ireland Government from 1951 to 1954, see Stephen Kelly, *Fianna Fáil, Partition and Northern Ireland, 1926–1971* (Dublin: Irish Academic Press, 2013), 147–150.

20   See comments by Conor Cruise O'Brien in his memoir, *Memoir, My Life and Themes, Conor Cruise O'Brien* (Dublin: Poolbeg Press, 1999), 185.

21   The previous inter-party government, under the direction of Taoiseach John A. Costello, and Minister for External Affairs, Liam Cosgrave, had followed a pro-western stance at the UN, focused on three underpinning principles. Addressing the Dáil, on 3 July 1956, Cosgrave laid out three loosely connected, but key, components of Irish foreign policy: the first was to adhere rigorously to the 'obligation of the Nation's United Charter'; the second was that 'Ireland should try to maintain a position of independence … and avoid becoming associated with particular blocs or groups as far as possible'; and lastly to 'do whatever the Country could as a member of the United Nations to preserve the Christian civilisation', of which Ireland was a part. Speech by Cosgrave, 3 July 1956. DE, Vol. 159, cols. 137–146.

22   Speech by Aiken, 3 July 1956. DE, Vol. 159, col.147.

23   Speech by de Valera, 28 Nov. 1957. DE, Vol. 164, col. 1255.

24   Conor Cruise O'Brien, 'Ireland in International Affairs', in Owen Dudley Edwards (ed.), *Conor Cruise O'Brien Introduces Ireland* (New York: McGraw Hill, 1969), 130.

25   Michael Kennedy and Joseph Morrison Skelly (eds), *Irish Foreign Policy, 1919–66: From Independence to Internationalism* (Dublin: Four Courts Press, 2000), introduction & 24. See also Noel Dorr's comments on Ireland's perceived 'golden years' at the UN from 1956 to 1960 in Dorr, *Ireland at the United Nations, Memories of the Early Years*, 37–39.

26 See Norman Macqueen, 'Frank Aiken and Irish Activism at the United Nations, 1957–61', *The International History Review*, Vol. 6, No. 2 (May, 1984), 210–231: 211.

27 Ronan Fanning, 'Raison d'État and the Evolution of Irish Foreign Policy', in Kennedy and Morrison Skelly (eds), *Irish Foreign Policy, 1919–66*, 323.

28 Ben Tonra, *Global Citizen and European Republic, Irish Foreign Policy in Transition* (Manchester: Manchester University Press, 2006), 44.

29 For the finest analysis of Aiken's involvement at the United Nations from 1957 to 1965, see Skelly, *Irish Diplomacy at the United Nations*. For additional readings, see Dorr, *Ireland at the United Nations, Memories of the Early Years*; Kennedy and Skelly (eds), *Irish Foreign Policy, 1919–66*; Michael Kennedy and Deirdre McMahon (eds) *Obligations and Responsibilities: Ireland and the United Nations, 1955–2005* (Dublin, 2005); Macqueen, 'Frank Aiken and Irish Activism at the United Nations, 1957–61', 210–231; T. D. Williams, 'Irish Foreign Policy, 1949–69', in J. J. Lee (ed.), *Ireland, 1945–70* (Dublin: Gill and MacMillan, 1979); Patrick Keatinge, *A Place Among the Nations, Issues of Irish Foreign Policy* (Dublin: Institute of Public Administration, 1978); and Patrick Keatinge, *The Formation of Irish Foreign Policy* (Dublin: Institute for Public Administration, 1973).

30 In 1965, alone, Aiken spent ninety-nine days in New York. See Bhreatnach, 'Frank Aiken and the Formulation of Foreign Policy', 40.

31 Michael Lillis, 'Aiken's Playpen,' *Dublin Review of Books*, Issue 30, 11 March 2013. The full review is available at http://www.drb.ie/essays/aiken-s-playpen (accessed 03/12/13).

32 Skelly, *Irish Diplomacy at the United Nations, 1945–1965*, 21.

33 Speech by Aiken, 6 Oct. 1960. *Ireland at the United Nations 1960, speeches by Mr. Frank Aiken* (Dublin: Brún agus Ó Nulláin Teo, 1961), 6–22.

34 South Tyrol, an alpine region of the Austrian–Italian border, was part of the Austro-Hungarian Empire until the aftermath of World War One, when it was ceded to Italy under the terms of the Treaty of St Germain. For further reading of Aiken's involvement with South Tyrol, see Joseph Morrison Skelly, 'National Interests and International Mediation: Ireland's South Tyrol Initiative at the United Nations, 1960–1961', in Kennedy and Skelly (eds) *Irish Foreign Policy, 1919–66*, 286–307. See also Dermot Keogh, 'Irish Neutrality and the First Application for EEC Membership, 1961–3', in Kennedy and Skelly (eds), *Irish Foreign Policy. 1919–66*, 291–304.

35 For example, Henry Patterson writes that Aiken was 'a bastion of traditional anti-partitionism'. See Henry Patterson, *Ireland Since 1939, The Persistence of Conflict* (Dublin: Penguin Ireland, 2006), 157.

36 See speech by Aiken, 6 Oct. 1960. *Ireland at the United Nations 1960, speeches by Mr. Frank Aiken*, 16.

37 Quoted in Skelly, *Irish Diplomacy at the United Nations, 1945–1965*, 94.

38 Conor Cruise O'Brien, *To Katanga and Back: A UN Case History* (London: Hutchinson of London, 1962), 15.

39 O'Brien fondly recalled that Aiken had read and enjoyed the former's book, *Parnell and his Party*. O'Brien, *Memoir, My Life and Themes, Conor Cruise O'Brien*, 162.

40 Michael Kennedy, 'Frederick H. Boland', *Irish Dictionary of National Biography* (http://dib. cambridge.org, accessed 18/04/13).

41 Keogh, 'Irish Neutrality and the First Application for EEC Membership, 1961–3', 267; footnote 9.

42 Writing in the mid-1980s, following Cremin's retirement from the Irish civil service, he wrote of his respect for Aiken, describing his former minister as 'distinguished'. See Con Cremin, 'United Nations Peace-Keeping Operations: An Irish Initiative, 1961–1968', *Irish Studies in International Affairs*, Vol. 1, No. 4 (1984), 83.

43 See National Archives of Ireland (NAI), Cabinet minutes, Cab/2/19–27, record of Cabinet meetings, 1959–1962 and UCDA, Fianna Fáil Party Papers, (P176)/447–448, record of parliamentary party meetings, 1959–1962.

44 Skelly, *Irish Diplomacy at the United Nations, 1945–1965*, 206.

45 Besides Lemass's obsession with EEC membership, there were other reasons for the Irish delegation's pro-western stance at the UN by 1961. The lives of Irish troops were endangered in the Congo, and the composition of the UN was changing drastically with the introduction of the new host of African and Asian countries. Furthermore, the Irish public's rapturous fascination with the J. F. Kennedy Presidency in the United States may have encroached upon Irish government thinking on foreign policy.

46 This paragraph is sourced from Skelly, *Irish Diplomacy at the United Nations, 1945–1965*, 208.

47 Lemass to Aiken, 11 Sept. 1961. UCDA, P104/6328.

48 Horgan, *Seán Lemass*, 193.

49 Horgan, *Seán Lemass*, 193.

50 Horgan, *Seán Lemass*, 340.

51 Lillis, 'Aiken's Playpen,' *Dublin Review of Books*, Issue 30, 11 March 2013.

52 Keogh, 'Irish Neutrality and the First Application for EEC Membership, 1961–3', 266–267.

53 Fanning, 'Raison d'État and the Evolution of Irish Foreign Policy', 324.

54 Williams, 'Irish Foreign Policy, 1949–69', 144–145.

55 See, for example, correspondence between Aiken and Lemass on Irish Government's policy at the UN, 13 Sept. 1961. UCDA, P104/6328.

56 Author's correspondence with Noel Dorr, 8 May 2013.

57 For an overview of Ireland's first application for membership of the EEC (1961–1963) and Aiken's limited role in this initiative, see Keogh, 'Irish Neutrality and the First Application for EEC Membership, 1961–3', 265–285. See also Sharp, *Irish Foreign Policy and the European Community*, 67–90. For a more general examination of Aiken's stance on the European federation and the UN, see Aoife Bhreatnach, 'Frank Aiken: Federation and United Nations Internationalism', *Irish Studies in International Affairs*, Vol. 13 (2002), 237–249.

58 Macqueen, 'Frank Aiken and Irish Activism at the United Nations, 157–61', 213.

59 Keatinge, *The Formation of Irish Foreign Policy*, 93. See also comments by Williams, 'Irish Foreign Policy, 1949–69', 145.

60 Keatinge, *The Formation of Irish Foreign Policy*, 93.

61 See copy of confidential conversation between Aiken and United States Secretary for Economic Affairs Mr George Ball, 17 Nov. 1961. UCDA, P104/5672.

62 Speech by Aiken, 11 July 1961. DE, Vol. 191, col. 664.

63 Speech by Aiken, 4 April 1963. DE, Vol. 201, col. 1075.

64 See, for example, correspondence between Aiken and Assistant Secretary of the Department of External Affairs Donal O'Sullivan, 1–9 Sept. 1966. UCDA, P104/5682.

65 See copy of Aiken's interview with the *Europa* magazine, Aug. 1963. NAI, Department of Foreign Affairs (DFA), 98/3/319.

66   Speech by Aiken, 10 Sept. 1957. *Ireland at the United Nations 1957, speeches by Mr. Frank Aiken* (Dublin: Brún agus Ó Nulláin Teo, 1958), 7.

67   Maud Aiken to Aiken, 11 Sept. 1957. UCDA, P104/5885.

68   De Valera to Aiken, 11 Sept. 1957. UCDA, P104/5919.

69   See, for example, Dáil Éireann debates, 23 Oct. 1957. DE, Vol. 164, No. 1.

70   Copy of confidential summary of the official reaction to Aiken's speech in the Hungarian debate at the UN, Oct. 1957. UCDA, P104/5929.

71   See Skelly, *Irish Diplomacy at the United Nations, 1945–1965*, 111–114.

72   Skelly, *Irish Diplomacy at the United Nations, 1945–1965*, 115.

73   Speech by Aiken, 23 Sept. 1957. *Ireland at the United Nations 1957, speeches by Mr. Frank Aiken*, 28.

74   Dorr, *Ireland at the United Nations*, 111.

75   See copy of a typed letter marked 'confidential', author unknown, Sept. 1957. UCDA, P104/5943.

76   See Sile Ni Lionnain to Aiken, Oct. 1957. UCDA, P104/5948.

77   Quoted in Keogh, *Ireland*, 236.

78   For an overview of Cardinal Spellman's attempt to alter the Irish vote on China, see O'Brien, *Katanga*, 21–25.

79   See series of correspondence between Lemass to Aiken, 20–23 July 1959. UCDA, P104/6165.

80   See speech by Aiken, 6 Oct. 1960. *Ireland at the United Nations 1960, speeches by Mr. Frank Aiken*, 13–14. In fact, Aiken's speech was inaccurate. It was Henry Harrison MP – not Charles Stewart Parnell – who stated that: 'the cause of nationality is sacred, in Asia and Africa as in Ireland'. See Dorr, *Ireland at the United Nations*, 42–43.

81   For an overview of the Algerian crisis and Ireland's involvement with the issue at the UN from 1955 to 1962, see Christophe Gillissen, 'Ireland, France and the Question of Algeria at the United Nations, 1955–1962', *Irish Studies in International Affairs*, Vol. 19 (2008), 151–167. See also Dorr, *Ireland at the United Nations*, 179–184.

82   Speech by Aiken, 20 Sept. 1957. *Ireland at the United Nations 1957, speeches by Mr. Frank Aiken*, 24–25.

83   Gillissen, 'Ireland, France and the Question of Algeria at the United Nations, 1955–1962', 157.

84   Speech by Aiken, 4 Oct. 1962. *Ireland at the United Nations 1962, speeches by Mr. Frank Aiken* (Dublin: Brún agus Ó Nulláin Teo, 1963), 15–17.

85   For example, Conor Cruise O'Brien gave a lengthy analysis of 'this general question of partition' in a debate on Korea and Vietnam in Oct. 1957. Frederick Boland also touched upon the subject during a First Committee debate on Cyprus in Nov. 1957. See Noel Dorr, '1969: A United Nations Peacekeeping Force for Northern Ireland?', in Kennedy and McMahon (eds) *Obligations and Responsibilities*, 254–255.

86   Dorr, '1969: A United Nations Peacekeeping Force for Northern Ireland?', 254–255.

87   Michael Kennedy, *Divisions and Consensus, The Politics of Cross-Border Relations in Ireland, 1925–1969* (Dublin: Institute for Public Administration, 2000), 160.

88   Skelly, *Irish Diplomacy at the United Nations, 1945–1965*, 171.

89   *The Irish Times*, 13 April 1959.

90   Speech by Aiken, 21 Sept. 1959. *Ireland at the United Nations 1959, speeches by Mr. Frank Aiken* (Dublin: Brún agus Ó Nulláin Teo, 1960), 4. See also UCDA, P104/6181.

91   See UCDA P104/6181–6197.

92   Aoife Bhreatnach, 'A Friend of the Colonial Powers? Frank Aiken, Ireland's United Nations Alignment and Decolonisation', in Kennedy and McMahon (eds) *Obligations and Responsibilities*, 186.

93   Bhreatnach, 'A Friend of the Colonial Powers? Frank Aiken, Ireland's United Nations Alignment and Decolonisation', 186.

94   See Brian J. O'Connor, 'Ireland and the United Nations', in *Tuairim* (April, 1961).

95   See, for example, Speech by Aiken, 14 Dec. 1965. *Ireland at the United Nations 1965, speeches by Mr. Frank Aiken* (Dublin: Brún agus Ó Nulláin Teo, 1966), 9197. See also Dorr, *Ireland at the United Nations*, 121–123.

96   The Dalai Lama to Aiken, 11 March 1961. UCDA, P104/6356.

97   For an overview of Aiken, the UN and Southern Africa, see Kevin O'Sullivan, *Ireland, Africa and the End of the Empire: Small State Identity in the Cold War, 1955–75* (Manchester: Manchester University Press, 2012).

98   On the subject of Southern Africa, Aiken also spoke out against the white-supremacy regime of Ian Smith in Southern Rhodesia (present day Zimbabwe). For further reading on this subject, see Bhreatnach, 'A Friend of the Colonial Powers? Frank Aiken, Ireland's United Nations Alignment and Decolonisation', 187–188.

99   Statement by Aiken '… on the question of Apartheid', 7 Dec. 1966. NAI, D/T/GIS/1/5.

100 Speech by Aiken, *Irish Press*, 23 Nov. 1959.

101 Irish government press release, 24 March 1960. NAI, DFA 305/94.

102 O'Sullivan, *Ireland, Africa and the End of the Empire*, 67.

103 O'Sullivan, *Ireland, Africa and the End of the Empire*, 72.

104 See statement by Aiken '… on the question of Apartheid', 7 Dec. 1966. NAI, D/T/GIS/1/5. See also UCDA, P104/6749.

105 Aiken to Lynch, 3 Jan. 1968. UCDA, P104/6966.

106 See UCDA, P104/6749.

107 See UCDA, P104/6745.

108 For further reading on this subject, see Michael Kennedy and Art Magennis, *Ireland, the United Nations and Congo* (Dublin: Four Courts Press, 2014).

109 Skelly, *Irish Diplomacy at the United Nations, 1945–1965*, 268–269.

110 Speech by Aiken, 6 Oct. 1960. *Ireland at the United Nations 1960, speeches by Mr. Frank Aiken*, 6–22.

111 Speech by Aiken, 28 March 1961. *Ireland at the United Nations 1961, speeches by Mr. Frank Aiken* (Dublin: Brún agus Ó Nulláin Teo, 1962), 3–12.

112 Remembering Aiken's decision to 'recall' me from my post in Katanga, O'Brien wrote, 'Mr Aiken was very upset. His attitude towards Máire and myself was paternal – that is to say, affectionate and a shade testy …'. O'Brien, *Memoir, My Life and Themes, Conor Cruise O'Brien*, 255. See also UCDA P104/7042–7053 for various correspondences between Aiken, Cremin, Boland, U Thant and O'Brien in relation to the latter's resignation, Sept. 1961 to Dec. 1962.

113 For an insightful examination of Aiken's views on the Arab–Israeli dispute during 1958, see UCDA, P104/6096–6114. For a general analysis of Ireland's involvement with the Israel–Palestine conflict, see Rory Miller, *Ireland and the Palestine Question: 1948–2004* (Dublin: Irish Academic Press, 2005).

114   Skelly, *Irish Diplomacy at the United Nations, 1945–1965*, 150.

115   For an in-depth examination of Aiken's role during the Six Day War, see Rory Miller, 'Frank Aiken, the UN and the Six Day War, June 1967', *Irish Studies in International Affairs*, Vol. 14 (2003), 57–73.

116   Handwritten comments and typed drafts of a speech by Aiken, 23 June 1967. UCDA, P104/6851.

117   Speech by Aiken, 24 Oct. 1962. *Ireland at the United Nations 1962, speeches by Mr. Frank Aiken*, 23–30.

118   See Joseph P. O'Grady, 'Ireland, the Cuban Missile Crisis and Civil Aviation: A Study in Applied Neutrality', *Eire-Ireland*, Vol. 30, No. 3 (fall, 1995). See also UCDA, P104/6491–6494.

119   Speech by Aiken, 20 Sept. 1957. *Ireland at the United Nations 1957, speeches by Mr. Frank Aiken*, 13–17.

120   Speech by Aiken, 17 Oct. 1958. *Ireland at the United Nations 1958, speeches by Mr. Frank Aiken*, 39–50.

121   For further reading on Aiken's involvement with nuclear non-proliferation at the UN between 1958 and 1961, see Catherine Manathunga, 'The Evolution of Irish Disarmament Initiatives at the United Nations, 1957–1961', *Irish Studies in International Affairs*, Vol. 7 (1996), 97–113; and Evgency M. Chossudovsky, 'The Origins of the Treaty on the Non-Proliferation of Nuclear Weapons: Ireland's Initiative in the United Nations, 1958–61', *Irish Studies in International Affairs*, Vol. 3, No. 2 (1990), 111–135.

122   Speech by Gilmore, 21 June 2012. DE, Vol. 769, No. 3, cols 566–567.

123   O'Brien, 'Ireland in International Affairs', 132.

124   Ronan Fanning, 'Frank Aiken', *Irish Dictionary of National Biography* (http://dib.cambridge.org, accessed 18/04/13).

125   The Frank Aiken Papers contain minimal reference to the Vietnam War. See UCDA P104/6806–6820 and P104/6900–6911.

126   Fanning, 'Frank Aiken', *Irish Dictionary of National Biography*.

127   Handwritten notes by Aiken, April 1967. UCDA, P104/7140.

128   See copies of speeches and handwritten notes related to Aiken's views re: Biafra, Feb. to May 1968. UCDA, P104/7152–7153.

129   Alvin Jackson, *Ireland, 1798–1998* (Oxford: Blackwell Publishing, 1999), 322.

130   Dorr, *Ireland at the United Nations*, 170.

131   Speech by Dillon, 2 July 1959. DE, Vol. 176, col. 558.

132   Speech by Dillon, 2 July 1959. DE, Vol. 176, cols 546–547.

133   Speech by Dillon, 4 April 1963. DE, Vol. 201, col. 1074.

134   Boland admitted that in 1957/1958 he pleaded with de Valera not to appoint Aiken as Minister for External Affairs. See Gerald Boland's unpublished handwritten memoirs, 7(x). See also file marked '1957–58' (pp. 3, 4).

135   Copy of a statement from Seán MacEntee, *Nuclear Weapons: Proposed Declaration*, 5 Jan. 1961. UCDA, P104/6364.

136   Chossudovsky, 'The Origins of the Treaty on the Non-Proliferation of Nuclear Weapons: Ireland's Initiative in the United Nations, 1958–61', 112.

137   Quoted in *Irish Press*, 19 May 1983.

PART ONE

Nationalist

CHAPTER ONE

Frank Aiken: family, early life and the revolutionary period, 1898–1921*

Eoin Magennis

Introduction

Frank Aiken lived his life in the public eye for six decades, from the age of sixteen until his retirement in 1973. Despite this he tended to avoid interviews, speaking to researchers rather than the media, and always reflecting government policy rather than his own opinions.[1] He was even more reticent to speak of his early years and activity in the War of Independence. A three-page typed autobiography, compiled around 1933, provides only sparse detail of his life between 1914 and 1923, and nothing before those years.[2] Neither an interview with Ernie O'Malley nor Aiken's papers offer much more.[3] Instead, his early years must be seen through the memories of others, which offer a picture of a relatively affluent background, an unusual family upbringing where both parents were dead by the time he turned fifteen, an attachment to the discipline and bravery involved

* My thanks to the archivists in University College Dublin Archives (UCDA); Cardinal Ó Fiaich Memorial Library and Archive (COFLA), Armagh; National Archives of Ireland (NAI); Kilmainham Gaol; and the Public Record Office of Northern Ireland (PRONI) for their assistance. Thanks also to Donal Hall, Matthew Lewis, Briege Rice and Patrick Quinn for generously sharing research findings with me. On a personal note, thanks are also long overdue to Kevin McMahon, Dr Rory O'Hanlon and the Magennis and Aiken families.

with soldiering, personal partisanship and a fully developed sense of the need for Ireland to be both independent and united. This chapter pieces together this detail on Frank Aiken's early years.

1898–1918

Parish records and a genealogical bookplate within a family bible reveal that Francis Thomas Aiken was born on 13 February 1898.[4] He was the seventh and youngest child of James and Mary Aiken of Carrickbracken, Camlough, County Armagh.

James Aiken was a significant local figure, important enough to merit extensive coverage of his death in August 1900.[5] James appears to have come to Camlough in the late 1870s, and may have migrated there from either Monaghan or Fermanagh, according to a family tradition that describes a nineteenth-century migration from the townland of Truagh. Further local lore in Fermanagh tells of Frank Aiken's grandfather leaving a townland near Ederney in the early nineteenth century. The reasons are unclear, and vary from links to the radical United Irishmen, to that the grandfather married a Catholic, excluding himself from his Presbyterian family circle.[6] The Ederney Aikens were said to be canny, strong farmers, and James Aiken followed in this tradition. By the time of his death, James had built up substantial landholdings and tenant houses in Carrickbracken and Derrymore townlands (near Camlough) as well as urban property on both sides of the county line in Newry (in Mary and Monaghan streets). This was amassed through both farming and a profitable building business, which specialised in church building.[7]

James was also a public figure sitting on Newry's Board of Poor Law Guardians, for the Camlough division, a body of which he became chairman. After the local government reforms of 1898, James was also elected onto Newry No. 2 Rural District Council, becoming its first chairman. He was a Justice of the Peace for County Armagh, and spoken of as a potential Member of Parliament for the South Armagh constituency. He was apparently noted for the independence of his views, which were strongly Nationalist. As one obituary in a Unionist newspaper noted, 'many of his actions while accompanying the chair at the meetings of local bodies came up for adverse criticism'. One that was certainly controversial was his casting vote against a resolution to welcome Queen Victoria's Irish visit of April 1900.[8]

James Aiken was twice married, making strong connections with local families. His first wife was Catherine Cardwell, from Camlough, who died in March 1885, after giving birth to a daughter Mary (who died before her third birthday in January 1888). He married his second wife, Mary McGeeney (of Carrowmannon, Belleek, County Armagh) in May 1887, and they had seven children together. Mary ran the family home and business after James's death in 1900 before her own early death in April 1913, aged 48. In the 1901 and 1911 censuses, Mary is mentioned as a widow and the owner of fourteen (of seventy-five) houses in Carrickbracken townland and two (of twenty-five) in Derrymore.[9]

James, Frank Aiken's eldest sibling, was born in March 1889, and went on to be a surgeon in Dulwich Hospital, London. He is noted in the 1911 census as a medical student and was qualified by 1916, when he served as locum Medical Officer for a cousin, Dr Frank McDermott of Donaghmore, outside Newry.[10] James nominated Patrick McCartan as the Sinn Féin candidate for the January 1918 South Armagh by-election, but he does not appear again in local politics.[11] Indeed, he seems to have gone to England at around this time, and lived and worked in London until he retired back to Dublin in the mid-1950s. James returned to Newry in his last months, and died there in June 1964.

The next child, Mary (or May as she was known by the family), was born in March 1890. She married a local auctioneer, Heber Magenis, lived in Poyntzpass and was seen as a Republican sympathiser, though not active, in 1923. May died in 1951 at the age of 61.[12] A third child, Annie (born July 1891), died in infancy while a fourth, Gertrude (born April 1893), died just after her fifteenth birthday. Another girl, Magdalene (known as Madge), was born in April 1895, trained as a schoolteacher and went to live and raise a family in Leicester, England, where she died. Closest in age and views to Frank Aiken was his sister Nano (born August 1896), who was to become very active in the republican cause in the revolutionary period, and reappears throughout his early life.

This domestic picture suggests a number of things. First, as Todd Andrews later noted, that Frank Aiken was born into comfortable surroundings with substantial property, a productive building business and involvement in local economic development.[13] Second, that the death of his father in 1900 and the medical training in Dublin of his oldest sibling meant that from his early teens Frank was the only resident Aiken male in Carrickbracken. This situation may well have forged the independence and self-reliance that became obvious at a later stage. Finally, the Aikens were a well-known family locally with marriage, business and political connections across much of South Armagh and into Newry. Frank Aiken's subsequent local rise becomes more explicable when the family's standing is taken into account.

In terms of education, there is a family story that Frank Aiken earned the nickname 'Corr Lá' (odd day) for his occasional attendance at school. We know that he attended Camlough National School and was photographed there in June

1908.[14] He went next to the Abbey Christian Brothers' School in Newry, where he passed his 'Inter' in 1914, and is photographed around the same time. Marginal notes in a surviving copy of William Neilson's *Irish Grammar*[15] give the sense that he went beyond the curriculum.[16] Although the 1929 University College Dublin Agricultural Science syllabus is to be found among the documents he kept, Aiken's papers support the idea that self-education was more important to him, particularly in fields such as agri-food, engineering and energy.[17]

According to his own account, Aiken's political life seems to have begun in 1914, when he was elected as secretary of the new company of Camlough Volunteers. There is no exact date for the formation of that company, but it is likely to have been between March and May 1914, when there was a surge in membership.[18] Locally, there was opposition to the Volunteers from the Ancient Order of Hibernians (AOH) whose leader, Joe Devlin, spoke against the movement in Newry in January 1914. And, in Aiken's own words, the Camlough company was short-lived: 'owing to the Great War and the split [into Irish and National Volunteers], the Company melted away in the autumn [of 1914]'.[19] So, while Newry and Dundalk had some contact with the 1916 Easter Rising, Aiken was completely 'out of touch', buying shotgun cartridges in case (or in the hope that) the fighting would spread beyond Dublin.[20]

In the absence of the Volunteer company, Aiken appears to have thrown himself into 'Irish Ireland' organisations, notably the Gaelic League and the Gaelic Athletic Association (GAA). He noted that he was secretary of his local League branch and that, in 1917, he was playing both hurling and football for Camlough's Shane O'Neills.[21] The League branch has left no records, and may have been subsumed into wider activity centred on Newry. The Newry branch, Craobh an nIúr, was the moving spirit behind summer schools in Colaiste Bríde in Omeath, County Louth, where Nano Aiken was a regular attender in 1915 and 1916.[22] Craobh an nIúr had a strong Republican presence from 1916, with Paddy Rankin and Bob Kelly (both interned in Frongoch internment camp, North Wales), as well as Roisín ní Beirne (ally of Nano in organising Cumann na mBan in Camlough from 1917), all on the committee. Aiken was named as an organiser in South Armagh for the 'Big Push' for the language in the winter of 1916–1917.[23] Interestingly, it is unclear how proficient Aiken was in the language at this time. Todd Andrews' memory in 1922 is of him consciously struggling to speak Irish.[24] George Colley's funeral oration noted that Aiken turned to learn Irish at a later (albeit undetermined) age, something that Colley took to denote determination.[25]

Despite the anger at the executions and internments after the Easter Rising, Republicans were not politically dominant in Aiken's home area in 1916. There was, firstly, a significant unionist community and electorate, some of whom supported plans to 'exclude' six Ulster counties (including Armagh and Down) from the Home Rule settlement.[26] Secondly, by-elections were to show how deeply divided nationalists in these counties were, with Sinn Féin facing a resilient Irish Parliamentary Party.[27] By 1917, these by-elections had become the bellwether of opinion and, as historian Michael Laffan writes, 'Sinn Féin was the fad or craze'.[28] Aiken got his first taste of electioneering in East Clare in July 1917, when he went to help with Éamon de Valera's campaign. There, he volunteered as a despatch rider for Sinn Féin honorary secretary Austin Stack and met de Valera for the first time, helping to keep order in Ennis on election night.[29]

Buoyed up by this experience, Aiken threw himself into organizing Sinn Féin in his own area. He became treasurer of the new branch in Camlough, and was appointed as organizer for the South Armagh constituency. The rival Irish Parliamentary Party, Ancient Order of Hibernians and United Irish League (UIL) organizations were all strong, although police sources believed that Sinn Féin's star was definitely on the rise, especially among the young.[30] In late 1917, Herbert Moore Pim, a former unionist who was regarded by police as an 'extreme republican', was invited to speak at a Sinn Féin meeting in Camlough. Although the local parish priest and UIL executive member Canon Charles Quinn prevented the meeting from taking place, Jack McElhaw later reported that the local Volunteer company was re-established and plans were laid for a Sinn Féin hall. Aiken's own account refers to tying 'the first Sinn Féin flag ever seen in the district to a tree opposite the police barracks' in Camlough in December 1917.[31]

The respective political strengths of nationalists and republicans in South Armagh were put to the test when a by-election was called after the sudden death of Charles O'Neill, the Irish Parliamentary Party MP, in January 1918. The Irish Parliamentary Party was to hold the seat by a majority of 1,019 votes in the poll in early February, but only after a bitter campaign.[32] The Sinn Féin candidate, Dr Patrick McCartan, had been involved in the abortive rising in Coalisland, County Tyrone, in 1916, while his rival, Patrick Donnelly, was a well-known solicitor and local councillor in Newry. A key factor of the campaign was that the 'partition question' became the focus rather than the 'Home Rule or Republic' debates elsewhere in the country.[33] During the by-election campaign Aiken's profile rose, particularly as his family premises became the local base for canvassers and some election committee meetings. In addition, James Aiken and Jack McElhaw nominated McCartan, adding to the sense of a Camlough and Aiken leadership of Sinn Féin in the area. The campaign saw verbal and written abuse about both candidates, as well as occasionally violent clashes between the AOH and the Volunteers. Aiken led bodies of Volunteers to provide defence at election meetings in Newtownhamilton and Bessbrook, County Armagh, at which Frank McGuinness, brother of Joe, the South Longford Sinn Féin MP, and de Valera spoke.[34]

Some Volunteers who came to South Armagh on the polling day to support McCartan left with jaundiced views about Ulster and the strength of 'Hibernianism' as well as loyalism.[35] Additionally, Aiken and other republicans used the campaign to recruit members and revive or establish Volunteer companies or branches of Cumann na mBan across the constituency.[36] The September 1918 Cumann na mBan convention reported that a Miss Cashel had been appointed as organiser in Newry district due 'to the spirit aroused by the South Armagh election'.[37] According to James McGuill, the election volunteers and 'the later recruits who joined up after the Election, although small in number when compared to areas in the South, gave a splendid account of themselves in the Black and Tan war'.[38] Many of these looked to Frank Aiken for leadership.

1918–1919

In the spring of 1918, national events began to have an impact in Aiken's local area. Joost Augusteijn describes the period as one of open defiance of the authorities, particularly through the act of drilling. At first the police were instructed not to intervene but only to note the illegal act, but, feeling that their position was intolerable, they began to single out the leaders.[39] In South Armagh the Volunteer companies were regularly drilling by February 1918, sometimes on their way to meetings and, at other times, to GAA matches. So too were republican women, organised in Camlough by Nano Aiken and Roisín ní Beirne under the banner of Cumann na mBan. The police arrested Frank Aiken for 'illegal drilling' in March 1918, and he was jailed for one month in Belfast. The trial in Newry offered a further opportunity for defiance, with the Camlough Volunteers marching to the courthouse to protest. Jack McElhaw was arrested for organizing the drilling outside the courthouse, and both men continued drilling and training on their release in June 1918.[40]

Political work also continued to be important for Aiken. He was secretary and then chairman of the South Armagh Sinn Féin Comhairle Ceanntair (district executive), constituency representative to the Ard Chomhairle (national executive) and, later, an organiser for the Dáil Loan, the national fundraising effort undertaken by Michael Collins. Aiken also led opposition to the Conscription Act, including breaking up a recruitment meeting in Newry in June 1918, which resulted in arrests and the jailing of six Volunteers.[41] The Volunteers were also called upon in the December 1918 general election. Aiken's Camlough company had been ordered by the Newry Brigade to go to Belfast on polling day, but at the last moment they were sent instead to Carlingford, County Louth, to prevent intimidation there. There were no clashes with rivals, but one statement records the Camlough Volunteers ordering the local Royal Irish Constabulary to return to barracks and them performing policing duties instead of a political role.[42] If true, this would suggest that this group of Volunteers, led by Aiken, had confidence in their training, and were openly defiant of the authorities.

Matthew Lewis argues that the Newry and South Armagh pattern was more advanced than elsewhere in the north-east, but not as developed as some areas farther south.[43] This raises a question as to what the restraining elements were at this time. Certainly, a lack of arms was critical. Edward Fullerton, a young Volunteer in Newry, recalls: 'during 1918 and 1919 we went into country districts around Newry very often and carried out military manoeuvres. We had little arms'.[44] Raids to seize weapons or attempts to buy them seem to have occurred later in this area than elsewhere.

A second restraining factor on the move from defiance to violence may have been the leadership. The Camlough Volunteer company was part of the Newry Brigade, which was formed in the winter of 1918–19 to direct activities in South Down and South Armagh, and continued to do this until the formation of the Fourth Northern Division in March 1921. Frank Aiken was elected commandant of the new Newry Brigade, but chose to serve under Paddy Rankin, who had a decade of republican activity behind him even before being in Dublin in Easter 1916. Later reminiscences tend to argue that the respected older leadership, men such as Paddy Rankin and Pat Lavery, acted as brakes on violence.[45] However, these memories should be viewed alongside the opinion, expressed in many places, that republican supporters were not keen on violence in early 1919, with hopes for the viability of the new parliament, Dáil Éireann.[46]

The mention of Paddy Rankin, an Irish Republican Brotherhood (IRB) leader from the 1900s, raises the question of whether Frank Aiken was a member of that well-established nationalist secret society. Aiken appears to have become a member of the IRB at some point in 1918, although his own account, and a separate one by his close ally, Johnny McCoy, stresses his recruitment by Rankin. Aiken emphasised to Ernie O'Malley that, by June 1920, the IRB was to have been dissolved into the IRA.[47] The organisation was certainly strong in the late 1890s and early 1900s in towns such as Newry, Dundalk and Armagh. Its role in combating Hibernianism and being the key vehicle for popular republicanism has been recently emphasised by historians, particularly Fergal McCluskey on East Tyrone.[48]

During the winter of 1918–1919, the formation of the Newry brigade did not result in any dramatic increase in Volunteer activity, with a continuing focus on drilling, training and political activity. After the general election, and the first sitting of Dáil Éireann, Aiken and his colleagues held Sinn Féin meetings in Newry, Armagh and Dundalk, organised welcomes home for released prisoners, and ensured that party halls across South Armagh and Down were bustling with activity.[49] As 1919 wore on, the balance shifted towards military activity. Aiken's autobiographical notes on 1919 record: '[I] was in command of a few small operations carried out by Volunteers in different parts of the Brigade'. Edward Fullerton's statement describes one action, which was led by the Newry brigade and provoked a wide response. This was an arms raid on Ballyedmond Castle, near Killowen, County Down, on 11 May 1919. The owner of the house, Captain Nugent, had been an officer in the British Army during the Great War, and there had been persistent rumours of an arms cache in the house.[50]

The raid involved companies from across South Armagh, North Louth and South Down, and was coordinated by the Newry brigade staff, specifically Aiken. Nothing of significance was found in the search, which lasted several hours, but there is a sense from later statements and contemporary press reports of a bold and well-planned operation. Up to 100 men travelled from meeting points in Newry and Omeath (from where they came by boat) to Ballyedmond. Once there, Volunteers were directed either to hold roads in and out of the area, to guard the house and its inhabitants, or to take part in the search, which Aiken led. Telephone lines were cut and, inside the house, floorboards were broken in the effort to find the elusive weapons.[51] The planning behind Ballyedmond built on an earlier action at Dromilly, County Armagh, in February 1919, where the 'big house' of the Cope family was raided by Volunteers in a search for arms. Again, the operation was led by Aiken and his closest allies, this time with the North Armagh companies in the forward role.[52]

At the same time as these raids, the new Dáil Éireann and Republican government were struggling to survive. In the autumn, the Minister for Finance, Michael Collins, issued the Dáil Loan Scheme, as mentioned above. The selling of 'Republican bonds' among supporters in Ireland and overseas, particularly the United States, had the aim of raising approximately £1 million by June 1920. The objective of the loan scheme was to support the fledgling Republican government, including administration costs and funding to procure arms for the IRA. At a local level, directors were appointed in each electoral constituency with targets for subscriptions. In South Armagh, Aiken was appointed director, and much of the autumn and winter was spent selling the bonds to an often sceptical public, concerned that their money would never be repaid.[53]

1920

In early 1920, decisions made nationally altered the pace of events at a local level. In February 1920, the Volunteer Executive endorsed open attacks on British forces and the destruction of police barracks.[54] At the same time, government policy oscillated between coercion and conciliation. Arrests were followed by releases and then rearrests. The murder of the Sinn Féin Mayor of Cork, Tomás MacCurtain, by disguised policemen in March 1920, marked a significant deepening of the crisis. Locally, the arrests (before April 1920) of Paddy Rankin, P. J. Berrill and Seamus McGuill meant that a new leadership came to the fore.[55] As in other areas, these were often much more active or perhaps radical Volunteers, younger and with fewer scruples about the use of violence.

The new leadership under Frank Aiken also found that communications between General Headquarters (GHQ) and the local brigade improved with the national reorganisation of the Irish Volunteers.[56] The attempted attack on Newtownhamilton barracks in February 1920, the attempt to burn the tax offices in Newry in April and the general burning of abandoned barracks in the same month all seem to have been either sanctioned by, or organised in conjunction with, GHQ. The accounts of the attack on Newtown barracks give a sense of Aiken's leadership and planning. British Army uniforms were procured, and Aiken went to the front door dressed in one. The intention was to get four disguised men in, and then overpower the Royal Irish Constabulary (RIC) men inside. Again, Volunteers from across County Armagh were mobilised, and orders given to secure the roads in and out of the strongly Unionist town. However, the RIC men were not fooled by the ruse, perhaps because it had been recently used elsewhere.[57] Attention then turned to destroying seven abandoned RIC barracks in and around Newry in April. The Newry brigade also followed GHQ orders to destroy local tax offices in Easter week. With Aiken in command, the bridge providing access to the Customs House was held for three hours while the IRA burned tax records and that part of the building that housed them.[58]

These attempts to hamper the operations of the state continued for the rest of 1920.[59] So too did the arms raids, with Unionist houses being particularly targeted in the South Down area. A general order from GHQ in August 1920 resulted in arms raids across what was to become the entire area of the Fourth Northern Division. However, this was a method that rarely delivered great numbers of weapons. Police reports in October 1920 estimated that a small number of rifles and shotguns had been seized, while the newspapers noted that some of the raiders were shot near Lurgan, County Armagh.[60] More direct methods for seizing weapons began to be used, despite the potential for clashes with the security forces.

In June 1920, plans were laid to ambush a company of soldiers who were acting as a convoy for the RIC men bringing explosives to Goraghwood quarry. Again, a significant group (perhaps twenty strong) was gathered outside Newry to carry out the ambush, led by Aiken and involving his closest collaborators (Jack McElhaw, Petie Boyle, John Quinn and Johnny McCoy). McElhaw's account presents a picture of what was fast becoming an Active Service Unit assembling overnight in Meigh, County Armagh (ten miles away), having access to motor vehicles, disguised, and armed with revolvers and hand grenades. The ambush was abandoned due to the absence of enough men to overpower the soldiers, which McElhaw attributed to a 'no-show' by Newry Volunteers.[61] Also in June 1920, at an Airidheacht (sports event) in Cullyhanna, County Armagh, a small, armed group led by Aiken demanded that three RIC men hand over their revolvers. Two revolvers were seized, but shots were exchanged and two men, IRA Volunteer Peter McCreesh of Aughanduff and RIC Sergeant Thomas Holland, were killed.[62] There had been deaths in Dundalk before June 1920, but Cullyhanna marked the beginning of a new phase in the War of Independence.

Despite these events, Aiken remained involved in politics, and does not appear to have taken the soldier's position of contempt for the political process that some historians have described.[63] Local government elections to county and district councils were held in June 1920, and Aiken won seats on Armagh County Council (in Forkhill ward), Newry No. 2 (Rural) Council (for Camlough ward) and Newry Board of Guardians.[64] The elections had two significant consequences from the republican viewpoint. The first was that Sinn Féin had now largely become the 'voice' of Irish nationalist opinion in counties Armagh and Down, although in Louth there was still a strong old nationalist vote.[65] The outworking of this shift could be seen in reports from Keady, where the old AOH/Republican divisions had been (perhaps temporarily) healed; their pipe bands marched together and fought alongside one another in a series of night-time clashes with local unionists in the town.[66] There was a problem with such incidents. In July, a crowd in Banbridge demanded that all premises close to mark the death of one of the town's inhabitants, who had been killed in a shooting in Cork. Two shops refused, and were attacked. When the mob threatened the public house of the Monaghans, Sinn Féin candidates in the election, a young man in the crowd was shot dead. On the next night the mob returned, and both the premises and

Monaghan house were burned to the ground. On the night of the first attack, Aiken was travelling by motorbike to Lurgan, and was fortunate to escape the angry mob in Banbridge.[67]

Politically, republicans now had local government bodies in which to push their case for recognition of Dáil Eireann. At a meeting of the Newry Board of Guardians at the end of June, Aiken proposed the motion to recognise the Dáil, which was seconded by Bob Kelly. When a unionist member said that he had lived eighty years under the British flag and hoped to die under it, Aiken responded 'I hope not'. The motion was passed.[68] A few weeks later, in Newry No. 2, Aiken proposed and John McCoy seconded a resolution 'acknowledging the authority of Dáil Éireann as the duly elected government of the Irish people and undertaking to give effect to all its decrees in so far as same affected the Council'. Despite unionist opposition, the resolution passed by seven votes to two.[69] There was also support for Dáil Courts and policing by republican 'vigilance committees', another element in the campaign to create an alternative state.[70]

In the summer and autumn of 1920, County Louth, under the leadership of the McGuills and Peter Hughes, was the focus of these efforts, especially in Dundalk and Ardee.[71] The rising temperature in the summer of 1920 came to a height with the death, after hunger strike, of Terence MacSwiney. This led to a series of political protests, a campaign to prevent dances and sporting events, and, after sectarian clashes in Belfast in which Catholics came off much the worst, the beginnings of the 'Belfast Boycott' in July 1920, which nationalist local authorities supported.[72]

At the same time, the military campaign went on. There were plans to destroy both occupied and abandoned barracks in Forkhill, evacuated by the RIC on 31 May 1920, and burned a few weeks later by the Mullaghbawn company, led by Aiken, and described in the press as '100 strange men'.[73] As the outlying barracks were abandoned (and then burned), a chain of fortified buildings remained, linking the main military (plus Black and Tans and Auxiliaries) garrisons in Armagh city, Castleblayney, Newry and Dundalk. Newtown was one of the key barracks, an 'enemy citadel, predominantly Orange, in the middle of the district', and so a second attempt was made to destroy it in May 1920.[74]

The twin aims were to burn the building and to seize arms, including what was believed to be a store of Ulster Volunteer Force (UVF) weapons. Again, the plan combined the mobilisation of large numbers of Volunteers to secure surrounding roads, and a core group (mainly of Camlough, Mullaghbawn and Newry men) using Aiken's engineering skills to force their way into the building. The town was secured before midnight, covering fire organised, and the lead group with Aiken in charge got into the public house next door, and twice drilled holes in the adjoining building before lodging explosives to blow a breach in the wall. On the second attempt, entry was gained by Aiken and Jack McElhaw, who forced the RIC men into a backyard and set the building alight. The police refused to surrender their weapons, despite a gun battle, which lasted the night. The statements of those involved stress the success of an operation in a unionist-dominated part of County Armagh, while the unionist press poured scorn on their efforts and accused the IRA men of spending much of the evening drinking the available alcohol. McCoy's account was critical of Aiken for not having 'constant contact between his post and the position in the ruins opposite the barracks and with the party engaged at the rear of the barracks'.[75]

Events in Newry caught up with the rest of the country in a shocking way in November 1920. This was due to the shooting of Head Constable John J. Kearney on 21 November as he left Sunday evening devotions in the Dominican chapel. The policeman was described in the local press as a 'marked man', and one who was fearless in his pursuit of republicans.[76] According to Edward Fullerton, an IRA man on duty that evening, Kearney 'took a prominent and active part in raiding for and arresting men on the run in the Newry district'. His assassination on Needham Street was ordered and carried out without hesitation, marking a definite hardening of approach by the IRA. It also provoked a reaction from the Crown forces, with halls (including the Gaelic League rooms, which were used for battalion meetings) and homes raided and reports of shots being fired at crowds by police.[77]

In December 1920, Aiken got agreement from GHQ for an ambitious operation. The target was the fortified blockhouse barracks, holding up to forty RIC and Special Constabulary men[78] in Camlough, with a secondary target being the military reinforcements coming from Newry. The discussion with Dick McKee in Dublin led to a plan to set the building on fire and demand surrender rather than using mines to explode their way into the building.[79] On the evening, however, many things went wrong, including the damaging of the fluid pump designed to force paraffin into the barracks, the failure to get arms out of dumps in South Down to arm the ambush party, and the bad weather. The failed attempt on the barracks pales alongside the disastrous attempt to ambush reinforcements at the Eygptian Arch on the Newry–Camlough road. The military pulled up out of reach of grenades and gunfire and used machine guns to attack the IRA emplacements, killing one Volunteer and mortally wounding two others.[80]

Aiken recorded the aftermath: '[I] had to go on the run after the attack on the local police barracks. Family home burnt out by Specials and police'.[81] Edward Fullerton notes that Volunteers made themselves scarce as 'the Crown forces were raiding all over Newry town and district'. In addition to Aiken's home being burned after three attempts, the military burned many other houses and premises in Camlough, as well as the Sinn Féin hall in Newry.[82] The military roadblocks made movement dangerous for armed men and civilians alike, two of whom were shot.[83] John McCoy urged that Aiken and his Camlough colleagues, McElhaw and Boyle, should move to Mullaghbawn for safety. Initially they refused, and moved from one abandoned farmhouse to another.[84] The aim was to pull their battalion together and launch an operation on the military in and around Camlough, and, in January 1921, they ambushed an RIC patrol passing the ruins of the Aiken family home, wounding two policemen.[85] After this, Mullaghbawn became the base for the Brigade staff from South Armagh, and Corrags became the same for the Newry-based men.

1921

In early 1921, Aiken intended to make it clear that the British did not entirely control the countryside. A decision was taken at a December 1920 meeting of the Newry brigade to order battalions to each carry out an operation.[86] Aiken and his staff put pressure on other areas beyond Newry and Camlough, and there was a sense of an activist leadership encouraging activity from a broader group of Volunteers. One example of this can be seen in an ambush organised by the Newtownhamilton battalion in January 1921. Aiken and his staff visited the battalion and the ambush was led, rather than supported, by the Camlough and Mullaghbawn contingent. In the event, they struck a police convoy accompanying a postman taking pension monies from Crossmaglen to Cullyhanna. After a heavy exchange of fire (although the lack of rifles was bemoaned by one Volunteer), the postman and two policemen lay dead.[87]

To encourage this activity, Aiken was on the move, mostly at night, throughout County Armagh and parts of South Down. As Brigade commanding officer (OC) he visited battalion areas and held discussions about the potential for local operations. John McCoy gave an account of one such visit to the Armagh battalion area in the first months of 1921. They stayed in a safe house for a few days, interviewed new officers (as their predecessors had been arrested), were given a general overview of the area they were in, and came away with confidence about the officers and their prospects.[88]

The impetus for a major reorganisation came from outside. This was the decision taken by GHQ in March 1921 to divisionalise the north of the island. The four Northern Divisions were born out of GHQ's desires, both to stir up activity outside Belfast, and to recognise what Robert Lynch calls 'Frank Aiken's rather unique fiefdom'.[89] The Richard Mulcahy Papers give an idea of the discussions behind the divisions, and show Aiken's growing influence. An early plan left his area without a division, giving North Armagh to Antrim and Down and South Armagh to Tyrone and Monaghan. The final decision, taken after a meeting in Dublin with the Ulster officers, saw the Fourth Northern area covering South and West Down, all of Armagh and North Louth, with Aiken as OC.[90] The decision was enforced locally after a meeting of battalion officers in Killeavy, County Armagh. The three brigades in the new division, and the divisional staff, were led by men trusted by Aiken, such as McCoy, Ivor Monaghan and John Quinn.[91]

The reorganisation led to GHQ intensifying its interest, and an influx of weapons, some procured by GHQ and shipped into Newry by an IRB member, followed.[92] Other arms were moved from areas of surplus (due to successful raids in North Louth in the 1919–1920 period) to areas of need. The attention paid by GHQ also meant that there was an added pressure to carry out operations, for example in April 1921, when Mulcahy ordered Aiken to revive morale in a few areas. One was the Mournes, County Down, from where Mulcahy had received a letter in February 1921, which complained that the company had called off an ambush on the Ulster Special Constabulary and was wary of provoking reprisals. Aiken was told to visit the area and 'see that he [the officer] understands what he should be doing'.[93] The other area was North Louth. The area had become quiescent after a long period of political activity.[94] The response was the attack on a house at Plaster, near Faughart, in April 1921, which brought men together from the first and second brigades. The plan was to ambush a convoy of military coming to relieve a guard on the house. The elements of the operation included detaining the guard in the house, ambushing the relieving lorry and preventing reinforcements coming from Dundalk. The problem arose when those surrounding the house began firing, alerting the military convoy to take a different route and causing the IRA to make a hasty retreat. McCoy regarded the operation as both a success (in mobilizing the north Louth men and getting away unharmed) and a failure (as the aim had been to capture the arms of the relief convoy). It also threw up a clear divide between the experienced men in the Division and those to whom operations, like the Plaster one, were either a very occasional or first-time occurrence.[95]

The period between February and June 1921 saw violence in Aiken's area rise to new levels, although he became less visible in the activity on the ground and more involved in directing operations. This was against the background of intense military activity in counties Armagh and Down in raids, swamping areas, burning homes[96] and reprisal shootings of both IRA Volunteers and civilians. The IRA made several attempts to ambush policemen, sometime at dances or public houses (in Barr and Camlough) and sometimes on patrol (in Newry, Corrags and

Warrenpoint). However, as Jack McElhaw put it, 'all that was possible at the time was to evade capture and to carry out reprisals for any acts of outrage carried out against our people by British forces'.[97] There were few large-scale operations, the exception being the attempt at Adavoyle, County Armagh, in June 1921 to derail trains returning from the opening of the new Northern Ireland parliament in Belfast. The aim was to take three trains, which were carrying the king's cavalry escort, off the tracks by using engineering skills rather than explosives. In the event, two trains got through and the third was derailed, killing two soldiers, a railway lineman and a large number of horses. This period, before the Truce was announced on 11 July, was one of greater violence in which twenty-seven people lost their lives. Civilians bore the brunt of the violence, both in IRA raids on houses and the shooting of alleged spies, and from reprisal actions by police and army, such as the shooting of four young men outside Newry in June, or the mutilation and murder of William Hickey in the same month.[98]

When the Truce was agreed in July 1921, a different period began for Aiken and his comrades. Outside of the new Northern Ireland state, the Truce provided a six-month period whereby tensions reduced and large numbers of young men joined the IRA. However, Belfast remained more violent than before the Truce had been signed, and the rest of the new state bristled with potential and actual violence.[99] Within those months there was a lessening of pressure on the Fourth Northern Division. The divisional HQ was moved from Mullaghbawn into Newry, where it operated quite openly. The later statements give a sense of men returning home after weeks or months on the run, and some relaxation being taken.[100]

It was also possible for Aiken to organise divisional training camps, such as the five-week-long effort held at Killeavy, County Armagh, in August to September 1921. However, training camps were technically breaches of the Truce, and had the potential to provoke trouble in the north, so other large camps were held in County Louth, at Dungooley, and at Giles' Quay, near Dundalk.[101] The camps emphasised training in different skills. The one at Giles' Quay focussed on the use of maps and the maintenance of weapons, while Killeavy had engineering classes. The camps were also visited by GHQ staff, including Mulcahy, who apparently gave the north Louth men a dressing down on one visit. Those attending the camps were then to bring their lessons back into the companies, where men were drilled in using signalling and first aid.[102] Seán McConville described how a series of battalion camps were ordered and held in his area in north Armagh before the end of 1921. Aiken was seen as being very keen on training, not only as a form of education, but also to keep the men disciplined during the Truce period. McConville noted how, in his area in Lurgan, 'at the end of all of these course [*sic*] of instruction the Divisional O/C held a general inspection at a parade of all of the officers and men of our battalion'.[103]

Another republican activity with which Aiken was involved during the Truce was the operation of Dáil Courts and associated policing. These operated openly, sometimes with the RIC actually present, in places such as Mullaghbawn, Camlough and Warrenpoint. This was seen as important, a sign of ignoring Northern Ireland. The courts actively involved Volunteers, as did the enforcement of the Belfast Boycott, in order to keep up morale within Northern Ireland.[104] The northern authorities, at least until December 1921, were willing to acknowledge, if not officially recognise, the liaison system that was in place across the island between the IRA and the State. John McCoy was Liaison Officer for County Armagh, a duty he reluctantly accepted from Aiken during recuperation after McCoy had been shot in April 1921. He presented his authorization from Dublin to the RIC in Armagh city, where he set up office in the Charlemont Hotel and announced to the local press that he was in business.[105] He found out quickly that it was a thankless task when word came of the arrests of six men in Keady who had been holding a Dáil Court to judge a man accused of burglaries. Despite McCoy's appeals, the local RIC insisted on charging the six men. Indeed, most of the cases he dealt with were complaints from the police about the local IRA carrying weapons, which McCoy then tried to resolve. Despite his appeals to Aiken to be released from this work, he had to carry on until the end of January 1922.[106] By then the Truce was virtually over within Northern Ireland, showing just how partition would complicate matters for the IRA, and particularly for Aiken and the Fourth Northern Division.[107]

The Anglo-Irish Treaty, 1921

The politics of the Treaty are important here for their local impact on Aiken and his men. They appear first with Michael Collins's visit to and speech in Armagh in September 1921. Jack McElhaw's account gives a vivid picture of the excitement among Volunteers at Collins coming north, his own disappointment when Aiken ordered him to stay behind at the training camp in Killeavy to organise a guard there against attacks, and the surprise visit the next day by Collins, Harry Boland and Aiken to inspect the men and arms.[108] The Armagh meeting, however, was more significant for Collins's speech, which people took to hint that the negotiations with Britain might result in something short of a republic. What has been described as his 'oddly moderate message' at Armagh caused disquiet among some republicans.[109]

Around this time, Aiken was privy to several semi-private discussions about the talks. He later told Ernie O'Malley that Collins's protégé, Eoin O'Duffy, was then telling Northern IRA commanders that Collins's tactic was to keep the talks going until the winter, when the war would begin again. Apparently, O'Duffy threatened to 'lose the head' if anything else was the result.[110] At another meeting in late October 1921, Mulcahy asked senior officers whether they would be prepared to settle for something short of a republic, and was told 'no'. Aiken's account gives a sense of the confusion and suspicion reigning at the time.[111] And yet, when the Anglo-Irish Treaty was signed in December 1921, including an acceptance of partition, Aiken was shocked but ambivalent. He told a close friend that he might have voted for the Treaty had he been in the Dáil, and suspected that it was a trick to buy time to plan a new campaign.[112]

Other reasons for Aiken's ambivalence were his preoccupation with keeping the Fourth Northern Division united, and the need for preparation to renew a campaign within Northern Ireland. This can be seen in early 1922 in the decision to move the divisional HQ to Dundalk after the Dáil had voted for the Treaty. One factor in the decision was Aiken's knowledge that his division was divided on the Treaty. Pádraig Quinn urged Aiken to move to Dundalk, not just for security but because he was afraid that pro-Treaty forces would take over the Military Barracks. Aiken was annoyed by such talk, wanting to trust Mulcahy and O'Duffy, but he did move to Dundalk to avoid the sort of crisis then gripping Limerick. Once there, in the interests of unity, Aiken took over the military barracks, and allowed the smaller police barracks in the town to be the base of the openly anti-Treaty North Louth (or 1st) Brigade, led by Seán Gormley and Patrick McKenna.[113]

The other factor behind the move to Dundalk was the intensification of pressure on Aiken's men by the Northern Ireland authorities. Heavily armed patrols began again to operate and, from February 1922, curfews were imposed in Newry and surrounding rural areas. McCoy's replacement as Liaison Officer in Armagh, Séamus Connolly, was arrested. In this context, Newry was becoming too dangerous, but Aiken was loathe to leave, because, as McCoy noted, 'there was no justification amongst our officers or men that they were being asked to take risks by us whilst we were enjoying the security of Southern Ireland territory'. However, Aiken finally gave in, sending first the papers to Dundalk, then munitions and finally the staff officers.[114]

Conclusion

With the Truce over, efforts to maintain neutrality within his division and farther afield were placing huge strains on someone about to turn 24. There was also the issue of what to do about Northern Ireland, especially as many of his men, like Johnny McCoy and John Quinn, were very keen to lead columns operating there. In conclusion, Aiken's early life and his leading role in the period between 1918 and 1921 offers several themes that recur in his later biography. First, his desire for Irish independence and unity, which was a driving force in his life from early teens, culturally, politically and then militarily. Second, the various accounts of Aiken's personal bravery and continuous placing of himself in harm's way. Third, the sense of self-sufficiency, coming from a combination of personal economic comfort, but also from being the head of his family by 1916, and a belief in the potential for the economic development of the country. Finally, Aiken was undoubtedly a partisan man with his likes and dislikes. This can be seen in the divisions over the Treaty and the increasing sectarian bitterness of 1922, but also in his lifetime adherence to his fellow IRA Volunteers from this period, both living and dead.

Notes

1   Contrast Robert Fisk to Frank Aiken, 10 April, 26 June 1979 (UCDA, Frank Aiken Papers (P104)/456, 450) to a series of plaintive letters from Michael McInerney, June–July 1974 (UCDA P104/450).

2   See UCDA, P104/1309.

3   See Ernie O'Malley diary entries. UCDA, Ernie O'Malley Papers (P17)b/90, 93.

4   The large bible is now held by Frank Aiken Jnr., and the records for Lower Killeavy parish can be seen in the COFLA.

5   *Newry Reporter*, 14 Aug. 1900.

6   UCDA, P104/457; John Cunningham, 'Belleek, Ballyshannon and Pettigo in the 1790s', *Ulster Local Studies*, 18 (1997), 95–101, 96.

7   UCDA P104/204.

8   *Newry Reporter*, 13 March, 14 Aug. 1900.

9   For the census material for 1901 and 1911, see http://www.census.nationalarchives.ie/, accessed 30/04/13.

10   *Frontier Sentinel*, 16 Sept. 1916.

11   Louis O'Kane, *History of Lower Killeavy parish*, (Newry: n.p., 1956). See also UCDA, P104/450(53).

12   PRONI, H.A./5/2303; UCDA, P104/214.

13   C.S. Andrews, *Dublin Made Me* (Dublin: Lilliput Press, 2001), 258.

14   See UCDA, P104/18.

15   William Neilson, *An Introduction to the Irish Language in Three Parts* (Dublin: Patrick Wogan, 1808)

16   Aiken later conceded that his memory of a former teacher, Br James Austin O'Reilly, was 'vague'; see Aiken to J.V. Hutton, 15 Dec 1955 (UCDA, P104/450). See also UCDA, P104/2–19.

17 UCDA, P104/3–5.

18 Gerry McAtasney, *Sean MacDiarmada* (Manorhamilton: Drumlin Publications, 2004), 62–83.

19 See NAI, CO 904/120, Monthly Reports, Jan. 1914 and UCDA, P104/1309.

20 See Bureau of Military History (BMH), Witness Statements (WS), 163 (Paddy Rankin); WS 171 (Peadar McCann); WS 664 (Paddy McHugh); UCDA, P104/1309.

21 See *Frontier Sentinel*, 20 May, 22 July, 21 Oct. 1916.

22 *Frontier Sentinel*, 10 June 1916.

23 *Frontier Sentinel*, 21 Oct. 1916; BMH, WS 634 (Jack McElhaw).

24 Andrews, *Dublin Made Me*, 259.

25 UCDA, P104/1211. However, Aiken was writing in Irish by the mid-1920s; see Aiken to Gerard Boland, 1 Dec. 1928 (UCDA, P104/464).

26 *Frontier Sentinel*, 18 Sept. 1915, 20 May 1916. For more general reading on partition, see Paul Bew, *Ideology and the Irish Question* (Oxford: OUP, 1994).

27 Eamon Phoenix, *Northern Nationalism: Nationalist politics, partition and the Catholic minority in Northern Ireland* (Belfast: Ulster Historical Foundation, 1994).

28 Michael Laffan, *The Resurrection of Ireland: The Sinn Féin Party, 1916–1923* (Cambridge: CUP, 1999), 94.

29 Liam Skinner, 'Frank Aiken', in *Politicians by Accident* (Dublin: Metropolitan Publishing, 1946), 84.

30 See Phoenix, *Northern Nationalism*, ch. 1.

31 See NLI, Joseph Brennan Papers, Ms 26172, police report 1915; BMH, WS 634 (Jack McElhaw); UCDA, P104/1309.

32 *Frontier Sentinel*, 9 Feb. 1918.

33 Siobhán McGuinness, 'The February 1918 by-election in South Armagh', *Creggan*, vii (1992), 6–18.

34 See, for example, *Irish News*, 21, 31 Jan. 1918; *Frontier Sentinel*, 19, 31 Jan. 1918; David Fitzpatrick, *Harry Boland's Irish Revolution* (Cork: Cork University Press, 2003), 99.

35 See UCDA, P17b/107, 105; UCDA, P7D94, 148; BMH, WS 378 (Robert Kelly).

36 BMH, WS 634 (Jack McElhaw), 3.

37 *Cumann na mBan Convention report* (1918), 17.

38 BMH, WS 353 (Seamus McGuill).

39 Joost Augusteijn, *From Public Defiance to Guerrilla Warfare* (Dublin: Irish Academic Press, 1996), 66–70.

40 BMH, WS 634 (Jack McElhaw), 3.

41 *Frontier Sentinel*, 18 June, 28 Aug. 1918.

42 BMH, WS 634 (Jack McElhaw), 6; WS 671 (Paddy Rankin), 2.

43 Matthew Lewis, 'The Newry Brigade and the War of Independence in Armagh and South Down, 1919–1921', *Irish Sword*, XXVII (2010), 225–32.

44 BMH, WS 890 (Edward Fullerton), 2.

45 See Skinner, 'Frank Aiken', 87. See also COFLA, LOK IV/B, John McCoy tapes, 2a/1.

46 Augusteijn, *Public Defiance*, 87–92.

47 See UCDA, P17b/90, 1.

48 Owen McGee, *The IRB: The Irish Republican Brotherhood from the Land League to Sinn Féin* (Dublin: Four Courts Press, 2005); Fergal McCluskey, 'Fenians, Ribbonmen and popular

ideology's role in nationalist politics: East Tyrone, 1906–9', *Irish Historical Studies*, XXXVII (May, 2010), 61–82.

49   See *Armagh Guardian,* 10 Jan. 1919; *Newry Reporter*, 2 Jan. 1919; *Frontier Sentinel*, 8 Feb. 1919.

50   BMH, WS 353 (Seamus McGuill), 56–9.

51   For various accounts of the raid see *Newry Reporter*, 13 May 1919; BMH, WS 353 (Seamus McGuill), 62; WS 634 (Jack McElhaw), 7.

52   BMH. WS 634 (Jack McElhaw), 6; WS 829 (Charles McGleenan), 5.

53   Arthur Mitchell, *Revolutionary Government in Ireland: Dáil Eireann, 1919–1922* (Dublin: Irish Academic Press, 1995), 115–20.

54   See Augusteijn, *Public Defiance*, 95. See also National Archives of the United Kingdom (NAUK), CO904/113, Inspector General Monthly Reports, Feb. 1920.

55   *Dundalk Democrat*, 7, 21 Feb., 27 March 1920; *Newry Reporter*, 23 March, 3 April 1920.

56   Lewis, Newry Brigade', 231.

57   BMH, WS 634 (Jack McElhaw), 7; BMH, WS 492 (John McCoy), 44–6. For a similar unsuccessful attempt in Newry, see WS 890 (Edward Fullerton), 6.

58   See, *Newry Reporter*, 8 April 1920; *Dundalk Democrat*, 10 April 1920; *Armagh Guardian*, 9 April 1920; BMH WS 890 (Edward Fullerton), 4–5.

59   Lewis, 'Newry Brigade', 228.

60   BMH, WS 640 (Hugh Gribben), 6; NAUK CO904/113, RIC County Inspector Report, Down, Oct. 1920; *Newry Reporter*, 7 Sept. 1920; *Dundalk Democrat*, 11 Sept. 1920; *Armagh Guardian*, 10 Sept 1920; BMH, WS 492 (John McCoy), 59–60.

61   BMH, WS 634 (Jack McElhaw), 16.

62   *Dundalk Democrat*, 12 June 1920.

63   See, for example, Tom Garvin, *Nationalist Revolutionaries in Ireland, 1858–1928* (Oxford: OUP, 1987). Aiken later lamented that 'we were great believers then in the power of the gun alone to cure all our evils'; see Trinity College Dublin, M.7847, Aiken to Director of Publicity (Mrs Childers), 18 Apr. 1924.

64   *Armagh Guardian*, 11 June 1920; *Newry Reporter*, 8 June 1920.

65   County Louth: 18 Sinn Féin, 8 Nationalist, 1 Labour and 1 Independent; County Armagh: 14 Unionist, 7 Sinn Féin, 1 Nationalist and 1 Independent [Unionist]; see *Newry Reporter*, 12 June 1920.

66   *Armagh Guardian*, 11 June 1920.

67   See *Newry Reporter*, 23, 27 July 1920. See also BMH, WS 492 (John McCoy), 57–59.

68   *Dundalk Democrat*, 3 July 1920; *Armagh Guardian*, 18 June 1920; *Frontier Sentinel*, 3 July 1920.

69   *Newry Reporter*, 13 July 1920.

70   Mary Kotsonouris, *Retreat from Revolution: The Dáil Courts, 1920–1924* (Dublin: Irish Academic Press, 1994).

71   *Dundalk Democrat*, 12 Aug. 1920.

72   *Dundalk Democrat*, 31 July 1920, *Newry Reporter*, 5, 10, 28 Aug. 1920.

73   BMH, WS 658 (John Grant), 3; *Newry Reporter*, 3 July 1920.

74   John McCoy, 'Sean Quinn (RIP)' (1945, n.p.).

75   BMH, WS 492 (John McCoy), 50–51; WS 658 (John Grant), p.2; WS 1148 (Patrick Casey), 2; WS 634 (Jack McElhaw), 11; *Newry Reporter*, 11 May 1920.

76   *Newry Reporter*, 23 Nov. 1920.

77   BMH, WS 890 (Edward Fullerton), 6–7; *Newry Reporter*, 23 Nov. 1920.

78   BMH, WS 492 (John McCoy), 75.

79   BMH, WS 492 (John McCoy), 67.

80   BMH, WS 890 (Edward Fullerton), 7–13; WS 634 (Jack McElhaw), 17–21; WS 492 (John McCoy), 69–74.

81   See UCDA, P104/1309.

82   BMH, WS 890 (Edward Fullerton), 14; WS 634 (Jack McElhaw), 22–23; *Newry Reporter*, 16 Dec. 1920.

83   BMH, WS 658 (John Grant), 4.

84   BMH, WS 492 (John McCoy), 77–79; WS 634 (Jack McElhaw), 22.

85   BMH, WS 492 (John McCoy), 79.

86   BMH, WS 658 (John Grant), 5.

87   BMH, WS 492 (John McCoy), 82–84; *Dundalk Democrat*, 15 Jan. 1921.

88   BMH, WS 492 (John McCoy), 84–85.

89   Robert Lynch, *The Northern IRA and the Early Years of Partition, 1920–1922* (Dublin: Irish Academic Press, 2006), 49.

90   UCDA, Richard Mulcahy Papers (P7)/A/17; BMH WS 458 (Sean Corr).

91   UCDA, P104/1408, 1412.

92   BMH, WS 1148 (Patrick Casey), 5.

93   UCDA, P7/A/17/203.

94   BMH, WS 492 (John McCoy), 85; WS 1148 (Patrick Casey), 5.

95   *Dundalk Democrat*, 23 April 1921; BMH, WS 492 (John McCoy), pp. 87–9; WS 1148 (Patrick Casey), 5; WS 658 (John Grant), 4. At a meeting in Newry, Aiken stated that the Dundalk brigade 'had become disorganised' and that such an operation 'would help their morale'; see WS 640 (Hugh Gribben), 8.

96   Some of the homes (between three and six) burned in Camlough in 1921 belonged to the Aiken family; see UCDA, P104/1309 and *Newry Reporter*, 11 Jan. 1921.

97   BMH, WS 634 (Jack McElhaw), 27.

98   The figures and details are taken from the local newspapers (*Armagh Guardian*, *Newry Reporter*, *Frontier Sentinel* and *Dundalk Democrat*) between mid-Feb. and 11 July 1921. The identification of IRA Volunteers came from Bureau of Military History witness statements.

99   Lynch, *Northern IRA*, 80.

100   BMH, WS 658 (John Grant), 8.

101   Police reports for Aug.–Dec. 1921 (NAUK, CO 904/151–154).

102   BMH, WS 658 (John Grant), 8; WS 1148 (Patrick Casey), 10.

103   BMH, WS 495 (Seán McConville), 11.

104   BMH, WS 658 (John Grant), 8; WS 890 (Edward Fullerton), 21–22; WS 634 (Jack McElhaw), 27–29.

105   *Armagh Guardian*, 25 Nov. 1921.

106   BMH, WS 492 (John McCoy), 103–112; COFLA, LOK 1/2). From the Northern Ireland State's perspective see 'Breaches of the Truce by Sinn Féin' (PRONI, HA/32/1/4).

107   Lynch, *Northern IRA*, 82–87.

108   BMH, WS 634 (Jack McElhaw), 28.

109   Fitzpatrick, *Harry Boland*, 229–232.

110 UCDA, P17b/93, 1.
111 UCDA, P17b/93, 2.
112 UCDA, P17b/90, 46.
113 See Pádraig Quinn's diary/memoir (Kilmainham Gaol Archives).
114 BMH, WS 492 (John McCoy), 112–114.

CHAPTER TWO

Frank Aiken's civil wars, 1922–1923

ROBERT LYNCH

On the afternoon of Friday, 20 May 1983, Frank Aiken was buried in a small churchyard at Camlough, County Armagh, less than a mile from his birthplace in the tiny rural hamlet of Carrickbracken. Despite a political career lasting over half a century, which had taken him to all corners of the globe and seen him rise to become one of the most important world statesman in the history of independent Ireland, it was this tiny corner of South Armagh that he had insisted would be his final resting place. Although he had not lived in the county for over fifty years, few of the hundreds of local people who had turned out to pay their respects seemed surprised by Aiken's decision. Indeed, most had fully expected it. One local woman, Mary O'Toole, whose husband had fought with Aiken in 1922, 'never doubted he would return to us in the end'.[1] Another, Mary Callaghan, stated that despite everything Aiken remained 'at heart a South Armagh man'.[2] Although he had few relatives left in the area, Aiken had retained strong links with local people. Archbishop of Armagh and Cardinal Primate of All Ireland Tomás O'Fiaich, another native of Camlough, recalled: 'I never heard of anyone … who was near death or dying that he didn't come to see and then came to the funeral'.[3]

It was here, between 1916 and 1922, that Aiken spent his formative years as a revolutionary IRA leader. Certainly at the time of his funeral in 1983, in the fervent aftermath of the hunger strikes, it was Aiken's revolutionary heritage that resonated the most.[4] For those present he was remembered principally as a man of integrity; an expert in guerrilla warfare, who had turned this small rural area into one of the most formidable fighting areas in Ireland during the whole revolutionary period. In his graveside oration, Fianna Fáil stalwart George Colley described Aiken as 'cool, brave, decisive and effective. Never was such an example as Frank Aiken gave us more needed by our people than now. Not for him was the uncaring killing and maiming of civilians'.[5]

However, for others this last part of Colley's oration struck a discordant note. Aiken's revolutionary career, while certainly marked by notable acts of courage and chivalry, was also punctuated by acts of murder and cruelty, typified by his role in the sectarian massacre at Altnaveigh in June 1922. Indeed for many, particularly the Protestant minority in South Armagh, he remained a war criminal responsible for some of the IRA's worst war crimes. Such wildly differing views of Aiken are not helped by the available historical sources. Unlike some of his revolutionary contemporaries, Aiken was loath to discuss his youthful role as an IRA leader. The fact that he wrote no books, gave few interviews on the period, made no apologies and sought no forgiveness, make this period of his life the most mysterious. As such, this chapter seeks to explore these two interpretations of Aiken through an analysis of his later revolutionary career, which, despite its many vicissitudes, remains strongly focused on the small rural borderlands of South Armagh – a place that for so many reasons was the most important place in Aiken's world.

The Northern Offensive, January–June 1922

When prompted to discuss Aiken's role in the Civil War, one is tempted to ask 'which civil war?' Aiken was a central figure in both of the internecine conflicts that blighted the early years of Ireland's two new states, being at times effective leader of the IRA on both sides of the border.[6] His command area itself, straddling the new frontier of Northern Ireland and within easy reach of both Dublin and Belfast, lay on the front line of north–south confrontation. It would become both a haven for the victims of violence such as refugees from Belfast and a conduit for those keen on instigating attacks against the six-county state. Similarly, Aiken was pitted against every counter-revolutionary force in Ireland, from the notorious Auxiliaries to the Ulster Special Constabulary and the Free State Army to the armed nationalist grouping, the Hibernians.

For good or ill, the signing of the Anglo-Irish Treaty in December 1921 marked a turning point for the fortunes of Aiken and the IRA in South Armagh. Despite Eoin O'Duffy's promises that the Treaty was 'only a trick', Aiken, ever the pragmatist, knew what the Treaty really entailed for northern Volunteers. As one

South Armagh veteran remarked: 'The Treaty was a tragedy when it came. We all knew that. We knew in the North that we had been left out'.[7]

Aiken's reaction to the wider splits in the republican movement was to occupy a position of unique neutrality and resolute opposition to both partition governments in Ireland. While Aiken's neutral position may appear impractical, it also reflected a consistent principle he had adopted throughout his revolutionary career. Ever an opponent of factionalism, Aiken felt that only through unity and the pursuit of consistent objectives could anything meaningful be achieved. Indeed, the ability to subsume disagreement was one of the hallmarks of Sinn Féin, and had sustained the heterogeneous movement throughout the many trials it faced between 1917 and 1921. There is little doubt that he felt he could provide a rallying point for disaffected republicans, and his constant and exhaustive attempts to broker some kind of peace deal are testament to the fact that his was a distinctly active form of neutrality.

Aiken's visits to Dublin during the first six months of 1922 were numerous. He intervened personally to prevent the holding of an Army Convention in January, and argued that all sides should await the publication of the constitution before deciding for or against the Treaty. Even after the military split in March, Aiken continued in his efforts to foster unity. On 16 May he was to play a significant role in fostering the Collins–de Valera electoral pact after convening a meeting with the key leaders on both sides of the Treaty split at the Mansion House.[8] Even after the outbreak of hostilities on 28 June, Aiken made a personal peace mission to meet Richard Mulcahy, Commander in Chief of the new provisional government Army, and the only Free State leader in whom he retained any trust by this time.

Meeting on 7 July, Aiken impressed on Mulcahy the need for an immediate truce, but met with little success.[9] On the next day, Aiken travelled west to Limerick to meet with Chief of Staff of the anti-Treaty IRA, Liam Lynch, and although he was able to participate in holding together the local truce in the city, he failed to make any headway with the anti-Treaty leadership.[10] Indeed, on the day after he left, fighting broke out in the city. Although Aiken's efforts to broker some kind of truce appear somewhat unsophisticated, what is most notable is his early willingness to engage in political debate in order to foster a compromise solution. Viewed in this light, Aiken was, unlike his other IRA contemporaries, an early convert to the increasing importance of politics as opposed to force of arms in furthering republican aspirations.

Neutrality also reflected a particularly northern way of looking at the conflict, and embodied the 'authentic' position of northern IRA units within Northern Ireland. Almost without exception they remained focused on the goal of impeding the establishment of the new Northern Irish state. John Grant, an IRA officer from Armagh, later explained his particularly northern perspective on the Treaty:

> As a Northerner and Six-Counties man I could not willingly accept partition. I do not mention this as an excuse for my anti-treaty attitude or as an apology for my republican activities as I realise that people born in any other part of Ireland were entitled to object on the same grounds if they so decided. The only difference, if any, is that in my case I did not have to ponder over the arguments used in the heavy Treaty debates in An Dáil at the time the acceptance of the Treaty was passed, to decide the difference between tweedledum and tweedledee. My reason for rejecting the Treaty ('partition') was all too evident at home.[11]

Indeed, while many declared themselves for one side or the other, usually in response to promises of material aid, in reality most were neutral. Patrick McCartan, the Tyrone Sinn Féin TD, noted in March 1922 that 'The I.R.A. in the six-counties are all anti-Treaty almost to a man. They, however, are out against partition rather than the Treaty. They feel they have been let down'.[12] Aiken himself stated that he would maintain his neutral position 'until an ordered state of Government attaining in the South – we could attack the North with a chance of getting a united Ireland, which was always the immediate job to us as Northerners'.[13]

Ironically, despite the devastating psychological impact of the Treaty, the first six months of 1922 saw the arrival of significant material support from southern IRA leaders, which for the first time made significant military operations viable for Aiken's Fourth Northern Division. In response to the growing rifts south of the border over the Anglo-Irish Treaty, both pro and anti-Treaty leaders, under the auspices of Michael Collins, Chairman of the provisional government, and Liam Lynch, Chief of Staff of the Anti-Treaty IRA, decided on a joint-IRA policy in Northern Ireland, effectively an attempt to avert a divisive civil war south of the border by starting a unifying one in the north. The Treaty would thus both elevate the status of northern IRA units, and also sow the seeds of its eventual destruction.

The attacks themselves were planned in large part by Eoin O'Duffy, Chief of Staff of the provisional government Army and Chief Truce Liaison Officer for Ulster, and involved the instigation of a guerrilla campaign along the border culminating in an all-out rising by IRA units across the province in late May 1922. In these plans, Aiken was to play a pivotal role. The geographical position of South Armagh –'jutting into the heart of Carsonia' – made it a perfect base to coordinate these attacks, and most crucially South Armagh was the natural conduit through which arms for the planned offensive could be ferried north into Belfast and other parts of Northern Ireland. As such, Aiken was appointed head of a new 'Ulster Council' to coordinate the attacks, effectively giving him control of all IRA units operating within Northern Ireland. He was prominent in all aspects of the planning, and personally travelled to Dublin on a number of occasions to transport weapons and equipment to his headquarters at Dundalk.[14]

The offensive itself launched on 22 May. Despite causing death and destruction in Belfast and elsewhere in the north, it proved to be a catastrophic failure. It had few clear aims, and in many ways was as limited as the people who had planned it. It also proved to be deeply counterproductive, and inspired the Northern Ireland government to introduce internment under the draconian Special Powers Act. Most startling, however, was Aiken's lack of contribution to the offensive. Despite his ostensible position as Commander of the northern rising, Aiken's men took no part in the intended assault. On the morning of 22 May, only a matter of hours before his division was due to go into action, Aiken called off the attacks. John Cosgrave, the leader of one of these columns, stated that he and his men were waiting in a barn ready to move on Armagh city when the countermanding order arrived just before noon.[15] One of Aiken's lieutenants, Patrick Casey, bemused by the last-minute cancellation, returned to see Aiken:

I returned to Dundalk that evening as directed and I saw Frank Aiken. I asked him what was the position and he replied that our Division was taking no part in the rising, but that there was no cancellation so far as the remainder of the Northern counties were concerned. He gave as his reason the fact that the Armagh Brigade was not fully equipped and for that reason he felt justified in withdrawing his Division from action. I pointed out that the South Down Brigade was fully armed and that we should be permitted to take our part. He was, however, adamant and his orders were paramount. I told him also that our failure (Armagh and South Down) would mean, if nothing else, increased concentration of enemy forces in the other northern counties, but this aspect of things did not appear to interest him. On the following morning the rising in the rest of the Six County area did take place and was quickly suppressed with considerable loss of life and arms on our part. I could never understand Aiken's real motive in not fighting his Division on this important occasion. He remained in Dundalk barracks inactive and remote from his command and so petered out this latest, and maybe the last, rising in the Ulster area.[16]

Certainly Aiken appears to have had little faith in the plots and conspiracies of Collins and O'Duffy, and little interest in the fate of his erstwhile comrades in Belfast and elsewhere. His curious decision to absent his men from the offensive, despite their detailed (if rather ambitious) plans, remains difficult to understand. For someone like Aiken, whose purported focus remained the undoing of partition, the offensive seemed like an ideal opportunity to perhaps fatally destabilise the Northern Ireland government.

In the confused atmosphere of late May, with such a variety of participants with differing motives, and considering the shambolic failure of the Second Northern Division, Aiken may have decided that the offensive was a doomed enterprise, and one that would have finished his Division as an effective fighting force. Suggestions by historians such as John Regan and Fearghal McGarry that the offensive was a pro-Treaty conspiracy designed to fatally compromise the IRA in the north are based on little supporting evidence.[17] It would appear rather that Aiken was simply wary of throwing in his lot with a pro-Treaty sponsored scheme over which, despite his nominal appointment at the head of the IRA in Ulster, he had little real control.[18]

Instead, in the face of the internment sweeps, Aiken withdrew his men across the border into a series of temporary camps, with his own headquarters at Dundalk. From here, his men launched a series of incursions across the border. Many of the attacks in Armagh were opportunistic, with small parties of IRA men moving across the border to await a chance to disarm, kidnap or shoot Crown forces. The attacks were effectively a resumption of the strategies of the War of Independence and the border campaign of early 1922, which were both similarly characterised as a constant, nagging war of intimidation and reprisal.

The failure of the IRA in Armagh and South Down to join the offensive was quickly made up for, however, by the brutal nature of these new attacks. The victims included not only the members of the Ulster Special Constabulary, but also members of the Catholic community, and above all innocent Protestant civilians. On 3 June, two Newry Volunteers, Eddie O'Hare and Edward Fullerton, shot dead James Woulfe Flanagan, a Resident Magistrate in the city.[19] Two days later a Special Constable, Thomas Sheridan, was shot dead at Annaghmore. In response, the Ulster Special Constabulary closed all of the bridges crossing the Newry Canal, effectively cutting the Division in two, and began a series of systematic and brutal raids in the border areas. Many young Catholic men were forced to cross the border each evening to sleep, with the poorest making do with barns or farmers' fields. James McElhaw, an IRA officer, commented: 'The whole atmosphere of the time as far as the civilian unionist and the civilian nationalist was concerned was one of something unpleasant if not horrible about to take place'.[20]

Altnaveigh, June 1922

That 'something unpleasant' would occur in the early hours of Saturday 17 June 1922, when a party of Volunteers from Aiken's own Fourth Northern Division launched a devastating raid on a small Presbyterian farming community in the townlands of Altnaveigh and Lisdrumliska, around a mile to the west of Newry.

According to the RUC report on the attack, six people were shot dead during the attacks, over twice as many injured, and numerous homes were bombed or burned out. The first victims were 67-year-old Thomas Crozier and his wife Elizabeth. The husband was shot in the chest as he opened his front door; his wife was then shot twice whilst comforting her dying husband. Shortly afterwards, another gang attacked the nearby home of John Heaslip. After hurling bombs through a window of the house, Heaslip and his son Robert, 19, were caught hiding in a stable after fleeing through the back door. Both were taken to the front of the house and shot dead. Despite the pleas of his family, Robert, who by all accounts was crying for his injured mother Isabella, was shot twice in the back of the head and three times in the groin. Two other fatalities were to follow. James Lockhart, 23, was shot dead in front of his mother and three sisters (all of whom were under the age of 7) after their house had been burned and they had been lined up along the road in their nightclothes. Next door, Joseph Gray, aged 20, was shot in the stomach after being dragged from his bed, dying later the next morning in hospital. Gray's father, who had tried desperately to stop the gunmen taking his son, was shot in both ankles after allegedly being told by his attacker, 'you have enough children already'.[21]

Well over a dozen of these attacks, from frenzied gun, bomb and arson attacks to cold-blooded executions, were made on local family homes. Along with the fatal attacks on the Heaslip, Crozier, Lockhart and Gray families, the properties of Margaret Reynolds, David McCullough, Sarah Richardson, James McKnight, Margaret Thompson, Sarah Williams and Joseph Little were also targeted. A police report calculated that if all the attacks made had succeeded – the woundings, arson attacks, bombs thrown into windows, or rigged to doors – the death toll could have reached as high as thirty.[22] After conducting the funerals of the victims, Reverend Patrick McKee said: 'We have been left with a bloody mile of roofless houses … even in war there is a certain limit to atrocity, a certain code of honour is practised by all but the vilest savage. In this, those who wrought Saturday's deed of shame have no share'.[23]

This incident, lasting barely forty-five minutes, has gone down in history as the 'Altnaveigh Massacre'. It is one of the most notorious atrocities carried out during the entire revolutionary period. For many it is Aiken's alleged involvement in organising and carrying out the attacks that remains for the most significant aspect of the Altnaveigh affair. For some it remains Aiken's great crime.[24]

While there is no direct evidence that Aiken himself ordered the attacks, the circumstantial evidence is compelling. At the time, many members of the IRA in South Armagh had little doubt Aiken was behind the attacks. Patrick Casey was appalled by the events:

> I remember my feeling was one of horror when I heard the details. Nothing could justify this holocaust of unfortunate Protestants. Neither youth nor age was spared and some of the killings took place in the presence of their families. Writing this, 35 years later, I still have the view that it was a horrible affair – nothing could justify such a killing of unarmed people. I was surprised at the time that Frank Aiken had planned and authorised this.[25]

An examination into the background to the events themselves leads one to the conclusion that, far from being on the periphery of the Altnaveigh attacks, Aiken was central to them. As demonstrated by his ability to restrain his men in May 1922, and also later in the Civil War period, his control over his IRA divisional area and the operations that occurred within it was unquestioned.

The Altnaveigh attacks showed the darker side of Aiken's character. Although noted by both friend and foe alike as a man of integrity, typified by his refusal to shoot unarmed prisoners, on many other occasions he had shown a streak of ruthlessness. For example, in March 1922, after a group of B-Specials had burned Catholic houses in the village of Roslea in County Fermanagh, Aiken, along with Monaghan IRA leader Eoin O'Duffy, set to work preparing a reprisal attack, which has notable similarities to that planned at Altnaveigh fifteen months later. Volunteer John Connolly, who attended the planning meeting, recalled:

> There were various expressions of opinion from some of the officers present as to the advisability of the [proposed] burnings and also as to

the number of Unionist houses which should be burned … After Aiken's arrival, O'Duffy and he started a discussion of the Roslea business – Frank Aiken did not at first approve of the burnings, as he thought that the 'B' men [i.e. 'B' Specials] would retaliate by burning double the number of nationalist houses. O'Duffy struck the table and said 'When you hit them hard they will not strike again'. Aiken then shouted: 'Well, burn them and their houses'.[26]

This is exactly what happened. Twenty-one houses in all were put to the torch, and two of the Specials and a Protestant civilian were dragged from their homes and battered to death. In South Armagh itself there were numerous attacks on civilians, show trials, the shooting of 'spies' and collaborators and other undesirables.[27] Strikingly, between 1919 and 1922 far more civilians were killed in South Armagh than combatants. For example, in July 1921, in response to the ambush at Adavoyle, four Catholic men were tortured and murdered by a party of B-Specials in the Altnaveigh area in the space of a week. A few weeks later, members of Aiken's own brigade shot dead two prominent Hibernians as spies.[28]

However, while such squalid atrocities on both sides increasingly defined the character of the revolution throughout Ireland, what marked out the violence in Aiken's border command was its deeply sectarian character. In many ways the Altnaveigh shootings were the culmination of a long period of escalating sectarian violence, which had increased dramatically after the deployment of the Ulster Special Constabulary in the area in the autumn of 1920, although even before then Protestant businesses had been burned in Dundalk as a reprisal for the August violence in Lisburn and Belfast.[29] Behind the facade of carefully planned ambushes and divisional directives, the conflict in South Armagh became an increasingly brutal and dirty war.

Outside of Belfast, this tiny area of South Armagh, with a population of barely 20,000 people, was notable for the intense bitterness of its sectarian violence. After the arrival of the Specials in the area, violence became increasingly indiscriminate and was turned against all manner of sectarian targets, including attacks on religious buildings and their congregations. Aiken himself held a Protestant church congregation in Creggan captive in April 1921, and the conflict witnessed the burning of Orange and Hibernian Halls, the defacement of religious statues and countless minor acts of harassment and humiliation.[30] As was common in many parts of Ireland during the spring of 1922, Protestants experienced vicarious punishment and intimidation at the hands of republican radicals. Prior to Altnaveigh, Protestant homes were raided and fired at in Dundalk, while notices threatening dire retributions were prominently displayed. Although Aiken appears to have intervened to halt sectarian intimidation in Dundalk, there appears to have been no similar sanction for operations across the border.[31] One veteran recalled: 'The shootings and outrages which took place before Altnaveigh happened were progressively getting worse, until at last the crescendo seemed to have been reached'.[32]

On the other hand, Altnaveigh was unique. This is most notable in terms of its timing. The attack occurred only days before the outbreak of Civil War in Dublin, when Aiken's eyes were very much fixed on the alarming divisions south of the border, and thus it was an odd time for him to choose to engage himself in a provocative showdown with the Northern Ireland authorities. Altnaveigh came at a time when he was very much on the defensive, holed up in Dundalk, and when the IRA in the north had almost disintegrated. The decision to carry out such a provocative attack at this time seems ill-judged, inviting embroilment in a war that could not be won.

Furthermore, if the argument is made that Altnaveigh was an attempt to instigate a belated unifying crusade against the Northern Ireland government, then the South Armagh IRA's choice of targets in the shape of Protestant civilians seems woefully inappropriate, doing little but to stiffen Protestant resolve and resistance, whilst at the same time outraging moderate nationalist opinion throughout Ireland. As T.K. Wilson's account of inter-communal violence in the period notes: 'Altnaveigh proved to be a watershed. It threw a huge question mark over the moral legitimacy of the 4th Northern Division [of the IRA]'.[33] If one does argue that the Altnaveigh attacks were part of an attempt to instigate a new unifying conflict along the border, then it begs the question as to why Aiken failed to make these attacks when they had far more chance of success on 22 May.

It is clear, though, that for attacks on the scale of Altnaveigh, a great deal of planning and coordination was required. One IRA veteran even recalls attending a divisional meeting with Aiken, where the plan to launch reprisal attacks was discussed.[34] Aiken himself, while not publicly admitting his role in the attacks, made references to his ordering of a significant reprisal at the time in which he 'directed operations which cursed the Specials of a tendency to carry out the Belfast pogrom tactics in Armagh & Down'.[35] As W.M. Lewis observes, no other events in May or June in Aiken's Divisional area apart from the Altnaveigh attacks come close to fitting this description.[36] Moreover, at the time of the massacre, other IRA units moved in to South Armagh, laying ambushes and trenching or mining roads in order to isolate the target area from police help. The Altnaveigh attacks were part of a coordinated campaign of ambushes and bombings right across South Armagh. Thus, while Aiken proved extremely reluctant to engage in large-scale operations during May and June, the Altnaveigh attacks, involving as they did almost the entire fighting capacity of the Fourth Northern Division, stand out in sharp relief.

A measured judgement of Aiken's involvement requires an examination of the causes of the Altnaveigh massacre and his response to them. What emerges is that the attacks were a reprisal for two very different, but equally savage, attacks on local Catholics. The first involved the shooting of two Catholic men, Patrick Creggan and Thomas Crawley on 14 June. Both men were abducted from their homes, bound and then shot in the back of the head. Their bodies were dumped on the Lislea road over two mine holes that had been dug by the IRA the previous evening.[37]

The attacks were also a response to an even more provocative incident, which occurred at almost the same time as the killings of Creggan and Crawley. This second incident involved a raid by a party of A-Specials from nearby Forkhill barracks on a local pub belonging to James McGuill, a prominent local republican and a close confidant and lifelong friend of Aiken.[38] It appears that the Specials had arrived with the intention of killing McGuill, something they had tried to do on numerous previous occasions. It is alleged that the Specials, outraged at McGuill's absence, began to smash up the pub and drink heavily on looted alcohol from behind the bar. When the women resisted, McGuill's heavily pregnant wife was dragged into an upstairs bedroom of the pub, thrown on the bed and there subjected to a gang rape by three members of this group of Specials. Her ordeal only ended when her mother and two servant girls broke into the room.[39] One of the servant girls, it is alleged, was also seriously sexually assaulted and savagely beaten. A doctor who later examined her in Newry claimed that he had never seen so many bruises and cuts on one body before. She also had a fractured skull from being repeatedly kicked in the head by her attackers. Another resident of the house, Mary McKnight, only managed to save herself from attack by throwing herself through an upstairs window.[40] In looking for the causes of the Altnaveigh attack, and Aiken's personal stake in it, this assault on McGuill's wife, for Aiken, may have been the final straw:

> I saw her the next day in the most frightful state, and I swore that if I could take it out of the skins of the men who did it I would do it. We went the following night and we laid ambush for the Specials from the Camp [i.e. Forkhill barracks] who were responsible for the attempted rape. We shot a few of them. I am sorry we did not get them all.[41]

Most tellingly, it was also from this pub that Aiken personally led an ambush party of fifty IRA Volunteers on the evening of the Altnaveigh attacks, five miles to the east. In the attack his men managed to kill one Special and severely wounded another. The response of the authorities to the attacks in Armagh led them to return to the pub and demolish it due to 'military necessity'. In subsequent years Aiken remained close to the McGuill family, and it was McGuill on whose behalf he advocated for compensation in the Dáil, vehemently and persistently.[42]

It is therefore clear that the one person who becomes most clearly identifiable with the Altnaveigh attacks remains Frank Aiken even if he was not there himself. The evidence, although largely circumstantial, remains compelling, and those who would seek to absolve him of responsibility must present a credible alternative explanation. Only he had the power to organise such an extensive, efficient and vicious assault. The unique provocation of the attack on the McGuill family, and his evident closeness to the people involved, suggest that the attacks were less a reprisal than a bitter personal vendetta.

The massacre at Altnaveigh demonstrated a number of key characteristics of Aiken's revolutionary career. Certainly Aiken showed little interest in the wave of denunciation that flowed from the British and Irish press in the aftermath of Altnaveigh. Indeed, while Altnaveigh brought an end to direct attacks on Protestant civilians, those on uniformed police were stepped up markedly in the ten-day period prior to the outbreak of civil war in Dublin. On 19 June, the day that news of the Altnaveigh atrocity filled the pages of the press, two more Specials were dragged from their bicycles near Keady and shot dead.[43] And in the following week there were four more attempted murders of Specials, numerous punishment beatings, shots fired at police barracks, mines exploded and the kidnapping of a number of other Specials.[44] For example, senior IRA man John Grant was detailed to kidnap four Specials, although he only managed to get three of them. He recorded that many other kidnap raids were ordered in late June.[45] All the kidnapped Specials were imprisoned in Dundalk and held as hostages under threat of death if any further outrages were reported in South Armagh. These hostages were only released by Dan Hogan when he and his provisional government troops took over Dundalk on 16 July. The body of Special Constable William Frazer, who was kidnapped by the IRA on his way to Newry less than a fortnight after Altnaveigh, was not discovered until 1924, found buried in a bog just over the border.

Throughout the period Aiken showed a consistently unsentimental lack of interest in the opinions of others, or in their opinion of him. Despite the titles that were heaped upon him during the revolutionary period, he was little flattered, and it did little to change his fundamental South Armagh outlook. Furthermore, he remained interested largely in his own area and his own men rather than the activities and fate of other Volunteers in the north. His major concern remained as ever his own divisional area, or even more precisely his particular heartlands of South Armagh and the welfare of the few hundred men under his control. He maintained a strong bond with his men long after he had left the area and embarked on his illustrious political career.

The Civil War, June 1922–May 1923

For IRA units in Northern Ireland, the Civil War itself was to prove catastrophic. The moral and material support that they had enjoyed from powerful elites south of the border during the first six months of 1922 disappeared almost overnight. Similarly, any pressure that they had managed to put on the Northern Ireland government, or at least the British government's toleration of its excesses, was lost as peace returned to Northern Ireland. The success of internment and the withdrawal of southern support meant that by the time of the attack on the Four Courts, in late June 1922, the northern IRA had all but ceased to exist.

As such, by the end of June 1922, Aiken's Fourth Northern Division was the only northern IRA unit that retained any cohesion. Aiken's decision to remain neutral during the early months of the Civil War itself was perhaps his most notable achievement. Despite his geographical isolation, being bordered in the north by the territory of Northern Ireland and to the west by the aggressively pro-Treaty Fifth Northern Division, under the control of his two old adversaries, Eoin O'Duffy and Dan Hogan, Aiken's borderland command – centred on Dundalk – remained largely united and determined.

Only two battalions and the staff of the First (Louth) Brigade under Patrick McKenna came out against the Treaty.[46] Tellingly, all of these units were outside of Northern Ireland, and had only been placed under Aiken's command in January 1921 as part of the IRA's divisional reorganisation. The notable loyalty that the bulk of his men showed him was extraordinary considering what was unfolding in other provincial units across Ireland. In his pronouncements to them Aiken offered little but harsh reality, explaining to them that 'the alternatives to joining [the provisional government Army] are starving or going back to Ulster to fight at a time that the disordered state of Southern Ireland ensures failure'.[47]

It was only after the most extreme provocation that Aiken was forced to side with the anti-treatyites. After returning to Dundalk from yet another fruitless peace mission in Dublin, Aiken and almost 200 of his men were arrested and imprisoned in Dundalk jail by members of the Fifth Northern Division. What came next, as recounted by Eoin Magennis, is fondly remembered as the 'hole in the wall' escape. On 27 July, Ivor Monaghan and fellow engineers blew a hole in the wall of the Dundalk jail to free approximately 100 prisoners.[48] After reuniting with his men in South Armagh on 14 August, Aiken recaptured the town, seized weapons and imprisoned the provisional government garrison.

Aiken's actions after the dramatic retaking of Dundalk, one of the few republican successes during the whole war in an unremitting story of defeat, have confused many historians.[49] His decision to abandon this major urban centre and retreat back into the shadowy borderlands of Louth and Armagh has been seen by many as a great lost opportunity. Whereas such a bold statement as the capture of Dundalk would have suggested a beginning to a new aggressive offensive (in fact, many at the time feared a march on Dublin), it instead signalled the end of Aiken's involvement in the conflict. His republican contemporaries were similarly bemused:

> Aiken's position is extra-ordinary. He has over 2000 men and must have 6 or 700 rifles and about 20 machine guns ... it seems to me that Aiken's eyes are on the Six Counties in which he has almost 1500 men and is saving himself to attack the Specials who are not doing us any harm at all.[50]

Indeed, despite his decision to ally with the Army Executive, Aiken did little to engage actively with his new comrades. His appointment as the head of a new anti-Treaty Northern Command was as uninspiring to Aiken as his selection as leader of the pro-Treaty Ulster Command eight months earlier. Ernie O'Malley noted in September that 'Aiken has not communicated with me – in fact he has sent no communication good, bad or indifferent'.[51]

He also took virtually no steps to organise his new area, or help those outside of it. When IRA commander Seán Lehane asked for help for his dwindling column in County Donegal, the last vestiges of the joint-IRA attacks, Aiken did nothing. 'The 3rd Northern Division are not aware of the formation of the Northern Command and Aiken apparently has never paid any attention to Belfast except to ask for arms and ammunition of which he has plenty already'.[52] Liam Lynch wrote that he had communicated with Aiken in December concerning 'his neglect in attending to GHQ orders and on the position of the forces in the six-county area not being active in the present war ...'.[53]

While such arguments may present Aiken as aloof or even incompetent, viewed in context such moves were consistent with his general attitude to the war. Aiken's heart was never really in the Civil War, or indeed the republican war effort in general. As with the May northern offensive, he seems to have recognised that extensive operations against overwhelming odds were futile. He retook Dundalk to maintain control of his fiefdom and to free his colleagues; the national significance of the capture of an urban centre was a secondary consideration. Above all, it was about re-establishing balance. As Todd Andrews, who took part in the attack, later wrote:

> With the captured rifles and machine guns together with the large quantity of arms already under his control, Aiken could have easily put together a force of one thousand disciplined men. In the circumstances of the time a force of even that size, led by a man of the military competence and character of Aiken, might have marched on Dublin with some hope of success. Marching on Dublin was far from Aiken's mind. He was determined that he would not participate in the Civil War nor would he allow it to be carried out in his area.[54]

Aiken's anomalous position was even highlighted perceptively by Assistant Minister for Local Government Kevin O'Higgins, who stated that:

> Mr Frank Aiken presumably is a Republican ... I do not know whether he is a Republican for thirty-two or twenty-six counties, but what I do know is that he is very glad of the benevolent protection of the border and of the Government in North-East, which, presumably, he does not recognise.[55]

The reality of Aiken's confused approach to the war, however, had less to do with cold, doctrinal paradoxes, but rather its inducement of a state of inertia brought on by sheer devastation at the calamity now unfolding. It is hard to overstate how devastating the collapse of IRA unity was to him personally. Recounting a famous meeting with Aiken in August 1922, Todd Andrews recalled the sheer despair:

> He was sitting on the bed and made no attempt to make me welcome. There was a chair in the room but I wasn't invited to sit down. He did not ask what I wanted. He looked at me in what he may have thought was a questioning manner but the muscles of his face did not appear to move. Finally a grunted 'well?' indicated that discussion should get under way. I explained the purpose of my visit ... He indicated by signs that we were about to leave and I was surprised to find a small Ford car with a red headed driver waiting outside the cottage door. The driver – who was named Peter Boyle – turned out to be a kind of Man Friday to Aiken. But beyond a monosyllabic direction to him, Aiken did not speak.[56]

Aiken's poor psychological state was graphically demonstrated in a letter to Richard Mulcahy, shortly after the death of Michael Collins on 22 August 1922, where he appeared to offer to sacrifice his own life to bring an end to the conflict:

> If you believed absolutely in the sincerity of the men opposed to you, you would stop the struggle. If that is true I'll prove to you if you wish. I'll die in order to prove to you if you guarantee to me that you'll stop this Civil War if I do so. For God's sake, Dick, agree to this and let one death end it all.[57]

While it is easy to put such pronouncements down to youthful hyperbole, the trauma of the Civil War was something that never left Aiken through his long life. In a 2008 interview with *The Irish Times*, his son, Frank Aiken Jnr., noted: 'my dad absolutely hated the Civil War … I still get emotional when I remember how much he hated it'.[58] On meeting Aiken in August 1922, Todd Andrews was moved to conclude: 'Nobody on either side liked having to take part in the Civil War, but I never met anyone who was so totally horrified or saddened by it as Aiken'.[59]

Certainly, while the Civil War was personally devastating for Aiken, militarily it proved to be calamitous. Whereas previously the southern side of the border had offered him a safe haven from which to conduct raids into Northern Ireland, it now became enemy territory. Aiken and his men were caught in a curious limbo, unwelcome in both Irish states, and roaming the marchlands in search of targets. Indeed, ironically, by late 1922, Aiken and his ever dwindling column had retreated back into Northern Ireland; a complete reversal of the position in the first half of the year. Operations against Free State forces were rare while he and his men spent most of their time staying alive. Indeed, the most notable actions carried out by the Fourth Northern Division after Dundalk were raids on small border villages to commandeer food and supplies. If Aiken did manage to achieve anything during the Civil War, it was to bring the vast majority of his men through the conflict in one piece.

His position was further compromised when, from December 1922, both Free State and Northern Irish governments began to exchange intelligence on his whereabouts. It was a very personal and at times hysterical manhunt. The RUC reported that he was seen dressed as a beggar walking the streets of Armagh city, or disguised himself as an old woman in order to cross over the border undetected. Aiken became the personification of the disorder that both states were seeking to end. Certainly, both governments were convinced that Aiken was planning a major offensive operation against them, was 'gathering forces' and 'readying himself to make a major move'.[60]

The capture of Aiken would have proved to be a major coup for the Northern Ireland government, especially as he was at this time being personally blamed for the massacre at Altnaveigh. For the Free State, Aiken's Column represented the one remaining cohesive republican unit still in existence, and the one that had carried out the one major republican coup of the war. Although in reality Aiken was a spent force militarily, his continued resistance proved a major embarrassment for Free State leaders.[61]

Aiken's appointment as republican Chief of Staff of the IRA in the last weeks of the Civil War was in many ways the final justification of his exhaustive attempts to arrange a peaceful solution and a vindication of his stance throughout the conflict. Much can be made of Aiken's increasingly rapid rise to a dominant position within republican ranks. Despite constant criticisms about his failure or willingness to organise resistance in his vast command, he was appointed Deputy Chief of Staff in January 1923. His appointment demonstrated the weakness of the IRA rather than its strength. Indeed, the more the republican cause floundered, the higher in the organisation Aiken rose. He was present, on 10 April, in the Knockmealdown Mountains in Tipperary, where his predecessor as Chief of Staff of the IRA, Liam Lynch, was killed, and appears to have been appointed to replace him more by default than any profound ideological shifts on the side of the republican leadership.[62]

However, it is unfair to view Aiken's rise to prominence as simply a case of being the last man standing. Above all it was his committed, if still crude, political instincts that lay at the heart of his growing authority. His often underrated achievement in ending the Civil War, while still allowing republicans to maintain their unity and political principles, made his reputation and laid the foundations for his later successful career. Far from being an inevitable compromise, Aiken's peace strategy reflected an underlying pragmatism, which, while often compromised by his impulsive reaction to any violation of his strongly held personal principles, had informed his actions throughout the revolutionary period. Typically, he refused both the possibility of abject surrender demanded by the Free State, and of continuing a futile guerrilla war, as favoured by republican diehards. His solution, a ceasefire with arms retained (although 'dumped') was typical of his personal vision of a third way between the uncompromising extremes of the Civil War. In many ways it was the policy of a true neutral.

Conclusion

Aiken's Civil War experience was unquestionably unique, and his actions subtly inspirational to later generations of Irish political leaders. Like his mentor Éamon de Valera, he listened to few but his own conscience. When comparing the two men who would do so much to shape the nature of independent Ireland, one South Armagh veteran may have shown more insight than intended: 'Dev was intelligent; Aiken was too, but he was wicked, he could fight'.[63] Aiken rarely suffered from self-doubt and, when he felt that a course of action was the right one, he would follow it through no matter what the opinion of others, reacting to condemnation with the same disdain with which he treated the numerous accolades that were bestowed on him throughout the period.

Aiken remained, in the most positive sense of the word, unsophisticated. Unlike many of his contemporaries he did not seek celebrity or easy populism, and did not fall into idle sentimentalism or sensationalism. As such, an analysis of Aiken's revolutionary career reveals a man who was above all else a practical person. While at times he offered ruthless or over-simplistic solutions to extremely complex problems, he remained realistic about the unsavoury practicalities of his position, inspiring a lifelong loyalty from the people with whom he served. At his funeral, the daughter of one veteran South Armagh Volunteer recalled her father telling her, when she asked about Aiken, 'Unlike some of the others he would never ask you to do anything that he wasn't prepared to do himself. We liked that. He was one of us'.[64]

Notes

1   *The Irish Times*, 21 May 1983.
2   *The Irish Times*, 21 May 1983.
3   *The Irish Times*, 21 May 1983.
4   The hunger-striker Raymond McCreesh, who died two years prior to Aiken's own passing, was buried in the same churchyard.
5   *The Irish Times*, 21 May 1983.
6   Formal partition of Ireland dates from June 1921, when the Northern Ireland parliament, as provided for in the Government of Ireland 'Partition' Act of 1920, was officially opened. Under the terms of the Act, two parliaments, one in Belfast the other in Dublin, were established with powers of local self-government. The Act granted local autonomy under a 'home rule' parliament to the six north-eastern counties of Ulster (Antrim, Armagh, Down, Fermanagh, Londonderry and Tyrone). Simultaneously, in the newly created twenty-six-county state of Southern Ireland, the revitalised Sinn Féin Party refused to contest the general election in May 1921, as stipulated under the terms of the Government of Ireland Act. The degree of self-governance conferred by the Act fell far short of Sinn Féin demands. Control of defence, foreign policy and finance remained with Westminster.
7   Patsy O'Hagan quoted in U. MacEoin, *Survivors* (Dublin: Argenta, 1980), 169.
8   Aiken to O'Donoghue, 9 Mar. 1953, National Library of Ireland (NLI), Florence O'Donoghue Papers, MS 31,421. See also 'Six County Position in the Present Crisis', May 1922. University College Dublin Archives (UCDA), Richard Mulcahy Papers, (P7)a/145.

9   See Aiken to Mulcahy, 20 July 1922. UCDA, Frank Aiken Papers (P104)/1248 and Aiken to Mulcahy, 6 July 1922. UCDA, P104/1239.

10   Michael Hopkinson, *Green Against Green: The Irish Civil War* (Dublin: Gill and Macmillan, 1988), 102. See also M. O'Hanlon, O'Malley notebooks. UCDA, Ernie O'Malley Papers (P17)b/106.

11   John Grant statement. National Archives of Ireland (NAI), Bureau of Military History (BMH) Witness Statement (WS) 658.

12   McCartan to Maloney, 31 March 1922 quoted in Enda Staunton, *The Nationalists of Northern Ireland, 1918–1973* (Dublin: Columba Press, 2001), 53.

13   'Position of the 4th Northern Division from January 1922–17 July 1922'. NLI, Thomas Johnson Papers, MS 17,143.

14   For the planning of the offensive see Robert Lynch, *The Northern I.R.A. and the Early Years of Partition, 1920–22* (Dublin: Irish Academic Press, 2006), 142–158. 'Carsonia' is Richard Mulcahy's phrase. See Mulcahy to O/C 4th Northern Division, 14 April 1921 (Mulcahy Papers, UCDAD, P7/A/17).

15   John Cosgrave statement. NAI, BMH, WS 605.

16   Patrick Casey statement. NAI, BMH, WS 1148.

17   See John M. Regan, *The Irish Counter-Revolution, 1921–36* (Dublin: Gill and Macmillan, 1999), 62; Fearghal McGarry, *Eoin O'Duffy: Self-Made Hero* (Oxford: Oxford University Press, 2007), 103. For an extensive discussion of the Fourth Northern Division's role in the offensive and Aiken's failure to act, see W.M. Lewis, 'Frank Aiken and the Fourth Northern Division: a personal and provincial experience of the Irish Revolution, 1916–1923', PhD Thesis, Queen's University Belfast (QUB), 2011, 140–154.

18   For Aiken's disputable authority over the Northern IRA, see 'Interview with Frank Aiken, 18 June 1952'. NLI, MS31, 421.

19   Edward Fullerton statement. NAI, BMH, WS 890.

20   James McElhaw statement. NAI, BMH, WS 634.

21   For details of the Altnaveigh attacks, see 'File relating to the burning of the homes of three Loyalists', Public Record Office of Northern Ireland (PRONI), Ministry of Home Affairs, (HA)/5/241.

22   'File relating to the burning of the homes of three Loyalists', Public Record Office of Northern Ireland (PRONI), Ministry of Home Affairs, (HA)/5/241.

23   *Northern Whig*, 21 June 1922.

24   See for example *Irish Independent*, 17 Dec. 2006

25   Patrick Casey statement, NAI, BMH WS1148.

26   John T. Connolly statement. NAI, BMH, WS 598.

27   The best estimate of casualty figures for the Fourth Northern Divisional area during the revolutionary period were sixty-eight killed and seventy-two wounded, almost half of the deaths (thirty-three) coming during the first six months of 1922. Thirty-one of those killed were civilians, with a similar number of woundings. For a full breakdown of these figures, see Lewis's exhaustive study of the revolution in Aiken's divisional area, 'Frank Aiken and the Fourth Northern Division: a personal and provincial experience of the Irish Revolution, 1916–1923', 90 & 166.

28   *Irish Independent*, 7 July 1921.

29   See statement of James McGuill. NAI, BMH, WS 353.

30 For details of these attacks see 'R.I.C. Bi-monthly reports, Jan–Dec. 1921'. PRONI, HA/5/152.

31 For a full discussion of Aiken's role in the sectarian attacks in Dundalk, see Lewis 'Frank Aiken and the Fourth Northern Division: a personal and provincial experience of the Irish Revolution, 1916–1923', 192–194.

32 Jack McElhaw statement, NAI, BMH WS634.

33 Quoted in T. Wilson, *Frontiers of Violence: Conflict and Identity in Ulster and Upper Silesia, 1918–1922* (Oxford: OUP, 2010), 169.

34 Statement of Patrick Casey, NAI, BMH WS1148. See also James McElhaw statement. NAI, BMH, WS 634.

35 Quoted in Lewis, 'Frank Aiken and the Fourth Northern Division',176.

36 Lewis, W.M., 'Frank Aiken and the Fourth Northern Division', 176.

37 File on shootings of Creggan and Crawley, PRONI, Ministry of Home Affairs files, (HA/5/239). See also Statements of John Grant, NAI, BMH WS658; John McCoy, NAI, BMH WS492.

38 Whilst on the run, Aiken had spent the Christmas of 1921 with the McGuill family.

39 Fourth Northern Division report, 15 Jun. 1922, NAI, Department of Taoiseach (DT), s5462.

40 For details of these attacks, see *The Irish Times*, 15 Nov. 1922; James McElhaw statement (BMH. WS 634); 'File on James McGuill-Grant from Special Fund'. NAI, DT, S845. See also Fourth Northern Division report, 15 Jun. 1922, NAI, DT, S5462.

41 Speech by Frank Aiken on compensation claims in Northern Ireland, 23 Oct. 1929. Dáil Éireann Debates (DE), Vol. 32, Col. 173.

42 Aiken raised the case of McGuill in the Dail on three separate occasions in various debates on the issue of compensation for northern nationalists; see DE, 17 Nov. 1927, 24 Oct. 1929 and again on 15 May 1930.

43 William Mitchell and Samuel Young were both found dead near Keady. They had been detailed to defend local farms after the Altnaveigh attacks, and had cycled into Keady for supplies, where by all accounts they were abducted by the IRA and driven a short distance away to be shot. R. Abbott, *Police Casualties in Ireland 1919–1922* (Cork: Mercier Press, 2000), 192.

44 For wider summary of attacks in the area both before and after Altnaveigh, see RIC (Royal Irish Constabulary) Bi-monthly reports, 1 Jan. 1922–31 Dec. 1922, Ministry of Home Affairs Files, PRONI, HA/5/152.

45 John Grant statement (BMH, NAI, WS 658)

46 James McElhaw statement. NAI, BMH, WS 634.

47 'Position of the 4th Northern Division from January 1922–17 July 1922'. NLI, O'Donoghue Papers, MS17143.

48 I wish to thank Eoin Magennis for granting this author permission to utilise his draft chapter, 'Frank Aiken: Early life (1898–1923) and some reflections on his later career'.

49 See for example Hopkinson, *Green against Green*, 171.

50 See 'D/org. to C/S, 22 Dec. 1922'. UCDA, Moss Twomey Papers (P69)/13 [80].

51 Ernie O'Malley, *No Surrender Here, The Civil War Papers of Ernie O'Malley, 1922–24* (Dublin: The Lilliput Press, 2007) 162.

52 D/Org to C/S, 22 Dec. 1922. UCDA, P69/13 [80].

53 Liam Lynch memo, 31 Dec.1922. UCDA, P69/13 [76].

54   C.S. Andrews, *Dublin Made Me* (Dublin: The Lilliput Press, 2008), 260.

55   *Northern Whig*, 8 Feb. 1923.

56   Andrews, *Dublin Made Me*, 258–259.

57   Aiken to Mulcahy, 27 Aug. 1922, UCDA, P7a/81.

58   *The Irish Times*, 13 Nov. 2008.

59   Andrews, *Dublin Made Me*, 261.

60   RUC report, Dec. 1922. PRONI, HA/5/152.

61   See, for example, the statement of Kevin O'Higgins in Dáil Éireann where he referred to Aiken as 'a mad dog'. *The Irish Times*, 8 Feb 1923.

62   For Aiken's description of the ambush, see Aiken to de Valera, 11 April 1923. UCDA, Éamon de Valera Papers (P150)/1752.

63   *The Irish Times*, 23 May 1983.

64   *Irish Independent*, 22 May 1983.

CHAPTER THREE

Frank Aiken and the IRA, 1923–1933

BRIAN HANLEY

In his biography, the veteran IRA leader Joe Cahill recounted how, while training in the south County Down area during 1938, he and his fellow Volunteers were tasked with a special mission. After a night on the border, however, they were ordered back to Newry without explanation. Cahill 'learned afterwards what the purpose of the mission had been. There had been some sort of agreement that units of the Free State Army were going to invade Northern Ireland. We were there to guide them in, to bring them across the border'. The troops 'meant to come across the border were known as Aiken's Volunteers', and the man behind the plan was the 'then Free State Minister for Defence, Frank Aiken'. Aiken, Cahill suggested, had 'always retained his basic republican principles. He often expressed concern for the beleaguered northern Catholic minority following partition'.[1] This story, which echoes similar rumours of invasion plans from the 1920s, confirms Aiken's image as an unreconstructed IRA leader with close ties to militant republicanism, even after Fianna Fáil's accession to power in 1932.[2] This chapter examines this belief in the context of Aiken's period as IRA Chief of Staff, his efforts to rebuild the organization, his support for Fianna Fáil and his attitude to his former comrades after Éamon de Valera's party came to power.

Keeping the Army intact

Aiken had been unanimously elected as the IRA's leader on 20 April 1923, shortly after the death of Liam Lynch. At the IRA Executive meeting at which he took charge, Aiken proposed that the 'Government and Army Council' should be empowered to 'make peace with F.S. [Free State] "Government" on the following basis':

1. The sovereignty of the Irish Nation and the integrity of its territory are inalienable.
2. That any instrument purporting to the contrary is, to the extent of its violation of above principle, null and void.[3]

The idea behind what were later referred to as the 'ceasefire proposals' was to offer an honourable way for the anti-Treaty IRA to cease fighting. The Free State government was in no mood for compromise, however, and in May Aiken was forced to order a dumping of arms and ceasefire.[4]

Following this, on 28 May 1923, Aiken issued instructions to his subordinates, reminding them that 'it is the duty of every officer to work energetically to see that all arms are safely dumped and ensure that all armed resistance ceases', but also that 'the dumping of arms does not mean that the usefulness of the IRA is past, or release any member of it from his duty to his country … it is clearly our duty to keep the Army Organisation intact'. He reminded them that 'we joined the IRA and enlisted men to firmly establish the Republic of Ireland. We fought for that, our comrades dies [sic] for it. Until we reach that objective it is our duty to push towards it, using at every moment the means at our disposal best suited to achieve our purpose'. Now, he continued, 'discipline must be maintained, ordinary routine work done and reports returned … Officers must do their utmost to safeguard their men and get them back to civilian work. The wounded and needy Volunteers must be cared for'. He also warned that 'Divisional O/Cs must give special care to men who are liable to be murdered, if captured. A list in code of the latter must be returned immediately to GHQ and arrangements will be made to have them transferred to other Divisional areas, if necessary'.[5]

This was a very necessary precaution because, despite the ceasefire, killings of anti-Treatyites by Free State forces, sometimes after capture, continued into the autumn.[6] In his instructions to his subordinates, Aiken also stressed that 'No man must leave Ireland unless ordered to do so by GHQ. It is the duty of every member of the IRA to live or die in [this] country until it is free unless ordered to leave to do some work for the cause, or to get strong after illness'. He reiterated that Volunteers should be politically active and:

… educate ourselves and the people around us in order to develop a healthy Gaelic civilisation that will have no use for Pro-British Irishmen.

For this purpose we must join the Sinn Fein Organisation and make sure that the nation is represented by men who have our ideals and objective.

Finally, he warned that: 'this nation has no use for slackers or those who throw their hands up in despair. We have work to do. It is our duty to do it'.[7]

At this point there were over 12,000 republicans in jail, large numbers emigrating, and dissension at leadership level. The Cork IRA leader Tom Barry left the organisation after several disputes, and there were small-scale splinter groups, including the short-lived 'Republican Defence Corps' in Dublin.[8] Despite the ceasefire order there were also several killings of Gardaí and civilians which were attributed to republicans.[9] Numerous armed robberies were also blamed on IRA members, though others, including Free State soldiers, were also involved in these activities. Complaining that 'some of our men take upon themselves so lightly the powers of peace and war', Aiken moved to reassert discipline, stressing that Volunteers could be 'liable to execution' for disobeying orders. In August 1923 a general election took place and, despite repression, forty-four Republican TDs were elected. This remarkable showing demonstrated that a popular base for anti-Treaty politics existed.[10] Aiken won a seat in Louth, topping the poll with 6,651 votes.[11]

Hunger strike

The IRA, however, soon faced a prison crisis. Aiken claimed that 'after the elections the enemy offensive to treat our prisoners as individuals and as criminals began'.[12] During October 1923, trouble erupted in Mountjoy, and soon spread to other prisons and internment camps. By November a mass hunger strike, involving up to 8,000 prisoners (including fifty women) was taking place.[13] Some cautioned against this tactic, but Aiken claimed not to have the power to order prisoners off it. Earlier in the year the IRA had decided that 'hunger striking was a matter for individuals'. Aiken claimed to believe that 'the best course was to let the prisoners go on with it or call it off themselves'. During the strike itself, however, Aiken stressed to the O/C of the Kilmainham prisoners that 'under no circumstances, even should a comrade die, are you to call off the hunger strike – of course you have no power to order any man off. I believe your fight will do more for the cause than a thousand years war'.[14]

But the huge numbers on strike meant that organisation was almost impossible and confusion soon reigned. Some prisoners broke relatively quickly, while others maintained their fast for over forty days. Two Cork prisoners died, and the strike came to an end in November. Nevertheless, Aiken claimed that the events were 'a success from a national point of view'. 'The deaths of Dinny Barry and Andy O'Sullivan', Aiken professed:

> ... clinched the victory the prisoners won [over] the materialism [and] Imperialism and selfishness that was sweeping the country. Even the bitter enemies of our country have great respect for the faith and endurance of the Volunteers who hungerstruck even for a few days.[15]

Between Christmas 1923 and July 1924, most republican prisoners in the Free State were released. Many of those north of the border were also freed, including Aiken's sister Nano, who had spent fifteen months in Armagh Jail, and was the last female republican prisoner on the island.[16] During this period Aiken oversaw the introduction of a new scheme of organisation to facilitate his army's reduced numbers.[17] The IRA numbered about 15,000 men in 1924, concentrated in the west and south of the Free State.[18] They had access to about 4,000 rifles, over 1,000 handguns and 100 machine guns of various types.[19] Aiken's leadership colleagues included Tom Derrig, Ernie O'Malley, P.J. Ruttledge, Seán Moylan, Liam Pilkington, Seamus Robinson, Peadar O'Donnell and Tom Maguire.[20] Despite Aiken's warning that 'the man who could live at home and who emigrates is giving (the British) voluntary help – he is Ireland's foe', many hundreds of republicans were leaving Ireland.[21] In order to combat this, the IRA formed a Foreign Reserve to ensure that all who left did so with official sanction and with a promise to return if conflict erupted.[22] The IRA also established an employment committee to help Volunteers find work, and set up a fund to provide financial aid for men on the run and for the families of men who had been killed. The focus of activity was still very much on the Free State (there were only about 600 Volunteers in Northern Ireland). During 1924, Aiken even had to answer charges from Richard Mulcahy that the Northern Ireland authorities were allowing the 'Irregulars' freedom to operate there.[23]

Were there any prospects for renewed action against the Free State? During the hunger strike the IRA had been approached by members of the Irish Republican Brotherhood (IRB) from Belfast, who had supported the Treaty, but now sought some form of cooperation. Aiken's response was to refuse to 'attend hole in corner conferences with men who recognised foreign authority and who carried on a war of extermination against Republicans'. In January 1924 the leadership ordered that 'IRA men will take no part in IRB activities'.[24] But contact was renewed in March 1924 during the so-called Free State Army mutiny.[25] The mutineers contacted the IRA, claiming that they could provide the information and means to capture Free State military posts. Aiken asserted that 'we would want more proof of their sincerity than their talk before we would think of touching them. We pointed out that the prisoners, for whose capture they were responsible, were still in jail'. According to the IRA leader, their attitude was 'if the mutineers were going to smash the Free State we would not put any obstacles in their way, but we were not going to rely on them or their help to do it'.[26]

A 'mere political party'?

Perhaps this was an opportunity for the IRA to use discord within the ranks of the state forces to move against the government. Aiken's organisation, though, was still recovering from the Civil War, and the mutineers included men who were believed to have carried out some of the worst atrocities of that conflict. The IRA let the opportunity pass and continued their low-level activities, primarily recruiting and drilling.[27] Politically, however, there was increasing friction. Some of this was featured in the weekly *An Phoblacht*, launched during 1925.[28] At Easter 1925, Aiken gave the oration in Dundalk, despite a large military presence around St Patrick's Cemetery. He reiterated that 'we all want peace, but there is not a man here who does not also know that a final peace cannot come until the British Government and her tools withdraw their interference in Irish affairs'.[29] Despite this rhetoric, there were those in the IRA who felt that Aiken was no longer committed to a military struggle. The state forces were aware that young IRA officers were pushing for more militant activity.[30] These issues came to a head when it became clear that some IRA leaders were supportive of proposals by Éamon de Valera that seats could be taken in Leinster House if the Oath of Allegiance were abolished. This issue came to the fore at the November 1925 IRA Convention; the organisation's first such meeting since 1922.[31]

The agenda illustrated the growing frustration with a Dublin motion asserting that the 'present policy of passive resistance is destroying the spirit and discipline of our Army', while the Cork No. 2 Brigade demanded that 'a definite time be laid down within which a revolution shall be attempted, say five years'. A motion from Donegal stated that, 'in view of the fact that the Government has developed into a mere political party ... the Army [must] ... sever its connexion with the Dáil and act under an independent Executive'.[32] The delegates voted to support this motion, meaning that the IRA became free of political control.[33] Amid strong criticism of the leadership, Aiken stepped down as Chief of Staff, to be replaced by Andy Cooney. The convention did not make a formal declaration, however, regarding the question of taking seats in parliament.

Aiken would claim that delegates accepted a compromise, that 'all volunteers who abided by the Army Constitution be allowed remain Volunteers, and that the question as to whether T.D.s should or should not enter Free State Parliament, if oath were removed, be left to Republican T.D.s'.[34] He also suggested that, while he was open about his support for allowing flexibility to the republican political leadership, most senior officers at the convention said nothing. 'Boiling the matter down, therefore, I have more right to speak for the Army in this matter then six of seven members of the Army Council'.[35] Aiken underplayed, though, how much opposition there had been. Though he was re-elected onto the IRA Executive, he came only twentieth out of thirty-six candidates. Of those associated with de Valera, only Aiken, Tom Derrig and Michael Kilroy retained their positions, while P.J. Ruttledge and Seán Lemass were voted off. The new IRA Executive, which included Mick Price, George Plunkett, Andy Cooney, Moss Twomey and Peadar O'Donnell, reflected a desire for militancy.[36]

'The height of foolishness'

Shortly afterwards, on 18 November 1925, Aiken wrote to his fellow officers to:

> … insist on my right to advocate when I think fit, outside Volunteer work, any honourable political policy for strengthening the nation to achieve independence. I insist on this right because I think it is the duty of Volunteers to insist on it; at the same time I am ready, as long as the Army Authorities abide by the Constitution, to serve as a Volunteer in any capacity in which I think I might be useful, and to uphold in public and in private the right and duty of Irishmen to be trained and armed without the control of any government hostile or inimical to the Republic of Ireland.[37]

Aiken was also:

> … greatly afraid that most of you are not, what I consider, far-seeing enough at the present time to appoint me or anyone holding my views to positions which I believe would be best filled in the interests of the Nation by people holding those views … it will probably take time and bitter experience to teach some Volunteers that it is the height of foolishness to debar in advance the people from using any honourable means to help them to secure our objective. [38]

In the same letter, Aiken argued that it was 'worse than foolishness, to put it mildly, to believe that the Nation should not have that much tactical elbow-room in theory and deny it to her now when she is in a life and death struggle in order to please some people who will not think the matter out until our enemies have won the fight'. Instead, he noted, it was 'an honourable policy to use the powers which the Free State or Six County governments possess in order to achieve the independence of our country, provided we don't have to admit their legitimacy by any oath or declaration or any other way whatsoever'. Aiken did not have 'much sympathy with people who would stake all the chances of success in our generation on the extremely remote possibility of a successful coup d'état', some of whom reminded him of those 'who threatened a lot about what they would do with the people who voted for the treaty and then discarded the sword when the civil war broke out', or 'the honest but foolish optimists who thought they could defeat the Free State in Civil War'.[39]

He concluded his letter claiming that:

> Volunteers believe that without the Army Ireland cannot gain her freedom. With a lot of our men this belief is only a human military instinct; they have never thought the matter out. I have thought it out; for, being as I was Chief of Staff, on me devolved principally its defence … It is because I have convinced myself with good, sound, clear reasons that without a good Volunteer Army, we cannot achieve freedom in our generation that I want to stabilise and strengthen ours and prevent it, if I can, from splitting over every disagreement regarding policy that is bound to arise between this and our goal.[40]

This was the reason why he believed that IRA officers should be free to endorse political actions. With the air of someone who knew that his arguments, despite their self-evident superiority, would be rejected, he concluded, 'Go dtuga Dia ciall daoibh' (May God give you sense).[41]

The interests of Fianna Fáil

With his position in the IRA leadership in flux, Aiken soon sought 'leave of absence to perform work for the Republic abroad'.[42] He spent from January to October 1926 in the United States, and was not in Ireland when the Fianna Fáil party was established during May.[43] But he soon made clear his support for this initiative, informing de Valera, in a letter dated 22 May 1926, that:

I am now more convinced than ever that the policy being worked now by Fianna Fail is the one political policy through which we have a chance of making progress towards the realization of our ideals, and that it is the duty of Republicans to give it a fair chance unless AND UNTIL the gloomy prophecies regarding Fianna Fail come true. If I were at home now I would give my utmost support to Fianna Fail and the Army. If Sinn Fein entered into the political fold as a rival to Fianna Fail, I would do my utmost to get the people to withhold support from it. [44]

He was also adamant that, while he did 'not know what arrangements are now in force regarding the expenditure of funds raised by the Mission here ... I would not stand for Government funds or any funds I helped to raise being given to Sinn Féin to spend on organising a political campaign in opposition to Fianna Fail'.[45]

In July, Aiken told de Valera that 'from this date ... until you instruct otherwise, I shall act as your representative in all matters affecting the interests of Fianna Fáil in the United States'.[46] From an early stage Aiken was 'extremely anxious ... to know as soon as possible how matters stand in Ireland and how funds raised here are to be distributed'.[47] Aiken was operating in an Irish-American milieu, which, though greatly weakened since the Civil War, was still capable of generating substantial support.[48] He was also still an IRA officer, 'General Aiken', with the credibility of having been Chief of Staff.

There were two main organisations that concerned him. The American Association for the Recognition of the Irish Republic (AARIR) had supported de Valera in 1922, but it had suffered a dramatic decline in membership, from an estimated 700,000 members in 1921 to just 13,870 by 1925.[49] The more secretive Clan na Gael, led by Joseph McGarrity, had around 5,000 members, including a substantial number of recent emigrants.[50] Aiken was hopeful that the 'overwhelming majority' of the AARIR could be won to supporting de Valera and, while the Clan na Gael were likely to 'support the Army only', he suggested that 'the majority of them are, however, I think in favour of (de Valera's) political policy'.[51]

Aiken openly stated his belief that 'Mr. De Valera's policy, is, in fact, the only one before the people of Ireland today which is likely, in the circumstances that exist, to achieve success for the cause for which our martyrs died'.[52] He also claimed that 'Fianna Fáil has already behind it the vast majority of Republicans who remained faithful during the last ten years'.[53] But he stressed most of all that there was no contradiction between supporting both Fianna Fáil and the IRA.

In an 'Open Letter to All Old IRA Men', Aiken asserted that 'Ireland Needs Both A Military And A Political Organisation'. He claimed that the history of revolutionary efforts in Ireland had shown that the 'success and failure of all movements to retain freedom, and to regain it when lost, were in direct proportion to the efforts of the national leaders of the day to develop both political and military organisations and to maintain the proper balance between them'. Thus, he continued:

> ... the Volunteers and organised citizens united to gain the Constitution of 1782; the Volunteers went out of existence and then came the Union. 1798, 1803, 1867, 1916, 1922–23, were military failures because the army was unsupported by the organised citizens; O'Connell, Butt, and Redmond were political failures because unsupported by military organizations. Grattan and Parnell succeeded in doing something when both military and political organisations existed, and failed when they failed to keep both alive. The lesson of 1918–21 should be well known to us all; the political and military organisations working in harmony and cooperation had the British Empire almost beaten. Michael Collins said that if the 'Treaty' were put through we would get plenty of arms and finish it by arms alone! I say again, and the history of the failures of the past bears out my opinion, which is based on my own experience, that success for our cause depends upon our having both a good army and a good political organisation. People who desire to see our cause succeed should, in my opinion, support both the Irish Republican Army and the Fianna Fail organisation. [54]

Fianna Fáil, Aiken explained, was 'the sole and only political organisation in Ireland today based on old Republican principles and adapted to suit the new conditions that exist today ... it is the old sword, which had got blunt, with a fresh sharp edge'.

For Aiken, there was no compromise with principle involved in using the political machinery of the Free State. While the administrations 'controlling the Twenty-Six and Six Counties respectively' were only 'pretending to be ruling them in the interests of the people of their areas', these 'so-called governments', he wrote, still controlled certain powers. These powers, he noted:

> ... like those of the old County Councils and District Councils, might be used to advance the national cause when worked by men who would proclaim openly they owed no allegiance to the British King and would recognize no authority as lawful in Ireland other than that which comes direct from God to the people, just as the powers of the County and

District councils when and where we could influence them to advance the interests of the nation, were used in 1918 and 1921 without obeying or recognizing the authority of the British King ... we Republicans worked in those local Councils six or eight years ago, and we used their powers to bring the nation to victory.[55]

Aiken admitted that he did not know whether Fianna Fáil would be:

... successful in removing the oath of allegiance or not at the next General Election; but certain I am that we have started a movement that will eventually draw into it all the elements who want to see Ireland free from British authority and living her own life in her own way, leaving only on the other side those who want England to dominate our country.

When that situation arose, he foretold, 'when the people of this generation get together once again on the firm rock of national principle ready to assert their own rights, and deny the supposed ones of the British – and if on that day there is a strong Volunteer Army to rely on, I care not a rap for devils nor Britishers'. 'A united Ireland', he declared, 'had nothing to fear from all the king's horses and the all the king's men'.[56] In making this appeal, as in several other public statements at this time, Aiken was careful to assure republicans that armed force had not been ruled out as a means of achieving their aims.[57]

Aiken's arguments met with some success. As he had predicted, the AARIR came on board, and in August 1926 announced 'that the Fianna Fail policy is the National Republican policy in Ireland'.[58] But Aiken was of course being disingenuous in claiming that the IRA and Fianna Fáil were the 'two legs of the nation'. During the summer of 1926, Andy Cooney was dispatched to the US by the IRA to ensure Clan na Gael realised that 'the I.R.A. was not neutral but had taken a definite stand against Mr. De Valera's program'.[59]

'Sweet reasonableness'

In response to communications from the IRA criticizing his activities, Aiken asserted that 'every act I have done since 1916, other than purely personal acts, was to secure as soon as possible recognition for the right of my country to be governed by a Republican Government of the free choice of her own people'. 'The question of my sincerity', he noted, 'is one which I won't argue with anyone. I note uncomplimentary statements people make regarding my motives principally as a guide to estimate their own wisdom and honesty'. Any confusion was the IRA's own fault: 'I wish to Goodness, now, that all the members of the Army Council had expressed their opinions fully at the Army Convention instead of quietly acquiescing in the let-the-matter-rest decision when the question of the new departure came up for decision'. He warned them not to:

> ... make the mistake of imagining that my 'sweet reasonableness' and avoidance of personalities is due to my being too timid to defend my reputation or to my lack of grip on my opinions; I am prepared to defend them when I think it necessary, no matter by whom they are attacked.[60]

These communications were private, and when Aiken arrived back in Ireland he was still an IRA officer. The IRA themselves admitted that 'there was no opportunity for judging as to whether he intended to be an active Volunteer or not'.[61] But the final break came when Aiken agreed to stand as a candidate in the June 1927 general election, in contravention of General Order No. 28, which forbade IRA members from becoming parliamentary candidates.[62] As a result, Aiken and nineteen other IRA officers were court-martialled, and left the IRA.[63] Despite this, Cumann na nGaedheal still referred to Aiken's 'army' and its alleged plans for war in their election literature.[64]

The crisis that followed the assassination of Kevin O'Higgins and new government legislation forced Fianna Fáil to take their seats.[65] From June 1927, Aiken was a Fianna Fáil TD, not an IRA officer, and by September he was sitting in Leinster House.[66] The relationship between the two organisations remained fluid. No senior Fianna Fáil figure was still a member of the IRA, but at rank-and-file level there was some crossover. On particular issues, such as the Land Annuities campaign, there was cooperation. A number of Fianna Fáil TDs publicly defended the IRA and denounced government moves against them, though Aiken was not particularly vocal on these matters.[67] Nevertheless, Special Branch did list him as a member of Fianna Fáil's 'left-wing', along with Séamus Robinson, Oscar Traynor and 'Briscoe the Jew', among others.[68]

'I am still fighting for Irish freedom'

During 1928, Aiken embarked on another US tour, this time raising funds for a new Fianna Fáil publication. The tour's publicity and the American press made much of the military exploits of 'General Fred Aiken ... Ireland's youngest and strongest rebel'; one Seattle paper even claiming in a feature about him that 'they don't croon babies to sleep in Ireland with "Mother Macree" or "When Irish Eyes are Smiling"... the children's lullaby of Ireland is "Freedom from England".'[69]

But Aiken's own views were more complex. In early 1932, in the midst of the security clampdown by the Cumann na nGaedheal government, he was forced to appear in court in a case involving the *Irish Press*, the newspaper established in support of Fianna Fáil in 1931. Aiken recognised the court; something that IRA Volunteers never did. He was questioned extensively about his attitude to military force. When asked whether he had 'tried to overthrow this State by force of arms?' he replied 'Yes'. When pressed as to whether he still held this view, he responded that 'I am still fighting for Irish freedom, and the only difference between myself and others is the best way of achieving this end … I never advocated force of arms when better means were available. [70]

When questioned as to whether he believed that 'better means' were available, he replied that he believed they were. As to the question of whether he still advocated force, he answered 'no … if I believed that I would be in the IRA..[71]

The security clampdown and attendant 'Red Scare' was in part an attempt by Cumann na nGaedheal to whip up fear of the IRA running amok in the wake of a Fianna Fáil victory in the forthcoming general election.[72] But it had the effect of forcing the IRA to support Fianna Fáil actively in the election, with the organisation admitting that 'owing to the Coercion Act, Terrorism, and the ill-treatment of prisoners, the hatred against the Coercionist regime was so intense that Volunteers could not be restrained from voting against their candidates'.[73] As a result, the IRA took part in Fianna Fáil's election campaign, which resulted in the party winning enough seats to form a government, but only with the support of the Labour party.

'Secure real national unity'

Two days after the election, Aiken made contact with IRA leader Moss Twomey, suggesting that 'the IRA and Fianna Fail must be fused at once', because 'a complete spontaneous fusing now would double the sum of their separate strengths'. 'The national morale', he advocated, 'would be strengthened a thousand fold, and many things that are impossible of achievement with divided forces would not only be possible but certain'. Aiken warned that there would be a determined attempt to undermine his party. He noted how:

> … the British papers are beginning to thunder already. All the usual re-actionary forces will be whipped up to force Labour and ourselves to agree to this Coalition, and the levers of the Eucharistic Congress, trouble with England, world depression, etc. will be used for all they

are worth. We will be on the defensive and may fail to secure the reains [*sic*] of Government unless you come to the national rescue by showing that you will accept our authority wholeheartedly when the oath is removed.[74]

Furthermore, Aiken stressed that:

> ... we have now a chance to secure real national unity against the re-actionaries which only comes once in a generation. You can round off a splendid record by an act honourable to the IRA and of everlasting value to the cause of freedom and social justice ... when a Fianna Fail Government gets control of the Governmental institutions of the twenty-six counties, and accepts and acts upon the principles contained in the Peace Proposals agreed by the Irish Republican Army published by the President, Eamon de Valera, on the 27th of April, 1923 ... the arms and services of the members of the IRA could then be placed at the disposal of that Government, and in my opinion it ought to be done immediately.[75]

Finally, Aiken warned that 'if the way is not cleared for a fusion of forces we are doomed to a period of indecision and weakness in dealing with the urgent international, financial and economic and social problems which will lead to a defeat of the Fianna Fail Government ... and the anti-national reactionary forces will again get control'.[76] In conversations with IRA leaders, Aiken suggested that the organisation might be able to play a military role under the new government, but clearly saw it as necessary that they accept Fianna Fáil's authority.

However, the IRA rejected these proposals, arguing that 'the Fianna Fail interpretation of the "Cease-fire" proposals is not ours'. Instead, they reiterated that 'the IRA be maintained as a distinct organisation ... retaining control of all arms and equipment [and] as the leadership of the National Revolutionary Struggle' they called 'upon the Fianna Fail Government, who claim to have as their objective the establishment of a Republic for all Ireland, not to hamper or impede the IRA in their activities'.[77]

Despite the lack of an agreement, one of the first steps of the government was to free all IRA prisoners. Aiken, now Minister for Defence, visited several of them in Arbour Hill just prior to their release. Anecdotal accounts suggest that the new government made no secret of their hostility to the state forces.[78] But on St Patrick's Day 1932, Aiken, along with Seán Lemass, visited Collins Barracks in Dublin and attended morning Mass with senior National Army officers.

He then travelled to College Green, where, along with Free State Army Chief of Staff (and Civil War adversary) Michael Brennan, Aiken removed his hat and took the salute while National Army troops, including armoured cars and artillery, paraded past.[79]

Talks with the IRA

At the same time, contact with the IRA was maintained. The conduit for these contacts was Tom Barry, who had applied to rejoin the IRA.[80] Barry had met de Valera in Cork, and the Fianna Fáil leader had suggested to him that war with Britain was likely and a new volunteer force for 'national defence' would be needed.[81] Barry suggested that the IRA might play a central role in this. During July 1932, he helped to arrange a meeting between Aiken and IRA leaders Moss Twomey, Seán MacBride and George Gilmore.

At the meeting, Aiken told the IRA men that he 'had been very busy', but would try to organise a meeting between them and de Valera. Barry then argued that there was a 'necessity for forming a military organisation under the Free State Ministry of Defence, pleading the necessity for a large military organisation to meet the crisis with the British'. Barry then stated that 'it was possible a military clash might arise', and in order 'to steady the country' the IRA should join such an organisation. The IRA officers noted that Barry had 'used identically the same arguments which Aiken had used in conversation last March'.[82] The IRA men, in contrast, argued that the 'essential need (was) agitation, and organisation of the people throughout the twenty-six counties' in a broad movement involving republicans and labour activists. To this, 'Aiken said very little and offered no information as to his plans in regard to the new force, except to say they intended launching it very soon'. Aiken explained that he hoped that the IRA 'will see their way to join it, especially since the Oath question is ended, the Land Annuities being fought, and the Governor General put in his place!'[83]

Asked about the further steps contemplated against the 'Treaty', Aiken said that they did not propose to exceed their mandate, but that they certainly were determined to carry it out at any cost. Aiken asked 'what we had in mind ... if a conference such as we proposed was held'? The IRA again stressed the need for mass mobilisation, but Aiken responded that 'the Fianna Fail government must control and direct the speed of the campaign and could not allow any other bodies to do this; that since they brought this situation around they should hold it and deal with it as they saw fit'. In the IRA's view, 'it was clear that Aiken was very cautious and not prepared to given even opinions on anything'.[84]

Ironically, while Fianna Fáil was offering the IRA something of a military role, albeit under their ultimate control, the IRA was more interested in a political campaign. It was clear that Aiken was somewhat frustrated by their lack of cooperation. The problem for the IRA was summed up by Twomey: 'Nobody visualised a Free State which Republicans were not supposed to attack! And that is just what we have today in the 26 Counties … We don't want the Cosgrave Imperial gang back, and we wish to avoid doing anything which may provide the pretext for their come back'.[85] This meant that the IRA backed Fianna Fáil again in the January 1933 general election, as it was the only way to drive out of 'public life a party that has sold itself to the British Empire'.[86] Secret contacts were maintained between the government and the IRA throughout 1933, but no agreement was reached.[87] In fact, conflict between the IRA and Fianna Fáil intensified as republicans stepped up street activities. IRA members were increasingly arrested and jailed.[88]

'Every ill-considered brain-wave'

There was some unease within Fianna Fáil at this, which was reflected in critical motions at the party's November 1933 Ard Fheis. It was Aiken who took the lead in dismissing these complaints. In response to a motion protesting about the imprisonment of IRA men, Aiken suggested that 'it would be more logical if the movers of the resolution submitted another: "That the Ard Fheis adjourn and that a dictatorship of the IRA Executive be set up in their stead to dictate Government policy".' He lamented that some Fianna Fail members were 'half-apologising for belonging to the greatest political organisation in the country'. Aiken claimed not to:

> … want to have anybody in jail [but asked] is there any one here or outside who will say there is a single man in prison for his political opinions – for his political opinions alone? (Voices – No, no) … there are men in jail because they took armed action or carried arms in public. They had to be dealt with of course, as leniently and generously as we could. Where are we going to go in this country if every fool who thinks he knows more than the collective wisdom of the whole people takes it upon himself to start a war of his own?[89]

He then referred again to the 'Ceasefire proposals', which in 1923 'were turned down, but … were in operation at the present moment' as the basis for the IRA ceasing armed activity.[90]

The mention of the 'Ceasefire proposals' sparked off a public debate with IRA leaders in the *Irish Press*. Aiken had retained copies of internal IRA correspondence when he left the organisation, and was able to force Seán MacBride to withdraw a claim that he had been 'kicked out of the Republican Army in 1925'. Aiken addressed the IRA's complaints with the patronising air of a frustrated parent: 'those must be restrained who act on every ill-considered brain-wave. The youngster or the courageous fool who does the right thing at the wrong time and in the wrong way must be treated as an indisciplined [*sic*] and disruptive individual and not as a hero'.[91]

'Protect all citizens … and property'

As Lar Joye examines in the following chapter, the reserve Volunteer Force of the Free State Army, which Aiken envisaged as a force republicans could join, was finally launched in 1934.[92] The IRA was divided on how to respond, but, in Kerry in particular, its members waged a violent campaign against 'Aiken's slugs'.[93] One of those jailed for involvement in these attacks was the son of a Tralee Fianna Fáil Councillor, who wrote to Aiken to complain about the treatment of his son. Aiken's reply illustrated both his lack of sympathy with the IRA and his belief that Fianna Fáil had been given a mandate to govern:

> I wish to point out to you that when the Government was seeking election it promised that it would protect all citizens and their person and property and that it would ensure that no one was interfered with unless in the process of law. The Government has been endeavouring to carry out its duty to the people with a minimum of force and restraint. I wish it were true that your son was in jail, as you say, 'simply because he refused to give an account of his movements'. [94]

In an unapologetic fashion, Aiken informed the councillor that his son was:

> … charged with being one of a mob which overpowered, stripped and beat a couple of unarmed Volunteers in a most brutal manner, and he acted before the Tribunal as if he were guilty and proud of it … There is no necessity to point out where these attacks would lead if they were allowed to continue. They must be stopped, whether if they were made by men just out for a mad stunt, or by men who are deliberately trying to prevent the Government from building up the National defences.

Aiken could not resist an added barb, concluding that:

> ... you may rest assured that everything ... possible will be done to take proper care of the prisoners' health if they co-operate with the prison authorities ... they have been doing so since Christmas Day and your son is in excellent health. He is 7 lbs. heavier than he weighed in Arbour Hill immediately after being sentenced.[95]

In summary, the evidence suggests that, despite his leadership position in the IRA, Aiken had come to the conclusion that military force was not a realistic option for the organisation as early as the mid-1920s. When still an IRA officer he was an important ally of de Valera in building Fianna Fáil, playing a vital role in convincing republicans that no principle was at stake in supporting the new party. It is also clear that, while he was prepared to try to co-opt the IRA in order to strengthen Fianna Fáil, he grew intolerant very quickly of militant republicans once in government.

Notes

1   Brendan Anderson, *Joe Cahill: a Life in the IRA* (Dublin: O'Brien Press, 2002), 27–30.

2   John Bowman, *De Valera and the Ulster Question, 1917–1973* (Oxford: Oxford University Press, 1982), 80.

3   Army Executive meeting, 20 April 1923. University College Dublin Archives, (UCDA), Frank Aiken Papers, P104/1263 (1–2).

4   Michael Hopkinson, *Green Against Green: the Irish Civil War* (Dublin: Gill and Macmillan, 1988), 256–258.

5   Chief of Staff (C/S) to all Officers, 'Our Duty in the Future' 28 May 1923. UCDA, P104/1312 (1–2).

6   Brian Hanley, *The IRA: a Documentary History, 1916–2005* (Dublin: Gill and Macmillan, 2010), 54–55.

7   Chief of Staff (C/S) to all Officers, 'Our Duty in the Future' 28 May 1923. UCDA, P104/1312 (1–2).

8   Chief of Staff to Executive Meeting Held 10 Aug. 1924. Aiken and Barry were involved in a public spat over these disputes during 1935. See *Irish Independent*, 4 June 1935 & UCDA, P104/1283 (1–5). See also UCDA, P104/1266 (6–9).

9   'Murders and principal outrages committed by Irregulars since the "Cease Fire" order, April 1923'. National Archives of Ireland (NAI), Department of the Taoiseach (D/T), S5864 A.

10   Richard Dunphy, *The Making of Fianna Fáil Power in Ireland* (Oxford: Oxford University Press, 1995) 38.

11   Brian W. Walker, *Parliamentary Election Results in Ireland, 1918–92* (Dublin: Royal Irish Academy, 1992), 113.

12   UCDA, P104/1266 (6–9).

13   Hopkinson, *Green Against Green*, 268–271.

14   Hopkinson, *Green Against Green*, 269.

15   UCDA, P104/1266 (6–9).

16   *Irish Independent*, 7 May 1924.

17   Army Council report for General Army Convention, 1925. UCDA, Moss Twomey Papers (MTP) P69/181 (82–91).

18   General Report for Executive Meeting, 10 Aug. 1924. UCDA, P69/179 (104–109).

19   Brian Hanley, *The IRA 1926–36* (Dublin: Four Courts Press, 2002), 29.

20   UCDA, P69/144 (141–142). Decisions of Executive Meeting, 10–11 Aug. 1924, to O/C's Divisions and Independent Brigades, 20 Sept. 1924. UCDA, P69/144 (141–142).

21   Gavin Foster, '"No 'Wild Geese' this time"? IRA Emigration after the Irish Civil War', *Éire-Ireland*, 47 1&2, Spring/Summer, 2012.

22   Hanley, *The IRA, 1926–36,* 161–162.

23   *Irish Independent*, 2 Feb. 1924.

24   Executive Meeting, 27/28 Jan. 1924. UCDA, P69/180 (3–10).

25   John M. Regan, *The Irish Counter-Revolution 1921–1936: Treatyite Politics and Settlement in Independent Ireland* (Dublin: Gill and Macmillan, 1999), 163–197.

26   UCDA, P104/1266 (6–9).

27   For a detailed chronology of events involving republicans, see Uinseann MacEoin, *The IRA in the Twilight Years, 1923–1948* (Dublin: Argenta Publications, 1997), 69–24.

28   Conor Foley, *Legion of the Rearguard: the IRA and the Modern Irish State* (London: Pluto Press, 1992), 53–54.

29   *Irish Independent*, 13 April 1925.

30   A/Commandant Dan Bryan to C/S (National Army), 2 Dec. 1925. UCDA, Desmond FitzGerald Papers, (P80)/849 (11).

31   J. Bowyer Bell, *The Secret Army: the IRA* (Dublin: Poolbeg, 1997), 52–54.

32   Agenda for Convention, 1925. UCDA, P69/179 (185–189).

33   Michael MacEvilly, *A Splendid Resistance: the Life of IRA Chief of Staff Dr. Andy Cooney* (Dublin: De Burca, 2011), 147–160.

34   Aiken to S. T. O'Kelly, 8 June 1926. UCDA, P104/2584 (15–16).

35   Aiken to S. T. O'Kelly, 12 Aug. 1926. UCDA, P104/2575 (4).

36   Executive, General Army Convention, 14–15 Nov. 1925. UCDA, P69/179 (190).

37   Aiken to Chairman, Army Council, 18 Nov. 1925. UCDA, P69/181 (77–78).

38   Aiken to Chairman, Army Council, 18 Nov. 1925. UCDA, P69/181 (77–78).

39   Aiken to Chairman, Army Council, 18 Nov. 1925. UCDA, P69/181 (77–78).

40   Aiken to Chairman, Army Council, 18 Nov. 1925. UCDA, P69/181 (77–78).

41   Aiken to Chairman, Army Council, 18 Nov. 1925. UCDA, P69/181 (77–78).

42   Record of Executive meeting 27 April 1927. UCDA, P69/48 (104).

43   For various accounts, see Dunphy, *The Making of Fianna Fáil Power in Ireland*; Noel Whelan, *Fianna Fáil: Biography of a Party* (Dublin: Gill and Macmillan, 2011); Donnacha Ó Beacháin, *Destiny of the Soldiers: Fianna Fáil, Irish Republicanism and the IRA, 1926–1973* (Dublin: Gill and Macmillan, 2010); and Kieran Allen, *Fianna Fáil and Irish Labour, 1926 to the Present* (London: Pluto Press, 1997).

44   Aiken to de Valera, 22 May 1926. UCDA, P104/2571 (3).

45   Aiken to de Valera, 22 May 1926. UCDA, P104/2571 (3).

46   Aiken to de Valera, 27 July 1926. UCDA, P104/2574 (1–2).

47   UCDA, P104/2571 (3). Aiken to de Valera, 22 May 1926.

48   Brian Hanley, 'Irish Republicans in inter-war New York', *Irish Journal of American Studies, IJASonline,* 1 (June, 2009) at http://www.ijasonline.com/BRIAN-HANLEY.html

49   AARIR membership figures, July 1925. UCDA, P104/2520 (55).

50   An Timithire, Clan na Gael, 20 May 1927. UCDA, P69/183 (47).

51   Aiken to de Valera, 27 July 1926. UCDA, P104/2574 (1–2).

52   Aiken responds to Sinn Féin (N/D). UCDA, P104/2575 (8).

53   'Open Letter to All Old IRA Men – General Aiken Appeals For Support For The Boys And People At Home'. (N/D). UCDA, P104/2573 (2–4).

54   'Open Letter to All Old IRA Men – General Aiken Appeals For Support For The Boys And People At Home'. (N/D). UCDA, P104/2573 (2–4).

55   'Open Letter to All Old IRA Men – General Aiken Appeals For Support For The Boys And People At Home'. (N/D). UCDA, P104/2573 (2–4).

56   'Open Letter to All Old IRA Men – General Aiken Appeals For Support For The Boys And People At Home'. (N/D). UCDA, P104/2573 (2–4).

57   Stephen Kelly, *Fianna Fáil, Partition and Northern Ireland 1926–1971* (Dublin: Irish Academic Press, 2013), 48.

58   AARIR Executive report, 16 Aug. 1926. UCDA, P104/2575.

59   Aiken to Seán T. O'Kelly, 8 June 1926. UCDA, P104/2584 (15–16).

60   Aiken to Chairman, Army Council, 12 Aug. 1926. UCDA, P104/2575 (9–10).

61   Executive report, 27 April 1927. UCDA, P69/48 (104).

62   'General Order No. 28. Volunteers as Parliamentary Candidates', 21 Oct. 1926. UCDA, P69/149 (38).

63   'Disobeyal of General Order No. 28, May 1927'. UCDA, P69/149 (6). It was at this point that Aiken was expelled from the IRA, contrary to the numerous accounts that the date of his expulsion was Nov. 1925. See for example, John Horgan, *Seán Lemass: the Enigmatic Patriot* (Dublin: Gill and Macmillan, 1997), 41.

64   Bowman, *de Valera*, 100–101.

65   Dunphy, *Fianna Fáil*, 131–132.

66   He was elected in June with 6,851 votes, coming second, but topped the poll in Sept. with 7,881. Walker, *Irish Parliamentary Elections Results*, 122 & 129.

67   Hanley, *The IRA, 1926–36*, 118–125.

68   'Report on revolutionary Organisations', 4 April 1930. Of Briscoe the report claimed 'it is often suggested that the Irish was not his first venture in revolutionary activities'. UCDA, P80/916 (3).

69   Press cuttings from Aiken's US tour, 1928. UCDA, P104/2488.

70   *Irish Independent*, 27 Jan. 1932.

71   *Irish Independent*, 27 Jan. 1932.

72   Richard English, *Radicals and the Republic: Socialist Republicanism in the Irish Free State 1925–1937* (Oxford: Oxford University Press, 1994), 138–163.

73   Army Council to Secretary, Clan na Gael, 7 May 1932. UCDA, P69/185 (298–302).

74   Aiken to Moss Twomey, 19 Feb. 1932. UCDA, P104/1322 (2–4).

75   Aiken to Moss Twomey, 19 Feb. 1932. UCDA, P104/1322 (2–4).

76   Aiken to Moss Twomey, 19 Feb. 1932. UCDA, P104/1322 (2–4).

77   AC to Secretary, Clan na Gael, 7 May 1932. UCDA, P69/185 (298–302).

78   Tim Pat Coogan, *Éamon de Valera: Long Fellow, Long Shadow* (London: Harper Collins, 1995), 465.

79   *Weekly Irish Times*, 26 March 1932.

80   Tom Barry to Moss Twomey, 13 May 1932. UCDA, P69/52 (63–64). See also, MacEoin, *The IRA in the Twilight Years*, 838.

81   British government and intelligence circles were also certain that such a conflict was likely. See Paul McMahon, *British Spies and Irish Rebels: British Intelligence and Ireland 1916–1945* (Woodbridge: the Boydell Press, 2008), 215–239.

82   C/S to O/C Cork No. 1 Brigade, 19 July 1932. UCDA, P69/52 (54–57).

83   C/S to O/C Cork No. 1 Brigade, 19 July 1932. UCDA, P69/52 (54–57).

84   C/S to O/C Cork No. 1 Brigade, 19 July 1932. UCDA, P69/52 (54–57).

85   Twomey to Joseph McGarrity, 25 Aug. 1932. UCDA, P69/185 (216).

86   *An Phoblacht*, 14 Jan. 1933.

87   Seán MacBride to Joseph McGarrity, 19 Oct. 1933. National Library of Ireland (NLI), Joseph McGarrity Papers, 17,456.

88   Foley, *Legion of the Rearguard*, 129–134.

89   *Irish Press*, 9 Nov. 1933.

90   *Irish Press*, 9 Nov. 1933.

91   *Irish Press*, 29 Nov. 1933.

92   See also Lar Joye, "'Aiken's slugs"; the Reserve of the Irish Army under Fianna Fáil', in Joost Augusteijn (ed.), *Ireland in the 1930s* (Dublin: Four Courts Press, 1999), 143–162.

93   Brian Hanley, 'The Volunteer Reserve and the IRA', *The Irish Sword* 83 (Summer, 1998), 93–104.

94   Aiken to D. Curran, 10 Jan. 1935. UCDA, P104/2801 (113).

95   Aiken to D. Curran, 10 Jan. 1935. UCDA, P104/2801 (113).

CHAPTER FOUR

Frank Aiken and the Volunteer Force of the Irish Army, 1934–1939

LAR JOYE

Frank Aiken was elected IRA Chief of Staff in April 1923 on the death of General Liam Lynch, as detailed earlier in this book. Along with six other anti-Treaty officers, he had been with Lynch when he was wounded at Crohan Peak in the Knockmealdown Mountains, where Lynch later died. Aiken held his position at the head of the IRA until November 1925. Remarkably, little more than six years later, he would find himself in charge of the very army he had opposed in arms so recently. On 9 March 1932, at the age of thirty-five, Aiken was appointed Minister of Defence. J.J. Lee has described this as an inspired choice: 'more acceptable to the Free State officers than any other possible appointment. He soon reconciled the army to the new regime'.[1] He was also the first minister since Richard Mulcahy to have military experience, and the fact that 'he had made strenuous efforts to prevent the civil war … counted for something with the army'.[2]

As a new minister, Aiken quickly settled down to attending state events and working with the Irish Army in preparing for the thirty-first International Eucharistic Congress held in Dublin from 22 to 26 June 1932. Over the next eight years he remained Minister of Defence until he was replaced by another famous War of Independence leader, Dubliner Oscar Traynor, in September 1939. As Brian Hanley explains in the previous chapter on entering government in 1932, Fianna Fáil still harboured doubts over the loyalty of the army, on the one hand,

and the activities of the IRA on the other. Aiken clearly occupied a bridging role between the army and recalcitrant republicans, and set about addressing these two concerns. As John Dulanty, Irish High Commissioner in London, told the British government in 1938, Éamon de Valera 'relies' upon Aiken to 'keep the IRA lot quiet and behind the government'.[3]

Contrary to army fears, Aiken did not radically change the army or create a new defence policy for the country. He left Chief of Staff Michael Brennan, a famous War of Independence leader from County Clare, in his position, along with the Adjutant General Liam O hAodha, the Quartermaster General J.J. O'Connell, and Assistant Chief of Staff Hugo MacNeill. At the same time, in a gesture to rump republicans, after his appointment he visited Arbour Hill Prison in the vicinity of Collins Barracks in Dublin and ordered the release of IRA prisoners. Over the next few years he closely monitored this situation and regularly communicated with the families of the prisoners, especially after the reintroduction of the Military Tribunal on 11 August 1933.[4] He wrote to one family on 7 March 1935: 'You must realise as well as I do that individuals or groups must be restrained from actions which aim to disrupt the country and prevent the government from building up our national defences and economic resources'.[5]

While Aiken's transition from local politician to government minister appears to have happened with ease, his official driver had problems adapting to the army life. Private Peter Boyle, a republican and long-time Aiken loyalist, who had joined the army to drive for the new Minister, refused to salute an Irish Army officer when he was being paid in February 1933, saying: 'I won't show respect for any officer, I do not Sir, or salute the Minister for Defence and won't sit with any of his officers. I came into the Army as driver for the Minister for Defence and am not in it for my own free will'.[6] Boyle's attitude summed up the slump in morale within the Irish Army. The army was not the force it had once proudly been. Following the end of the Civil War, the permanent force in Ireland was scaled down from a height of 50,000 men in 1923 to a peacetime level of 5,000.

Therefore, the army was in a poor state when Fianna Fáil took power in 1932; 45,000 men had experienced demobilisation, leaving the army with 5,315 regular officers and soldiers, and 7,816 reservists.[7] By the early 1930s the Irish Army was relatively neglected, under-strength, and its men poorly trained. Despite the fact that an army of this size could be housed in the Curragh Camp in County Kildare, it was spread around the country in twenty-eight barracks. Any attempt to close a barracks in the 1920s and 1930s was opposed by local people, and in particular shop owners, and was not to be tackled by the new minister. Most of the army was confined to looking after these barracks, rarely carrying out large exercises, and not equipped to fight a modern war.[8] The army was rarely seen outside the barracks wall, and it was also difficult 'to retain skilled men for the various technical corps, as employment in Britain was a very attractive alternative for anyone with qualifications'.[9] This change in the army's fortunes has been described by Theo Farrell thus: 'a politically powerful and strategically savvy IRA was succeeded by a politically wimpish and strategically idiotic Irish army'.[10]

The situation was not helped by the fact that many of officers left in the army in the late 1920s were a 'ragbag of obscure lightweights'.[11] Overseeing the army was the Department of Defence, and in particular the Department of Finance, which instinctively opposed nearly every army proposal to spend money. This was particularly noticeable in 1939 when, at the outbreak of the Second World War, the army was underequipped, unable to launch an offensive and practically restricted to guerrilla resistance to invasion. Naturally, the training of officers and in particular future generals is essential in any army, and in 1927 six Irish officers trained with the American Army, including at West Point. When they returned they established the Defence Plans Division to create future plans for the army. By sending officers to the United States it was intended to 'broaden the horizons of the new army and to lessen the dependence on the British approaches to military organisations'. This, of course, was more acceptable to the new government.[12]

This chapter concentrates on Aiken's biggest reform of the Irish Army in the 1930s: the creation of the Volunteer Force. This new reserve force, later nicknamed 'Aiken's slugs', was planned to constitute a large proportion of the army.[13] This force was the precursor to the Fórsa Cosanta Áitiúil (FCA), or local force, established in 1947.[14] It is not clear from the papers held in the Military Archives, Cathal Brugha Barracks, Dublin or in the Frank Aiken Papers in University College Dublin who decided to create this new army. But in August 1932, four months after the new government came to power, the General Staff of the Irish Army submitted a document that created a new reserve army entitled 'The Volunteers'.[15] This new army was to be a nationwide militia based upon the British Territorial Army. Over the next year the plan was to be developed and reviewed, although there is no record of Aiken's opinion of the force. It was left to Seán Lemass, the new Minister for Industry and Commerce, to underline the merits of the new force to his ministerial colleagues. He did so on 23 October 1933, writing to inform them that:

> ... the primary purpose of any Volunteer scheme in the present circumstances of the Saorstat is a political one, i.e. the provision of an opportunity of military training in a manner beneficial to the State, to young men to whom military manoeuvres are an attraction and who if they do not get the association they desire in an official organisation may be induced to seek it in illegal organisations.[16]

Furthermore, he felt that: 'The provision of effective military forces to strengthen the existing army and fit in with present or contemplated army organisation is, while important, only a secondary consideration for the present at any rate'.[17] This statement would best define what can be described as the defence policy for Ireland in the 1920s and 1930s: the weakening of internal illegal organisations. Because of its small size, the Irish Army would leave broader external strategic defence to the European powers. The new Volunteer Force, thus, was to serve primarily as a tool against the IRA and the fascist-inspired Blueshirts.[18] Indeed, initially Aiken and his Fianna Fáil Cabinet colleagues considered that the IRA would become the new Volunteer Force, although this never materialised. The IRA refused to disband, believing that the Fianna Fáil government would be unable to achieve the Holy Grail of an Irish Republic in the face of British opposition.[19]

Eventually, on 8 December 1933, the Cabinet officially approved the new Volunteer Force, which was to cost £250,000 in its first year. This was nearly 20 per cent of the annual Defence Budget of £1,318,458.[20] Clearly, the Cabinet and the Department of Finance were fully supportive of this proposal. Again, the response from the Irish Army's General Staff is not recorded regarding the loss of much of their budget. As well as being such a large project, it was intended that the regular army would train this new reserve. Interestingly, twenty-one former anti-Treaty officers were now commissioned into the army as organisers for the new Volunteer Force. They were known as Area Administration Officers (AAOs), and consisted of twenty captains and one lieutenant. De Valera admitted in the Dáil that the AAOs 'had taken up arms in defence of the Republic which had been proclaimed at that time'. However, he expressed full confidence in them when he stated: 'every one of them will be expected to make a declaration accepting the authority of the elected representatives'.[21] The appointment of the officers circumvented the official promotional procedure, which was by an officer cadetship in the military college in the Curragh. The officers themselves came from all over the country, and had vast experience, including Capt. Martin O'Donnell and Capt. Manus O'Boyle, who had fought alongside Aiken during the Civil War.

On 7 February 1934, Aiken announced the formation of the new Volunteer Force in the Dáil. He set out the form that the new reserve would take, which was interestingly still very much based on the Territorial Army in England. Volunteers were organised into three lines. First-line Volunteers had to be aged between eighteen and twenty-five. Men over twenty-one with special qualifications or old IRA Volunteers with some active service prior to the Truce in July 1921 could also be considered for the first line. Enlistment in the reserve was for twelve years. The first five years of service were spent in the first line, after which the Volunteers transferred to the second line. The third and last line was comprised of men aged between forty-five and fifty-five, with specialist qualifications that could be mobilised in the case of a national emergency.[22]

It was envisaged that, once properly trained and organised, the Volunteer Force would constitute a large proportion of the Irish Army, with three fully integrated brigades, with their own artillery, infantry, medical, transport and signal units. The Fianna Fáil government estimated that approximately 12,000 Volunteers would be enrolled by 1935. The perceived military roles of these three brigades were to defend Ireland from foreign invasion. In reality, however, the Irish Army was severely under-resourced, with the regular army not having the equipment and materials necessary for fighting modern wars.[23] From the outset, therefore, the Volunteer Force was arguably not fit for purpose.

To integrate the Volunteer Force into the local communities, civilian-area committees known as 'The Sluagh' were appointed by the local AAO, who assisted him in matters not directly of a military character. The area committees were to comprise 'two members of the local County Council, two representatives of the local employers or farmers union, and two trade union nominees'.[24] Aiken outlined their role as follows:

> In each Sluagh area there will be built or hired halls for the purpose of training, administering and promoting the various activities of the Sluagh and the Sluagh Committee will help in seeing that these activities are property co-ordinated and efficiently carried out.[25]

The Sluaighte soon acquired the nickname 'Aiken slugs' because the Minister for Defence confirmed all appointees to the committees.[26] This was, though, something of a misnomer. The chief source of discontent within the 'slugs', as discussed below, was the refusal to grant unemployment assistance to Volunteers attending overnight camps and test mobilisations. This unpopular aspect of life in the 'slugs' was not down to Aiken, but to Lemass, Minister for Industry and Commerce and, as mentioned above, an early champion of the Volunteer Force. The removal of unemployment benefit for those stationed in camps was a favourite tactic of Lemass in this period. He is to be found advocating similar policies (with similarly unsuccessful results) to a range of other camp labour schemes in the 1930s.[27] Aiken's Department of Defence in fact protested to Lemass's Department of Industry and Commerce about these harsh measures, only to be dismissively told that 'the loss of one day's Unemployment Assistance twice a year is rather trifling'.[28] This logic did not sit well with the recruits themselves, most of whom were from rather disadvantaged socio-economic backgrounds, and discontent persisted within the ranks.[29]

Between 11 and 14 April 1935, a test mobilisation of the Volunteer Force was held in the Eastern, Western and Southern Commands. In total, 4,287 Volunteers reported for duty from 4,500 called. The mobilisation was regarded as a huge success. Indeed, within a year of its creation the Volunteer Force had 11,594 members.[30] In April 1935, Aiken rejoiced that the 'outstanding fact of importance in the life of the army during the year has been the development of the Volunteer Force'. 'Applicants for enrolment', he said, 'have exceeded all expectations'.[31]

On 28 August 1935, the first Volunteers received their commissions in the Curragh's Pearse Barracks from President of the Executive Council, and Minister for External Affairs, de Valera. The president addressed the new officers after the ceremony, saying that 'what this force is to become depends on your devotion to work'.[32] Matt Feehan, who worked for the *Irish Press* and, in 1942, at the age of twenty-nine, became a Lieutenant Colonel during the Emergency in charge of the Forty-First Battalion, later wrote:

> The circle in which I moved was composed of young men of the same age group and political outlook, in other words we were sons or brothers of people who were on the losing side of the Civil War; for us to join the army of the State at that time was asking quite a lot in view of the recent wounds and bitterness which was very much alive.[33]

Volunteers paraded in public for the first time in Dublin at the St Patrick's Day Parade in 1935. The parade took twenty-three minutes in all to pass the saluting base in College Green. The salute was taken by Frank Aiken himself, but, notably, was marred by a small, hostile crowd who protested against the Volunteer Force.

Ultimately, the new Volunteer Force was not a success, and despite Aiken's efforts it was to undergo a series of organizational changes from 1936 to 1939. The force faced several problems, including the inability of the regular army to provide training courses, the poor standard of recruits and insufficient administrative resources. As mentioned above, it was originally planned that there would be 12,000 Volunteers by 1935, and a full 20,000 by 1936.[34] In the initial year over 11,000 did join, but the numbers began to decline thereafter.

A report by the General Staff of the Irish Army in 1936 highlighted that, from the outset, attendance at local drills was poor, averaging just 30 per cent. The Sluagh Committees for the most part served their purpose, but 'many never functioned in the practical sense and latterly there had been a general decline in activities and enthusiasm'.[35] The report believed that this situation would not change until the committees were composed entirely of Volunteers. On the issue of annual training, it was clear that 'over forty per cent of those called are not prepared to fulfil their obligations'.[36] Later revisions to the terms of employment as one of 'Aiken's slugs' continued to prejudice its members. As a sweetener, grants were introduced in addition to normal pay. However, these grants were regarded as 'means' by Lemass's department, thereby debarring recipients from other public entitlements for which many would have ordinarily qualified, such as food vouchers.[37] These issues were not dealt with until just before the outbreak of the Second World War.

The failure to rectify financial disincentives led to a significant drop off in turnout for 1935. As noted above, the first mobilisation of the Volunteer Force during Easter of 1935 had seen a 94 per cent response. However, because unemployment assistance was revoked for the Easter mobilisations, the turnout for annual training in the summer of 1935 fell to 44 per cent of those called, only 2,799 first-line Volunteers out of approximately 6,300 reported. By April 1938 there were just 9,525 Volunteers, compared to its peak of 11,594 in 1935. Moreover, attendance at local training for the force had decreased to an average of 29 per cent, with the result that thirty hired halls were surrendered.[38]

In response to the low morale, Aiken proposed another reorganisation of the Volunteer Force, but by this stage the die was cast. The impact of the Spanish Civil War, and also of the Munich Crisis of September 1938, focused the Irish state and the army on potential world war. Under de Valera's instructions the army drew up a scheme for the establishment of two reinforced brigades with a combined strength of 37,560, consisting of the permanent Irish Army, the Reserve and the Volunteer Force. In line with the reorganisation of the force in early 1939, all existing Volunteers were discharged but given the option of re-enlisting. On 1 March of that year there had been 7,278 Volunteers left, of whom 3,731 re-enlisted while the remainder resigned. With war on the horizon, however, recruitment began to increase. At the time of Ireland's declaration of neutrality in September 1939, 237 officers and 6,429 Volunteers reported for duty.[39]

Conclusion

On 8 September 1939, only days after the outbreak of war in Europe, Aiken left the Department of Defence and was appointed to the important Ministry for the Coordination of Defensive Measures. During this anxious period, as Bryce

Evans explains in the following chapter, Aiken's immediate preoccupation was with military recruitment for the Irish Army. Thus, his ongoing efforts to reform the Volunteer Force were absorbed into the recruitment drive for the army.

In assessing Aiken's involvement with the Volunteer Force, one must acknowledge that from the outset the new force suffered from the fact that the Irish Army was under-resourced and unable to supply even the basic equipment or personnel. The calibre of recruits that the force attracted also failed to live up to Aiken's expectations. These deficiencies were compounded by the fact that as a part-time reserve it depended on Volunteers freely giving their time, but without adequate monetary compensation. This, therefore, naturally impacted on the overall morale of the force. Moreover, Aiken and his Fianna Fáil government colleagues had ulterior motives for establishing the Volunteer Force. Deciding to place the force outside direct military control, but within the structure of the army, exposed Aiken's distrust of the existing army and his desire to create a force that exhibited strong republican credentials.[40]

Despite the Volunteer Force's innate military and structural deficiencies, the movement left a lasting legacy upon the Irish Army. Today the Irish Defence Forces consist of 9,500 permanent full-time men and women responsible for defending the state at home and aiding the United Nations in peacekeeping duties abroad. This small army is supported by Irish Reserve Defence Forces (RDF), or local defence forces, comprised of 4,069 members.[41] The RDF has its origins in the part-time Volunteer Force, 'Aiken's 'slugs', established under the watchful eye of the Fianna Fáil government in 1934.

Notes

1   J. J. Lee, *Ireland 1912–1985, Politics and Society* (Cambridge: Cambridge University Press, 1989), 176.

2   Eunan O'Halpin, *Defending Ireland, the Irish State and its Enemies Since 1922* (Oxford: Oxford University Press, 1999), 97.

3   Robert Fisk, *In Time of War, Ireland, Ulster and the Price of Neutrality, 1939–45* (Dublin: Gill and Macmillan, 1983), 81.

4   University College Dublin Archives (UCDA), Frank Aiken Papers, P104/2801–22.

5   UCDA, P104/2804.

6   Army Report in relation to complaints concerning Private F. Boyle, 20 Feb. 1933. UCDA, P104/2844.

7   See John P. Duggan, *A History of the Irish Army* (Dublin: Gill and Macmillan, 1991), 161–166.

8   Duggan, *A History of the Irish Army*, 163.

9   Eunan O'Halpin, 'The Army in Independent Ireland', in Thomas Bartlett and Keith Jeffery (eds), *A Military History of Ireland* (Cambridge: Cambridge University Press, 1996), 414.

10   Theo Farrell, 'The Suicidal Army: Civil–Military Relations and Strategy in Independent Ireland', in Tom Garvin, Maurice Manning and Richard Sinnott (eds), *Dissecting Irish Politics: Essays in Honour of Brian Farrell* (Dublin: University College Dublin, 2004), 48.

11   O'Halpin, *Defending Ireland, the Irish State and its Enemies Since 1922*, 37.

12   O'Halpin, *Defending Ireland, the Irish State and its Enemies Since 1922*, 97.

13   An excellent analysis of the political and military significance of the Volunteer Force is examined by Labhras Joye in '"Aiken's slugs": the Reserve of the Irish Army under Fianna Fáil', in Joost Augusteijn (ed.), *Ireland in the 1930s, New Perspectives* (Dublin: Four Courts Press, 1999), 143–162.

14   The FCA was renamed the Reserve Defence Forces (RDF) in 2005.

15   Joye, 'Aiken's slugs',147.

16   Memorandum to Cabinet from Seán Lemass 23 Oct. 1933. National Archives of Ireland (NAI), S6327.

17   Memorandum to Cabinet from Seán Lemass 23 Oct. 1933. NAI, S6327.

18   Officially called the Army Comrades' Association, later the National Guard, the Blueshirts were paramilitary and fascist in form, with drilling and uniforms (mimicking the Italian Blackshirts and German Brownshirts) and fascist salutes and slogans. Led by Eoin O'Duffy, previously Commissioner of the Garda Síochána, the Blueshirts were outlawed in 1933. Its members, however, along with the National League, were absorbed into Cumann na nGaedheal, leading to the establishment of a new party, Fine Gael.

19   This chapter examines the Volunteer Force from a military perspective. For those interested in the relationship between the new force and the IRA, see Joye, 'Aiken's slugs', 144–147.

20   Joye, 'Aiken's slugs', 148.

21   Joye, 'Aiken's slugs', 148.

22   Joye, 'Aiken's slugs', 150.

23   Joye, 'Aiken's slugs', 150.

24   Brain Hanley, 'The Volunteer Reserve and the IRA', *The Irish Sword*, Vol. XXI (No. 83), 94.

25   Speech by Aiken, 7 Feb. 1934. Dáil Éireann (DE), Vol. 50, col. 1131.

26   Hanley, 'The Volunteer Reserve and the IRA', 94–104.

27   See Bryce Evans, *Seán Lemass: Democratic Dictator* (Cork: Collins, 2011), 108–109.

28   Joye, 'Aiken's slugs', 156.

29   Joye, 'Aiken's slugs', 159.

30   Joye, 'Aiken's slugs', 152.

31   Speech by Aiken, 3 April 1935. DE, Vol. 55, col. 1798.

32   Joye, 'Aiken's slugs', 153.

33   Lt. Col. M. Feehan (retd). 'A Personal Reminiscence of the Volunteers', *An Cosantoir*, Feb. 1978, 42.

34   Joye, 'Aiken's slugs', 153.

35   Report on Volunteer Force, 3. Military Archives (M.A.), A.C.S. G2/0044.

36   Report on Volunteer Force, 4. M.A., A.C.S. G2/0044.

37   Joye, 'Aiken's slugs', 158.

38   See Joye, 'Aiken's slugs', 156–160.

39 See Joye, 'Aiken's slugs', 160–161.
40 Joye, 'Aiken's slugs', 161.
41 See Irish Department of Defence and Defence Forces, Annual Report 2012, 14. Available at http://www.military.ie/fileadmin/user_upload/images/Info_Centre/documents/Annual_Reports/an_report_2012_en.pdf (accessed 22/11/2013).

CHAPTER FIVE

'The Iron Man with the Wooden Head'? Frank Aiken and the Second World War

BRYCE EVANS

On 8 September 1939, Frank Aiken became Minister for the Coordination of Defensive Measures. The new department was a product of the major Irish Cabinet reshuffle carried out by Taoiseach Éamon de Valera to meet the demands of the Second World War ('the Emergency'). In the anxious days of September 1939, Aiken's immediate priority was military recruitment, and he oversaw an increase in the number of men under arms in the state from 7,000 to 19,000 within his first month in the job.[1] But the new brief comprised much more than mere mobilisation. This chapter explores Aiken's dealings with the IRA; external powers; the neutrality principle; censorship; and the food and fuel crisis.

Aiken was to remain at this post for almost six years. As the war continued, the activities of the Minister for the Coordination of Defensive Measures would become the subject of vitriol, controversy, and even ridicule. Much of the flak that pock-marks Aiken's record has been aimed at his fastidious exercise of one of his key responsibilities: censorship. To his most cutting and influential antagonist of the period – the bombastic Robert 'Bertie' Smyllie, editor of *The Irish Times* – Aiken was a bigoted buffoon, 'unintelligently impossible' to deal with.[2] Neither has posterity been kind. Common perception has it that Aiken's neutral stance

133

was driven by a narrow-minded and recidivistic anti-partitionism. His unswerving position jars with that staple of western popular historical memory: the belief in the righteousness of the wartime anti-fascist struggle. Contemporary Dublin wits dubbed Aiken 'the iron man with the wooden head'.[3] And the mud, for reasons outlined in this chapter, has largely – if not always deservedly – stuck.

The Irish 'Sudetenland': Aiken, the IRA, and the Nazis

At the outbreak of hostilities in Europe, the Irish government's top security priority was the neutralisation of the IRA, whose members had been blowing up British cities for much of 1939 and had established links with Nazi Germany.[4] As the senior member of de Valera's administration responsible for coordinating defence, Aiken fully subscribed to the suppression of the IRA. And yet there have been persistent rumours that 'given half a chance, Aiken would order an attack on the Six Counties'.[5] This hard-line republican image was augmented by one of the most infamous episodes in Aiken's ministerial career: his 1941 meeting with Franklin Delano Roosevelt, during which his steadfast anti-partitionism drove the American President to near-apoplexy (more of which later). But did Aiken's commitment to a united Ireland lead him to adopt a pro-German or pro-IRA disposition during the war?

In the popular mentality, Aiken stood apart from his Cabinet colleagues. The image of the tough northern gunman cast a long shadow. The 'iron man' caricature was based on his perceived sympathy for the IRA and, following the logic of 'the enemy of my enemy is my friend', Nazism. At the outbreak of war, Dublin gossip had it that de Valera had ordered Aiken's arrest and that he was being detained in Arbour Hill prison.[6] This perception was not confined to bar-room whispers. Among IRA men active in Northern Ireland, it was hoped that Aiken would use the war as a pretext for a border incursion by the Irish Army.[7] As the conflict ground on, the rumours continued. In the run-up to the liberation of Europe in July 1944, British intelligence warily reported on Aiken's presence at a reception for Axis diplomats hosted by the Spanish legation in Dublin.[8] According to a confidential British memorandum written as late as 1947, 'he believed in German victory and probably hoped for it'.[9] It is even claimed that Hermann Görtz, the senior Nazi agent-at-large in Ireland during the war, secretly met with Aiken to discuss German invasion plans.[10]

It is true that from the earliest stages of the European conflict Aiken believed that Britain was, on the whole, a more serious military threat to Ireland than Germany.[11] On the other hand, he was not ignorant of German expansionism. During the Munich Crisis of September 1938, he wrote to Minister for Finance

Seán MacEntee stressing the need for 'urgent action' to protect Ireland's shores and by April 1939 had overseen the establishment of a coast-watching service.[12] An early supporter of an Irish Air Force, he organised Ireland's air-raid precautions throughout the war, including plans for the mass evacuation of people from Dublin.[13] None of these early ministerial moves indicates Nazi/IRA sympathy where it really mattered: at policy level.

It was not until the fall of France in June 1940 that the reality of world war and, with it, the realistic prospect of German victory, really hit home. The early stages of the war were soon eclipsed by this event, which radically shifted the entire dynamic of the Irish Emergency. The American Representative in Ireland, David Gray, warily noted at the time that 'what the IRA were now, General Aiken had been but a decade before'.[14]

With anxiety about invasion palpable, Aiken insisted that the Irish Defence Forces would challenge any invader, British or German (a point of principle lost, as outlined below, on Roosevelt). He hurriedly issued instructions to the Irish people: 'remain in your own house'; 'don't cooperate with, or assist the enemy'; 'obey all instructions issued by the Army'.[15] These were repeated in the pamphlet *Civilian War Duties*, which was distributed to the public throughout July 1940 at the rate of 100,000 a day.[16] For the remainder of 1940, Aiken oversaw a further expansion in recruitment. There were 41,000 men in the army by March 1941, and a total of 180,000 in the auxiliary Local Security Force (LSF) and Local Defence Force (LDF) by October 1941.[17]

But if Aiken was gearing up to repel an invasion, could he hope to appeal to the IRA to come onside? Here again, the fall of France forced the pace he adopted. According to some sources, Aiken visited the hunger-striking republicans Larry Grogan and Peadar O'Flaherty in Arbour Hill prison in the spring of 1940. At this meeting, he offered the IRA an amnesty and incorporation into the Irish Army.[18] When it is considered that the IRA's Magazine Fort raid of a few months earlier had deprived the state of much-needed arms and ammunition, this alleged offer was generous. The deal, however, was refused. Consequently, in April 1940 the renewed government assault on the IRA commenced and, after France fell in June 1940, the state's military court, which would hand down the death penalty to IRA men, was instituted. With the global shift towards war proper, Aiken's attitude towards domestic dissidents had hardened. Gray wrote to Roosevelt on 28 June 1940 changing his tune, and confirming this: 'Aiken, as I wrote to you, has been suspect as a fifth columnist, but on the best authority I can get, this is untrue'.[19]

Meanwhile, in coordinating Irish defence, the Minister for Coordination of Defensive Measures chaired a small inter-party 'Defence Conference', which met eighty-five times between 1940 and 1944. The minutes of this committee reveal that no love was lost between Aiken and Fine Gael's Richard Mulcahy, whose military authority he had defied during the Civil War. Aiken's authoritarian control of information, analysed below in relation to censorship, quickly became an issue, even for this small body. Mulcahy later claimed that the opposition had to 'grub for information' at these Defence Conferences, 'like hens scratching'.[20]

This committee's records are revealing of Aiken's attitude towards German aggression. Oddly, the German bombing of Wexford in August 1940 – in which three people were killed – was not discussed at that week's Defence Conference meeting.[21] After the first German bombs fell on Dublin in January 1941, Aiken 'hoped, and believed personally, it was mistakes … due to weather conditions' which were to blame.[22] It is uncertain whether Aiken held this benign view when it came to the more destructive German bombings of the North Strand in May 1941 because he was away in America at the time. At the meetings from which Aiken was absent, there was freer discussion of the unpreparedness of the LSF to deal with a potential German paratrooper attack and public hostility to the Irish Army firing on planes illuminated by its searchlights.[23] Nonetheless, in a meeting with the American Assistant Secretary of State Dean Acheson at around this time, Aiken proved himself alert to the possibility of a German airborne attack on Ireland, even if his estimate that a German invasion force of Ireland would consist of '50,000 to 200,000 men' appears over the top.[24]

In his broader recruitment work for the Irish Army, Aiken consistently invoked a 'Step Together' spirit. In doing so, he repeatedly disparaged the IRA for its lack of patriotism. He admitted the Irish Army's need for 'finer and better equipment', and acknowledged that drilling without action was monotonous, but insisted that the spirit of 'moral resistance' would prevail and 'rouse the laggards to action'. Laggards and dissident republicans aside, there were other notable exclusions from Irish mobilisation. Aiken, who enjoyed the self-image of the 'big man', deliberately cited the big men of Irish history when attempting to whip up morale at parade grounds, invoking the likes of Owen Roe O'Neill, Cú Chulainn, Brian Boru, Red Hugh O'Donnell and Thomas Davis.[25] This emphasis on *male* fighting potency reflected the conventional sexism of the age. In mid-1940, Mulcahy brought the issue of national service for women before the Defence Conference. Mulcahy had received a letter from a female 'IRA veteran' who envisaged a role for Irish women similar to that of the British Auxiliary Territorial Service: the women of this force would have their own uniform and would assist the army as drivers, typists and cooks.[26] Aiken poured cold water on the idea. Women, he said, could assist the national effort by volunteering for the Red Cross.[27]

For pressing political reasons, Aiken would not have been as dismissive towards a male member of the 'Old IRA'. With the Fianna Fáil government now executing IRA men and allowing others to die on hunger strike, uncomfortable parallels with the treatment of republicans by the Free State during the Civil War arose. Like many republicans before and after him, Aiken now resorted to juxtaposing the 'good' old IRA with the current 'bad' crop. Distinguishing between anti-state and state republicanism, he bluntly informed a Dundalk crowd in 1940 that 'the difference in the two causes is the difference between treason and patriotism'.[28] The IRA was a 'small anarchical group'. Its volunteers were contravening the historical lesson that Irish nationalism was best served by a 'single national authority in control of policy'. Since this statement obviously defied the logic of the anti-Treaty position in the Civil War, he awkwardly squared his logic by arguing that the Anglo-Irish Treaty of 1921 had contravened the republican constitution while the 1937 Constitution had restored these ideals.[29] He appealed specifically to veterans of the anti-Treaty IRA 'to form the disciplined back-bone of the nation so that we may hold on to what we have won until we achieve that unity and independence for the whole of Ireland which our comrades died to secure'.[30]

Pointedly, in August 1941, when a military tribunal sentenced Dundalk IRA man Richard Goss to death, Aiken was the only deputy representing County Louth who did not appeal for clemency.[31] Remarkably, though, rumours of his affinity with the IRA did not cease. A key reason for this was Aiken's relative responsiveness to the complaints of IRA prisoners. He 'made personal investigations' into claims that IRA prisoners in Arbour Hill had been 'beaten and kicked and treated like savages' at Christmas time, 1941. Exhibiting his belief that he could turn his hand to just about anything, he visited the prison to carry out medical examinations on each of the prisoners himself. Visiting them in their cells, he concluded that their injuries had been exaggerated. 'I examined him carefully and found no traces of bruises or injury'; he had 'no sign of cuts on his forehead'; 'his eye was practically normal again'. He countered any sympathy he might have felt for these men through the adoption of a detached pseudo-medical tone. These men were not 'gangsters', he wrote, but their violence was 'like a contagious disease which the more it spreads … the more virulent it becomes'.[32]

Another reason for the persistence of the popular Aiken–IRA association was his publicly truculent anti-partitionism. For example, in 1941 Aiken responded to a claim by Randolph Churchill (Winston's son) that Irish partition functioned to protect Britain's 'strategic safety' by claiming that Churchill, as a 'fair-minded Englishman', would therefore surely not mind if Stalin 'demands the remainder of the continent of Europe' for the 'strategic safety of Russia'.[33] This was strident rhetoric all right, but if his desire for a united Ireland was implacable, he never publicly supported the IRA's activities to that end.

To the disappointment of radical republicans, Aiken was marching firmly in line with government policy: his anti-partitionism was clearly limited to the defence of 'the twenty-six counties which we have liberated'.[34] Asked in mid-1940 whether he had any thought of using the situation to overcome the border by force, he replied: 'No ... If we had an enormously strong army we would feel we had a moral right to take the Six Counties by force [but] we knew that that would not settle the problem but would leave us with a "Sudetenland" problem. We hoped to win their hearts rather than overcome their opposition by force'.[35]

This was an unequivocal rebuttal of the 'border incident' rumours, so why have they lingered? Firstly, the British vilification of Aiken as a republican hardliner was well established. It is exemplified in a British tabloid newspaper description of him from 1925 in which a 'Plot Against the Irish Free State' was reported. 'The mastermind behind this plot is a republican leader named Frank Aitken [sic] who works independently of de Valera', it claimed. 'Aitken is a law unto himself. He has as much consideration for the mandates of de Valera as he had for those of the British Government'.[36]

Secondly, this image of Aiken as an anti-British bogeyman suited the strategic interests of Irish policymakers during the Second World War. In October 1938, the Irish High Commissioner in London, John Dulanty, bad-mouthed Aiken to an MI5 contact. 'In the strictest confidence', Dulanty stated that he was an ineffective minister and 'an extremist (left)'. Historian Eunan O'Halpin judges these remarks to have been made deliberately. If so, the ploy was effective: Dulanty's remarks were repeated at a British Cabinet meeting a month later. Moreover, two-and-a-half years later, when Aiken visited the White House to meet President Roosevelt (as discussed below), US military intelligence repeated the briefing. Aiken, Roosevelt was informed, was 'of the extreme left wing'.[37]

Crucially, in cementing the policy of neutrality, it suited de Valera to portray Aiken as a republican 'iron man' because it cast the Taoiseach in a more moderate light. Whether deliberately or not, Dulanty's remarks confirmed the long-established British suspicion that Aiken was 'a law unto himself', that 'Mr Aiken represents the IRA organisation and Mr de Valera relies on him to keep the IRA lot quiet and behind the government'.[38] If de Valera genuinely regarded Aiken as a loose cannon, there is no doubt that in placing him in his new ministerial role in

1939 he ensured that he no longer held overriding control over the Irish military and its intelligence network. On the other hand, many claims about Aiken's desire for a border incursion or German invasion seem to have little evidence other than that he was a native of Armagh.[39] Scrupulously neutral rather than pro-Nazi, he was first and foremost loyal to the neutrality principle. Yet the hard-line image was influential, and was repeated in polite diplomatic table talk throughout the Emergency. 'Mr de Valera would be so much freer to act if Mr Aiken was not in the cabinet', sighed the wife of the Canadian high commissioner at a dinner party in Ottawa in 1942.[40] It was an opinion that Aiken's trip to the United States in 1941 did nothing to dispel.

The Trip to America

By June 1940, the German occupation of France and Norway had ensured that Hitler's warships and U-boats were significantly closer to the Atlantic convoy routes, not to mention the British coast. Amid the anxiety, Malcolm MacDonald, the former British Dominions Secretary, travelled to Dublin to convey an attractive proposal. Britain, facing a German invasion, would accept the principle of a united Ireland if Ireland would join the Allied war effort.

When assessing Aiken's standpoint here, a crucial consideration is the extent of de Valera's control of the situation. De Valera met privately with MacDonald four times prior to the Cabinet meeting on the morning of 27 June 1940, when he hand-picked Aiken and Minister for Supplies Seán Lemass to meet MacDonald.[41] When MacDonald discussed this offer with Aiken, he found him 'extremely rigid in his opposition to our plan' and wary of the vague promise of 'the principle of a United Ireland'.[42] But MacDonald also 'got the impression that de Valera had not passed on to his colleagues the assurance I gave him that the declaration of a United Ireland should settle the issue once and for all'. Later on, when MacDonald emphasised the finality of unification to Aiken, he actually thought that he 'was impressed'.[43] Days later, the British improved the offer by proposing that Northern Ireland and Éire cooperate as a joint body assisted by Britain. These terms were not brought to the Cabinet by de Valera, who personally vetoed the offer.[44] Therefore, what Aiken's opinion on the improved offer would have been is uncertain.

If Aiken had been quietly 'impressed' by the British offer, he showed no signs thereafter, and stuck doggedly to de Valera's neutral stance. The Irish writer Denis Johnston conducted a bad-tempered interview with Aiken for America's National Broadcasting Corporation a month after the meeting with MacDonald, in July 1940. When asked whether he would be prepared to give up neutrality for union with Northern Ireland, Aiken replied: 'Most certainly not. We want union and sovereignty, not union and slavery'.[45]

The following year, in February 1941, and in the midst of an ever-tightening British supply squeeze, de Valera decided to send Aiken to America. He was to gather material and moral support for Ireland's neutrality policy.[46] The reasoning behind the selection of Aiken for the 'mission' is the subject of some dispute. Was de Valera rewarding him for his steadfast maintenance of the neutral line, or was he setting him up for a fall? As discussed below, the trip did not hold out much prospect of success. Northern IRA folklore has it that de Valera was punishing Aiken in sending him to Washington because he had been pushing too hard for the fabled 'international border incident'.[47] According to the British representative in Ireland, John Maffey, his American counterpart David Gray had suggested the trip because he thought that, although it would not achieve any of its objectives, it would be 'educational'.[48] If anyone needed convincing of the virtue of the Allied war effort it was Aiken, but when interviewed in the late 1970s, he simply claimed that he was the default choice after Tánaiste Seán T. O'Kelly turned down the trip.[49]

So, in March 1941, Aiken embarked on the journey. In his original account of the trip, which he composed back in Ireland a few months later, he recalled arriving in New York on 18 March, where the mayor of the city placed his car at his disposal. The following day he was joined by Robert Brennan, the Irish Representative in Washington. When the two men met with Head of the State Department, Sumner Welles, on 21 March, Aiken outlined Ireland's neutral position. Welles's response was 'that England should win'. He said this with 'great emphasis and significance'.[50] Aiken responded in kind. Dismissing British policy as 'foolish', he told Welles that 'there was no point in talking to the Irish people about a potential aggressor when they were facing an active aggressor'.[51]

This was Aiken's first experience of a bullish State Department attitude towards Irish neutrality. But given what was to follow when he met with President Roosevelt, these meetings of late March and early April were very much the calm before the storm. On 20 March 1941, Brennan was suddenly and unexpectedly informed that Roosevelt was leaving Washington immediately for a fishing trip 'for a week or ten days'.[52] Aiken now had two weeks to kill. He met various Irish-American cardinals and bishops, and claimed that he was 'pretty fairly reported in the newspapers' at this point. He and Brennan also set about lobbying Congress and Senate, where they were buoyed by declarations of support.[53] A key contact was Senator John McCormack of Massachusetts, a man whom Brennan described as 'one of the few men who have access to Roosevelt who talks back to him'. Brennan reported that they also visited 'some old friends' of Aiken's, 'who are as staunch as ever'. During their fortnight waiting for a presidential audience, Brennan and Aiken enjoyed several late nights with members of the Irish-American community. The trip was even leant some glamour by the presence of Hollywood star Maureen O'Sullivan, famed as 'Jane' in the *Tarzan* films, who had heard that 'General Aiken' was in town and resolved to visit him.[54]

By contrast, the meeting with Roosevelt, which took place two weeks later, was tempestuous. After pleasantries were exchanged, with the president enquiring after de Valera's health, Roosevelt told Aiken that he meant to speak frankly and asked him why he had said that Ireland had nothing to fear from a German victory.[55] Aiken denied that he had said this. But, going on to speak about the severity of the British supply squeeze being applied to Ireland at the time, he found it 'very difficult to outline the purpose of my mission'. 'I had to interrupt the president and keep talking against his attempts to interrupt me in what would be a boorish way in dealing with an ordinary individual'. Roosevelt promised Aiken that he would grant Ireland supplies if Britain consented. Aiken instructed the president to 'use his own initiative and save the British from their own folly'.[56]

Roosevelt was not used to being talked to like this. The audience was 'scheduled to last ten minutes', but 'lasted three quarters of an hour', according to Aiken, and one hour and fifteen minutes, according to Brennan.[57] Holding out against the persistent attempts of the president's aide-de-camp to interrupt, their meeting was 'finally terminated in the presence of three or four negroes who entered and placed the president's lunch on the table', wrote Aiken. At this point, according to his account, Aiken asked Roosevelt whether he would support Ireland in 'our stand against aggression'. 'German aggression, yes' replied Roosevelt. 'British aggression too', retorted Aiken. According to Aiken's sanitised version of events, the meeting finished there. On his way out, Aiken claims that he asked Roosevelt to get Winston Churchill's assurance that Britain would not attack Ireland, and for a 'definite reply' on Ireland's request for 'ships and arms'. He promised that he would, and 'we bade him good bye'.[58]

Understandably, Aiken omitted the most remarkable detail from the official report, which Brennan admitted in a newspaper piece years later, in 1958. When Aiken had replied 'British aggression too', Roosevelt lost control of his temper in a quite spectacular fashion. Roaring 'nonsense', he pulled the tablecloth from the table, sending cutlery flying around the room.[59] Remembering the meeting many years after the event, Aiken admitted that Roosevelt had lost his temper, but inserted a quip, which he claims inflamed Roosevelt. When the president asked him how high Ireland's defences were, Aiken supposedly replied: 'you'd need a good horse to get over them'.[60]

Brennan, in his 1941 report, tells a different (and probably more accurate) story. Resisting Aiken's appeal for arms, Roosevelt claimed that Ireland was flat and therefore easy to invade. Aiken countered that the country was broken by rivers, mountains, bogs, hedges, ditches and stone walls. Roosevelt replied: 'well you can hunt all over the country', to which Aiken responded sarcastically that it would take a very good horse. But Brennan claims that it was not this remark that enraged Roosevelt. As the president settled down to lunch, signalling the end of the meeting, Aiken, standing over the paraplegic president, sought his assurance against British aggression. This prompted Roosevelt to bellow 'preposterous!', 'absurd nonsense!', and 'ridiculous nonsense!' at him. Clearly, the president had lost his temper with the man from Camlough. Yet, in Brennan's 1941 report, there is no mention of the cutlery flying around the room. Brennan did not reveal this until 1958.[61]

Following this meeting, Aiken reported that, on his urging, Irish-American Senator Joseph O'Mahoney saw the president and again raised the question of a guarantee against aggression from Churchill. Roosevelt demurred, instead giving his 'personal guarantee' that Britain would not invade Ireland. That day, 1,000 Masses across the USA were dedicated to the preservation of Irish neutrality. Later on in the trip, responding to the prospect of conscription in Northern Ireland, Aiken told the American press that this would constitute a 'monstrous outrage'.[62] The Secretary of the Department of External Affairs, Joseph Walshe, recalled Aiken to Dublin on 17 June 1941, writing that the 'Taoiseach would be glad to have Frank's help at home as soon as possible'.[63] At a farewell dinner at the Waldorf Astoria, Aiken claimed that 'interviews with the press were extremely satisfactory'.[64] It was up to Brennan to circumvent the spin, cabling Dublin to urge that a strong statement should be issued against the British threat to introduce conscription in Northern Ireland because 'Frank's interview [on the subject] got little or no publicity'.[65]

When Aiken returned on 27 June 1941, he was greeted by de Valera at Dublin airport.[66] Despite the upbeat tone of his reports, there was little disguising the fact that the lengthy trip had been a diplomatic disappointment. In his absence, his rival Richard Mulcahy had been sniffing around as to the success of the mission. Repeatedly informed that 'no definite news' had been received, Mulcahy smelt a rat.[67] Typically, Aiken had instructed his censorship team to mute all domestic criticism of him while he was away, a task that they undertook diligently.[68] Weeks later, when details of a speech Aiken had delivered in San Francisco were revealed, Mulcahy questioned the diplomatic wisdom of Aiken's revelation that pressure was secretly being applied from some quarters in America in an effort to defeat his mission.[69] While the bombing of Dublin's North Strand deflected some of the subsequent criticism of Aiken,

Mulcahy won an assurance from de Valera in June 1941 that, from that point on, only the Taoiseach would make statements on external affairs.[70] Mulcahy branded Aiken's 'soap box diplomacy' as 'appalling'.[71]

On his return to Ireland, Aiken was also obliged to report on his trip to Mulcahy and other members of the Defence Conference. It was a masterclass in censorship. He stated that he had 'met the President whose attitude was friendly', and that 'the President promised that the question of supplies for Ireland would receive his consideration'. He noted that he 'was shown the latest development in military equipment' and 'was cordially received' by Irish organisations in several American cities.[72] In fact, when interviewed about the trip many years later, the wounds still festered. Aiken felt that in all his statements to the American press he had maintained a neutral and 'anti-fascist' line, but that his comments were given a negative twist. He recalled what he perceived to be a WASP hostility to him and the Irish case. On a tour around an arms factory, he felt that 'they were regarding me as a big buck nigger. They took me to their firing ground and pumped up a few shells from their guns. It was meant to impress me'.[73]

American commentators, relying heavily on the papers of the hibernophobe American representative in Ireland David Gray, portrayed Aiken as intransigent and his mission disastrous.[74] Others have claimed that 'the only result of the meeting was a good deal of bad blood'.[75] Undeniably, the upshot of the trip was a low in Irish-American relations. Aiken professed to be in America to secure 'moral support for Ireland's stand against aggression'.[76] Although this was achieved in all the predictable Irish-American circles, overall it floundered. To be precise, though, the trip was not a dead loss. The negative appraisals of the trip are, in part, based on the misconception that all Aiken was seeking from the Americans was arms and ammunition. He requested both from Dean Acheson, and repeated the request to Roosevelt five days later. But just as important was his quest for aid, which was a success, albeit a limited one. He was able to secure valuable supplies of grain, two ships, and the promise of coal. Given the material hardship in Ireland in mid-1941, half a million dollars worth of food for the civilian population was substantial.

Aiken's achievement is all the more remarkable given that, before the trip, Brennan reported to Dublin that the acquisition of ships was highly unlikely and arms impossible. In January 1941, State Department officials had told him, in no uncertain terms, that Ireland was 'not playing the game' and 'will not benefit [from lend-lease] unless we fall in line'. 'No one is interested in providing credit for countries not in the line-up', Brennan was bluntly told.[77] The trip therefore held slim prospects of success. To what extent Aiken was aware that his mission was likely to fail is a matter of conjecture.

Importantly, Aiken's small achievement helped to alleviate some of the significant pressures upon his beleaguered colleague Seán Lemass at Supplies. Compounded by Lemass's failure to establish a merchant marine in the 1930s, Ireland was experiencing a supply squeeze so severe that it threatened the very existence of the state. With Winston Churchill unflinching in his pursuit of economic warfare against Ireland, and with Lemass facing searching questions in the Dáil about his complacency on the supply issue, Aiken's acquisition of two ships – the *West Hematite* and the *West Nerris*, later renamed *Irish Pine* and *Irish Oak* – was crucial. Not only did it kick-start the celebrated Irish Shipping Ltd. (for which Lemass took the credit); it provided food and the promise of fuel at a time when Ireland's material situation was truly perilous and starvation a distinct possibility.[78] As the government acknowledged, 'Ireland's need for these ships is great, and the possession of them might well mean the difference between extreme hardship and a hardship which would be tolerable'.[79]

A full assessment of the trip therefore demands an examination of how Aiken was briefed before entering the corridors of power in Washington. Crucially, his determined attitude was shaped by a rather self-righteous Irish Department of Foreign Affairs briefing. It informed him that most sinkings of British ships by German U-boats occurred between 300 and 600 miles from Irish shores. This confounded the Royal Navy's insistence on the utility of the 180-mile radius afforded by the use of the port at Berehaven, which, the report informed Aiken, 'could be of no more advantage to the British than Plymouth'. 'If England seized the Irish ports it would be like them seizing Calais and Boulogne', the report went on, claiming that Ireland, in its resolution 'to save the remnant of our race from destruction', had done more than any other nation to keep alive 'the principles of liberty and justice on which the American nation was founded'.[80] He was prepared, too, for hostility from the US State Department. The Secretary of External Affairs, Joseph Walshe, briefed Aiken that 'No government with which we have direct diplomatic relations has been so grudging to admit our separate statehood as the American government'.[81]

If Aiken's public admission of American pressure to defeat his mission was diplomatically wooden-headed, this pressure was far from imaginary. As Robert Brennan later commented, 'the dice had been loaded against the Minister from the very start'.[82] Brennan recalls that Roosevelt kept Aiken waiting for seventeen days for an audience, during which time Aiken 'had got fed up with the situation'. In a farewell dinner of 23 June 1941, Daniel Cohalan, the prominent Irish-American politician, misjudged Aiken by describing him as 'tactful'. On the other hand, Cohalan claimed that he had been subjected to 'cajolery', 'coercion', 'argument and persuasion' on his trip: charges that all held weight.[83]

Roosevelt, for his part, was under pressure from the British to force concessions from the Irish. In stressing the tragic heroism of the British merchant fleet in braving U-boat attacks in the Atlantic, Churchill had convinced the American public that ideologues in neutral Ireland were responsible for hundreds of sinkings and thousands of deaths.[84] The State Department adhered closely to the British line on the issue, regarding the washing up of bodies on Irish shores as a direct consequence of Irish neutrality. Prior to crossing the Atlantic, Aiken was conveniently delayed for nine days in Lisbon, during which time Lord Halifax, the British ambassador in Washington, received a full briefing from his counterpart in Dublin, John Maffey, on the imperative that Aiken return 'in chastened mood'.[85] The State Department approved Aiken's visit on 1 March 1941, but according to the president no one had informed him. This remark was brushed off by Brennan as a typical Rooseveltian bluff; nonetheless, the State Department's failure to tell the White House that Aiken was visiting implied discourtesy on Aiken's part.[86] British Foreign Office sources also had a hand in ensuring that Roosevelt was fed the old story that Aiken was a poisonous ideological mixture of ardent leftist and pro-German. Consequently, Roosevelt was unwilling to let Aiken speak his piece, and may even have come away from the meeting with the false impression that Ireland would not defend itself if Germany invaded.[87]

Finally, his cause was not helped by the activities of that Iago of the Irish wartime diplomatic scene, the American representative in Dublin, David Gray; a man who regularly smeared Ireland, found Aiken 'as friendly as a disappointed rattlesnake',[88] and whose wife happened to be an aunt of Eleanor Roosevelt. Gray delighted in the fact that Aiken's visit had 'created bad effect' because it exposed his 'spirit of blind hostility to England'.[89] But while Aiken was in America, Gray wrote an extraordinary letter to his wife Maud, claiming 'I like Frank very much'. He enclosed a clipping from the gossipy 'Washington Merry-Go-Round' newspaper column, which described Aiken as 'tall, genial' and 'eloquent in his praise', not only of 'British courage' but also President Roosevelt's policy of making the United States 'the arsenal of democracy'.[90] The wily Gray, who rarely had a good word for Aiken, was using the inaccurate article in a disingenuous attempt to see how the Irish political establishment might respond to an ostensible change of tack by Aiken. De Valera, to whom he also sent the clipping, saw through the ploy. In a curt reply, he told Gray that 'newspaper comments on the one side or the other, at a time like this, are no fair index of Mr Aiken's views'.[91]

It was neither the first nor the last time that Machiavellian elements within the American administration had used the 'Washington Merry-Go-Round' as a mouthpiece to smear Aiken and the Irish legation. Later, in an attempt to stall the transfer of the two ships Aiken had acquired, the column alleged that Brennan had used 'violent language' against the use of lend-lease as an instrument of politics.[92] The passage of the ships was duly delayed even further. In Dublin, Walshe concluded, 'we are being made the sport of petty departmental indignation and resentment'. Reaching a high point during Aiken's visit, Ireland had been subjected to 'prevarications, meaningless assurances and last-minute changes of plan'. 'It is more than any country's national dignity could stand', wrote Walshe.[93] And yet it seems that Aiken, despite these efforts, was not a man to be bullied.

Censorship

If the sideswipes about his American trip rankled, the strongest criticism Aiken faced related to wartime censorship. The most important of a raft of Emergency Powers Orders relating to censorship was his ministerial entitlement to prevent the publication or dissemination of any material that he deemed 'prejudicial directly or indirectly to the public safety or to the preservation of the state'.[94] Answerable to Aiken was a censorship team headed by the Controller of Censorship. Thomas Coyne, the Controller from 1941 onwards, was particularly loyal to Aiken, and with one very good reason. Through Aiken, Coyne, who suffered from lung problems, was able to secure one of the extremely rare exceptions to the Emergency ban on private motoring, gaining special permission on health grounds to use his car.[95]

Bolstering his ministerial power, Aiken integrated officials from the Department of Justice and Government Information Bureau more closely in eliminating 'alarmist' news pieces.[96] From the earliest stages of the Emergency, this censorship drive came under fire. In response to criticism of the censorship of TDs' speeches, Aiken prepared a landmark memorandum, submitted to the Cabinet in January 1940, outlining the reasons behind the policy's fastidiousness. As the IRA commander who had issued the ceasefire in 1922, he knew that the prospect of a renewed civil war over whether to back Britain or Germany would not make for comfortable reading, and he duly raised this spectre. Propaganda, he asserted, was a critical weapon in the era of total war, and one that the Dáil had endorsed through the passage of the Emergency Powers Act in 1939. The halcyon days of the old Hague conventions was one thing, he argued; the 'terrific and all-prevailing force of modern warfare' quite another.[97] He was to uphold the ban on atrocity stories, even when those perpetrated by the Axis powers began rolling in with a grim regularity from 1942 onwards. It is worth noting that the British and the Americans devoted similar energy to suppressing news of Allied atrocities.[98] To Aiken, such news pieces were 'supplied by foreigners with the purpose of stirring up hatred and blinding reason'.[99]

Aiken may have had all the pragmatism of a war-torn world on his side, but his rhetoric was also, and unrepentantly, illiberal. He condemned 'self-styled democrats who would hold on to the liberalistic trimmings of democracy while the fundamental basis of democracy was being swept from under their feet'. If this was an articulate defence of the limits to liberty, his later elaboration that *any* opponent of his censorship policy was 'either a foolish democrat or an agent provocateur for those who want to embroil us in civil or foreign war' shows the extent to which Aiken was, as de Valera's son Terry put it, 'prone to contradiction and argument'.[100]

Ultimately, censorship officials answered to Aiken and, at times, the decisions were excessive. Examples are legion: an image of Minister for Posts and Telegraphs P.J. Little nervously ice-skating around Dublin's Herbert Park was deemed unsuitable for publication, or the mutilation of film classics *Casablanca* and *Gone with the Wind*. On occasion, Aiken could be petty. In December 1940, the Seanad heard a passionate condemnation of censorship by Sir John Keane, a senator who happened to be a director of the Bank of Ireland. Prior to the speech, Aiken had pleaded with Keane not to speak out. Characteristically, in seeking to persuade Keane, he managed to link criticism of censorship with the partition issue. Anglo-Irish relations were at that point 'explosive', and any negative criticism would be seized on by the British press, he claimed. Aiken (again, typically) merged the carrot with the stick: 'words can be a lot more dangerous than any bomb thrown by Hitler or the British ... good intentions might lead you to a certain place which is paved with them'.[101] Keane made the speech regardless. Two days later, Aiken took his revenge-of-sorts: an *Irish Times* photograph of LSF volunteers drilling outside the Bank of Ireland was censored by the removal of the royal coat of arms from the bank's pediment.[102]

Similarly, Aiken's thoroughgoing republicanism saw him object to the 'Royal National Lifeboat Association', claiming that it could not simultaneously be both 'royal' and 'national'.[103] There was a hard-headed logic to all this, but when he attempted to use censorship to purge the country of the cultural remnants of Anglo-Ireland, such as place names, he was opposed, even by the loyal Coyne.[104] Aiken's 'Irish Ireland' cultural disposition was surely also behind his declining of an invitation by British representative John Maffey to attend one of the first screenings of Laurence Olivier's patriotic adaptation of Shakespeare's *Henry V*, which had been filmed in Ireland, in February 1945.[105]

More seriously, Aiken was also responsible for episodes of naked political favouritism: stifling criticism of himself; allowing friendly press organs such as the *Dundalk Examiner* greater leeway; gagging outspoken socialists and republicans. His censorship even made political interventions against the Labour Party during the hotly contested general election of 1943.[106] In 1942, reports alleging that his wife, Maud, was contravening fuel restrictions by using the State car to travel into Dublin in the evenings were forwarded to Aiken by Lemass.[107] A member of the public had written to Lemass claiming that Maud's flouting of privilege made him 'boil with anger', and that he was informing the press.[108] Aiken, naturally, used his powers to suppress the scandal.

Despite his self-righteousness, Aiken was well informed about press censorship laws in other countries, and did not feel that the Irish variant was excessive.[109] Donal O'Drisceoil, in his comprehensive appraisal of Emergency censorship, claims that Aiken played his part in a certain 'slippage towards authoritarianism' in Emergency Ireland.[110] But, as O'Drisceoil himself points out, it is significant that his censorship team were civil servants based at Dublin Castle, and not military officers.[111] Censorship also protected minority groups from slander. For example, anti-Jewish diatribes linked to the wartime black market were removed.[112] Home-grown ultra-nationalist tomes were given similarly short shrift, and even Catholic bishops, if their messages 'cut across' those of the state, faced censure.[113]

Written without access to the Aiken papers, O'Drisceoil's otherwise excellent study overlooks characteristics for which Aiken is not renowned: a sense of humour, and an occasional humility. With the lifting of censorship at the end of hostilities, he invited all newspaper editors to a dinner at which his ebullient enemy, *Irish Times* editor Bertie Smyllie, held court with his stories of cleverly evading the censorship. Aiken 'smiled benignly on the proceedings'.[114] The magnanimity was genuine. Around the same time, he wrote to an editor who had taken advantage of the lifting of censorship to criticise Aiken's 'brutal and callous use of powers for political purposes'. Aiken apologised 'for any unnecessary inconvenience or annoyance', and referred to himself as a 'humble politician'.[115] Although such language lends itself to a more cynical reading, it is evident that Aiken's tongue was only very slightly in his cheek. At the lifting of censorship his sentiments were overwhelmingly conciliatory and good-natured. He dubbed his formal invitation to Smyllie to attend the end-of-censorship dinner 'the liberation of Dublin Castle'. Under 'dress options', Aiken drily wrote: 'Dinner Jacket optional. Rapier de rigueur. Dagger verboten'.[116]

Smyllie's and Aiken's game of cat and mouse was, however, a Dublin affair. To rural Irish society, a more unpopular aspect of censorship was the removal of news on market conditions in the agricultural sector. O'Drisceoil aptly terms the Irish censorial bent one of 'moral neutrality'. Just as important, though, was the theme of moral *economy*. Responding to accusations that censorship was destroying the viability of the sector, Aiken raised the moral economic standard. The censorship of agricultural strikes and price fluctuations was carried out, he argued, to protect 'supplies essential to the life of the community'.[117] 'When the life of this country is at stake, it is necessary for some disciplined, united effort' to protect 'the community generally'.[118] In the same breath, he could praise Ireland's farmers as 'magnificent' while reminding them of their 'privileged position' and 'duty to the community at large which helped them to get possession of the soil'.[119] It was *their* moral economic duty to prevent starvation and *his* to ensure that they did not receive information that would lead them to shirk from the task.

Thus, *The Farmers' Paper*, which constantly toed the state line in urging its readers to work harder to prevent starvation, found itself censored for merely calling on the government for a 'fair and generous price' for wheat.[120] Likewise, a press release by the Fine Gael Agricultural Committee, stating that its members were discussing the price of wheat, was pulled by Aiken. In the ensuing bad-tempered exchanges in the Dáil, Aiken's bête noire, Richard Mulcahy, accused him of putting 'the hand of the censorship over everybody else's mouth' but his own. Was Mulcahy, Aiken retorted, 'trying to argue that every galoot in the country should have the power to try and advocate starving people'?[121]

Food and Fuel

It is fitting to end this analysis of Aiken's Emergency with a consideration of his role in Ireland's material survival, a story so often overlooked in favour of the racier diplomatic narratives. As the threat of invasion receded, the threat of starvation replaced it. Ireland's economic isolation, compounded by a British trade squeeze, and Lemass's complacency in securing supplies, impelled Aiken to apply his militaristic 'step together' spirit to the government's 'Grow More Food!' campaign. Workers and farmers now became 'soldiers in the campaign for food'.[122] Partly inspired by the success of Mussolini's pre-war 'Wheat Campaign', he took to the food campaign with his customary rigour.[123]

A believer in national self-sufficiency, Aiken possessed a well-thumbed copy of *Grow Your Own Food Supply*, an English publication of 1939.[124] He was aware that, while Ireland's farmers could sustain the population with vegetables and meat, the country's food supply challenges lay mainly in the production of cereal crops. In 1941 he prepared a witty memorandum for the Cabinet, 'On the necessity of Strong Wheat – for those who don't like their water neat', which outlined the importance of water absorption levels in wheat.[125] Speaking in 1943, he referred to 'the near-panic situation' that arose in towns when bread supplies were restricted.[126] It was imperative that the urban poor received enough bread, and he used the press to urge greater production of home-grown wheat.

Ireland's perilous food supply situation soon raised the prospect of famine. Although Aiken allowed the dreaded F-word to appear in the press, he cut some of the more vivid accounts of starvation in Europe.[127] While cutting stories of military atrocities, he continued to refer to the 'dire distress' of mass starvation in Europe throughout the conflict.[128] Although privately he was acutely aware of the negative effect on productivity of Seán Lemass's failure to secure chemical fertilisers and agricultural machinery,[129] publicly he flippantly claimed that 'there are much more important growth factors – sunshine and rain'.[130] He was powerless to stop the BBC reporting on the 'shortages of bread, tea, oil, coal', 'distress amongst the poor' and 'the problems of the Irish housewife' in the form of Denis Johnston's 'overseas recordings' from Dublin.[131] However, realizing how serious the material situation was, in 1942 he agreed to Lemass's extraordinary request that private mail that contained the barest hint at a contravention of rationing regulations be forwarded to the Department of Supplies.

In fact, if there was a 'slippage towards authoritarianism' in Emergency Ireland, it was Lemass leading the way, not Aiken. During the Emergency, the Special Criminal Court heard more cases concerning the black market than the IRA.[132] Privately, Aiken also entertained criticism of Lemass for failing to administer rationing and price control successfully.[133] These failings were laid bare in early 1941, when the British trade squeeze tightened. Aiken responded by drafting his own 'policy and plan for meeting complete blockade'. Overstepping his ministerial boundary, he bemoaned the absence of a 'clear-cut policy and plan' to ensure the equitable distribution of resources in order to prevent 'social and economic chaos'.[134] When, in August 1941, Lemass resumed control of the Department of Industry and Commerce, as well as the mammoth Department of Supplies, the reaction of his Cabinet colleagues was hostile. Even the usually mild Minister for Agriculture, James Ryan, complained angrily to de Valera about this unprecedented concentration of ministerial power in one man.[135] Aiken channelled his criticism more surreptitiously, by temporarily un-muzzling his very own attack-dog: Bertie Smyllie. When *The Irish Times* made a similar point to Aiken's criticism of Lemass, Coyne deleted the article. Intriguingly, though, Aiken refused to authorise Coyne's action, and instead instructed him to write to Smyllie admitting regret on behalf of the censorship officials, claiming that the deletions were an error and granting permission for the criticisms to be published.[136]

But while Lemass gobbled up more ministerial power over food and fuel supply, Aiken's ideas were overlooked by the Cabinet. Far from the wooden-headed buffoon of caricature, Aiken privately displayed touches of the Renaissance man, advising the Emergency Scientific Research Bureau to carry out investigations into a plethora of innovative food and fuel schemes. These included plans for the conversion of potatoes into fuel; for the turf-fuelling of Dublin's gas supply; for the recovery of methane gas from urban sewage; for the use of heather in paper-making; for the manufacture of penicillin; for the manufacture of lubricating oil from animal fats; for fruit punnets made from peat; and – at the wackier end of the scale – designs for a 'large rotary nutmeg grater'.[137] He was, in the words of a British officer who dined with him in 1940, 'the most enthusiastic of amateur inventors'.[138]

The more quixotic of Aiken's designs lent themselves to criticism by Todd Andrews, head of the Turf Development Board. To Andrews, Aiken possessed a certain impracticality borne of his 'easy' farming background, meaning that he 'had never the experience of earning a living', and therefore 'could not distinguish between poverty and frugal comfort'.[139] But if Aiken at times possessed the air of the mad scientist, all of his ideas were grounded in his social desire to increase employment. In 1942 he urged de Valera to alleviate unemployment and emigration through a state road-concreting scheme,[140] and envisaged employment in the 'mass production of cheap windmills suitable for lighting and heating of isolated houses'.[141] His own windmill, which he constructed near his house in Sandyford, Dublin, is still standing at the time of writing.

Aiken also believed that the banking sector should primarily serve the public interest and that the state should provide social credit.[142] In 1943 he is to be found advocating increasing national health insurance payments for working-class people.[143] As his broader views on national finance are discussed in the following chapter, they are not detailed in depth here. It is clear, though, that the wartime British economic squeeze and the consequent intensification of self-sufficiency confirmed his left-leaning economic views. When Aiken arrived at the Department of Finance after the war, his belief that the Central Bank should provide capital for public projects pitted him against its deflationary tendencies.[144] Frustrated, he pilloried this ideological outlook in a humorous 1939 memo written from the perspective of a 'Finance departmenteer' (a fatalistic and unimaginative clerk) to whom any policy that attempted to rectify Ireland's adverse trade balance, to increase public expenditure, or to find markets other than the UK was 'DOOOOMED to failure!'[145]

Conclusion

Frank Aiken's ability to point out the hypocrisy in Anglo-American economic and political orthodoxy was one of his strengths, even if diplomatic tact was not. He did not hold back from telling American audiences that the British supply squeeze was a 'gratuitous interference with our economic life'.[146] He derided Richard Mulcahy's proposal of a post-war military alliance with Britain, which was as meaningless as 'the diplomacy of the man who heard that his neighbour's cow had fallen into a ditch', and told him 'the next time your cow falls into a ditch let me know and I'll help drag her out'.[147] Neither did he entertain the overblown admiration for the United States typical of some of his contemporaries. When the Americans threatened to halt the export of American movies to Ireland in retaliation for the banning of the film *A Yank in the RAF*, Aiken thundered: 'Our policy in censorship is not directed to please foreigners or to prevent their ill-will but for the purpose of keeping our own people together', before dismissing Warner Brothers' wartime output as 'crude propaganda'.[148]

But with Allied victory in the war, accompanied by the revelation of Axis atrocities, such scrupulous neutrality appeared increasingly narrow-minded. Comparatively, the neutral Swiss and Swedes allowed more wartime freedom of expression and imbued their censorship with less of the sanctimonious sentiment of 'moral neutrality', as O'Drisceoil points out.[149] And yet these countries also profited from trade with Nazi Germany under the veil of wartime neutrality. When held up in Lisbon prior to his trip to America in 1941, Aiken met Portuguese leader António de Oliveira Salazar. Salazar told Aiken that Portuguese efforts to obtain 'war material' from the United States had come to naught. Portugal, like Ireland, was being punished by Britain and America for her neutrality. 'It is the neutrals who are paying for this war', he informed Aiken. Under these circumstances, Portugal, like Spain, resorted to limited trade with Nazi Germany. Irish neutrality, by contrast, could not and did not reap comparable economic benefits.[150]

Herein lay the principle of Aiken's twin application of 'moral neutrality' and 'moral economy': political principle would, albeit painfully, trump short-term economic relief. Joining the Allied war effort would bring immediate material gains, admitted Aiken in 1942, but it would compromise Irish sovereignty. 'If we want to build decent houses for our people we must make sure that we *hold on to the site*, otherwise we will be building castles in the sky for another 700 years'.[151] It was with such obdurate and unbending conviction that Aiken defended de Valera's controversial decision to offer his condolences on the death of Hitler in May 1945.

Aiken does bear responsibility for some of the more niggling and conformist features of the 'slippage towards authoritarianism' during the Emergency, even if he legitimised his actions by pointing to the horrors of total war and starvation. By the end of the conflict, however, he could relax into liberal language. Ireland, 'as a wise and grown-up people', could 'take a just pride in the fact that the vast majority of our young men of all classes and creeds had the wisdom and guts to defend our neutrality in the midst of warring giants', he wrote. But, acknowledging those who did fight, the iron man proved that he did not, at least, possess a wooden heart: 'may they all rest in peace who fell fighting for what they believed right; and in some manner, in the inscrutable ways of Providence, may their combined sacrifices bring a just and lasting peace to the stricken peoples of Europe, victor, vanquished, and neutral'.[152]

Notes

1   Emergency Defence Plans (65), 60–67, MA, cited in Peter Young, 'Defence and the New Irish State, 1919–1939', in Dermot Keogh and Mervyn O'Driscoll (eds), *Ireland in World War Two: Neutrality and Survival* (Cork: Mercier Press, 2004), 32.

2   Smyllie to Mulcahy, 21 May 1941. University College Dublin Archives (UCDA), Richard Mulcahy Papers, (P7)/C/113.

3   Cited in Robert Fisk, *In Time of War: Ireland, Ulster and the Price of Neutrality* (Dublin: Gill and MacMillan, 1983), 306.

4   See T. Ian Adams, *The Sabotage Plan: The IRA Bombing Campaign in England, 1939–1940* (Titchfield: Lulu, 2010); David O'Donoghue, *The Devil's Deal: The IRA, Nazi Germany and the Double Life of Jim O'Donovan* (Dublin: New Island, 2010).

5   Tony Gray, *The Lost Years: The Emergency in Ireland, 1939–45* (London: Sphere, 1997), 34.

6   Joseph Carroll, *Ireland in the War Years* (New York: David and Charles, 1975), 22.

7   Joe Cahill, *A Life in the IRA* (Dublin: O'Brien Press, 2003), 127.

8   Eunan O'Halpin, *Spying on Ireland: British Intelligence and Irish Neutrality during the Second World War* (Oxford: OUP, 2008), 280.

9   Memorandum on 'Mr F. Aiken'. National Archives of the United Kingdom (NAUK), Prime Minister's Office files (PREM) 8/824.

10   According to John Duggan, this meeting took place in Autumn 1940 after the fall of France. Given the lack of evidence, it seems highly unlikely. See John Duggan, *Neutral Ireland and the Third Reich* (Dublin: Gill and MacMillan, 1989), 218.

11   Fisk interview with Aiken, 12 April 1979. Cited in Fisk, *In Time of War*, 574.

12   Michael Kennedy, *Guarding Neutral Ireland: The Coast Watching Service and Military Intelligence, 1939–1945* (Dublin: Four Courts Press, 2008), 17–21.

13   Minutes of Defence Conferences, 30 May 1940 – 15 Dec. 1944. UCDA, Frank Aiken Papers (P104)/3534.

14   David Gray, 'Lifting the Emerald Curtain', 8–12 June 1940, in Paul Bew (ed.), *A Yankee in De Valera's Ireland: the Memoir of David Gray* (Dublin: Royal Irish Academy: 2012), 174.

15   *Irish Press*, 15 July 1940.

16   Defence Conference minutes, 15 July 1940. UCDA, P104/3534.

17   Eunan O'Halpin, *Defending Ireland: The Irish State and Its Enemies since 1922* (Oxford: OUP, 2000), 161–164.

18   See Conor Foley, *Legion of the Rearguard: the IRA and the Modern Irish State* (London: Pluto, 1992), 198. Aiken appealed to them on the basis of small-nation nationalism, a rationale noticeable in his speeches around this time. See UCDA, P104/3375.

19 Gray, 'Lifting the Emerald Curtain', 24 June – 2 July 1940, 228.

20 Donal O'Drisceoil, *Censorship in Ireland, 1939–1945, Neutrality, Politics and Society* (Cork: Cork University Press, 1996), 262.

21 Minutes of Defence Conference, 29 Aug. 1940. UCDA, P104/3534.

22 Minutes of Defence Conference, 3 Jan. 1941. UCDA, P104/3534.

23 Minutes of Defence Conference, 5 and 11 June 1941. UCDA, P104/3534.

24 Meeting of Aiken and Acheson, 2 April 1941, Washington Embassy file. National Archives of Ireland (NAI), Department of Foreign Affairs files (DFA) 10/P/35.

25 See Aiken's various speeches at conventions, parades and exhibitions at UCDA, P104/3374.

26 Joan Murray to Richard Mulcahy, 17 June 1940. UCDA, P104/3536.

27 Minutes of Defence Conference, 12 June 1941. UCDA, P104/3534.

28 Aiken speech in Louth 1940. UCDA, P104/3375.

29 Aiken speech in Mullingar, 5 May 1940. UCDA, P104/3377.

30 Aiken memo. on meeting members of Dublin Chamber of Commerce, 30 May 1940. UCDA, P104/3378.

31 Donnacha Ó Beacháin, *Destiny of the Soldiers: Fianna Fáil, Irish Republicanism, and the IRA* (Dublin: Gill and MacMillan, 2010), 180.

32 Aiken notes c. 1939. UCDA, P104/3711.

33 Aiken letter to editor, *The Irish Times*, c. 1941. UCDA, P104/3527.

34 Aiken speech 23 June 1940. UCDA, P104/3375.

35 Aiken memo. on meeting members of Dublin Chamber of Commerce, 30 May 1940. UCDA, P104/3378.

36 Excerpts from *The People*, 11 Feb. 1925. UCDA, Moss Twomey Papers (P69)/181 (136).

37 O'Halpin, *Spying*, 37–38 and 144.

38 Thomas Inskip note, 20 Oct. 1938. NAUK, Cabinet Papers (CAB) 53/42.

39 See, for example, Trevor Allen, *The Storm Passed By: Ireland and the Battle of the Atlantic, 1940–41* (Dublin: Irish Academic Press, 1996), 148.

40 John Hearne to Joseph Walshe, 19 Jan. 1942. NAI, DFA, secretary's files, P12/5.

41 Meeting of the government, 27 June 1940. NAI, Department of the Taoiseach (DT), 2001/6/500.

42 Geoffrey Roberts, 'The British Offer to End Partition, June 1940', *History Ireland* (spring 2001), 5–6.

43 Cited in Carroll, *Ireland in the War Years*, 55.

44 See Bryce Evans, *Seán Lemass: Democratic Dictator* (Cork: Collins, 2011).

45 Johnston–Aiken interview, 6 July 1940. UCDA, P104/3577.

46 Walshe to Brennan, 24 Feb. 1941. NAI, DFA, secretary's files, P2, NAI.

47 Cahill, *A Life in the IRA*, 127.

48 John Maffey to Dominions Office, 24 Feb. 1941. NAUK, Foreign Office (FO) files, 371/29108.

49 Fisk, *In Time of War*, 306.

50 Aiken's report of trip to United States, 5 Aug. 1941. UCDA, P104/3585.

51 Robert Brennan to Frederick Boland, 26 March 1941. NAI, DFA, Washington Embassy file, 10/P/35, NAI.

52 Robert Brennan to Frederick Boland, 20 March 1941. NAI, DFA, Washington Embassy file, 10/P/35.

53 Aiken's report of trip to United States, 5 Aug. 1941. UCDA, P104/3585.

54   Brennan to Boland, 26 March 1941. NAI, DFA, Washington Embassy file, 10/P/35.

55   Robert Brennan to Joseph Walshe, 10 April 1941. NAI, DFA, Washington Embassy file, 10/P/35.

56   Robert Brennan to Joseph Walshe, 8 April 1941. NAI, DFA, Washington Embassy file, 10/P/35.

57   Robert Brennan to Joseph Walshe, 8 April 1941. NAI, DFA, Washington Embassy file, 10/P/35.

58   Aiken's report of trip to United States, 5 Aug. 1941. UCDA, P104/3585.

59   Robert Brennan, 'My War-Time Mission in Washington', *Irish Press*, 7 May 1958.

60   Cited in Fisk, *In Time of War*, 308.

61   Robert Brennan to Joseph Walshe, 10 April 1941. NAI, DFA, Washington Embassy file,10/P/35.

62   Aiken to Walshe, 23 May 1940. NAI, DFA, Washington Embassy file, 10/P/35.

63   Joseph Walshe to Robert Brennan, 17 June 1941. NAI, DFA, secretary's files, P35.

64   Aiken's report of trip to United States, 5 Aug. 1941. UCDA, P104/3585.

65   Brennan to Joseph Walshe, 23 May 1941. NAI, DFA, secretary's files, P70.

66   See *Irish Press*, 27 and 28 June 1941.

67   Minutes of Defence Conference, 18 April 1941 and 24 April 1941. UCDA, P104/3534.

68   Coyne to Oscar Traynor, 23 May 1941. UCDA, P104/3573.

69   Minutes of Defence Conference, 14 May 1941. UCDA, P104/3534.

70   Minutes of Defence Conference, 5 June 1941. UCDA, P104/3534.

71   *Irish Independent* (censored), 19 May 1941. UCDA, P104/3587.

72   Minutes of Defence Conference, 3 July 1941. UCDA, P104/3534.

73   Fisk, *In Time of War*, 309.

74   Joseph L. Rosenberg, 'The 1941 Mission of Frank Aiken to the United States: An American Perspective', *Irish Historical Studies*, 22 (1980–81), 162–77; Raymond James Raymond, 'David Gray, the Aiken mission, and Irish Neutrality, 1940–41', *Diplomatic History*, 9, 1 (1985), 55–71.

75   Allen, *The Storm Passed By*, 148.

76   Undated transcript of Aiken radio interview. UCDA, P104/3581.

77   Brennan to Walshe, 31 Jan. 1941, NAI, DFA, Washington Embassy file, 10/P/35.

78   'Record of Activities'. NAI, Industry and Commerce files (IND) EHR/3/15, pp. 22–23.

79   Walshe to Brennan, 13 May 1941. NAI, DFA, secretary's files, P35.

80   'Copy of Material given to Mr Aiken for his visit to the USA'. NAI, DFA, Washington Embassy file, 10/P/35.

81   Walshe to Aiken, 28 Feb. 1941. NAI, DFA, secretary's files, P35.

82   Robert Brennan, 'My War-Time Mission in Washington', *Irish Press*, 7 May 1958.

83   Cablegram from Washington Legation to Dublin, 26 June 1941. UCDA, P104/3572.

84   For Gray's smears see Booth-Staunton telephone conversations, 5–8 Dec. 1942. UCDA, P104/3510; Rooney–McGlinchey telephone conversations, 22–24 March 1944. UCDA, P104/3513. See also Fisk, *In Time of War*, 102.

85   Walshe to Brennan, 15 March 1941. NAI, DFA, secretary's files, P35.

86   Brennan to Walshe, 18 March 1941. NAI, DFA, Washington Embassy file, 10/P/35.

87   Brennan to Sumner Welles, 15 July 1941. NAI, DFA, secretary's files, P35.

88   O'Drisceoil, *Censorship*, 144.

89 Brennan to Walshe, 29 April 1941. NAI, DFA, Washington Embassy file, 10/P/35.

90 Gray to Maud Aiken, 12 May 1941. UCDA, P104/3513.

91 Kathleen O'Connell to Gray, 17 May 1941. FDR Library, David Gray papers Box 2, (http://www.fdrlibrary.marist.edu).

92 Brennan to Walshe, 18 Sept. 1941. NAI, DFA, Washington Embassy file, 10/P/35.

93 Walshe to Brennan, 19 Sept. 1941. NAI, DFA, Washington Embassy file, 10/P/35.

94 'Emergency Powers (No. 5) Order'. UCDA, P104/3431.

95 Leydon to Aiken, 22 Dec. 1943. UCDA, P104/3763.

96 Minutes of meeting, March 1940. UCDA, P104/3507.

97 Aiken's memorandum on censorship, 23 Jan. 1940. NAI, DT S11586A.

98 See Karen Slattery and Mark Doremus, 'Suppressing Allied Atrocity Stories: The Unwritten Clause of the World War Two Censorship Code', *Journalism and Mass Communication Quarterly* 89, 4 (Winter, 2012), 624–642.

99 Aiken letter to unidentified editor, c. 1945. UCDA, P104/3450.

100 Terry de Valera, *A Memoir* (Dublin: Currach Press, 2005), 120.

101 Telephone conversation between Aiken and Frank McDermott, 11 Nov. 1944. UCDA, P104/3439.

102 Robert Cole, *Propaganda, Censorship And Irish Neutrality in the Second World War* (Edinburgh: Edinburgh University Press, 2006), 74

103 Gray, *The Lost Years*, 157.

104 O'Driscoeil, *Censorship*, 109–111.

105 Aiken to Maffey, 9 Feb.1945. UCDA, P104/3747.

106 Donal O'Drisceoil, 'The Neutralisation of Irish Public Opinion', in Brian Girvin and Geoffrey Roberts (eds), *Ireland during the Second World War: Politics, Society, Remembrance* (Dublin: Four Courts, 2000), 180.

107 Lemass to Aiken, 3 Nov. 1942. UCDA, P104/3753.

108 Horgan to Leydon, 22 Oct. 1942. UCDA, P104/3753.

109 J.W. Dulanty to Michael Rynne, 2 March 1940. UCDA, P104/3438.

110 O'Drisceoil, 'The Neutralisation', 179.

111 O'Drisceoil, *Censorship*, 13

112 See Censor's Report for Dec. 1944. UCDA, P104/3502.

113 Censor's Reports, Oct. 1939. UCDA, P104/3464.

114 Todd Andrews, *Man of No Property* (Dublin: Lilliput, 1982), 124.

115 Aiken letter to unidentified editor, c. 1945. UCDA, P104/3450.

116 Invitation to 'Liberation of the Press Censors of the Castle' dinner. UCDA, P104/3747.

117 Office of the Controller of Censorship (OCC), 8/7, MA.

118 Aiken speech, 4 Feb. 1942. Dáil Debates (DE), Vol. 85, col. 1753.

119 Excerpts from speech of Sept. 1941. UCDA, 104/3374.

120 OCC, 8/24, MA.

121 Aiken speech, 4 Feb. 1942. DE, Vol. 85, col. 1752.

122 Aiken speech, Dungarvan, 22 Jan. 1944. UCDA, P104/3389.

123 UCDA, P104/3390.

124 UCDA, P104/3387.

125 'On the Necessity of Strong Wheat', 23 Oct. 1941. UCDA, P104/3390.

126 Aiken speech in Carlow 18 Jan. 1943. UCDA, P104/3389.

127   Censor's Report for Feb. 1942. UCDA, P104/3486.

128   See, for instance, Aiken speech 20 Dec. 1943, Wexford. UCDA, P104.

129   Aiken, 'Proposal for the consideration of the Cabinet Committee on Economic Planning', 17 April 1945. UCDA, P104/3696.

130   Aiken speech in Clonmel, 26 Feb. 1943. UCDA, P104/3389.

131   Denis Johnston, BBC Overseas Recordings, 1 Sept. 1941 and 3 Nov. 1941. UCDA, P104/3441.

132   See O/CC 7/50 MA. Censorship already covered any statements regarding 'shortages of essential supplies'. See also Memorandum on the Censorship of Communications and the Press. UCDA, P104/3434.

133   Untitled memorandum, Feb.1941. UCDA, P104/3398.

134   'Policy and Plan for Meeting Complete Blockade'. UCDA, P104/3420.

135   Ryan to de Valera, 13 Jan. 1941. NAI, DT, S/11402.

136   Smyllie–Coyne correspondence 10 and 13 Oct. 1940. NAI, Department of Justice files (DJ) no.3.

137   Various ideas are detailed in UCDA, P104/3391.

138   Carroll, *Ireland in the War Years*, 44.

139   Andrews, *Man of No Property*, 125.

140   Aiken to de Valera, 24 Feb. 1942. UCDA, P104/3679.

141   Memorandum of 20 Sept. 1944. UCDA, P104/3410.

142   For the material Aiken was reading on banking systems in the 1940s, see UCDA, P104/3632–3675.

143   Aiken to de Valera, 12 July 1943. UCDA, P104/3681.

144   Leon Ó Broin, *No Man's Man: A Biographical Memoir of Joseph Brennan, Civil Servant & First Governor of the Central Bank Dublin* (Dublin: Institute of Public Administration, 1982), 153.

145   Aiken, 'Between me and the wall or a Finance departmenteer discusses with himself the 'notes on the economic situation' in November 1939 for consideration by the executive council'. UCDA, P104/3671.

146   Aiken speech, 28 June 1941. UCDA, P104/3581.

147   Aiken speech at Louth, 26 Nov. 1944. UCDA, P104/3375.

148   Aiken untitled memorandum, 30 Oct. 1943. UCDA, P104/3445.

149   O'Drisceoil, 'Neutralisation', 154.

150   See Bryce Evans, *Ireland during the Second World War: Farewell to Plato's Cave* (Manchester: Manchester University Press, 2014).

151   Aiken speech, 11 Oct. 1942. UCDA, P104/3375.

152   Aiken letter to unidentified editor, c. 1945. UCDA, P104/3450.

CHAPTER SIX

An experiment or a new departure? Aiken in Finance, 1945–1948

CONOR KEELAN

Introduction

The contribution of Fianna Fáil to economic development in independent Ireland has been portrayed largely as Seán Lemass in frequent conflict with Seán MacEntee, with many other Cabinet members as bit players.[1] This interpretation overlooks the fact that Frank Aiken held the Finance portfolio for three years from 1945 to 1948. Lemass's career and contribution in economic matters has been analysed in a succession of biographies.[2] MacEntee's contribution to Ireland's economic history has been the subject of one biography to date.[3] By contrast, there has been no critical examination of fiscal and financial policy during Aiken's tenure to date, and this analysis aspires to be the first such attempt in this vein.

In general, there have been mixed views recorded about Aiken's time spent in the Finance portfolio. When Aiken left office in 1948, Joseph Brennan, Governor of the Central Bank from 1943 to 1953, said that he was one of the few ministers who had made an effort to study the merits of public finance.[4] Brennan recalled in his memoirs that Aiken 'had the great advantage that whenever I got him to accept reluctantly some proposal I made to him, he was able more than any other

Minister to secure the agreement of [Éamon] de Valera who had the utmost trust in him'.[5] This correlates with the findings of another study, which concluded that Aiken was more highly regarded by the officials in the Department of Finance than those on the opposition benches gave him credit.[6]

John Horgan, in his biography of Lemass, gives a different opinion. In 1948, James J. McElligott, Secretary of the Department of Finance from 1927 to 1953, noted during a conversation with Lemass that he might not be retained in his position by the new inter-party government. Lemass allegedly told him: 'You're safe, anyone who can get economics into Frank Aiken's head will be alright'.[7] In examining Aiken's career in Finance, a contemporary, Patrick Lynch, wrote that he could have been regarded, prematurely, as a Keynesian in light of his studentship of the English theorist Clifford Hugh Douglas's social credit scheme.[8] In his history of the Department of Finance, Ronan Fanning described Aiken's tenure in office as: 'marked by a growing concern within the Department with the need to reduce state expenditure'.[9] It has also been argued that Aiken carried out a strongly deflationary policy while in office.[10] Aiken, together with MacEntee, has also been portrayed as a consistent opponent of Lemass's bolder plans when they were in the Cabinet together.[11] Another recent analysis has argued that not only were Cabinet members such as MacEntee and Aiken traditionalists, but they were also in favour of creating an economic autarky and conservative state based on Catholic doctrines.[12]

Coming to Office

The 1945 Irish presidential election was the first such election to be held in the Irish Free State. Seán T. O'Kelly, Fianna Fáil Tánaiste and Minister for Finance, was the odds-on favourite against General Seán MacEoin of Fine Gael and Patrick McCartan, the Independent Republican candidate.[13] Although the margin of victory was not as comfortable as Fianna Fáil had predicted, O'Kelly was elected President of Ireland on 14 June 1945. Two vacancies arose at Cabinet level at this time. Opinion was shared among the political correspondents that the position of Tánaiste would be allocated to Seán Lemass, given his performance in building up the Department of Industry and Commerce since 1932, and subsequently in Supplies during the years of the Emergency. Meanwhile, the consensus was that Seán MacEntee would almost certainly make a return to his former Department of Finance; the portfolio he had held until he had been replaced by O'Kelly in a previous reshuffle.[14]

It came as a considerable shock and surprise, therefore, that Aiken was appointed to the Finance portfolio on 19 June 1945. The *Irish Independent* political correspondent commented: 'the general anticipation even in the Fianna Fáil party had been that there would have been some reshuffle of the government which would have provided Mr. Aiken with a different post'.[15] Referring to Aiken's appointment, the *Cork Examiner* political correspondent wrote: 'Aiken's translation to the Ministry of Finance from the Ministry for Co-ordination of Defensive Measures – now redundant with the coming of peace – must be regarded largely as an experiment'.[16] Even a sympathetic biographer like Liam Skinner expressed surprise that Aiken had been appointed to the Finance portfolio in his pen portraits of Fianna Fáil ministers.[17] Praise for Aiken's appointment came from the unusual source of the *Catholic Standard*, which labelled him as a reformer.[18]

As will be explored, however, Aiken had a significant interest in economics, which was appreciated by his Cabinet colleagues. It is now known that Aiken requested this appointment directly from de Valera.[19] Given the close relationship between Aiken and de Valera, it is extremely unlikely that the appointment would have gone ahead were it not for the trust the Taoiseach had in his minister. This chapter shall examine his time in this role through an analysis of his budgetary and banking policies during his tenure in office. In addition, the chapter also examines his contribution and views on economic policy during the 1950s and later during his time on the opposition benches and in government.

Financial initiatives pre-appointment

During his time in various portfolios he held before assuming Finance, Aiken made a number of interventions on economic policy. For example, the 1936 census, the results of which were produced in 1939, provoked considerable cause for concern regarding trends for population decline. De Valera, conversing with his economic adviser Professor Timothy Anthony Smiddy, proposed a system of family allowances to families with weekly wages of under £3 10s. per week, or £38 per annum for farmers. Aiken sent a memo to the Cabinet on family allowances, proposing payments to agricultural workers and small farmers in mid-1939.[20] In July 1939, the Cabinet decided to request that the Department of Local Government and Public Health investigate the matter, despite the opposition of Minister for Finance, Seán MacEntee.[21] A committee was formed made up of Aiken, Lemass, Patrick Joseph Ruttledge, James Ryan and Thomas Derrig, but this committee did not meet until April 1940 as Ruttledge was absent due to illness. Lemass was very unhappy with the delay, and this policy became increasingly associated with him.

The coming of family allowances into law was a tortuous process, and has been regarded as a battle between forces of modernisation and resistance within the party, which Lemass won.[22] However, it has been suggested that this analysis does not give a sufficient contribution to de Valera's role in helping the legislation become law, and it would be with his consistent support that the proposal eventually became enacted as policy, despite the opposition of MacEntee and Finance.[23] While Aiken's initial proposal for allowances was for those involved in agriculture and rural families, it became subsumed into the wider scheme. From correspondence and advice he received from diplomats abroad, it is apparent that Aiken remained a supporter of allowances. He read about equivalent schemes in France and Australia and in the UK, as a way of mitigating poverty in its most extreme form.[24]

Lemass, as well as Aiken, had a substantial interest in the development of Ireland's natural resources. Lemass felt that Ireland had more resources than was stated and that the state should go out and look for them. This resulted in the creation of the Institute for Industrial Research and Standards.[25] During the Emergency years, Aiken established the Emergency Science Research Bureau. Research was conducted on natural resources and imported raw materials with a view to creating new by-products for the general population at large and Irish industry. Among the products experimented upon were potato flour, phosphate deposits from County Clare and gas from bog peat. Attempts were also made to extract pesticide from tobacco offal and sulphur from the spent oxide of gas works. While work with peat charcoal proved expensive, a plant to produce formalin from methyl alcohol was acquired, and it was eventually taken over by Irish Alcohol Factories Ltd.[26]

Perhaps the greatest example of the utilization of natural resources was in the development of the bogs. Aiken was fascinated by the possibilities of using turf as a source of fuel, and was influenced by fellow Fianna Fáil TD Tom Harris, who showed him how a successful local market could operate.[27] C.S. Andrews also described Aiken as 'the last of the Sinn Féiners', in terms of economic policy going back to Arthur Griffith, and credited the development of the bogs as largely down to him.[28] He and Aiken chose the name Bord na Móna for the new turf board, and while at times several of his ideas proved impractical to implement, such as turf as a source for wax and motor oil, his consistent support made it easier to deal with civil service resistance.[29] It has been suggested that two of Aiken's ministerial colleagues, Gerald Boland and Oscar Traynor, favoured a policy of decentralised industry based on the development of natural resources. This would have seemingly brought them into conflict with Lemass, who favoured manufacturing, based if necessary on imported raw materials.[30]

The Banking Commission of 1934 to 1938, established to examine the feasibility of creating a Central Bank, contained many fiscal conservatives among its members who were hostile to Fianna Fáil. It also included William O'Brien, who was a representative of the trade union movement. Aiken and Lemass were vocal on this subject. It has been suggested that the need for substantial independence of the Central Bank and the need for more powers to be transferred to it was also an area of common ground between the two in opposition to the MacEntee–O'Kelly axis. Apparently, de Valera tried to achieve a form of consensus while favouring the progressive opinion.[31] It was not until 1942 that the Central Bank was established. Even when it was, the extent to which it could act as a restraint upon government spending was very limited. While the Central Bank could discipline the government, it could not do the same to the banking system. It had a duty to safeguard the integrity of currency and the control of credit, but in practice was powerless to do either.[32] Keynesian economics did not feature at the debates of the Banking Commission – a testament to the conservative nature of its contributors. In its absence, vocationalist theories were debated as alternatives to the present banking system.[33]

A variety of these vocationalists did attempt to fight a rearguard action to try and secure the inclusion of at least some Catholic social principles into government policy. Several adherents to both vocationalism and social credit theory sent de Valera a tentative draft of the minority report in September 1937 in an attempt to persuade him that there should be a significant divergence between the minority and majority reports. De Valera saw the usefulness in this in placating the radical wing of his party, and to ensure that he could not have been accused of abandoning self-sufficiency as an ideology. Peadar O'Loghlen, a constituency colleague of de Valera, was a member of the Banking Commission, and reported its proceedings back to him.[34] The report, which was written by a Fr. Cahill, Bulmer Hobson and Mrs. B. Berthon Waters, was presented as a third minority report, and was signed by O'Loghlen.[35]

Aiken was an enthusiastic advocate of social credit theory and its potential application in Ireland.[36] The theory derived from the work of Major Clifford Hugh Douglas, a renowned British engineer, who attempted to re-engineer the economy and the banking system. Douglas was a critic of classical economics, especially with regard to money and banking. He criticised the ability of banks to act like governments, in that they wielded significant powers to create money, and sometimes assumed ownership of the money thus created. Meanwhile, there was a need to bridge the gap between purchasing power and prices. Social credit proposes a means for the creation of debt-free money, whereby a country creates money using its tangible, physical wealth and natural resources. Given his own background as an engineer, it can be seen how the theories of Douglas, who sought to apply engineering principles to economics, appealed to Aiken. The theory was quite popular throughout the British Commonwealth, particularly in Canada, where social credit governments had been elected in the 1930s. Other theorists included the British Professor Frederick Snoddy, who was a Nobel laureate in chemistry, and who published four books arguing for an economy to be rooted in physics, specifically the law of thermodynamics, as the economy was, in his view, essentially a machine.[37] Aiken was also aware of the extent of Snoddy's theories.[38] Among the criticisms levelled at social credit are that it ignores the quantity theory of money, and that its frequent references to usury contain anti-semitic undertones.[39]

Social credit transcended Irish political boundaries. Luke Duffy, one of the general secretaries of the Labour Party and a member of the Banking Commission, was influential in encouraging his party to shift their economic policy from effectively abandoning support for a worker's republic to supporting a system of system of social credit lest they be subject to clerical attack. It seems that Duffy was influenced by his friendship with Professor Alfred O'Rahilly of University College Cork, who was also an advocate of the theory.[40] It has also been argued that Seán MacBride was a strong supporter of social credit.[41] It seems that he was heavily influenced by Mrs B. Berthon Waters, who wrote economic memoranda for him.[42]

Budgetary Policy

Aiken's first budget as Minister for Finance in early May 1946 was generally considered to be a 'good news' budget. Press reaction was almost universally positive. *The Irish Times* praised the reduction in income tax to six shillings six pence in the pound, together with the reduction in duties on goods such as sugar, petrol and turf, and the abolition of the excess corporation tax.[43] The paper, having praised Aiken for his 'excellent budget', wrote further: 'Mr Aiken has distributed his favours with a discriminating hand, giving something to everybody'.[44] Local press reaction was also favourable, with the *Dundalk Examiner* welcoming the budget for bringing a measure of relief to taxpayers.[45] The *Dundalk Democrat*, typically supportive of the Fine Gael party, also welcomed the budget for its progressive character.[46] The *Dublin Evening Mail* struck a different note, however, arguing that it was the worst budget in history for savers as the 2.5 per cent rate on bank deposits had been cut to 2 per cent for the first £300 and 1.5 per cent thereafter. This was a break in a tradition dating back to 1888. The paper claimed that Aiken had granted relief to industrialists and big business while hitting savers.[47] Partially overshadowing the budget was concern about the fate of the republican hunger striker Seán McCaughey in Portlaoise Prison, which was also discussed in the Dáil.[48]

Army expenditure, which was the single biggest outlay in the previous four to five years, had been practically halved due to army demobilisation, at a saving of over £4m.[49] The budget allowed for capital expenditure, together with tax reductions. The excess corporation profits tax and the excess surtax were both abolished.[50] There was also a reduction in the price of turf and oils. Duties on wines and spirits were increased, by way of contrast, and the reduction in the interest rate on deposits provoked some disquiet, but can be seen as trying to encourage money to be spent in the local economy.[51] The resumption in shipping trade with Lisbon, again a benefit of the end of hostilities, had benefited customs duties.[52] With knowledge of Aiken's views on natural resources, it is not surprising that there were concessions to encourage the extension of mining activity throughout the state, and the budget made provision for borrowing for capital projects at Bord na Móna (£400,000), rural electrification (£1m), tourism (£350,000) and for activities at Aer Lingus (£1.4m).[53]

Arguably the most innovative aspect of the budget was the proposal to set up a Transition Development Fund for the next two years, from which contributions would go to extra capital expenses of state organisations and local authorities, attributable to post-war transitional difficulties such as the shortage of equipment and the high price of material. The plan proposed to borrow £5m in 1946 for the fund, which would operate for two years. Priority projects would be in the Gaeltacht and large urban areas where desirable schemes might be postponed otherwise. It would be legalised in the Finance Bill, and could also be used for farm improvements and housing, increased productivity and better health services.[54] Furthermore, there was also £1m towards rates relief for agricultural landowners. The budget emphasised the need for tackling unemployment, and Aiken saw agriculture as a future growth avenue for the future.[55] However, the summer of 1946 would prove to be one of the worst on record, which would ultimately impact upon the subsequent harvest, which failed, and in turn led to the introduction of bread rationing in 1947.[56] Joseph Connolly foresaw the likely difficulties in obtaining additional supplies from abroad, particularly from Britain, and recommended to Aiken that an export corporation be established, financed by American dollars, to charter steamers from the United States to deliver the requisite cargoes of grain, coal and raw materials.[57] This advice was not acted upon.

Aiken's second budget, containing expenditure worth £61,131,500, was delivered on 7 May 1947, and saw income tax rates remain unchanged. However, personal tax allowances were increased from £120 to £140 in the case of a single person, and from £220 to £260 for a married couple, which proposed to remove some 27,000 people from the tax net.[58] Aiken raised the tobacco duty significantly; a move that received the most media comment.[59] Import duty on tobacco rose to twenty-three shillings and ten pence, which resulted in a corresponding rise in a packet of twenty cigarettes by three pence. Tobacco prices also rose by three pence an ounce. This gave rise to a concern that there would be an increase in cross-border smuggling, although tobacco prices had risen in the United Kingdom in the equivalent budget there. The budget also proposed new forms of entertainment tax, which would raise the cost of operating cinemas. Stamp duty on stocks, shares and marketable securities was also doubled in the budget. Additional licence duties were imposed on auctioneers and house agents.[60]

The reaction to these duties proved to be quite unpopular. Although *The Irish Times* praised Aiken for his 'sound budget' despite the new duties, the paper issued a cautionary note that public expenditure was continuing to rise and would need to be addressed in subsequent budgets.[61] The *Dundalk Democrat* commented that the increase in tobacco and amusement taxes was less than expected, and the average taxpayer escaped relatively lightly.[62] The *Dundalk Examiner* also praised Aiken's 'sound budget', as might be expected, despite the increased duties on cigarettes and cinema seats.[63] The *Irish Independent* took a more caustic view of the budget, making particular reference to the cost of living, which the paper argued the government was keeping artificially high, and that the effect of the increase in personal allowance rates would simply be absorbed by the rising cost of living.[64] Recognising difficulties in the agricultural market, creameries were aided by the introduction of guaranteed prices for butter and milk.[65] The harsh winter of 1946 to 1947 gave rise to a severe fuel crisis, which had a significant impact on industry and transport.[66] As a way to attempt to counteract the situation, fuel subsidies worth £1.5m were included in the budget, together with £2.2m for turf development.[67] Disappointedly, Aiken noted that there had been little expenditure from the Transition Development Fund in 1946, but sums totalling £1.25m had been committed for a variety of projects.[68] The rural electrification programme was to be expanded, and by the year end a further twelve districts were due to be linked to the ESB network, with another twenty more during the course of installation. Some £2m was provided in the estimates for this purpose.[69]

Continuing with capital expenditure, a sum of £8.2m was borrowed. The schemes to benefit included improvement and expansion of the telephone network, tourism, local loans, air service expansion and turf development. Some 1,000 local authority houses had been completed in 1946, and it was hoped that

1,500 would be completed in 1947. There was also borrowing provided for this purpose. Savings certificates were to be used to assist in funding the borrowing programme as well, and funds were available at a rate of 2.5 per cent.[70] A new initiative of the budget, and one promoted by Aiken, was the glasshouse production scheme.[71] The aim of the scheme was to improve living standards in the Gaeltacht, and glasshouses would be erected on 100 smallholdings in that area. In addition, poultry production could be extended in these areas also.[72]

In discussing the feasibility of the scheme, James Ryan, Minister for Agriculture, observed that several applications had come from non-landholders, and some of those most interested in the scheme were among the more affluent in the community. He felt that the only export market for the crop was the UK, and that there was potential for the cultivation of cucumbers also.[73] Despite Ryan's concerns, the scheme proceeded. One problem in developing it further was that Aiken did not invest in the necessary infrastructure to complement it.[74] Aiken again continued with his policy of support for the Irish language through raising the sum for existing Gaeltacht scholarships to £130 per annum, and creating fifty more such scholarships per year to students from outside the area to do university courses through Irish.[75]

Despite an average outflow of 30,000 people per annum emigrating from the country between 1945 and 1947, there continued to be high unemployment, standing at 9.3 per cent in 1947.[76] While industrial employment did recover to some extent, the number of people employed in 1946 was only the same number as those employed in 1938. By 1948, employment in this sector would grow by another 10 per cent, while savings only accounted for 4.5 per cent of Gross National Product, and fixed investment was only 9 per cent of Gross National Product by 1947. There was significant industrial strife in the country at this time.[77] This was caused, chiefly, by people's concerns over inflation and the cost of living. The consumer price index had risen by 31 per cent alone between August 1946 and August 1947.[78]

On 15 October 1947, Aiken was compelled to introduce a supplementary budget to the Dáil as a reaction to the shocks to the economy. This contained a number of measures that remain controversial to this day, and with which his tenure in office is most commonly associated. The budget was a mixed combination of subsidies on essentials and increased taxation on so-called luxury goods. These new subsidies totalled £5,765,000, and the additional taxation measures were expected to yield approximately £4.7m. This £4.7m would meet the deficit from existing taxation measures previously agreed. As the price of wheat had risen, and the wages in mills and bakeries had also increased, it was estimated that an additional £3.4m would need to be raised to keep the price of bread at current levels. Total subsidies for bread and flour combined for the year now amounted to some £5.6m.

The Irish Times commented that the government acted with 'strange courage', particularly in the political context of three outstanding by-elections.[79] The purchase and distribution of various necessity products was subsidised at the expense of other goods. The supplementary budget halved the price of tea, and reduced the price of sugar by two pence per pound. The price of a four-pound loaf would be reduced by three and a half pence due to subsidies on flour. However, necessities such as tea, sugar and bread continued to be rationed at this time, so any reduction in their prices would not have had any considerable effect for Irish families. By contrast, spirits cost an additional sixpence a glass after the budget, the excise duty having risen by 30 per cent, which was expected to yield £935,000. Beer would cost an additional three pence a pint, the excise duty having nearly doubled, which was expected to yield an additional £830,000. Increased duty on wines was expected to yield an extra £220,000.[80] The price of cigarettes was to rise by four pence on a packet of twenty cigarettes, while pipe tobacco was to rise by between four and a half and five pence per ounce, with an expected yield of £1,960,000. Regarding personal taxation, Aiken announced that he intended to raise rates by six pence in the pound beginning in 1948, with the intention of yielding an additional sum of £600,000 in the first year.[81]

The Irish Trade Union Congress said of the supplementary budget that it was: 'a costly hoax calculated to fool the workers and assure to profiteers their ill-gotten gains'.[82] A letter from Patrick Brady, a treasurer of the Fianna Fáil party, to Éamon de Valera, was quite illuminating. He expressed disappointment at the government's banking policy. Referring to problems in the economy, he argued that agriculture was in a terrible state and that no effort had been made to drain many areas, and that there had been a shirking of forestry as a policy. In addition, mineral resources had not exploited to their potential, and emigration continued unabated. Brady felt that many voted for Fianna Fáil because there seemed to be no alternative other than a complete surrender of the national ideal.[83] This could be seen as a foreshadowing of Clann na Poblachta appearing on the horizon to challenge the party's electoral hegemony. The views of James Cadden, expressed in a letter to Aiken after the supplementary budget, demonstrated how unpopular the measures proved for some. Cadden had closed down his licensed premises following the budget and the rise in the price of stout, and blamed religious influence for the rise in duty. He hoped that Fianna Fáil would suffer electorally due to public dissatisfaction, while he would be either on the dole or have to emigrate to support his family.[84] It could be argued that the supplementary budget measures had a disproportionate effect against the less well-off, particularly given the designation of luxury and necessity goods, especially at a time of continued rationing and high unemployment.

Banking Policy

One significant area of financial policy not addressed by Fianna Fáil upon assuming office in 1932 was that of banking policy. Essentially, the party's policy remained indistinguishable from that of the previous Cumann na nGaedheal administration. The party had spoken of change before 1932, when Seán MacEntee spoke of creating a State bank. However, his stance in opposition proved different from his stance in government, and this policy was soon dropped. The department was highly supportive of the status quo in this area, and also of maintaining the Sterling link. Banking and finance circles were not a core constituency for Fianna Fáil, but they did not go out of their way to address the manner in which the banks dealt with the electorate, or the economy at large, during their time in office.[85] In 1938, another chance to challenge the pre-eminent order was passed up regarding the Banking Commission. As has been discussed, Aiken was regarded as an outlier in press and political circles when appointed to Finance. There were concerns in the Department of Finance as well. Much of this arose from his awareness of issues such as social credit and how they had been applied in other countries. There was also a fear that immediately upon assuming office, he would adopt an aggressive, expansionist stance to stimulate the economy similar to Hugh Dalton, his counterpart in Britain.[86] A young T. K. Whitaker was appointed as Aiken's adviser on monetary theory at the imprimatur of McElligott.[87]

On 24 June 1945, Aiken inquired of the Central Bank Board whether it was feasible to lower lending rates. At a meeting between the Governor of the Central Bank, Joseph Brennan, and Aiken, the latter pressed for rates to be lowered. In response, Brennan told Aiken that such a sudden initiative would be inopportune, and that a policy of cheap money was not economically advisable at this time.[88] No reduction in lending rates would occur, and Irish bank rates would remain fixed at 3 per cent from October 1939 to 1952. Aiken also had a discussion with Gabriel Brock, the Acting Deputy Governor, regarding the British government's financial policies, which incorporated large-scale borrowing from banks at low rates of interest. Aiken wondered about the adaptability of such policies to Ireland. Brock advised that the British would have to fund a large part of its floating debt and that the new money, in excess taxation, would then have to be found from savings. For his part, Aiken disagreed, but did not pursue the matter again.[89] These were some of Aiken's attempts at making capital more available in Ireland for public purposes, mirroring the Daltonian example.[90] He came up against the firm resistance of the Department of Finance and the Central Bank, and reluctantly listened to their advice. The Irish banks had operated an informal cartel arrangement since 1919, and the Irish Banks Standing Committee rigidly operated a system to reduce competition and virtually freeze the banking network until the 1950s. The Committee also dictated the interest rates charged and paid by banks.[91] There existed a substantial difference in the margin of four percentage points between lending and deposit rates, which gave rise to claims about inadequate competition between the banks.[92]

The deliberate policy of Irish banks putting their reserves overseas, chiefly in Britain, was a bone of contention with Aiken. In 1933 he had asked his Cabinet colleague, Joseph Connolly, for a memorandum on the knock-on effects of this policy on the Irish economy, which made Irish investors very reluctant to invest and speculate in Irish enterprises and greatly impacted on securing finance for industry and housing.[93] Brennan, by way of contrast, had long argued that the banking system owed its stability to its investment policy, and that there was no need to urge the banks to invest at home – indeed, he feared that this could lead to partial nationalisation.[94] Aiken found common ground with Lemass at Cabinet level in this regard, but, despite strong rhetoric and occasional threats, they did not compel the banks to change their policy, and as a party Fianna Fáil took no firm action, following the example of previous governments.[95]

In 1945, McElligott wrote to the Irish Banks Standing Committee on Aiken's behalf, expressing his minister's disappointment that the committee did not agree to his request to take up the proposed issue of 1.75 million exchequer bills a month at one and one-eighth per cent. Aiken had commented that banks should 'benefit the community' and 'behave in the best traditions of Irish banking' by advancing exchequer bills at suitable rates of interest.[96] In December 1945, Aiken submitted a proposal to the Department of Finance and to the Central Bank in which he proposed to issue £10m in 1946 over and above the present floating debt, which the Central Bank would agree to re-discount at a rate of 5 per cent.[97] As might be expected, significant concerns over inflation were expressed by the banks, while the Central Bank Board also said that it was undesirable to re-discount given the current money supply, the large increase in same in recent years, the small turnover and the need for prudent management.

Throughout much of this period, the stance of the banks and the Central Bank Board was indistinguishable. Aiken was quite angry in response, and circulated a memorandum regarding the commercial bank's actions to his

Cabinet colleagues calling it 'an act of undeclared war upon our people'. In his opinion, Irish banks had been offered the same terms as their British counterparts and had turned them down, i.e. £1.8m bills bearing interest at the same rate as in Britain.[98] Aiken felt that British banks would never at any time in the last six years have held out against such a request by their government. This exposed a significant deficiency in the Central Bank, which had insufficient powers since the time of its inauguration, while also exposing the prevalent laissez-faire attitude of the government towards the banks.

Despite Aiken's anger, no action was taken by the government against the banks. He rejected the offer of an advance of 1 per cent, and instead a decision was taken to obtain ways and means advances through the selling of State assets (which was not a good bargain, but accepted as necessary). On 1 January 1946, Aiken secured government approval to compel each bank to deposit within the state approximately 10 per cent of the sum by which deposit liabilities within the state exceeded assets on that date. This was met with significant opposition from the Central Bank in the form of Joseph Brennan, who assumed a new role as President of the Institute of Bankers that same year.[99] Nothing came of this policy proposal. On 15 February 1946, McElligott sent a final appeal to Lord Glenavy, chairman of the Irish Banks Standing Committee, emphasising the need to invest in capital projects and hoping for a favourable interest rate, which would have the knock-on effect of not severely impacting on the national debt. Glenavy was not impressed, and tritely responded that the state should borrow from the public. This resulted in increased foreign borrowing, and the state would ultimately borrow from its citizenry through increased indirect taxation.[100]

In early 1946, Aiken sought a new issue of exchequer bills from the Central Bank of up to £10m, and again entered into correspondence with the Irish Banks Standing Committee. He highlighted how emigrants would be returning to the State with the end of the Second World War and that this, together with demobilisation, brought with it an increased risk of debt. He expressed much anger about how the refusal of the banks to grant a discount on the bills was 'contrary to the welfare of the people'.[101]

As noted by Brennan in his memoirs, some concessions were made to Aiken during his time in office, and this was particularly the case regarding the proposed stock issue.[102] The Central Bank Board was opposed to Aiken's Finance (Miscellaneous Provisions) Act of 1945, which allowed for funds from An Post Savings Bank to be reinvested in the stock of local authorities. The Board went as far as to lodge a formal protest. Brennan was particularly annoyed that he was not consulted in advance about the scope of the proposed powers of An Post Savings Bank and the remit of advances of the local loans fund.[103] He recommended that the Act be amended for a more limited period. For his part, Aiken did not want private arrangements between the An Post Savings Bank and the local authorities. Subsequently, an agreement was reached over exchequer bills and the value of the rediscount rate.[104]

This initiative also attracted the interest of MacEntee, Aiken's Cabinet colleague, as it concerned his current and former departments. In a memorandum to McElligott, MacEntee wrote that he agreed that it was desirable to have a public stock issue rather than an expansion of bank credit through the suggested arrangements from the Bank of Ireland or Dublin Corporation. MacEntee's inflationary concerns would dissipate if the bank disposed of the whole or greater part of the credit subsequent to taking up the issue. However, he did not agree that the corporation loan would attract public interest.[105] McElligott, in response, was supportive of Aiken here against his former minister, who expressed some doubts about the enthusiasm of banks for investing in low-yielding corporation stock with the apparent certainty of a heavy capital loss. MacEntee continued to retain an interest in this quarry. On 9 October 1945 he queried the benefits of the scheme with the Department of Finance. He was concerned about the amount of borrowing proposed by the Bank of Ireland, and favoured the local loans bill, which was similar to that which already existed in Stormont. He recommended that local authorities be allowed only to borrow from the government, and only with State approval, and that the banks should make advances to the State for capital development at rates not less than those already existing in Britain.[106]

Aiken had established the local loans bill on 26 July 1945 upon coming to office, which provided for local authorities being able to borrow from a local loans fund, with the loans issued at a rate of interest at parity with Britain and linked directly with the credit of the British exchequer. The Minister for Finance acted as the underwriter over any public issue of stock by the council in the exercise of an option to redeem existing stock.[107] Thomas Joseph Barrington, of the Department of Local Government and Public Health, wrote to McElligott on 13 October 1945 stating that 'The Minister for Local Government and Public Health is not convinced that there is a need for provision by the state of cheap short term loans to councils to warrant extraordinary steps to provide them at rates as low as 2 percent'.[108] Barrington argued that there was a considerable cost involved, and the money would need to be either subsidised or borrowed by the State itself. In essence, Barrington wrote that a cheap money policy could result in a loss for the exchequer, and he argued that the issue could still be raised on the open market.[109] Subsequently, it was agreed that the true rate of interest should fall from 3.25 per cent to 2.75 per cent as per MacEntee's recommendations. If the stock issue were open to public subscription on terms not less favourable, the government would support the issue if required. Finally, the Minister for Finance agreed to consult with the Central Bank regarding cooperation with the commercial banks to ensure adequate capital for future such initiatives.[110] On 29 October 1945, the Irish Banks Standing Committee indicated to the Bank of Ireland that they would not intervene in it and that the scheme would be a public issue.[111] Their desire was to mitigate the inflationary effects of the stock issue. In November 1945 the banks confirmed to MacEntee that they would not be underwriting the stock issue. Rather, the government would.[112]

On 19 November 1945, the Department of Posts and Telegraphs also expressed some concerns. Aiken's proposal to lower the existing 2.5 per cent interest rate, which had been maintained since 1861, was the chief concern of the minister, Patrick J. Little. He intimated his worries, given how An Post Office Savings Bank had made a profit since its inception, about how it would be affected by a cheap money policy.[113] Little was not opposed, however, to the replacement of savings certificates through the issue. In December 1945, Aiken wrote to the Central Bank stating that he hoped they would assist in getting the commercial banks to ensure the availability of capital in sufficient volumes and at low interest rates (like in Britain) for capital development purposes by the State, local authorities and the semi-state bodies.[114] It was further agreed to allow a £2,333,333 loan be raised by Dublin Corporation at 2.75 per cent, redeemable in 1963–1983. This would be a public issue again to mitigate inflationary effects, and the banks would not act as the underwriter.[115]

Later that same month, Dublin Corporation wrote to criticise Aiken and the government over the terms of the scheme. The Corporation was angry that the short-term loan had an interest rate of 3 per cent per annum. Apparently, they could have secured these terms privately if they had accepted its own banker's offer to underwrite at 3 per cent to the public. This had been rejected by the government as contrary to the public interest. The Corporation said that they would hold the Ministers for Finance and the Minister for Local Government and Public Health up to public odium and criticise their perceived blunder on the issue.[116]

Compounding his distractions, Aiken was dragged into the Locke Tribunal, and would be called as a witness to testify to it. On 12 September 1947, Arthur Cox & Co. solicitors wrote to the Department of Finance on behalf of George Eindiguer, who was trying to acquire Locke's distillery County Westmeath, enquiring whether Aiken would grant permission under Emergency Powers (Finance) (No.7) Order 1941 for the transfer of shares to Eindiguer. Department of Finance officials said that Aiken had no objection to transfer, provided that payment was made in either US Dollars or Swiss Francs.[117] The allegations made by Fine Gael TD Oliver J. Flanagan chiefly focused on the alleged role of other ministers such as Seán Lemass and Gerald Boland. The tribunal had investigated allegations that Lemass and others had made financial gains from the sale of the distillery. The judges censured Flanagan for his testimony and declared that there was no evidence of corruption, regardless the perception persisted that the party elite had benefited through corruption.[118]

An Experiment or a New Departure?

In conclusion, Aiken's appointment as Minister for Finance in 1945 was a considerable surprise at the time. He was, however, no stranger to economics, and had ideas that he wanted to implement upon assuming office. He was clearly a devotee of the practical benefits of social credit policy, and would remain such throughout his life, as shown when he briefly replaced MacEntee in the 1950s, but there was little deviation in overall monetary policy throughout his tenure. This was particularly true in the case of banking policy, despite much rhetoric on the matter. This was a continuation of the policy of previous Fianna Fáil governments, which had shown deference to the banks in failing to adopt a significant shift in banking policy from that of their predecessors in office, Cumann na nGaedheal. Both the banks and the Department of Finance played their part in this, as their policies frequently went hand in hand to resist Aiken. Equally, Joseph Brennan and his successors in the Central Bank were consistent resistors of change. His department officials, the Central Bank and the commercial banks all had a collective interest in maintaining the status quo regarding monetary policy, and they frustrated Aiken's efforts to change it. However, this experience demonstrates both how intertwined officialdom and the banks were, and the special relationship that the commercial banks had with central government, before and after the creation of the Central Bank. Social credit and Hugh Dalton-like ideas would remain heretical concepts.

While it is overly simplistic to dismiss Aiken's period in office as entirely having a deflationary bent, it is for his budgetary policy that he is remembered, particularly the supplementary budget of 1947. Aiken's first budget contained a provision for a Transition Fund to act as a form of economic stimulus to the local economy, but it did not reach its targets. Despite attempting to assist in the development of the economy, particularly the development of natural resources, agriculture and through investment in infrastructure, Aiken became, in effect, a Minister for Austerity. Bread rationing had to be reintroduced due to harvest failure. In addition, the severe winter of 1946 and 1947 led to a fuel crisis that crippled industry and transport. Furthermore, the country was beset with severe industrial relations problems. Dissatisfaction about these economic issues, particularly the cost of living, would be the ultimate cause of the defeat of Fianna Fáil in the 1948 general election. In this respect, Aiken's time in Finance was an experiment. He was forced to react to events, as internal and external shocks to the economy derailed most of his initiatives. At the same time, he was trying to address a legacy issue, from O'Kelly's tenure in office, of tackling the public finances and reducing State expenditure while still favouring borrowing for capital projects in order to increase investment.

Problems of rising prices resulting from inflation would also result in the defeat of the government's successor in 1951. The first inter-party government had embraced John Maynard Keynes' state capital investment programme, but by 1951 there was a substantial balance of payments crisis, and attempts to correct it would have deflationary consequences. This apparent profligacy, and Fianna Fáil's re-election that year, led some senior figures in the party, such as Aiken, MacEntee and de Valera, to conclude that the people had expressed a desire for the restoration of stable non-coalition government and a return to the old policies of the previous Fianna Fáil governments instead of the irresponsible socialism of the coalition.[119] Upon returning to office, de Valera no longer retained the External Affairs portfolio and appointed Aiken in his stead. It has been suggested that, had de Valera appointed his son Vivion to that office, it would have been a direct continuance of de Valera-style foreign policy and would have enabled Aiken to remain in Finance.[120] However, a return to the days of pre-coalition budgetary policy required the return of Seán MacEntee to deliver the necessary conservative medicine.[121]

Fianna Fáil's victory in 1951 was illusory, however, as the party only gained one additional seat when compared to 1948. This was in Dublin, where, it has been argued, voters at that time backed Noel Browne and Fianna Fáil in opposition to the coalition's perceived surrender to the Catholic Church.[122] As a result, Lemass argued for a shift in party policy to appeal to these voters. This was ignored by de Valera, and the impact of MacEntee's budget in 1952 would see the party lose power again in 1954. On 12 August 1953, the Cabinet decided to create a National Development Fund 'to finance desirable projects of development of a public character', to be administered by the Department of Finance. The £5m in the fund was to be financed by the banks on the basis of a similar Treasury deposits receipts scheme to the one that ran in Britain during the Second World War. Lemass had initially insisted upon £20m or £30m, but there was resistance from the Department of Finance and Seán MacEntee. However, Lemass and Aiken were strong proponents of the fund, and won the support of de Valera. It was also Aiken who suggested the name.[123] Part of the fund was earmarked for spending in Gaeltacht areas, and was talked up during the Galway South by-election campaign that year.[124] The fund would operate until 31 March 1957.

In late summer 1953, MacEntee underwent tests for suspected cancer, which dulled his opposition to the operation of the National Development Fund.[125] Aiken acted as Minister for Finance at this time as well as holding his External Affairs portfolio. In September 1953, Aiken would again raise with McElligott, who was now the Governor of the Central Bank, his predilection for using interest rates to create a cheap money policy. On 30 September 1953, Ireland reduced interest rates by 0.25 per cent in response to Britain reducing her interest rate by 0.5 per cent, from 4 to 3.5 per cent.[126] It was not until the party's second significant period in opposition from 1954 to 1957 that Fianna Fáil realised that it needed to update its party organisational structures and develop new policies to appeal to the electorate. Chiefly, it was Lemass who took the lead in both tasks.[127] Based on his experiences from serving on the Fianna Fáil National Executive, Michael B. Yeats felt that Aiken was dismissive of criticism and of new ideas from within and without the organisation. Once, having made a policy suggestion to Aiken at a committee that he chaired, Aiken dismissed him, saying: 'tá tú óg' [you are young].[128] David Andrews commented that Aiken could be regarded as reserved, if not austere, and agreed that he felt that economic development should focus on agriculture first.[129]

It has been argued that the differences between Lemass and MacEntee over economics were not only apparent internally, but were known across parties. Gerard Sweetman quoted Aiken's economic views in the Dáil, when he was the Fine Gael Minister for Finance, to try and set him apart from his colleagues.[130] In 1956, when replying to emergency measures that the coalition government was enacting, Aiken gave a traditional protectionist response. In reply, the government sought to highlight known policy differences between Lemass and MacEntee.[131] Aiken was a traditionalist in terms of the way in which he wanted to develop the economy, having come from being an advocate of old-style Sinn Féin theory and Fianna Fáil protectionism, which would likely place him at opposite sides with economic modernisers. The party would take contradictory positions during the 1957 general election, with Aiken and MacEntee emphasizing that when they had left office in 1948, and again in 1954, the State's finances had been sound and its credit high. In their eyes, this had been destroyed by the coalition's inflationary policies. Lemass concentrated on blaming the outgoing coalition for causing the depression.[132] In office, post 1957, a new direction was taken with economic policy, which began when de Valera's Cabinet endorsed T. K. Whitaker's proposals for economic development, and which expanded under Lemass's time as Taoiseach. At this time, Aiken would embark on a distinct new departure by putting his own unique stamp on Irish foreign policy.

Notes

1   Brian Farrell, *Seán Lemass* (Dublin: Gill and Macmillan, 1983), 39.

2   See Paul Bew and Henry Patterson, *Seán Lemass and the Making of Modern Ireland 1945–66* (Dublin: Gill and Macmillan, 1982); Tom Garvin, *Judging Lemass, The Measure of the Man* (Dublin: Royal Irish Academy, 2009); and Bryce Evans, *Seán Lemass, Democratic Dictator* (Cork: The Collins Press, 2011).

3   Tom Feeney, *Seán MacEntee: A Political Life* (Dublin: Irish Academic Press, 2009).

4   Maurice Moynihan, *Currency and Central Banking in Ireland, 1922–60* (Dublin: Gill and Macmillan, 1975), 399.

5   Leon Ó Broin. *No Man's Man: A Biographical Memoir of Joseph Brennan* (Dublin: Institute of Public Administration, 1982), 153.

6   T. D. Williams, 'De Valera in Power', in F. MacManus (ed.), *The Years of the Great Test 1926–39* (Cork: Mercier Press, 1967), 40.

7   John Horgan, *Seán Lemass: The Enigmatic Patriot* (Dublin: Gill and Macmillan, 1997), 134. On this matter, Horgan gives a private source.

8   P. Lynch, 'The Irish Economy since the War 1946–51' in K. D. Nowlan and T. D. Williams (eds), *Ireland in the War Years and After 1939–51* (Dublin: Gill and Macmillan, 1969), 187.

9   Ronan Fanning, *The Irish Department of Finance, 1922–1958* (Dublin, 1977), 393.

10   D. R. O'Connor Lysaght, *The Republic of Ireland* (Dublin: Mercier Press, 1970), 140, and Richard Dunphy, *The Making of Fianna Fáil Power in Ireland 1923–48* (Oxford: Oxford University Press, 1995), 255.

11   Evans, *Seán Lemass*, 154.

12   D. Ó Beacháin, *Destiny of the Soldiers: Fianna Fáil, Irish Republicanism and the IRA, 1926–73* (Dublin: Gill and Macmillan, 2010), 387.

13   McCartan, TD in the first and second Dáils, had previously quit politics due to disillusionment. His candidacy was supported by the Labour Party and Clann na Talmhan Oireachtas members. He secured 19.6 per cent of the final vote. D. McCullagh, *A Makeshift Majority: The First Inter-Party Government 1948–51.* (Dublin: Institute of Public Administration, 1998), 16.

14   *Irish Independent*, 14 June, 1945.

15   *Irish Independent*, 20 June 1945.

16   *Cork Examiner*, 20 June, 1945.

17   Liam Skinner, *Politicians by Accident* (Dublin: Dublin Metropolitan, 1946), 174.

18   *Catholic Standard*, 14 Dec. 1945. See also University College Dublin Archives (UCDA), Frank Aiken Papers, P104/4393. It is possible that Aiken received this praise due to his studentship of social credit and interest in monetary reform. It is unclear what Aiken thought of this opinion, but given that he had been previously excommunicated, and in light of subsequent clashes with Catholic prelates, it may have been tongue in cheek.

19   Fanning, *The Irish Department of Finance, 1922–1958* (Dublin, 1977), 392.

20   UCDA, P104/676.

21   M. Cousins, *The Birth of Social Welfare in Ireland 1922–52* (Dublin: Four Courts Press, 2003), 107.

22   J. J. Lee, *Ireland 1912–1985; Politics & Society* (Cambridge: Cambridge University Press, 1989), 277.

23   Cousins, *The Birth of Social Welfare in Ireland 1922–52*, 121.

24   See UCDA, P104/3627.

25   Horgan, *Seán Lemass*, 126–127.

26   Cormac Ó Gráda, *A Rocky Road: The Irish Economy Since the 1920s* (Manchester: Manchester University Press 1997), 9.

27   C.S. Andrews, *Man of No Property* (Dublin: Mercier Press, 1982), 118–119.

28   Andrews, *Man of No Property*, 125.

29   Andrews, *Man of No Property*, 160–161.

30   Horgan, *Seán Lemass*, 353.

31   Moynihan, *Currency and Central Banking in Ireland, 1922–60*, 289. De Valera's views on economics are not, however, widely known.

32   Mary E. Daly, *Social and Economic History of Ireland* (Dublin: The Educational Company, 1981), 155.

33   Cousins, *The Birth of Social Welfare in Ireland 1922–1952* (Dublin: Four Courts Press, 2003), 84–85.

34   F. O'Driscoll, 'Social Catholicism and the Social Question in Independent Ireland: The Challenge to the Fiscal System', in N. Cronin and J.M. Regan (eds), *Ireland: The Politics of Independence 1922–49* (New York: St. Martin's Press, 2000), 133.

35   Fr. Edward Cahill, a Senior Jesuit; Bulmer Hobson, the former IRB figure and then civil servant and Mrs B. Berthon Waters, an economist, and member of the Labour Party.

36   Fanning, *The Irish Department of Finance, 1922–1958*, 392.

37   *The New York Times*, 11 April 2009. While dismissed as a crank in his day, four of his five principal theories have now become accepted into modern economic practice, including abandoning the gold standard, allowing exchange rates to float, the creation of a consumer price index and the use of surpluses and deficits as macroeconomic policy instruments to counter cyclical trends. He retains many admirers within the field of ecological economics.

38   See UCDA, P104/2958. Newsletter The Age of Plenty and Social Economist Review, Autumn 1932.

39   Douglas, C. H., *The Birmingham Debate* (The New Age Vol: LII(23), 1933); Janine Stingel, *Social Discredit, Anti-Semitism, Social Credit and the Jewish Response* (Montreal: McGill Queen's University Press, 2000), 13. It should be made clear that Aiken was never associated with these viewpoints, however.

40   Niamh Puirséil, *The Irish Labour Party 1922–1973* (Dublin: UCD Press, 2007), 85. Their programme advocated implementation of the second minority report of the Banking Commission, support for the Dignan Plan and elements of social credit theory. See also Bryce Evans, *Ireland during the Second World War: Farewell to Plato's Cave* (Manchester: Manchester University Press, 2014), for a comprehensive overview of the popularity of O'Rahilly's work *Money* (1942) during the Emergency.

41 Puirséil, *The Irish Labour Party 1922–1973*, 120–121.

42 MacDermott, *Clann Na Poblachta*, 61.

43 *The Irish Times*, 9 May 1946.

44 *The Irish Times*, 9 May 1946.

45 *Dundalk Examiner*, 11 May 1946.

46 The editor, O. B. McGahon, was a political opponent of Aiken's. Aiken had dismissed his father, the previous editor, as 'the scribbler of Earl Street'. See Matthew Potter, *A Century of Service: A History of the Association of Municipal Authorities of Ireland 1912–2012* (Nenagh: The Association of Municipal Authorities of Ireland, 2012), 249–250.

47 UCDA, P104/3853. See also *Dublin Evening Mail*, 13 May 1946.

48 McCaughey died on 11 May 1946.

49 *Irish Press*, 8 May 1946.

50 Dunphy, *The Making of Fianna Fáil Power in Ireland 1923–48*, 249. Aiken acceded to Lemass's request to abolish the excess corporation profits tax, for which the latter had long argued. Dunphy argues that Lemass believed that it would be used to reduce prices, but in fact the abolition proved to be an encouragement to excess profits and led to increased prices.

51 See UCDA, P104/3846. Budget Speech, 8 May 1946.

52 Agenda and Report of Budget Committee Meeting April 1946. UCDA, P104/3845.

53 *Irish Press*, 9 May 1946.

54 Skinner, *Politicians by Accident*, 176; *The Irish Times*, 9 May 1946.

55 Skinner, *Politicians by Accident*, 177–178.

56 F. S. L. Lyons, 'The Years of Adjustment 1945–51' in Nowlan and Williams (eds), *Ireland in the War Years and After 1939–51*, 68.

57 See UCDA, P104/4248. Confidential letter from Joseph Connolly to Frank Aiken re the difficulty of grain shortages.

58 *Irish Press*, 8 May 1947.

59 *Irish Independent*, 8 May 1947.

60 *Irish Independent*, 8 May 1947.

61 *The Irish Times*, 8 May 1947.

62 *Dundalk Democrat*, 10 May 1947.

63 *Dundalk Examiner*, 10 May 1947.

64 *Irish Independent*, 8 May 1947.

65 £2,200,000 was provided for bread and flour subsidies in this budget out of a total food subsidy budget of £4,636,000, including fertilisers. UCDA, P104/3855. Budget Speech 7 May 1947.

66 Lyons, 'The Years of Adjustment 1945–51', 68.

67 *Irish Press*, 9 May 1947.

68 See UCDA, P104/3855.

69 *Irish Press*, 3 May 1947.

70 UCDA, P104/3855.

71 UCDA, P104/3855.

72 UCDA, P104/4270.

73 UCDA, P104/4270.

74 Andrews, *Man of No Property*, 125.

75 *Irish Press*, 8 May 1947.

76   Kieran Kennedy and Brendan Dowling, *Economic Growth in Ireland: The Experience Since 1947* (Dublin: Gill and Macmillan, 1975), 200.

77   Kieran Allen, *Fianna Fáil and Irish Labour; 1926 to the Present* (London: Pluto Press, 1997), 88–93. The Irish Women Workers Union went on strike at the end of 1945. The next major dispute concerned 1,000 farm labourers who were members of the Workers Union of Ireland. The Irish National Teachers Organisation then began a national strike in March 1946. Workers in the flour mills were intent on beginning strike action in May 1947, which was prohibited through special powers that effectively banned strikes. Road and turf workers later began strike action for better pay that same year, and unskilled ESB workers in Roscommon, road workers in County Dublin, insurance staff in Irish Life and employees in the Dublin wholesale drug trade were among the varied groups to go out on strike. In September 1947, bus workers also went on strike. This encouraged the railwaymen to consider striking for better conditions, and shop stewards at the ESB also considered taking some form of joint action. Banking staff would begin strike action in 1947 also.

78   Moynihan, *Currency and Central Banking in Ireland, 1922–60*, 337.

79   *The Irish Times*, 17 Oct. 1947.

80   *Cork Examiner*, 16 Oct., 1947.

81   Also, customs duties on cosmetics were to be doubled, with an approximate yield of £35,000. Entertainment taxes in cinemas, dance halls, greyhound tracks and boxing matches were also to rise in January 1948, and were expected to raise an additional £150,000. Motor tax was also increased, but the way that this was levelled provoked comment as the chief burden fell on small and medium cars, which was expected to yield an additional £203,000. (Ibid.)

82   *Cork Examiner*, 17 October 1947.

83   UCDA, P104/3986. Letter to Éamon de Valera from Patrick Brady, Treasurer of Fianna Fáil party, 15 Dec. 1947.

84   UCDA, P104/3905. Letter from James Cadden to Aiken, 15 Jan. 1948.

85   Dunphy, *The Making of Fianna Fáil Power in Ireland 1923–48*, 172–173.

86   Hugh Dalton, the Labour Party Chancellor of the Exchequer, pursued a cheap money policy in Britain through the use of low interest rates. He ultimately had to resign from office after he gave some details of his 1947 budget speech to a journalist.

87   Fanning, *The Irish Department of Finance, 1922–1958*, 393.

88   Moynihan, *Currency and Central Banking in Ireland, 1922–60*, 324–325.

89   Ibid.

90   Ó Broin, *No Man's Man: A Biographical Memoir of Joseph Brennan*, 153.

91   Ó Gráda, *A Rocky Road: The Irish Economy Since the 1920s*, 175.

92   Ó Gráda, *A Rocky Road: The Irish Economy Since the 1920s*, 176.

93   UCDA, P104/2939. Connolly subsequently became a Director of the Central Bank himself.

94   Moynihan, *Currency and Central Banking in Ireland, 1922–60*, 292.

95   Dunphy, *The Making of Fianna Fáil Power in Ireland 1923–48*, 253.

96   J. J. McElligott to S. Hegan, Secretary Irish Banks Standing Committee, UCDA P104/3954.

97   Statements and Memoranda from the Department of Finance and the Central Bank Board re the Minister for Finance raising funds. UCDA, P104/3952.

98   Statements and Memoranda from Department of Finance and Central Bank Board re Minister for Finance raising funds, UCDA P104/3952, c. December 1945.

99   Moynihan, *Currency and Central Banking in Ireland, 1922–60*, 332–334.

100 Dunphy, *The Making of Fianna Fáil Power in Ireland 1923–48*, 256–257.

101 Aiken and McElligott letters to Irish Banks Standing Committee, Joseph Brennan, Governor Central Bank. UCDA, P104/3964.

102 Ó Broin, *No Man's Man: A Biographical Memoir of Joseph Brennan*, 153.

103 UCDA, P104/3945. Minutes from McElligott of a meeting between Central Bank Governor and Aiken re Finance (Miscellaneous Provisions) Bill, 11 Dec. 1945.

104 Moynihan, *Currency and Central Banking in Ireland, 1922–60*, 326–330.

105 UCDA, P104/3918. McElligott to Aiken re MacEntee's memo, 29 Nov. 1945.

106 UCDA, P104/3923. Memo from Department of Finance on proposed stock issue by Dublin Corporation, 9 Oct. 1945.

107 UCDA, P104/3915. Government Loans Bill, 26 July 1945.

108 UCDA, P104/3925. Memo from T.J. Barrington to J.J. McElligott re proposed stock issue by Dublin Corporation, 13 Oct. 1945.

109 UCDA, P104/3925. Memo from T.J. Barrington to J.J. McElligott re proposed stock issue by Dublin Corporation, 13 Oct. 1945.

110 P. O'Kennedy (Parliamentary Secretary to the Department of Finance) to the Private Secretary Minister of Finance. UCDA, P104/3929. 17 Oct. 1945.

111 S. Hegan, Secretary Irish Banks Standing Committee to Secretary Bank of Ireland. UCDA, P104/3932. 29 Oct. 1945.

112 P.J. Hernon, Dublin Corporation Manager to Secretary Department of Local Government and Public Health re letter from W. W. Foster, General Manager Bank of Ireland. UCDA, P104/3938. c. 13-16 Nov. 1945.

113 Memorandum from the Department of Posts and Telegraphs on 'Interest Rates on Saving Certificates and Post Office Savings Bank Deposits'. UCDA, P104/3941. 19 Nov. 1945.

114 Frank Aiken note to Central Bank, c. Dec. 1945. UCDA, P104/3947.

115 Department of Finance Memorandum Interest Rates on State and Local Authority Borrowings. UCDA, P104/3944. 1 Dec. 1945.

116 Dublin Corporation to Frank Aiken, c. 21 Dec. 1945. UCDA, P104/3953.

117 UCDA, P104/4294. Confidential Note from the Department of Justice re Locke's distillery, 27 Oct. 1947.

118 G. Kerrigan and P. Brennan *This Great Little Nation: The A–Z of Irish Scandals of Controversies* (Dublin: Gill and Macmillan, 1999), *190–191*.

119 Bew and Patterson, *Seán Lemass and the Making of Modern Ireland 1945–66*, 61.

120 Lee, *Ireland 1912–1985*, 322. Given Aiken's closeness to de Valera, he could have been seen as a natural successor to his chief's time in External Affairs.

121 Frank Pakenham (Earl of) Longford, and Thomas P. O'Neill, *Eamon de Valera* (Dublin: Houghton Mifflin, 1970), 439.

122 Lysaght O'Connor, *The Republic of Ireland*, 146.

123 See Daly, *Social and Economic History of Ireland*, 420; Fanning, *The Irish Department of Finance, 1922–1958*, 497; and Feeney, *Seán MacEntee*, 193.

124 Daly, *Social and Economic History of Ireland*, 416.

125 M. Mac an Tsaoi, *The Same Age as the State: The Official Biography of Máire Cruise O'Brien*. (Dublin: The O'Brien Press, 2003), 206.

126 Moynihan, *Currency and Central Banking in Ireland, 1922–60*, 408–409.

127 Horgan, *Seán Lemass*, 159.

128   M.B. Yeats, *Cast a Cold Eye: Memories of a Poet's Son and Politician* (Dublin: Blackwater Press, 1998), 49.

129   Interview with David Andrews, 20 Feb. 2013.

130   Bew and Patterson, *Seán Lemass and the Making of Modern Ireland 1945–66*, 91.

131   Bew and Patterson, *Seán Lemass and the Making of Modern Ireland 1945–66*, 94.

132   Bew and Patterson, *Seán Lemass and the Making of Modern Ireland 1945–66*, 103–104.

1. Aiken and his mother, in a Keogh Brothers portrait, 1901.

2. Aiken with a donkey foal on his shoulders, Inishere, Aran Islands, late 1920s.

3. Aiken with cigarette in mouth, beside windmill, c. 1937.

4. Air Corps shot of the Aiken home, Sandyford, Dublin, 1932.

5. Aiken and Maud outside the National Library of Ireland, Dublin, c.1932.

6. Aiken and Maud posing with bows and arrows, c.1932.

7. Aiken, the family, and their dog on a child's scooter, c. 1939.

8. Aiken, dozing off while reading, c.1940.

9. Frank and Maud on their wedding day, October 1934.

10. Aiken on the hustings, Dundalk, c. June 1943.

11. Aiken at a potato alcohol factory in Cooley, Co Louth, c. 1946.

12. Aiken and Éamon de Valera beside a concrete hut, c.1944.

13. Group portrait of Éamon de Valera and Frank Aiken, wearing garlands, standing with Martin Higgins by their aeroplane at John Rogers Airport, Honolulu, 25 April 1948.

14. Frank Aiken at Dublin airport before leaving to go to the UN General Assembly in New York, pictured with DFA officials Conor Cruise O'Brien, Counsellor, Political Section, Con Cremin, Secretary, Hugh McCann, Assistant Secretary, 1958.

15. Signing the nuclear non-proliferation treaty in Moscow, 1 July 1968.

16. Aiken, George Colley and Con Cremin at the UN, 1967.

17. Aiken looks on at Winston Churchill and Éamon de Valera, Downing Street, c.1955.

18. Aiken, Seán Lemass and John Foster Dulles, US Secretary of State, at the Lincoln Monument, Washington DC, c.1962.

CHAPTER SEVEN

From anti-partitionism to *realpolitik*? Frank Aiken, partition and Northern Ireland, 1948–1954

STEPHEN KELLY

Introduction

This chapter examines Frank Aiken's attitude to partition and Northern Ireland from 1948 to 1954. This was a period when Aiken moved from the continual usage of sterile anti-partitionist rhetoric to an acknowledgement – albeit reluctantly – that action and not words would deliver Fianna Fáil's purported Holy Grail: a united, all-Ireland, thirty-two-county republic. The study commences by examining Aiken's participation in the ill-fated Fianna Fáil-sponsored worldwide anti-partition campaign from 1948 to 1951 and his attitude to the British-inspired Ireland Act of 1949. It concludes by analysing Aiken's attitude to partition and Ulster Unionism during his first period as Minister for External Affairs from 1951 to 1954. Aiken is revealed as a politician who continually grappled with his past; a past consumed by a deeply held sense of injustice following the formal division of Ireland under the Government of Ireland Act in 1920, and the establishment of the State of Northern Ireland the following year.

Despite his deep-rooted political prejudices towards the Belfast and London governments, Aiken sought to confront the realities of the changed nature of North-South relations in the post-war era. In particular, he slowly came to realise that Ulster Unionists represented a formidable stumbling block in the national drive to end partition. The problem he faced, however, was his inability, excluding some improvements in cross-border economic cooperation, to formulate constructive policies that might entice Ulster Unionists into a united Ireland. Aiken, therefore, may be best described as holding a confused and at times contradictory attitude to partition in the years immediately following the Second World War.

It is not intended here to offer a full overview of Aiken's attitude to partition during the course of his political career; this is examined elsewhere.[1] Rather, this chapter presents a specific insight into Aiken's public and private attitude to the emotive subject of partition in the immediate post-war years. The historiography related to Aiken and partition is limited. Apart from this author's publication on the history of Fianna Fáil's Northern Ireland policy from 1926 to 1971, little has been produced. In general, the available literature is misleading, one-dimensional and rather biased. On the one hand, Aiken is accused of failing to pursue the partition question with any 'vigour', which could distinguish him from many of his Fianna Fáil colleagues.[2] On the other hand, however, writers have presented Aiken as a northern 'bigot', a politician consumed by his hatred for partition.[3] Henry Patterson, for example, describes Aiken as 'a bastion of traditional anti-partitionism …'.[4] Ronan Fanning explains that Aiken was omitted from the Irish delegation during the Anglo-Irish negotiations of 1938 because he was perceived as 'the most Anglophobic of de Valera's ministers'.[5]

This perception of Aiken as an anti-partitionist Anglophobe was certainly held, and indeed nurtured, by the London government. An anonymously authored British intelligence report, dated 1947, noted that Aiken's earlier career within the IRA greatly influenced his 'political prejudices'. Though now 'somewhat mellowed', he was reported to have 'always had a violent anti-British bias', to have believed in a German victory during the Second World War, and even to have 'probably hoped for it'.[6] Even on the eve of his ministerial retirement in 1968, a Whitehall memorandum claimed that because Aiken hailed from County Armagh, and was a Fianna Fáil TD for the border county of County Louth, this still 'embitters his outlook [on partition]'.[7] Indeed, writing in 1971, British Ambassador to Ireland Sir John Peck maintained that, due to Aiken's 'Northern background', he still felt 'strongly about partition'.[8]

It is unfair to portray Aiken simply as a one-dimensional anti-partitionist, devoid of political empathy. In fact, he sought to accommodate his own prejudices and political sensibilities to the changed post-war environment. Eunan O'Halpin best describes Aiken's views regarding Northern Ireland. Aiken, he writes, was 'fatalistic rather than fanatical about partition'.[9] This chapter concurs with O'Halpin's observations. It contends that, while Aiken always remained an outspoken critic of partition, his attitude during the early to mid-1950s demonstrated his genuine commitment to seeking a solution to this perennial question. The problem Aiken faced, however, was that he found it almost impossible to translate his willingness to find a solution to partition into any practical policies that either the Belfast or London governments might possibly consider.

Aiken and anti-partitionism: The Fianna Fáil worldwide anti-partition campaign, 1948–1951

Following the conclusion of the Second World War, Éamon de Valera stipulated that a worldwide anti-partition campaign would constitute a central plank of Fianna Fáil's official post-war partition policy.[10] Why did de Valera make this policy decision? In the post-war climate, partition represented a conundrum for Fianna Fáil. Due to Irish neutrality during the war, Northern Ireland's participation in the war effort, and the strategic importance of the island in the event of a future war, both Britain and America – not to mention Ulster Unionists – categorically rejected the prospect of a united Ireland.

Therefore, having previously admitted that he was unable to offer an immediate solution to partition,[11] de Valera instead maintained that a Fianna Fáil government offered the best chance, when the 'circumstances arose', of securing Irish unity.[12] Propaganda, therefore, became Fianna Fáil's last resort. Relegated to the opposition benches following Fianna Fáil's defeat at the 1948 general election, de Valera, working alongside his confidant Aiken, finally decided to undertake Fianna Fáil's anti-partition worldwide campaign. Never before, or after, did Fianna Fáil place such importance on the employment of anti-partition propaganda.

In March 1948, de Valera and Aiken commenced the first stage of the tour. Over the subsequent nine months, hardly spending a day away from one another, the two political colleagues travelled approximately 50,000 miles, visiting America, Australia, New Zealand, India, Great Britain and Northern Ireland. The first stop of their anti-partition campaign was America, the country of de Valera's birth. De Valera and Aiken arrived in New York on 4 March 1948. The Irish delegation received a warm welcome from the Irish-American community. Frank Gallagher, Director of the Irish Government Information Bureau from 1939 to 1948, recalled that a parade through New York's main thoroughfares in honour of de Valera and Aiken was the biggest seen since the end of the Second World War.[13] Writing to his wife Maud, who remained in Ireland, Aiken enthusiastically captured the welcome they received, the 'like of which was never before seen'.[14]

Over the course of three weeks, de Valera and Aiken travelled 10,000 miles, visiting Boston, Chicago, Detroit, Los Angeles, Oklahoma, San Francisco and Philadelphia. Gallagher recalled that half a million people marched in Boston to welcome the Irish delegation.[15] In San Francisco, Gallagher reminisced that 1,000 horsemen were present at the welcoming procession to greet de Valera and Aiken upon their arrival.[16] The campaign in America highlighted that anti-partition propaganda had now become more important than ever for Fianna Fáil. The tour, as Aiken noted, was the ideal opportunity to propagate the anti-partitionist orthodoxy that laid claim to Northern Ireland as the stolen six-counties of Ireland.[17] De Valera's speeches in America had four dominant themes: that the partition of Ireland was illegal and a 'crime';[18] that the British government should make a declaration in support of Irish unity;[19] that there was a need for a federal solution to end partition;[20] and that the Ulster Unionist government of Northern Ireland was illegitimate.[21]

During their time in America, Aiken acted as de Valera's right-hand man. Writing once more to Maud on 7 March 1948 from New York, Aiken noted that he was having 'a lovely trip'. 'I did not say very much', he wrote, 'but the Chief did'.[22] This was characteristic of Aiken's time abroad. De Valera, not Aiken, represented the public face of the anti-partition campaign. Aiken refrained from delivering speeches, and was instead content to work tirelessly behind the scenes. He was responsible for logistical issues, planning the itinerary, arranging appointment after appointment and always on hand, as he phrased it, to distribute to assembled pressmen 'leaflets containing a map showing the original four provinces of Ireland and with Northern Ireland divided from the remainder of the country by a red line'.[23] Indeed, in a genial letter to Maud, de Valera admitted that while he was the 'gentleman' of the anti-partition tour, 'poor Frank ... has to listen to my speeches hours on end'. Humorously, de Valera noted that Aiken 'should get some cotton wool for his ears'. 'He braves it politely', de Valera wrote, 'I hope his purgatory, if he deserves any, will be shortened in proportion to the length of the speeches he has to put up with'.[24]

Politically, the Fianna Fáil delegation's trip to America was a failure. The Dominions Office in London, which kept a file on de Valera's American speeches, reported that 'Mr de Valera's United States tour had little effect in influencing general United States opinion on the Irish partition issue'.[25] The Commonwealth

Office recorded that 'Irish politics seemed to have ceased to be an issue of the moment to the mass of Americans'.[26] Most revealing was the verdict of the Director of the US State Department's Office of European Affairs, Jack Hickerson. Hickerson informed the newly appointed American Minister to Ireland, George Garrett, that America's attitude towards Ireland in the light of recent world events was 'that any interference on our part in the issue [of partition] would, of course, be construed as an affront to the United Kingdom'.[27]

From America, in late April 1948, de Valera and Aiken commenced the next leg of their anti-partition journey, where over several weeks they visited Australia and New Zealand. On the invitation of Reverend Daniel Mannix, Archbishop of Melbourne and former President of St Patrick's College, Maynooth, de Valera and Aiken arrived in Sydney on 28 April. From Australia, on 24 May, they travelled to New Zealand, where he had a two-hour meeting in Wellington with New Zealand Prime Minister, Peter Fraser.[28]

Despite Aiken's description of the southern hemisphere anti-partition tour as a 'magnificent' success, the campaign was not well received by the vast majority of either Australians or New Zealanders.[29] In truth, the campaign in the southern hemisphere was a flop. Irish Minister Plenipotentiary to Australia, Thomas J. Kiernan, reported that the Australian people seemed little interested.[30] The High Commissioner for the United Kingdom in New Zealand, Patrick Duffy, recorded that de Valera's visit had caused Fraser 'some embarrassment'.[31] He said that during a meeting between de Valera, Aiken and the New Zealand Cabinet, the latter felt that they were 'being lectured' by the Irish delegation, particularly by Aiken.[32]

The main issue of contention for many Australians and New Zealanders was Ireland's decision to remain neutral during the Second World War. According to reports from British officials in Australia, the presence of de Valera and Aiken 'provided evidence of little sympathy for Éire's attitude during the war ...'.[33] On several occasions, de Valera was forced to defend Ireland's policy of neutrality. He reminded his audiences that 'until Ireland had complete independence, it would be strange to ask her to join a crusade to gain independence for other countries'.[34] He asked: 'why should Ireland enter a war in which she would not be able to defend herself?'[35] His arguments, however, were not sympathetically received by his hosts. This was not surprising, considering that over one million Australians and approximately 200,000 New Zealanders had fought as part of the Commonwealth forces during the Second World War.

From Australia, de Valera and Aiken arrived at the next destination of their anti-partition propaganda campaign, Calcutta, India, on 14 June 1948. Unlike the guarded reception that the Irish delegation had received from the American,

Australian and New Zealand governments, their arrival was warmly welcomed by the Indian government. Aiken reported that, upon first arriving in Calcutta, 'we were met by a huge crowd who nearly tore Mr. de Valera to pieces'.[36] On their first night in Calcutta, de Valera and Aiken dined with the Governor of Bengal, Chakravarthi Rajagopalachari.[37] This reception was followed later in the day with a meeting with the Indian Prime Minister, Jawaharlal Nehru.[38] De Valera had a 'long chat' with Nehru, and the Irish delegation enjoyed a meal at the prime minister's home.[39] Writing to Maud, Aiken explained that Nehru and de Valera exchanged prison experiences.[40] Privately, Nehru expressed to de Valera his 'deep sympathy' for the partition of Ireland, and remarked that he saw Ireland as an ally to India in her quest for independence from Britain.[41] The following day, on 15 June, de Valera and Aiken travelled to Delhi, where they lunched with the Governor General of India, Lord Louis Mountbatten. This was one of the Viceroy's last official functions in his capacity as Governor General, as he was succeeded the following week by Rajagopalachari.[42] Indeed, Aiken recalled that on their arrival Lord and Lady Mountbatten were in the process of 'packing up to leave and we had the interesting experience of being the last guests of the British regime'.[43]

Following five months' respite back in Ireland, in October 1948, de Valera and Aiken commenced the final leg of their worldwide anti-partition campaign. Accepting an invitation from the Anti-Partition of Ireland League of Great Britain, between October 1948 and February 1949 the Irish delegation travelled throughout Britain, visiting a series of centres of the Irish diaspora. In a letter dated late September 1948, Aiken reflected positively on the forthcoming anti-partition campaign to Britain. 'I feel', he wrote, 'that these meetings will do a great deal to bring home to the British people the disaster … in maintaining partition'.[44] In separate correspondence during this period he explained that he had 'great hopes that these meetings will bring home to the British people the foolishness of maintaining the Tory crime of Partition in the present state of world affairs …'.[45]

De Valera and Aiken opened their campaign at a monster meeting in Liverpool, and over the subsequent weeks attended similar anti-partition rallies in Glasgow, Cardiff, Cambridge and Manchester. After a break for Christmas, in February 1949, they travelled to Birmingham, Newcastle, London and Sheffield.[46] In contrast to his time in America and the southern hemisphere, in both Britain and Ireland Aiken regularly spoke out against partition. Indeed, his speeches during this period were notable for their attack on the maintenance of partition and Ulster Unionism. The Northern Ireland government, Aiken told the Dáil in July 1948, had maintained an intensive 'pro-partition propaganda' campaign to defeat Irish nationalists' legitimate rights for Irish unity.[47] Aiken decried the continued division of Ireland during a speech at his home town of Camlough, County Armagh, in February 1949, referring to it as a 'disastrous division'. The British government, he said, 'deny by the force of arms' the unity of Ireland. The present dominance of Ulster Unionism in the north, he continued, is 'based on gerrymandering constituencies and an out-of-date register …'.[48] The following month, in March 1949, Aiken again accused the Ulster Unionist government of keeping 'your party in power' by the threat of physical force and the use of the B-Specials, or, as Aiken described them, 'the "B" men'.[49]

Such attacks by Aiken against Ulster Unionism, during the height of the anti-partition campaign, revealed the naiveté of Fianna Fáil's attitude to partition. By waging a propaganda offensive against Ulster Unionists, Aiken was attacking the very people whose support was required to achieve Irish unity. This bold expression of anti-partitionism merely helped to propagate the notion that unionism and Irishness were incompatible – that there could only be one or the other. Seán Ó Faoláin, writing several years earlier in 1941, recorded that this form of nationalist, anti-partitionist thinking had only consolidated rather than helped to end partition. 'The problem', he wrote, was not 'primarily the problem of partition'. Instead, he argued that 'it calls not so much for the destruction of the political Border so much as for a mental Barrier'.[50]

Both Aiken and de Valera were victims of this 'mental Barrier'. Speaking in 1947, de Valera had acknowledged that the support of Ulster Unionists was required if partition was to be undone.[51] This was a point that Aiken, albeit reluctantly, also acknowledged.[52] Indeed, Aiken's outcries against the partition of Ireland were usually qualified by a realisation that Irish unity was a long-term aspiration rather than a short-term objective. 'No one who appreciates the situation', he admitted in February 1949, 'will promise a speedy end to partition'.[53] Aiken, however, failed to realise that the two sides of Fianna Fáil's partition policy contradicted one another. On the one hand, the Fianna Fáil leadership sought to build a relationship of goodwill, which it hoped could persuade 300,000 Ulster Unionists to agree to a united Ireland. On the other, the Fianna Fáil-sponsored worldwide anti-partition campaign wished to expose the 'evils of partition' and reveal the extent to which Ulster Unionists discriminated against the Catholics of Northern Ireland.

Moreover, Aiken (like the vast majority of senior Fianna Fáil members) failed – or simply chose not to acknowledge – that Northern Ireland's integration into the British welfare state at the end of the Second World War had further strengthened the Ulster Unionists' case against entering a united Ireland. While Aiken opportunistically claimed that if Ulster Unionists agreed to a united Ireland then they 'could have far higher social services for the same of less [*sic*] taxation in a united Ireland than they had to-day', the reality was altogether different.[54] Compared to citizens south of the border, the people of Northern Ireland were enjoying a comprehensive health service and increased sickness and pension benefits.[55] The weak Irish economy was further evidence to Ulster Unionists for rejecting any calls from Dublin for Irish unity. In reality, the economic protectionism of Fianna Fáil governments since the 1930s appealed little to Ulster Unionists. Northern Ireland's industrialised economy, which witnessed a boom during the war years, and which depended heavily on export markets, could not be sustained in a protectionist all-Ireland market.

One point, however, must be recorded. Although a vocal critic of partition during Fianna Fáil's years in the political wilderness from 1948 to 1951, Aiken routinely spoke of his opposition to the use of physical force to achieve a united Ireland. Similar to de Valera, Aiken warned against the 'use of guns' to deliver Irish unity.[56] The uptake of armed revolt to secure the political aspirations of Irish nationalists, Aiken informed the Dáil on 2 March 1949, 'would only end in disaster'.[57] Several days later, in an open letter to Northern Ireland Prime Minister Sir Basil Brooke, Aiken noted that he had no intention in pursuing 'force' to achieve his political goal of a united Ireland. Rather, he hoped that 'the border will have melted away peacefully'.[58] Importantly, throughout his political career, Aiken routinely maintained that the Irish people had a 'moral right' to use force to end partition;[59] an argument de Valera had habitually employed since the early 1920s.[60] During Fianna Fáil's early years of existence, Aiken believed that if peaceful methods failed, Irish nationalists had a legitimate right to take up arms to secure Irish unity.[61] By the early 1930s, however, Aiken qualified this argument, maintaining that he opposed the 'force of arms' if 'better means were available'.[62] Although he was 'not a pacifist', by this juncture of his political career Aiken claimed that the use of physical force was impractical and thus unlikely to succeed.[63] In making this subtle but important transition, Aiken adhered to de Valera's traditional objection to the use of force on the grounds that it was unlikely to succeed.[64] In particular, Britain's military superiority, as glaringly revealed during the Second World War, convinced both Aiken and de Valera of the futility of the use of armed insurrection.

Despite their objections to the use of force, neither Aiken nor de Valera recognised (or simply chose not to admit) that their anti-partition propaganda campaign and aggressive speeches had helped to encourage violence. Seán MacEntee, a senior member of Fianna Fáil, later recalled that harsh anti-partition speeches, such as those made by Aiken, merely drove some young people into taking their own 'unauthorised and unguided action'. MacEntee said that he always urged the Fianna Fáil leadership to 'stay away from the North. It is the only way'.[65]

During the Fianna Fáil-sponsored anti-partition campaign, both at home and abroad, Aiken's partition speeches were noticeably different from those delivered by de Valera on one distinctive point. In what became a hallmark of Aiken's stance on partition as Minister for External Affairs during the 1950s and 1960s, he routinely vilified the division of Ireland from an international comparative perspective. 'As far as we Irishmen are concerned', Aiken explained in a speech in February 1949, 'we shall continue until victory comes to assert the right for our own country which Britain denies to us, but which she advocates for Greeks and Czechs, and Hungarians – the right to have a democratically elected Government ...'.[66]

Addressing a gathering in Newtownbutler, County Fermanagh, in July 1953, Aiken compared Ireland's division to the continued partition of Germany. 'The principles and the considerations which demanded that Germany should be re-united under a government freely elected by all her people ...', he said, was 'equally demanded' by the people of Ireland.[67] Indeed, Aiken regularly used the comparison of a divided Germany and Ireland as a reason for maintaining Irish neutrality. Speaking in February 1953, for example, he explained that in the event of the outbreak of war, Irish policy would first focus on fighting for a united Ireland before fighting for the freedom of others. It would be a 'bit thick', he said, 'that a partitioned Ireland should be forced to join in a war to reunite Germany'.[68]

Overall, the anti-partition campaign abroad represented something of a waste of time and of resources. Apart from the diplomatic success of the Irish mission to India, there was little political appetite abroad for the campaign, particularly in America, Australia and New Zealand. While Aiken publicly claimed that Fianna Fáil must 'avoid stunts, political or otherwise, in connection with Partition ...', this was precisely how the campaign was perceived by both the international community and the Irish population at home.[69] If the Fianna Fáil delegation's trip to America and the southern hemisphere had not been a success in propaganda terms, their campaign in Britain was doubly difficult. Ironically, it was possibly the previous Fianna Fáil government's greatest achievement – securing and maintaining Irish neutrality during the Second World War – that had altered the circumstances so drastically. De Valera, Aiken and their fellow 'soldiers of destiny' failed to grasp that, due to Ireland's neutrality and the strategic importance of the island in the event of a future war, Britain, and indeed America, would not permit a united Ireland. Simply put, in the eyes of the world, Ireland's splendid isolation meant her continued division.

Aiken, the repeal of the External Relations Act and the Ireland Act

In September 1948, during a State visit to Canada, Taoiseach John A. Costello confirmed reports that the government intended to repeal the External Relations Act, and that Ireland would be leaving the Commonwealth.[70] Costello, Seán MacBride and William Norton, leading figures in the main coalition parties, Fine Gael, Clann na Poblachta and Labour, had all been bitter opponents of the External Relations Act passed by the Fianna Fáil government in 1936. Costello was determined to repeal the Act, and informed his Fianna Fáil political opponents that the inter-party government intended to withdraw from the Commonwealth and to introduce the 'Republic of Ireland Act' in its place.[71]

Aiken was bitterly opposed to the repeal of the Act. Like de Valera, he was pessimistic about the benefits of such a move, having always justified Ireland's tenuous link with the Commonwealth, through the External Relations Act, on the grounds that the Act was necessary 'bait' for Ulster Unionists.[72] Addressing the Dáil in November 1948, Aiken argued that it was 'not necessary to pass an Act of Parliament to describe the republic as a republic'.[73] In protest, Aiken and his Fianna Fáil Party refused to participate in national celebrations organised on behalf of the inter-party government to mark the coming into operation of the Republic of Ireland Act, scheduled for Easter Monday, 18 April 1949.

Speaking in the Dáil in early December 1948, Aiken rejected an amendment that 'the date on which the Bill would come into operation should be named Independence Day'.[74] Aiken also snubbed a proposal that the day the Act came into operation should be a public holiday.[75] He had strong feelings against celebrating any political or constitutional event short of the full reunification of the whole island as a republic. The very use of the name 'Republic' agitated Aiken, as he felt that the term was sacred, and could only be used when the entire island of Ireland was united. However, Aiken must accept part of the responsibility for the Irish government's decision to repeal the Act and remove Ireland from the Commonwealth. The Fianna Fáil-sponsored anti-partition propaganda campaign forced the hand of the inter-party government, prompting them to play the 'green card'. As British Representative to Ireland, 1939-1949, Lord Rugby (formerly Sir John Maffey) pointed out to the London government, 'each party must now outdo its rivals in a passionate crusade for Irish unity'.[76]

The repeal of the Act had major consequences for Fianna Fáil's partition policy. The introduction of the Republic of Ireland Act, together with the anti-partition campaign, witnessed intense lobbying of Whitehall from within Ulster Unionist circles for the introduction of counter legislation. The Dublin government's establishment of the All Party Anti-Partition Committee in January 1949, consisting of the four major political parties, Fine Gael, Labour, Clann na Poblachta and Fianna Fáil (Aiken, de Valera and Cavan TD Patrick Smith represented Fianna Fáil on the committee), further exasperated relations between Dublin and Belfast.[77] Northern Ireland Prime Minister Sir Basil Brooke was incensed by the committee's organisation of a campaign fund outside local churches in support of Northern Nationalist anti-partitionist candidates in the Northern Ireland general election set for 10 February 1949.[78]

In private correspondence with Brooke, British Prime Minister Clement Attlee explained that because of Irish 'aggression' in the context of Dublin's anti-partition campaign and the Republic of Ireland Act, he was fully prepared 'to make it clear' that the British government condemned Ireland's interference in Northern Ireland's affairs.[79] Attlee was particularly unhappy about Fianna Fáil's 'intensified' anti-partition campaign in Britain and America, believing that such escapades merely embittered Dublin's relationship with London and Belfast. He found it 'ludicrous' to suggest that 'if the anti-partitionists had their way and Northern Ireland were made part of the Irish Republic, there would be a united Ireland'.[80]

Consequently, the inter-party government's decision to repeal the External Relations Act compelled a reluctant Labour administration in Britain to introduce counter legislation. On 3 May 1949, the British government formally announced, under the title 'The Ireland Act':

> That Northern Ireland remains part of His Majesty's dominions and of the United Kingdom ... that in no event will Northern Ireland ... cease to be part of His Majesty's dominions and of the United Kingdom without the consent of parliament of Northern Ireland.[81]

The doctrine of consent, which was enshrined within the Act, reassured Northern Ireland's constitutional position within the United Kingdom. Most significantly, the Act effectively witnessed the passing of the veto of Irish unity from London to the custody of the Ulster Unionists.

On hearing of London's decision, Aiken was furious. Speaking in the Dáil in mid-May 1949, he described its introduction as a British conspiracy against

Irish nationalists' legitimate rights to a united Ireland. 'Whatever clauses the British now wrote into their Acts of Parliament purporting to bind any portion of Ireland to Great Britain', he said, 'would, with the help of God … go the way of hundreds of other "Ireland Acts" passed in London during the last seven centuries'.[82] Writing privately to Attlee, Aiken passionately compared Britain's justification for a partitioned Ireland to Adolf Hitler's rationale for invading 'Sudetenland, Czechoslovakia, Austria and Poland'. The British maintenance of partition, he wrote, 'undermined the morale' of not merely Irishmen and women, but of all 'Europeans'.[83]

The impact that the Ireland Act had for partition was dramatic. The introduction of the Act forced Aiken to acknowledge that his use of propaganda to help end partition had proved futile. Not since the introduction of the Government of Ireland Act in 1920 had partition been so resolutely confirmed. From this moment onwards, arguably as never before, Aiken and the Fianna Fáil hierarchy were forced to concede that the ending of partition was a long-term aspiration rather than a medium-term objective.

It is, therefore, no coincidence that by 1950 the Fianna Fáil leadership abandoned its anti-partition propaganda campaign. On visits to Birmingham, Cardiff and Newry in the early months of 1950, de Valera did not speak of partition.[84] Similarly, during visits to France, Switzerland, Italy, Greece and Israel in April 1950, once again he decided not to mention partition in any of his speeches.[85] In Ireland Aiken was, likewise, reluctant to bang the anti-partitionist drum. Addressing a crowd of over 7,000 people in Lisnaskea, County Fermanagh, in February 1950, he was noticeably conciliatory towards Ulster Unionists. Instead of placing the responsibility for partition in the hands of northern Protestants, he spoke of how 'England had deceived' the people in the Six Counties. 'It was not Protestants who had set up partition', he explained. Rather, partition had 'been thought of by the British in their own interests …'.[86]

On the eve of Fianna Fáil's return to government in the summer of 1951, Aiken realised (albeit reluctantly) that the use of propaganda to preach the injustice of partition was a policy of futility. As Aldous Huxley poetically noted: 'the propagandist is a man who canalises an already existing stream. In a land where there is no water, he digs in vain'.[87] Aiken now came to terms with the fact that he had been digging in vain. He had learned the valuable lesson that propaganda only offered superficial success. As is explained below, he therefore acknowledged that the 'sore-thumb'[88] approach of stressing the injustice and crime of a partitioned Ireland had run its course.

From anti-partitionism to *realpolitik*? Aiken and Dublin–Belfast cooperation, 1951–1954

As we have learned in the Introduction to this book, and despite some raised eyebrows, on his return to government in June 1951, Aiken was appointed to the prestigious portfolio of Minister for External Affairs. Importantly, de Valera trusted Aiken to follow his line on partition. He was one of de Valera's 'closest friends',[89] and as a Central Intelligence Agency (CIA) report noted in 1949, was 'politically devoted' to 'his Chief'.[90] Indeed, writing in 1952, Lord Pakenham recalled 'I gained the impression that [the minds of] both Mr de Valera and Mr Aiken … clearly work in close harmony'.[91]

On securing his new ministerial portfolio, Aiken recorded that ending partition and securing a united Ireland would dominate the Irish government's 'external policy' in the field of international relations.[92] He routinely demanded an end to partition, and emphasised Britain's responsibility towards securing this goal.[93] For example, addressing a gathering at Castleblaney, County Monaghan, in April 1954, Aiken declared that Fianna Fáil had 'succeeded in getting rid of the British bag and baggage out of the 26 Counties and he had no doubt that, with the help of God, the Irish people would get rid of them bag and baggage out of the remaining Six Counties'.[94]

Aiken, however, was to find this self-appointed mission an arduous task, not least because of London's antipathy towards Dublin's overtures. In his rare meetings with British government ministers, Aiken spoke of securing an end to partition in the context of the impending threat of a third world war; a nuclear war that, he predicted, could destroy humanity.[95] During a meeting with the Secretary for Commonwealth Relations, Sir Patrick Gordon-Walker, in July 1951, Aiken warned of a possible Russian invasion of Ireland in the immediate future and requested that London make a statement 'to the effect that it was a British interest that Partition should come to an end'.[96] His protests, nonetheless, were continually ignored.

Consequently – and uninspiringly – Aiken decided to return to two central tenets of Fianna Fáil's traditional attitude to Irish unity. Firstly, that London should make a declaration in support of Irish unity, and secondly that the best method to secure an end to partition was a federal agreement between Dublin and Belfast.[97] Aiken and his Cabinet colleagues were to be disappointed. Within weeks of entering government, Fianna Fáil's wish to secure a declaration in favour of Irish unity and the government's offer of a federal agreement was rejected by London. When Aiken attempted to raise the issue of partition with London he was greeted by a wall of silence.[98] British politicians now disliked 'having to touch it [partition]'.[99] There was reluctance in London even to meet

Aiken, knowing that they would inevitably be greeted with 'the familiar text of partition'.[100]

Aiken's plight, and that of his Fianna Fáil government, was further exasperated following the arrival of a Conservative-led administration in October 1951. Irish Ambassador in London Freddie Boland noted that the Conservative government did not wish to 'touch partition'.[101] For example, in February 1952, during a rare meeting between Aiken and the recently appointed Secretary of State for Commonwealth Relations, Lord Ismay, the latter informed an infuriated Aiken that partition could not be discussed by 'minnows like himself [Lord Ismay]'.[102]

London's unwillingness to maintain a debate on partition forced the Fianna Fáil government to initiate a new partition policy that sought to 'let the temperature drop', as noted by Seán Nunan of the Department of External Affairs.[103] Except for Aiken's outbursts and frustration over the Coronation Oath and the official title of Queen Elizabeth II (the first British monarch to specifically use the term 'Northern Ireland' in her title), during this period his tone was notably conciliatory.[104] Aiken came to realise that the continual stressing of the division of Ireland, as espoused by his predecessor in the Department of External Affairs Seán MacBride, had run out of steam.

Henceforth, as Aiken outlined in October 1952, the Fianna Fáil government's policy was directed towards letting 'the temperature drop to a point at which Partition could be ended on the basis of reason and goodwill'.[105] Privately, Aiken routinely admitted that the Fianna Fáil government could 'not expect any immediate spectacular results' on partition.[106] Given London's refusal to sustain a debate on Irish unity, Fianna Fáil's attention therefore turned towards Belfast and Ulster Unionists: this was to mark a significant shift in policy. Aiken, together with the vast majority of his Cabinet colleagues, now moved away from a policy of supposing that partition existed merely by the virtue of the political, economic and military power of the British government. Aiken recognised, reluctantly, that Fianna Fáil could no longer ignore Ulster Unionists' opposition to Irish unity. The advancement of cross-border economic cooperation between north and south was Fianna Fáil's desired new approach to the thorny partition question.

Dublin's sudden shift in emphasis from London to Belfast marked an important cornerstone of Aiken's approach to partition in the early 1950s. Guided by a policy of persuasion, specifically on issues of cross-border economic cooperation, he tried to reassure Ulster Unionists of the benefits of an economically and politically unified Ireland. Under the personal guidance of de Valera and Aiken, Fianna Fáil targeted three areas of cross-border cooperation of particular importance: the Great Northern Railway (GNR), the Erne Hydro-Electric Scheme and the Foyle Fisheries.

Unlike the previous inter-party government's anti-partitionist policy towards Ulster Unionism, the new Fianna Fáil administration followed a more pragmatic and persuasive partition policy. The 'whole aim of Fianna Fáil's approach', as recorded by Freddie Boland in discussions with Lord Pakenham in late 1951, was to 'bring about the political circumstances and the climate of opinion, which would make the ending of partition easier and more feasible'.[107] This was to be achieved, he explained, by 'direct dealings with Dublin and Belfast in connection with the Erne development, Foyle Fisheries and the Great Northern Railway'.[108]

The Fianna Fáil government's willingness to work side by side with Ulster Unionists on issues of mutual cross-border concern showed that Dublin was eager to engage openly with the Northern Ireland government for the first time since the December 1925 London Agreement, which was signed in the aftermath of the Boundary Commission Agreement fiasco. Nonetheless, the Fianna Fáil government's new policy of persuasion was fraught with numerous difficulties, not least because Ulster Unionists viewed the initiative with scepticism.

There was a belief within Fianna Fáil that if the Dublin government offered Ulster Unionists economic concessions on north–south cooperation, Belfast would simply agree to a united Ireland. Aiken was himself a victim of this misconception. In July 1953, for example, he publicly said that the recent uptake in cross-border cooperation between Dublin and Belfast, coupled with the 'logic of geography', meant that it was 'reasonably easy' to envisage the union of Ireland.[109] Indeed, Aiken's pronouncements during this period that the 'political re-union' of Ireland would inevitably witness the end of sectarian and 'unchristian and destructive religious antagonism', merely confirmed his naivety towards Ulster Unionism.[110]

Aiken was, therefore, willing to concede that the support of Ulster Unionists was required to secure an end to partition. Yet, this concession was always half-hearted. Aiken was unable to acknowledge that Ulster Unionists held the veto on Irish unity, and that only with their consent could partition be ended. Writing privately to Miss Alexandria Howson in August 1953, Aiken could not hide his deep-rooted convictions. 'The Six County Administration', he snappily wrote, 'is subsidised by the British taxpayer'. Northern Ireland, he concluded, 'is based on the antagonism so fermented'.[111]

Indeed, Aiken's public support on behalf of the Irish government in 1953 for the 'Fogarty Resolution' confirmed his engrained opposition to the argument that Ulster Unionists were constitutionally entitled to reject Irish unity. After years of tireless work, under the auspices of the American League for an Undivided Ireland, American Congressman John E. Fogarty managed to secure the safe passage of a resolution through the Foreign Affairs Committee of the United States Senate. The Fogarty Resolution demanded that Ireland should have the right 'in the maintenance of international peace and security' to be permitted to settle the question of the reunification of her territory through a free plebiscite of all the people of Ireland.[112]

Such a plebiscite, Aiken argued, 'would reveal a majority in favour of Irish unity of at least 4 to 1'. 'It is only the short-sighted view that the partition of Ireland is a British interest', Aiken wrote, 'that is responsible for the maintenance of this evil in present world conditions'.[113] Therefore, the resolution (which had Aiken's full support) was a rejection of Ulster Unionists' legitimate right to vote themselves out of a united Ireland, as enshrined under the Ireland Act of 1949. Rather, the Fogarty Resolution stipulated that if 'the clear majority of all of the people of Ireland' voted in favour of Irish unity, then this was a legitimate aspiration.[114]

Although Northern Ireland Prime Minister Basil Brooke (raised to the peerage as Lord Brookeborough in 1952) was not averse to the Fianna Fáil overtures for cross-border cooperation, he would not agree to formal north-south relations while Dublin refused to recognise the constitutional position of Northern Ireland. In June 1951, Brooke spoke of a 'hands across the border' policy, citing recent advances in 'matters of common interest, such as transport, fisheries and drainage'.[115] His pronouncements were, however, always measured by a warning that cross-border cooperation, on a significant scale, could never occur before recognition was granted.[116]

Aiken was equally stubborn. Although he publicly admitted that he favoured economic cooperation between Belfast and Dublin, he refused to acknowledge the constitutional status of Northern Ireland, a policy to which he rigidly adhered throughout his political career.[117] Like de Valera,[118] Aiken was unwilling to move on such a fundamental point of principle. Ireland's constitutional claim over Northern Ireland was non-negotiable, even if this meant the end of north-south cooperation. Indeed, Aiken steadfastly refused to use the descriptive term 'Northern Ireland' when referring to the six north-eastern counties of Ulster, because in his mind this would have represented an acknowledgement of the *de facto* existence of the state of Northern Ireland.[119]

The Fianna Fáil government's refusal to acknowledge the Belfast government reinforced Ulster Unionists' belief that Aiken's latest attempt to encourage north-south cooperation was merely a veiled plot aimed at securing some concessions on partition. Their scepticism seemed warranted. Behind the façade of seeking to encourage cross-border cooperation with the Belfast government and ending its anti-partition propaganda campaign, the Fianna Fáil government's partition policy had changed little in a generation.

By the time Fianna Fáil exited government in the summer of 1954, Aiken still remained unwaveringly loyal to core principles of his party's traditional stance on partition. Namely, he maintained that the British government, irrespective of the passing of the Ireland Act, had a moral obligation to make a declaration in support of Irish unity; that a federal agreement constituted a workable solution to partition; that Ulster Unionists had no right to vote themselves out of a united Ireland; and that Fianna Fáil would not recognise the constitutional position of Northern Ireland.

It was Aiken's overall inability to progress beyond the above policies that ultimately undermined his desire to find a workable solution to partition, particularly in his dealings with Ulster Unionism. First and foremost, Aiken was a man of principle. Economic concessions to Ulster Unionists were one thing, but this did not mean that he would tolerate constitutional concessions, and particularly official recognition, either *de facto* or *de jure*, of the Northern Ireland government.

Conclusion

For the remainder of Aiken's political career, the partition question was never too far from his heart. On his reappointment as Minister for External Affairs, under the Fianna Fáil administration from 1957 to 1961, Aiken wasted little time in voicing 'the case against Partition', as expressed by the Fianna Fáil magazine, *Gleas*.[120] Though now 'somewhat mellowed', he was reported by the British Embassy in Dublin to have 'always had a violent anti-British bias',[121] and remained a man who saw partition as the 'supreme issue'.[122]

In one particular meeting with the British Ambassador to Ireland, Alexander Clutterbuck, in July 1957, Aiken reportedly exclaimed that 'it was ridiculous to divide Ireland on the pleas of self-determination for local majorities ...'.[123] More than any other Fianna Fáil politician during the late 1950s – and this included de Valera – Aiken repeatedly drove home to British officials and ministers the 'injustice' of partition.[124] He focused on the 'gerrymandering' practices in Northern Ireland against the Catholic minority, which he described as 'disastrous',[125] and on how it was in Britain's 'interest' to see Ireland united.[126]

As Minister for External Affairs throughout Seán Lemass's reign as Fianna Fáil leader and Taoiseach from 1959 to 1966, Aiken's central interest lay not with partition, but with Ireland's involvement in the United Nations. Under Lemass's leadership, Aiken was of the firm opinion that Northern Ireland policy was a constitutional issue, and thus not his concern.[127] As he explained to the Dáil in 1967, partition was 'regarded as an internal affair', and was therefore not the responsibility of the Department of External Affairs.[128]

Under Jack Lynch's leadership, following Lemass's retirement as Taoiseach in November 1966, Aiken followed his new leader's conciliatory approach towards Ulster Unionism.[129] That said, Aiken could still be relied upon to deliver the occasional anti-partition rant. For example, in February 1967, to the infuriation of Northern Ireland Prime Minister Terence O'Neill and the displeasure of Lynch, Aiken declared in the Dáil that the British Prime Minister Harold Wilson publicly favoured a united Ireland if the people of north and south could agree on a workable solution. If Dublin and Belfast arrived at an agreement for Irish unity, Aiken recorded, 'Prime Minister Wilson', would give his 'blessing'.[130]

By the time the Troubles exploded in Northern Ireland in the summer of 1969, Aiken found himself exiled to the back benches. Lynch's decision not to reappoint him as Minister for External Affairs, following Fianna Fáil's general election victory in April 1969, signalled the end of a long and successful ministerial career. Aiken's absence around the Irish Cabinet table during the turbulent years from 1969 to 1971 was acutely felt, particularly in mid-August 1969, when some Fianna Fáil ministers, notably Neil Blaney and Charles J. Haughey, advocated sending the Irish Army into Northern Ireland. Aiken acted as a voice of reason and, most importantly, moderation, helping to galvanise Taoiseach Lynch's resolve as the latter fought desperately to win support both from within Fianna Fáil and the general public for his conciliatory, non-violent partition policy.[131]

How, by 1969, did Aiken come to represent a voice of reason on the partition issue within Fianna Fáil? This was a man who, after all, throughout his political career was a staunch opponent of partition, and on occasions Fianna Fáil's most vocal anti-partitionist. The answer becomes clear if one traces Aiken's stance on partition in the post-war period, particularly during the 1950s. In the aftermath of Fianna Fáil's shambolic anti-partition campaign both at home and abroad from 1948 to 1951, Aiken came to understand that Irish unity could not merely be solved by the will of the British government. Rather, he gradually realised that the attainment of a united Ireland also required support from among the Ulster Unionist community. This explains his attempts during the early 1950s to nurture cross-border cooperation between the Dublin and Belfast governments.

The problem Aiken faced, however, was that he was continually impeded by his own nationalist beliefs. Consequently, Aiken was caught between a rock and a hard place, motivated by a genuine desire to improve relations between north and south, but at the same time unwilling to dilute his strongly held republican principles.

Notes

1   For a general overview of Aiken's attitude to partition from 1926 until his retirement from politics in 1973, including his relationship with Éamon de Valera from 1926 to 1959, Seán Lemass during the 1960s and his role during the Arms Crisis of 1970, see Stephen Kelly, *Fianna Fáil, Partition and Northern Ireland, 1926–1971* (Dublin: Irish Academic Press, 2013).

2   See Donnacha Ó Beacháin, *Destiny of the Soldiers, Fianna Fáil, Irish Republicanism and the IRA, 1926–73* (Dublin: Gill and Macmillan, 2010), 387.

3   Fine Gael's James Dillon believed Aiken to be 'a Northern bigot … intolerant and dictatorial'. See Maurice Manning, *James Dillon, a Biography* (Dublin: Wolfhound Press, 1999), 160–161. See also Henry Patterson, *Ireland Since 1939, The Persistence of Conflict* (Dublin: Penguin Ireland, 2006), 61.

4   Patterson, *Ireland Since 1939*, 157. Indeed, some of Aiken's Fianna Fáil colleagues believed him to be 'deeply anti-British'. Patterson, *Ireland Since 1939*, 61.

5   Ronan Fanning, 'Frank Aiken', *Dictionary of Irish Biography* (http://dib.cambridge.org, accessed 18/04/13).

6   Character profile of Frank Aiken, 1947. National Archives of the United Kingdom (NAUK), Prime Minister's Office (PREM) 8/824.

7   Character profile of Frank Aiken, 1968. NAUK, Dominions Office (DO) 182/149.

8   This was the opinion of British Ambassador to Ireland (1970–1973), John Peck, May 1971. NAUK, Foreign and Commonwealth Office (FCO) 33/1599.

9   'Frank Aiken', *Oxford Dictionary of National Biography*, entry by Eunan O'Halpin.

10   At both the 1945 and 1946 Fianna Fáil Ard Fheiseanna, the National Executive, under de Valera's instructions, issued separate resolutions stating that Fianna Fáil 'believes that the time has come to launch a worldwide propaganda campaign to expose the inconsistency, futility and injustice of the partition of Ireland …'. See *The Irish Times*, 7 Nov. 1945. See also the record of partition resolution issued at the 1946 Fianna Fail Ard Fheis, *Irish Press*, 9 Oct. 1946.

11   See speech by de Valera, 24 June 1947. Dáil Éireann (DE), Vol. 107, col. 84. Aiken made a similar frank acknowledgment in Feb. 1949. See comments by Aiken, *Irish Press*, 10 Feb. 1949.

12   See comments by de Valera. *Irish Press*, 19 Oct. 1948.

13   Unpublished biography of Éamon de Valera. National Library of Ireland (NLI), Frank Gallagher Papers, MS 18375 (2).

14   Aiken to Maud Aiken, 1 April 1948. University College Dublin Archives (UCDA), Frank Aiken Papers P104/4823.

15   NLI, Gallagher Papers, MS 18375 (2).

16   NLI, Gallagher Papers, MS 18375 (2).

17   See *Sunday Independent*, 17 Oct. 1948.

18   *Irish Press*, 26 Oct. 1948. See also speech by de Valera, New York, 3 April 1948 and UCDA, Éamon de Valera Papers P150/2947, speech by de Valera, 13 April 1948. Additionally, see Maurice Moynihan, *Speeches and Statements by Eamon De Valera 1917–1973* (Dublin: Gill and MacMillan, 1980), 497–505.

19   Speech by de Valera. DE, 24 June 1947. Vol. 107, cols. 78–81. See also, speech by de Valera, San Francisco. *Irish Press*, 17 March 1948; speech by de Valera, Los Angeles. *Irish Press*, 18 March 1948 and lastly, UCDA, P150/2948, speech by de Valera, 30 March 1948.

20   See for example speech by de Valera, Tulsa, Oklahoma. *Irish Press*, 12 March 1948.

21   Speech by de Valera. *Irish Press*, 3 April 1948.

22   Aiken to Maud Aiken, 7 March 1948. UCDA, P104/4820.

23   See *Sunday Independent*, 17 Oct. 1948.

24   De Valera to Maud Aiken, 7 May 1948. UCDA, P104/4840.

25   Kate O'Malley, *Ireland, India and Empire, Indo-Irish Radical Connections, 1919–1964* (Manchester: Manchester University Press, 2008), 159.

26   Lord Innverchapel to Bevin, 16 April 1948. NAUK, DO 35/3938.

27   Seán Cronin, *Washington's Irish Policy 1916–1986* (Dublin: Anvil Books, 1987), 193.

28   Speech by de Valera. *Irish Press,* 1 May 1948.

29   Aiken to Kiernan, Irish legation, Canberra, Australia, 5 Oct. 1948. UCDA, P104/4767.

30   Kiernan to unknown recipient in the Department of Foreign Affairs, autumn/winter, 1948. National Archives of Ireland (NAI), Department of Foreign Affairs (DFA), 305/14/21.

31   Duffy to Secretary of Commonwealth and Relations Office, Philip Noel-Baker, 1 June 1948. NAUK, DO 35/3931.

32   Duffy to Noel-Baker, 1 June 1948. NAUK, DO 35/3931.

33   Williams to Sir E. Machtig, 11 June 1948. NAUK, DO 35/3929.

34   Speech by de Valera. *Irish Press*, 15 June, 1948.

35   Speech by de Valera. *Southern Cross*, 26 May 1948.

36   Aiken to Kiernan, Irish legation, Canberra, Australia, 5 Oct. 1948. UCDA, P104/4767.

37   For further reading on de Valera's and Aiken's visit to India, and in particular the former's relationship with Nehru, see O'Malley, *Ireland, India and the Empire, Indo-Irish Radical Connections, 1919–64*, 159–178.

38   Itinerary of de Valera's visit to India, 14 June 1948. UCDA, P150/2955.

39   Aiken to Kiernan, Irish legation, Canberra, Australia, 5 Oct. 1948. UCDA, P104/4767.

40   Aiken to Maud Aiken, 17 June 1948. UCDA, P104/4837.

41   See UCDA, P150/2955, Nehru to de Valera, 18 June 1948. Nehru devoted several chapters of his work, *Glimpses of World History,* to de Valera and Ireland's fight for independence. See Jawaharlal Nehru, *Glimpses of World History* (India, 1934).

42   O'Malley, *Ireland, India and the Empire*, 167.

43   Aiken to Kiernan, Irish legation, Canberra, Australia, 5 Oct. 1948. UCDA, P104/4767.

44   Aiken to Brother Boylan, principal Irish Christian Brothers, Melbourne, 28 Sept. 1948. UCDA, P104/4766.

45   Aiken to Mr J. J. Kelly, Tasmania, 5 Oct. 1948. UCDA, P104/4767.

46   Record of de Valera's visit to Britain, Oct. 1948 – Feb. 1949. UCDA, P150/2968.

47   Speech by Aiken, 20 July 1948. DE, Vol. 112, col. 840.

48   Copy of speech by Aiken, 10 Feb. 1949. NAI, DFA 305/74/1.

49   Speech by Aiken. *Irish Press*, 19 March 1949.

50   See Seán O'Faoláin, 'Ulster', *The Bell*, Vol. 2, No. 4 (July, 1941), 4.

51   See de Valera's comments, 24 June 1947. DE, Vol. 107, cols. 79–82.

52   Comments by Aiken. *Irish Press*, 19 March 1949.

53   Comments by Aiken. *Irish Press*, 10 Feb. 1949.

54   See comments by Aiken. *Irish Press*, 21 Feb. 1950.

55   Patterson, *Ireland Since 1939*, 120.

56   See comments by Aiken. *Irish Independent*, 3 Dec. 1948.

57   Speech by Aiken, 2 March 1949. DE, Vol. 114, col. 811.

58   See comments by Aiken. *Irish Press*, 19 March 1949.

59   See, for example, copy of 'A call to unity' by Frank Aiken, 19 June 1926 (UCDA, P104/1499); and comments by Aiken, 2 March 1949. DE, Vol. 114, col. 811.

60   See, for example, comments by de Valera, 22 Aug. 1921. DE, Vol. 4 cols. 28–29 and comments by de Valera, *Irish Independent*, 14 Sept. 1927.

61   See copy of 'A call to unity' by Frank Aiken, 19 June 1926. UCDA, P104/1499.

62   See comments by Aiken. *Irish Independent*, 27 Jan. 1932. This information is sourced from Brian Hanley's chapter within this edited collection.

63   Speech by Aiken, 2 March 1949. DE, Vol. 114, col. 811. See also speeches by Aiken, 11 May 1959 and 6 Dec. 1960, *The Irish Times*.

64   Since at least 1921, de Valera maintained that the use of physical force was impractical in the attainment of Irish unity. See comments by de Valera, 22 Aug. 1921. DE, Vol. 4, cols. 28–29.

65   *The Irish Times*, 13 Dec. 1979.

66   See comments by Aiken. *Irish Press*, 10 Feb. 1949.

67   Copy of speech by Aiken 'The common name of Irishman', Fermanagh County Feis, 19 July 1953. NAI, Department of the Taoiseach (D/T)/GIS/1/1. See also 'handwritten and typescript letter' by Aiken, 3 April 1954 (UCDA, P104/8043) and separate comments by Aiken, *The Irish Times*, 5 April 1954 and 18 Jan. 1962.

68   See copy of a statement by Aiken, 23 Feb. 1953. UCDA, P104/5836. See also speech by Aiken, 'Mr. Eden now in Molotov's camp', *Irish Press*, 4 April 1954.

69   Comments by Aiken. *Irish Press*, 20 April 1949.

70   Earl of Longford and Thomas P. O'Neill, *Eamon de Valera* (London: Hutchinson, 1970), 432.

71   The Act declared that the *description* of the State would be the 'Republic of Ireland'. However, the Act did not change the official name of the State (this remained 'Ireland', or 'Éire' in Irish).

72   John Bowman, *De Valera and the Ulster Question, 1917–1973* (Oxford: Oxford University Press, 1982), 268.

73   See also comments by Aiken, 26 Nov. 1948. DE, Vol. 113, col. 690.

74   See comments by Aiken. *Irish Independent*, 3 Dec. 1948.

75   See comments by Aiken. *Irish Independent*, 3 Dec. 1948. See also meeting of Fianna Fáil parliamentary party, 2 Dec. 1948. UCDA, P176/446.

76   Bowman, *De Valera*, 269.

77   For further analysis of Fianna Fáil's participation on the All-Party Anti-Partition Committee, see Kelly, *Fianna Fáil, Partition and Northern Ireland, 1926–1971*, 131–138.

78   Brooke announced that 'partition was the main issue' of the Northern Ireland general election. *Irish Press*, 28 Jan. 1949.

79   Memorandum entitled 'Ireland Bill Defence of Northern Ireland', undated. University of Oxford (UO), Bodleian Library (BL), Clement Attlee Papers, MS. Dep. 82 Fols. 176–77,

80   Memorandum entitled 'Secret Ireland Bill – Partition Question', undated. UO, BL, Attlee Papers MS. Dep. 82 Fols. 256–57.

81   *Irish Press*, 4 May 1949.

82   See comments by Aiken. *The Irish Times*, 14 May 1949.

83 See, Aiken to Attlee, undated, May 1949 (it is unclear if Aiken sent a version of this letter to Attlee). UCDA, P104/4649.

84 *Irish Press*, 26 Jan. 1950, 27 Jan. 1950 and 3 Feb. 1950.

85 Record of de Valera's anti-partition world tour; section III, July 1948–April 1951. UCDA, P150/2996–2997.

86 See comments by Aiken. *Irish Press*, 21 Feb. 1950.

87 Aldous Huxley, quoted in David Welch, *The Third Reich, Politics and Propaganda* (London: Routledge, 2002), 9.

88 See Conor Cruise O'Brien, *Memoir my Life and Themes* (Dublin: Poolbeg Press, 1999), 162.

89 Longford and O'Neill, *Eamon de Valera*, 463.

90 This was the opinion of a secret CIA report dated 1 April 1949. See Seán Cronin, *Washington's Irish policy 1916–1986* (Dublin: Anvil Books, 1987), 254–245.

91 Meeting between de Valera, Aiken and Pakenham in Dublin, 2 May 1952. UCDA, P104/8035.

92 Speech by Aiken, 30 Jan. 1952. DE, Vol. 129. col. 48.

93 See, for example, confidential Department of External Affairs memorandum compiled on behalf of Aiken, Oct. 1951(UCDA, P104/8601); and record of an interview Aiken gave to a gathering of assembled press in Dublin, 17 Dec. 1952 (UCDA, P104/8038). See also comments by Aiken, *Irish Press*, 18 Dec. 1952 and *The Irish Times*, 25 July 1953.

94 Speech by Aiken, *Irish Press,* 26 April 1954.

95 Speech by Aiken, 28 Nov. 1957. DE, Vol. 164, col. 1204.

96 Record of meeting between Aiken and Gordon-Walker, 11 July 1951. UCDA, P104/8030.

97 Confidential memorandum on partition signed by Seán Nunan, 21 Aug. 1951. NAI, DFA, 305/14/192.

98 See conversation between Aiken and Lord Ismay, 14 Feb. 1952. UCDA, P104/8724.

99 Document entitled 'Membership and Representation on Inter-Parliamentary Groups', record of meeting between de Valera and a collection of British MPs, 9 Feb. 1949. UCDA, P150/2970.

100 Sir John Maffey to Dominions Office, 26 July 1946. NAUK, DO 35/2095.

101 Boland to Nunan, 22 Jan. 1952. UCDA, P104/8033.

102 Conversation between Aiken and Lord Ismay, 14 Feb. 1952. UCDA, P104/8724.

103 See Seán Nunan's comments. Confidential memorandum on partition signed by Seán Nunan, 21 Aug. 1951. NAI, DFA 305/14/192.

104 See Aoife Bhreatnach, 'Frank Aiken and the Formulation of Foreign Policy, 1951–1954; 1957–1969' (M.Phil thesis, National University of Ireland, Cork, 1999), 11–14.

105 Meeting between Aiken and Lord Salisbury, Leader of the House of Lords, 28 Oct. 1952. UCDA, P104/8037.

106 See meeting between Aiken and Lord Salisbury, Leader of the House of Lords, 28 Oct. 1952. UCDA. P104/8037.

107 Meeting between Boland and Pakenham, 29 Nov. 1951. NAI, DFA P203/1.

108 Meeting between Boland and Pakenham, 29 Nov. 1951. NAI, DFA P203/1.

109 See comments by Aiken, *The Irish Times*, 20 July 1953.

110 See comments by Aiken, *The Irish Times*, 20 July 1953.

111 Aiken to Miss Alexandria Howson, Bedford College, Regent Park, London, 6 Aug. 1953. UCDA, P104/8747.

112   See copy of extract of the Fogarty Resolution for the Eighty-Third Congress, First Session, 3 Jan. 1953. UCDA, P104/8711.

113   Files containing Department of External Affairs memorandum relating to the 'Fogarty Resolution', Aug. 1953. UCDA, P104/8713.

114   See copy of the 'Fogarty Resolution'. UCDA, P104/8713.

115   Michael Kennedy, *Divisions and Consensus, The Politics of Cross-Border Relations in Ireland, 1925–1969* (Dublin: Institute for Public Administration, 2000), 152.

116   See comments by Brooke. *Northern Whig*, 25 June 1951.

117   Throughout his political career, Aiken refused to acknowledge the *de jure* constitutional legality of the Northern Ireland government and State. See, for example, speech by Aiken, 14 June 1937. DE, Vol. 68, cols. 386–387. See also Secretary to the Department of External Affairs, John Molloy to Secretary in the Department of Education, 27 Sept. 1963 (NAI, DT S 10467/ F/64); and lastly, series of correspondence between T. K. Whitaker and Miss T. J. Beere, including some reported comments by Aiken, 4–5 Aug. 1965. UCDA, P104/8815.

118   See comments by de Valera. *Northern Whig*, 25 June 1951.

119   For example, against the wishes of his party leader Seán Lemass, during the 1960s Aiken refused point blank to use the term 'Northern Ireland' to replace the 'Six Counties'. See file relating to political terminology and the descriptive usage of the term 'Northern Ireland', June–Aug. 1960 (NAI, DT S 1957/63).

120   UCDA P104/8766, copy of *Gleas*, No. 35, Oct. 1957.

121   Character profile of Frank Aiken, 1947. NAUK, PREM 8/824.

122   See letter from British Embassy, Dublin to Commonwealth and Relations Office, London, recording Aiken's views on partition, 3 March 1958. NAUK, PREM 11/2374.

123   Meeting between Aiken and Clutterbuck, 8 July 1957. NAUK, DO 35/7812.

124   See, for example, meeting between Aiken and Home, 22 March 1958. UCDA, P104/8050.

125   See Aiken's comments. *Irish Press*, 28 Nov. 1958.

126   See comments by Aiken during a meeting with Home, 4 July 1958. NAI, DFA P203/2.

127   Fanning, 'Frank Aiken', *Dictionary of Irish Biography*, 55.

128   Comments by Aiken, 9 Feb. 1967. DE, Vol. 226, cols. 284–285.

129   See, for example, record of comments by Aiken, Jan. 1968. UCDA, P104/8788.

130   Speech by Aiken, 9 Feb. 1967. DE, Vol. 226, cols. 984–985.

131   For further reading into Aiken's stance on Northern Ireland during the emotive years from 1969 to 1971, see Kelly, *Fianna Fáil, Partition and Northern Ireland, 1926–1971*, 301–322 and 352.

PART TWO

Internationalist

CHAPTER EIGHT

Frank Aiken at the United Nations: some personal recollections

NOEL DORR

Frank Aiken was Minister for External Affairs when I joined the Irish Department of External Affairs in January 1960. As a Third Secretary, the most junior rank in the diplomatic service, and a recent entrant at that, I could expect in the normal course of events to have little if any contact with the minister. But External Affairs was still a very small department, where junior staff might on occasion be summoned to deal directly with the secretary or even with the minister. This could be disconcerting for a very junior officer working alongside senior and experienced colleagues.

During my first year I was assigned to the small Political Section, which dealt with the United Nations (UN). I could not have asked for a more interesting area – not least because it came under the responsibility of Conor Cruise O'Brien, who was then still a middle-level official in the department. It was also an aspect of the department's activities that engaged Frank Aiken's particular interest during his long term of office as our minister.

In this chapter I offer some personal memories of Aiken during that period, and an account of a few selected issues on which he took a particularly active role as leader of the Irish delegation to the UN General Assembly.[1]

Background

At the time I joined the department, Ireland was still a relatively new UN Member State. It was admitted only in December 1955, and attended its first General Assembly session in 1956. The UN in those years was very different from what it is today. Most UN Member States belonged to one or other of the two rival Cold War 'blocs', the Security Council was split between 'East' and 'West', and there was limited representation from the developing world. This gave an opportunity for a few small- and medium-sized States to play a helpful role on occasion in the Assembly. These States did not form an organised group; they were simply seen as 'good UN members', concerned to make the system work by promoting compromise.

As a small Western-European State that was not a member of an alliance, and which emerged to independence after a long struggle, Ireland easily identified itself with this loose grouping of small- and medium-sized States. Ireland would probably have been equally positive in its attitude under any Irish minister or any Irish government. But the personalities and political outlook of individual ministers make a difference, and Frank Aiken, who took office in a new Fianna Fáil government in 1957, brought a new and distinctive approach to Ireland's participation in the General Assembly. The UN was at the centre of his interests, and he had ample time in his long tenure of office to create a reputation there, which, heightened somewhat in retrospect, still has around it something of a golden afterglow in the memories of many Irish people of a certain age. In this chapter I hope to convey an idea of his personality as well as discussing some of his policies.

I cannot claim much direct knowledge of the period before I joined the department in January 1960. But after a few months handling the copious UN files and documentation in the Political Section, and working with a handful of senior colleagues who had worked closely with Aiken as part of the UN delegation at successive annual sessions of the General Assembly, I came almost to feel that I too had been there in New York with them over the previous two and a half years. As it happened I *was* there for the Assembly session a year later in the autumn of 1961, and again in each of the four years from 1966 to 1969 – five sessions in all. Four of these were led by Aiken as Minister for External Affairs, so I served under him at the UN over a total of some twelve months in all.

Aiken's personality

I think I can say that I came to know Aiken reasonably well as minister over that period. It would of course be too much to say that I knew him well personally.

I was not a family friend, but a relatively junior – and appropriately deferential – official dealing with a minister old enough to be my father, if not my grandfather. He was accustomed to spending long periods in New York – much longer than any Irish Foreign Minister could afford to do today – and he was not a man to stand on ceremony. The delegation was small, and I was assigned to a committee that dealt with some issues in which he took a particular interest. I also sat behind him from time to time when he took the Irish seat in the Assembly or in a committee, which gave me the chance to observe him closely enough in those later years of his career. I have to say that the more I think now about his role at the UN, the more I regard him with respect, tinged with a kind of affection.

Aiken, as I recall him, was a tall man with a small, neat toothbrush moustache who cut quite a distinguished figure at the UN. He was kindly but also taciturn, and he spoke in a rather clipped voice – not with what we in Ireland call a strong northern accent, but with definite traces of his origin and background in Armagh. He was a man of great and gritty integrity, conviction and, be it said, stubbornness. He had been Minister for Finance for a time in the late 1940s and, whether it was the effect of that experience or his innate instinct, he was always appropriately cautious, not to say parsimonious, about anything that involved increasing State expenditure. In the view of his officials he was much too reluctant about seeking to expand the department. He was cautious too about allowing Irish diplomats, or the state as such, to seek election to international bodies of any kind since that would put additional pressure on the department and might entail additional expenditure. He did, however, allow Freddie Boland to run successfully for election as President of the General Assembly in 1960, Lieutenant General Seán McKeown to become Commander of the UN peacekeeping force in the Congo, and Conor Cruise O'Brien to become Representative of the Secretary General in Katanga.

Aiken spoke Irish reasonably well, though not perhaps with the complete ease and fluency that would have been necessary for the conduct of all his ministerial business in that language.[2] He had a habit of beginning a discussion briefly in Irish and then reverting to English. He was not given to wasting words in either language, and a laconic annotation 'aontúim' ('I agree') was his way of approving a submission or a recommendation. I remember, often enough, walking with him from the offices of the Irish UN mission to the General Assembly a short distance away, and as we walked, feeling, foolishly, that it was my duty to make conversation. Sometimes, having duly opened up a promising topic, and in Irish too, I would be met by a rather curt 'seadh' ('yes') or 'ní h'eadh' ('no'), which, though not unkindly meant, was a conversation-stopper, and left me groping for something else with which to catch his interest.

He came from an older, more austere generation of leaders within his party, and he must have been somewhat uncomfortable about the attitude of a newer kind of leader who came to the fore in Fianna Fáil during Ireland's relative prosperity in the 1960s – as no doubt they were with him. The Irish phrase Oisín i ndiaidh na Féinne' ['Oisín, lonely after the Fianna'] comes to mind.[3] I saw evidence of this on a day in the late 1960s when the then Minister for Finance, Charles J. Haughey, was in New York. The local offices of the various Irish semi-state agencies handled his visit and, for no very obvious reason, included in it a courtesy call on the UN Secretary General, U Thant. As the cavalcade of limousines flying the Irish flag swept in towards the tall building that housed the UN Secretariat, Aiken, whose role as minister was to deal with the UN and its Secretary General, and who normally walked to the UN and elsewhere, sat at his desk in the Irish UN Mission office a short block away and took no notice whatever of the impressive spectacle outside.

I often thought that he was, at heart, an engineer. He certainly had an inventive cast of mind – evident in a variety of 'gadgets' that he had devised from time to time and put to good use himself. These were spoken of by his officials – though not to his face – with knowing amusement: we regarded them with the understanding tolerance appropriate to an austere uncle's mild eccentricity. But it appears now that he may have been ahead of his time: something very like the 'spring-heeled shoe', for example, which we joked about then, can now be found on sports footwear from manufacturers such as Nike or Adidas.

Aiken's view of the importance of the UN

If I try in retrospect to identify the single theme that was most fundamental to Aiken's thinking about international issues in those years, it would have to be his belief in the importance of the UN. He was not blind to its weaknesses, but he saw it as an organisation whose very existence would both guarantee the independence of smaller states like Ireland, and provide a forum to which peoples struggling for independence could appeal for support. In the General Debate on 6 October at the 1960 Assembly session, he described the UN as:

> ... a body in which the small nations have an influence such as they have never before possessed in their history: an influence quite out of proportion to their material power and resources; an influence moreover, which will disappear if this Organisation should fail.[4]

He attached importance to the peacekeeping role of the UN, and over a number of years in the 1960s he took a lead role and fought tenaciously to ensure that its peacekeeping capacity would be adequately financed.

Of course, any Irish foreign minister, then or since, would, broadly speaking, share these views. Support for an ordered international system and the rule of law in international affairs have been fundamental principles underlying Ireland's approach to foreign policy since the foundation of the state. But in Aiken's case more than most there was underlying these ideas a strong conviction, based on his own personal experience, of the existential importance of the UN for smaller and weaker Member States, and a fear of what might happen if it were to fail. Two points in particular in his background seem to me to have been important in this.

One would certainly have been his participation in Ireland's own independence struggle, and the memory he must have had of the unsuccessful efforts by representatives of the first Dáil Éireann to gain recognition for that independence at the Paris Peace Conference in 1919 after the First World War. As he told the Assembly in 1960:

> In 1913 I became a volunteer in our national revolutionary army. We had few weapons. We armed ourselves largely with the weapons we captured. We fought elections as well as guerrilla battles until we established our government, with the active support of three-fourths of our people. And that revolutionary government was, of course, refused official recognition. Although one of the Fourteen Points proclaimed the right of small nations to self-determination, our delegates were turned from the door of the Paris Peace Conference in 1921 [sic]. We had no international forum to appeal to, no United Nations to support our struggle for freedom.[5]

The fact that he could refer back to his own guerrilla days as well as the strong anti-colonial position of the Irish delegation gave him a particular authority when he advised, as he sometimes did, against the resort to 'armed struggle' by national liberation movements now that the United Nations existed as a forum to which they could take their case for national independence.

The other event that influenced his thinking, and the sense he conveys at times that the very existence of the UN could come into question was, I think, his memory of the virtual collapse of the League of Nations, the predecessor of the UN, in the 1930s. As Minister for Defence, and someone close to Éamon de Valera, he would certainly have remembered the slow, unedifying death of the League in that decade as Member States failed to uphold its Covenant. This personal commitment to the UN as an organisation whose very existence provided assurance to smaller states and national liberation movements comes through clearly in all his speeches.

As Minister for External Affairs from 1957 to 1969, Aiken attended twelve Regular Sessions, and several Special Sessions and Emergency Special Sessions of the General Assembly. He also took the Irish seat on the Security Council during the Cuban missile crisis, which occurred in 1962, while Ireland was serving a one-year term on the Council. This is a record of involvement with the UN unequalled by any other Irish Foreign Minister – or, most probably, by any other foreign minister of recent times.

Disengagement of forces in Central Europe: Aiken and the 'Areas of Law' initiative

Aiken was deeply concerned about the very serious dangers to world peace arising from the confrontation of the North Atlantic Treaty Organization (NATO) and Warsaw Pact forces in Central Europe in the late 1950s, and particularly about the situation in a divided Berlin. This is evident from a controversial proposal for a reciprocal withdrawal of forces along agreed lines of latitude, which he first put forward in the General Assembly in 1957.

Towards the end of October 1956, Soviet forces had brutally suppressed a nationalist rising in Hungary. The Soviet action was widely condemned at an Emergency Special Session of the UN General Assembly held almost simultaneously with another Emergency Special Session that addressed the Suez crisis. The Assembly called for the withdrawal of all foreign forces, and it established a five-nation investigative committee, but, as Aiken put it on 10 September 1957 when he addressed the Assembly in the debate on the committee's report, 'the United Nations was unable to intervene in any effective way and the Hungarians were crushed by overwhelming and ruthless force'.[6]

In the course of the polemic between East and West that followed the Soviet actions, the Soviet leader Nikita Khrushchev repeated an earlier offer to withdraw Soviet troops from Eastern Europe if the US would withdraw its troops completely from the European continent. This was widely dismissed on the western side as mere propaganda. In his address to the Assembly, however, Aiken suggested that Khrushchev's proposals might 'present a possibility worth exploring'.[7] He noted that the cases were not of course comparable: American troops in Western Europe had been invited by democratic governments; there had been no free elections in Eastern Europe since the victorious Russian troops entered the countries in that area twelve years before. Nevertheless, he suggested that there should be an effort to seek agreement 'on a fair and reasonable drawing back of the non-national forces on both sides from the border of Russian-occupied Europe'. He explained further what he had in mind:

> To avoid prolonged negotiations and the great emotional difficulty of deciding what country must be evacuated in exchange for what other, we suggest that the drawing back should take place along latitudinal lines from either side of the border for an equal number of kilometres. In other words for every step Russian troops take to the east along a given line of latitude, American troops will take a step westward along the same line of latitude.[8]

This was not a spur-of-the-moment addition to his speech, but a much worked-over proposal to which he was deeply attached, and which he held to despite the very considerable misgivings of Ireland's UN Representative, Ambassador Freddie Boland. He subsequently linked it to a related idea for 'Areas of Law', of which Central Europe could be one. This was another idea that he proposed as a step towards 'effectively controlled world disarmament and the universal rule of law',[9] and one to which he returned in other speeches, year after year.[10] The states in such an area would guarantee to abide by the UN Charter, to uphold the rule of law in their international relations, not to acquire nuclear weapons or weapons of mass destruction, and to subject themselves to UN inspection. In return, the other members of the UN, and the nuclear powers in particular, would bind themselves in advance to defend the states in such an area by means of a standing UN force.[11]

The reaction of western countries such as the UK and the Federal Republic of Germany to Aiken's disengagement proposal ranged from cool to very negative; the Warsaw Pact attitude was 'lukewarm'.[12] European members of the North Atlantic Treaty Organization (NATO) at the time saw the presence of American forces in Europe as an important guarantee of their security against possible aggression by the Soviet Union, and it may be that some of the negative reaction to Aiken's proposal was due to a mistaken belief that his proposal meant that they would have to withdraw completely from the area. More generally, however, to those engaged in high-level political and security issues on both sides of the great divide in Europe, his suggestions must have seemed the very 'far out' ideas of an amateur. I can even recall one of my own irreverent colleagues in the department commenting to me sardonically later that 'all you need to make Irish foreign policy these days is an atlas and a ruler'.

Yet in retrospect there was something admirable, even if naïve, about Aiken's ideas. Maybe, though not accepted, they were not so naïve after all. In the months after Aiken first put his idea forward in September 1957, two other eminent figures came forward with suggestions that bore at least some similarity to his. Speaking at the UN on 2 October 1957, the Polish Foreign Minister, Adam Rapacki, proposed the creation of a nuclear-free zone covering East and West Germany, Poland and Czechoslovakia; the distinguished American strategist and diplomat, George Kennan in a public lecture on the BBC on 24 November referred to 'the common assumption that the Western Powers would be placed at a hopeless disadvantage if there were to be any mutual withdrawal of forces from the heart of Europe'. For him this was one of the 'element[s] of Western thinking about the German problem that might well stand further examination'. He went on to say that it seemed to him to be 'far more desirable on principle to get the Soviet forces out of Central and Eastern Europe than to cultivate a new German army for the purpose of opposing them while they remain there'.[13] These various ideas, like Aiken's own, were highly sensitive at the time since they were seen as running counter to the integration of West Germany into the NATO alliance, and ultimately pointing instead towards the possibility of a neutralised, reunited Germany in the heart of Europe.

I have some reason to think that this was not too far from Aiken's own thinking. I still have, yellowing with age, a carbon copy of a note I prepared of a discussion over a lunch given by the American Ambassador, Grant Stockdale, at the US Embassy in Dublin on 13 September 1961 for Aiken and three of his officials, of whom I was one, before we left for New York for the annual session of the UN General Assembly. Berlin was much in the news at the time – the building of the infamous wall had started just one month earlier. The Ambassador,[14] who was accompanied by two diplomats from the Embassy, asked, a little apprehensively perhaps, whether the minister intended to take an initiative on Berlin at the forthcoming UN session. Aiken doubted that it would be on the agenda, although it would be referred to in debates. In the discussion that followed, he said that the problem could be solved only in a much broader context. He referred to his own proposals for a phased withdrawal in Central Europe: the only real solution would be to make it an 'Area of Law' within which nuclear weapons would be prohibited and conventional weapons limited.

The Russians, he went on, were no longer Communists in the classic sense: they were primarily Russians, and it would be a great mistake to look to communism in tracing the motivation for their current behaviour. Historically, they had no great love for the Poles. Furthermore, they had only an empty Siberia between themselves and China, and would now have to make preparations everywhere against the inevitable rise of China as a world power. During the last war, the western powers had recognised Russia's legitimate interest in ensuring that it would be protected against another German attack – he recalled seeing a recognition of this in *The Times* in 1943. Russia was now only trying to secure what had already been recognised as a legitimate interest by the West. The great Russian fear in his view was of a Germany armed with nuclear weapons. He felt that this was justifiable. Khrushchev, he was sure, would not go to war over Berlin, but he seemed to be determined to frighten the western powers out of it.

The important thing was that the West should seek a solution that would bring the German people along with it. The Germans would be willing to pay a price for unity. They would therefore agree to disengagement, and to the sacrifice of some of the attributes of a great power. They would not want to be the cockpit of Europe since they knew that they would be the first to be wiped out in any war. Aiken said that he thought the present pressure by the Russians would continue. The feeling 'better Berlin red than Englishmen dead' would grow within NATO and weaken the alliance. As this belief that freedom for Berlin was not worth dying for grew stronger, the effort to retain (West) Germany as a member would actually weaken the NATO alliance. The Russians seemed to be relying on this. For this reason, he thought, disengagement would actually be in the interests of Britain and the US.

It is clear that the idea of 'Areas of Law' in various parts of the world, and the related concept of reciprocal disengagement in Central Europe, were very personal to Aiken. These imaginative ideas were not taken up. To his worldly-wise contemporaries in other delegations, particularly those of the larger states in the rival alliances, they must have seemed hopelessly idealistic.

A fuller study of Aiken's years at the UN would have to deal with a great variety of issues: apartheid in South Africa, Tibet, Namibia, anti-colonialism, the Congo, the Middle East, Algeria, peacekeeping, the financing of peacekeeping operations, and so on. But I will limit myself to considering just three other selected issues to illustrate both his personality and how that determined his approach to policy at the United Nations. The first was his initiative on nuclear non-proliferation: this was a success, and he is still remembered for it outside Ireland. The second was the position he took on the representation of China: here his approach caused great controversy, but within a few years a change in the way the issue was presented allowed him to moderate, without openly abandoning, Ireland's initial voting position. Finally, because of the historic importance of the event in question, I will conclude with a brief account of how Aiken responded to the Cuban missile crisis during the tense month of October 1962.

Aiken and preventing the spread of nuclear weapons

On rare occasions, a new idea, raised by a Member State in the UN General Assembly and then pressed with determination and political skill, can eventually lead to the opening up of a new and important area for international negotiation. This was true of the courageous, far-sighted initiative Aiken took in the late 1950s to direct international attention to the dangers that would arise from the further spread of nuclear weapons.

He raised the issue for the first time at the 1958 Assembly session, having got clearance for it during an informal discussion in government a short time before.[15] At that session he submitted a draft resolution that took a limited approach designed to gain wider attention for the problem: it simply recommended that the Assembly establish a committee to study the dangers and make recommendations to the 1959 session. The general climate, even for such a limited initiative, was far from favourable at the time. The idea of yet another arms control committee won little favour; some UN Member States were concerned about freezing the inequality between nuclear 'haves' and 'have-nots', and there was the vexed question of the 'verification and effective control' of any agreement that might be reached.

In October 1958, it became clear that his proposal would not gain sufficient support. So, on the advice of his officials, he took a prudent tactical decision to withdraw the resolution. However, he asked the committee to vote on a single paragraph in the preamble that recognised the dangers inherent in the spread of nuclear weapons. It was approved by thirty-seven votes to none, with forty-four abstentions. The USSR and its allies voted in favour; the US and its NATO allies abstained.[16]

He returned to the issue in 1959. First he got agreement to have a new item – 'Prevention of the Wider Dissemination of Nuclear Weapons' – put on the Assembly agenda. Then he submitted a cautiously phrased draft resolution. It simply *suggested* that a new Ten-Nation Disarmament Committee, which was shortly to meet in Geneva, 'should consider appropriate means' to avert the danger of nuclear proliferation, 'including the feasibility of an international agreement subject to inspection and control ...'.[17]

In presenting the resolution, Aiken showed considerable prescience about a danger that is of even greater concern today: that nuclear weapons might not be confined to states:

218

Revolutionary organisations and groups can come into possession of such weapons by various means, and they are ever more likely to do so according as these weapons become more numerous, more easily transportable and part of standard military equipment.[18]

The Irish resolution was adopted by the General Assembly on 20 November 1959 by sixty-eight votes to none, with twelve abstentions. This time the US and its allies, except for France, voted in favour; the USSR and its allies in the Warsaw Pact switched to abstention. However, the Ten-Nation Disarmament Committee in Geneva broke down before it even got around to addressing the question. So Aiken, with admirable persistence, returned to the 1960 Assembly session with a new draft resolution. This time he had four other Member States – Ghana, Japan, Mexico and Morocco – as co-sponsors with Ireland for his proposal. The resolution called on nuclear states, as a temporary and voluntary measure pending a permanent agreement, to refrain from relinquishing control of nuclear weapons to any nation not possessing them and from transmitting the information necessary for their manufacture; and non-nuclear states to refrain from manufacturing these weapons or otherwise attempting to acquire them.[19] The Assembly adopted the resolution, on 20 December 1960, by sixty eight votes to none, with twenty-six abstentions. This was significant progress achieved over two years.

In 1961, Aiken brought the issue back again to the Assembly. By now his persistence was beginning to pay off. At the start of the session the US and Soviet representatives had issued a joint statement agreeing on certain principles to govern disarmament negotiations. Shortly thereafter, each of the two separately issued another statement setting out his government's position in greater detail. Somewhat surprisingly, these two separate statements by the two superpowers contained almost identical language on nuclear non-proliferation, which seemed to echo Aiken's ideas. Naturally he was heartened by this, and in submitting a new resolution in late November he pointed to the similarities between the US and the Soviet positions.[20]

This new resolution for the first time focused specifically on the need to negotiate an international agreement on non-proliferation. This time, Ireland was the sole sponsor. The text was short and relatively simple. The key paragraph was as follows:

Calls upon all States, and in particular upon the States at present possessing nuclear weapons, to use their best endeavours to secure the conclusion of an international agreement containing provisions under which the nuclear States would undertake to refrain from relinquishing control of nuclear weapons and from transmitting the information necessary for their manufacture to States not possessing such weapons, and provisions under which States not possessing nuclear weapons would undertake not to manufacture or otherwise acquire control of such weapons.[21]

Now, at last, three years after he first raised a lone voice, the omens were favourable. The Assembly adopted the resolution unanimously on 4 December 1961. I am glad to say that I was present in the Assembly for that historic vote.

I think it is indeed fair to describe the vote that day as 'historic', and those who write about the issue of nuclear proliferation today recognise it as such. At a time when debate about a variety of other disarmament proposals amounted to little more than Cold War jousting, the General Assembly, in a clear and unanimous vote, called for the negotiation of a treaty to deal specifically with the particular problem to which Aiken had patiently, but insistently, drawn attention over a period of three years. Of course, a vote of this kind – even a unanimous one – could be only a first step towards an actual treaty. Seven long years of difficult negotiation between the major powers lay ahead. Eventually, the Treaty on the Non-Proliferation of Nuclear Weapons was agreed on 1 July 1968, and opened for signature simultaneously in three capitals: London, Moscow and Washington DC. Even though Ireland had no diplomatic relations with the Soviet Union at that stage, Aiken went to Moscow at the invitation of the Soviet government to sign the treaty there. At a dinner in Moscow on the following day, he presented Ireland's formal instrument of ratification to the Soviet Foreign Minister, Andrei Gromyko, with the result that Ireland was the first state to ratify the new Treaty, just as it had been the first to raise the issue at the UN just ten years earlier.[22]

The Treaty came into force two years later, on 5 March 1970. It has now been signed and ratified by more states than any other arms-control or disarmament agreement. Although it is under pressure, the Treaty has served reasonably well so far as a barrier against the spread of nuclear weapons.

A conference to review the Treaty is held every five years, and at the 1995 conference it was agreed to extend it indefinitely.

Aiken and the representation of China

The single issue that involved Ireland in the greatest controversy during Aiken's time at the UN was his decision in 1957 that Ireland would vote in favour of an Indian proposal to put the issue of the representation of China on the Assembly agenda.

China was a founder member of the United Nations and, as 'the Republic of China', it is named in the Charter as one of the five permanent members of the Security Council. When the UN was founded, the 'Nationalist' or Kuomintang government of Chiang Kai Shek was recognised internationally as the legitimate government of China, but the Nationalists were engaged in a long-running civil war with Communist forces under Mao Zedong. In the late 1940s, the Communists decisively defeated the Nationalists. Mao took power in Beijing, and proclaimed the state to be 'The People's Republic of China'. Chiang Kai Shek, with the remaining Nationalist forces, fled to the offshore island of Taiwan, where they suppressed local opposition and established themselves in power.

Now that it controlled the whole Chinese mainland, Mao's People's Republic claimed the right to represent China in the United Nations. The Nationalist regime in Taiwan, however, still claimed to be the legitimate government of all of China and, with strong support from the US, it continued to sit in China's seat in the UN. Neither side would accept that there were 'two Chinas': both were adamant that there was only one, and that it included Taiwan as well as mainland China. The question was who was to represent it in the Security Council and in the General Assembly. In 1950, under pressure from the US, the Security Council rejected a proposal to discuss the issue of Chinese representation there and, as result, the Soviet Union walked out in protest. The Assembly, too, rejected an Indian proposal to seat the Beijing government and approved a Canadian proposal to maintain Nationalist representatives in the Chinese seat, pending a report by a special committee. Year after year thereafter, the Assembly, though by a diminishing majority, voted down proposals to put the question of the representation of China on its agenda for discussion.[23]

In 1957, his first year in the Assembly, Aiken decided that Ireland would vote in favour of an Indian proposal to put the issue of China's representation on the agenda for discussion.[24] The proposal was defeated by twenty-nine votes in favour to forty-three against, with nine abstentions.[25] In explaining why Ireland had voted in favour, Aiken condemned China's aggression, but argued that the aim should be 'to win acceptance for the principles of the Charter in China and ... self-determination for the people of Korea'. Progress on these points, he said, could best be made by having 'a full and open discussion of the question of the representation of China in this Assembly'.[26]

Ireland's vote was attacked as being 'a vote for Red China'. It raised quite a storm in some Irish-American circles, and also among some – though by no means all – American Catholic bishops. Some diocesan papers, such as the *Catholic News* in the New York Archdiocese and the *Tablet* in Brooklyn, bitterly denounced Aiken's position. Aiken's vote also had repercussions at home. Some

Irish bishops criticised the minister strongly, and Catholic newspapers such as *The Irish Catholic* and the *Catholic Standard* echoed and amplified the criticisms of their American counterparts.

Faced by this storm of criticism, Aiken maintained his position. Though he appeared staunch, there is reason to think that behind his strong outer perimeter the hail of criticism may have had some effect. Furthermore, by 1959 the new Taoiseach, Seán Lemass, undoubtedly favoured a more western-oriented approach. The effect of this change in the political weather can be seen from various subtle nuances, including the insertion of conditions, which become evident in Aiken's presentation of his position at the UN in subsequent years.[27] In 1957, for example, his view was that 'progress can best be made' towards winning 'acceptance for the principles of the Charter in China' and 'self-determination for the people of Korea' by having a full discussion of the representation of China in the Assembly. By 1959 he favoured a prior negotiation. Before any decision to seat Beijing:

> ... a United Nations effort should be made through negotiation to secure from the Peiping [i.e. Beijing] Government an undertaking to refrain from using force against any of their neighbours, to give religious freedom to the Chinese people and to allow the people of all Korea to decide their destiny in an internationally supervised election.[28]

His call for negotiation, however, was subtly phrased: there should be an 'effort ... to secure an undertaking', but he did not make it a requirement that China respond positively. This was a distant echo of de Valera's position on the admission of the Soviet Union, another Communist state, to the League of Nations twenty-five years earlier: he had strongly urged the Soviet Union to guarantee 'the rights of liberty of conscience and freedom of worship', but he spoke and voted in favour of admitting the Soviet Union.

The initiatives that Aiken took in relation to Tibet in those years involved him in criticisms of China's actions, which helped to blunt some of the criticism of his 'China vote'. Furthermore, in 1961, a change in the way the issue of Chinese representation was presented greatly eased the pressure he had come under since his initial vote in favour of discussion in 1957. The political complexion of the Assembly was changing as new Member States joined the UN, and the US, no longer certain of being able to command a majority, took a new approach. Instead of opposing discussion, it argued that a decision on admitting Beijing would require a two-thirds rather than a simple majority. The issue turned on the Charter provision that 'Decisions of the General Assembly on important questions shall be made by a two-thirds majority of the members present and voting'.[29] Was China's representation an important question or not? In ordinary language, yes, of course: it would involve not only the seating of the People's Republic in China's seat, but the concomitant exclusion of the Nationalist Chinese delegation. In parliamentary language, however, it could be argued that this was merely a procedural issue: it did not involve the admission of a new Member State (China was a founder member of the UN) and so was simply a matter of deciding whose credentials to accept as representatives of China.

In the vote that year, Ireland supported a resolution stating that it was 'an important question' that would require a two-thirds majority for adoption. The Assembly adopted that resolution by sixty-one votes to thirty-four, with seven abstentions.[30] Aiken and the Irish delegation were now 'off the hook' and restored to a respectable position. Ireland could continue to vote in favour of discussing the representation of China, as it had done every year since 1957, while voting also for the proposal – which to an outsider would seem no more than common sense – that the issue of who should represent China should be treated as 'an important question', a decision on which would require a two-thirds majority.

Each year thereafter, throughout the 1960s, the outcome was broadly similar. In 1964, however, Aiken took a new approach. The People's Republic was now the fifth nuclear power, and he thought it desirable to have the five nuclear powers occupy the five permanent seats on the Security Council. He then made a novel suggestion:

The Secretary General and the four nuclear Powers in the Security Council should be asked to negotiate with Peking [i.e. Beijing] and Taiwan ... to find out whether agreement could be arrived at on the following basis: that Taiwan would take a seat in the Assembly and that Peking would assume the position of a permanent member of the Security Council, accepting to be bound by the Purposes and Principles of the Charter, by a non-dissemination agreement and by an agreement that all other nuclear States would go to the assistance of a non-nuclear State attacked by a nuclear Power.[31]

Aiken maintained this position in speeches at the 1965 and 1966 Assembly sessions, and elucidated it further. In 1965 he spoke of 'the ancient nation of Taiwan', which ought to be admitted in its own right to the Assembly.[32] In 1966 he spoke of the right of its people to self-determination and to be represented in the UN as a sovereign independent state.[33]

Other Member States had shown reluctance about seating the People's Republic at the cost of expelling Taiwanese representatives, but no one, so far as I know, had previously spoken of self-determination for 'the ancient nation of Taiwan' and of its right to be represented in the UN as a sovereign independent state. There were, to say the least, some difficulties. For one thing, neither Beijing nor Taiwan would accept. Each believed that there was only one China, that Taiwan was a part of it, and that it was itself the legitimate government of that China, to the exclusion of the other. But Aiken's approach went further: by talking of 'the ancient nation of Taiwan' and the right of its people to self-determination, he was by implication referring to the indigenous people of the island and questioning the legitimacy of the Nationalist government of Chiang Kai Shek, which had taken control of the island and suppressed its native inhabitants in the closing stages of the Chinese civil war.

The idea, so far as I know, was Aiken's own: I do not recall that he ever elaborated on it in discussions with his officials before he left office in 1969. I do recall our misgivings, but, having fixed on the idea, he was not easily to be dissuaded. Looking back now, it seems to me quite characteristic of the man and the minister: courageous, off-centre and quirky in its way, but rooted in deep conviction about the right to self-determination that had its origins in his own involvement in the Irish struggle for independence nearly half a century before.

As a postscript, I might add that in 1971, as American President Richard Nixon was preparing to go to China, the Assembly decided that a simple majority would suffice. It then voted – by more than two-thirds as it happened – to seat the People's Republic in China's seat.

Ireland, where Dr Patrick Hillery was now minister, voted with the majority to seat the Beijing representatives.

The Cuban missile crisis

Finally, I want to touch briefly on the position Aiken took during the Cuban missile crisis of 1962. In October of that year, US intelligence agencies detected moves by Khrushchev's Soviet Union to station offensive medium-range missiles with nuclear warheads and a range of several thousand miles in Cuba, some ninety miles off shore from the continental US. On 22 October, American President John F. Kennedy in a television address to the nation made an ominous announcement: the US was imposing, unilaterally, a naval and air quarantine of Cuba, and the US would:

... regard any nuclear missile launched from Cuba against any nation in the Western Hemisphere as an attack by the Soviet Union on the United States, requiring a full retaliatory response against the Soviet Union.[34]

The president also addressed a personal letter to a number of leaders of the governments of other countries, including the Taoiseach, Seán Lemass, asking for their support.

The world was shocked at these developments, and there was widespread fear that a confrontation over the issue between the two superpowers could turn to nuclear war. In the days that followed, the US asked for an emergency meeting of the UN Security Council. The Council met on 23 October and the following days in an atmosphere of high drama. Its meetings were televised around the world. On 25 October, the US Representative to the UN, Adlai Stevenson, challenged Valentin Zorin, his Soviet opposite number, to deny that the Soviet Union 'has placed, and is placing medium and intermediate-range missiles and sites in Cuba'.[35]

When he received no reply, Stevenson produced aerial photographs by US spy planes to confirm what he had said. He then put forward a resolution calling for the withdrawal of the missiles from Cuba under the supervision of UN observers. At this stage, Russian vessels with additional missiles were still sailing towards Cuba, and there was serious danger of a confrontation at sea with US naval vessels, which had been ordered to intercept them and maintain the blockade. In the meantime, the UN Secretary General, U Thant, had been urged by many Member States to intervene. On the evening of 24 October, he sent messages to Kennedy and to Khrushchev. The messages were identical: they asked for the voluntary suspension of all arms shipments to Cuba, and the voluntary suspension of the quarantine measures involving the searching of ships, for a period of two to three weeks.

At the time, the Security Council had eleven members in all – five permanent and six elected members. Coincidentally, during the crisis Ireland was ten months into a one-year term as an elected member of the Security Council, having agreed to split the usual two-year term with Liberia. As events unfolded at the UN, Lemass was on an official visit to Germany. He gave a press conference in Bonn, at which he expressed Ireland's support for the US position. At the time he had been pressing the six EEC Member States to open negotiations on Ireland's application for membership, and he wanted to ensure that there would be no misunderstanding of its international position. At his press conference he went further in committing Ireland to a 'pro-western' position than any other Irish leader, then or since:

We are not in NATO, but that does not mean that we should be regarded as neutral. On the contrary we have emphasised over and over again that we are on the side of the western democracies …[36]

He had taken a similar tone on 5 September, some two months previously:

We do not wish, in the conflict between the free democracies and the communist empires, to be thought of as neutral. We are not neutral and do not wish to be regarded as such, even though we have not got specific commitments of a military kind under any international agreements.[37]

Aiken was in New York at this time to attend the annual session of the UN General Assembly. Lemass spoke to him on the phone from Bonn, and they agreed that Ireland would speak and vote for the US resolution in the Security Council. Ireland had already supported the US position on two related issues that came before the Council earlier that year: in February it helped to vote down Cuba's attempt to have the Council consider the decision of the Organization of American States (OAS) to expel it; and in March it voted against Cuba's request to have the Council seek an advisory opinion from the International Court of Justice in the Hague on the legality of the actions taken against it by the OAS, which included an economic boycott as well as expulsion.

Aiken took the Irish seat in the Security Council, and spoke in the debate on 24 October. There must have been no doubt at that point that Ireland would support the US position as already agreed on the phone with Lemass. Although this was clear enough, his speech was, nevertheless, reasonable and moderate in tone.

He was critical of both the Soviet Union and Cuba. 'The leaders of the Cuban Revolution', he said, 'chose to regard the part played by United States interests in Cuba as the source of all their country's ills', and 'Castroism … was inspired by a propagandist zeal which prompted it actively to pursue the spread of its ideas to other countries in Latin America'. He went on to note the successive stages in the quarrel between the US and Cuba: the Castro government's confiscations of US interests in Cuba; US economic reprisals; the economic and political rapprochement between Cuba and the Soviet bloc; Cuba's emergence as a Marxist-Leninist state, which had inevitably injected the Cold War into inter-State relations in the Americas; and US retaliation against Cuba. It was understandable that the Cuban government was concerned about their national security – all the more so because 'of the attempt by Cuban refugee elements to invade their territory' (a reference to the Bay of Pigs attack in April of the previous year).[38] It was only natural that the Cubans should seek to strengthen their defences, but it was a far cry from that to a military build-up of the kind that the Cuban government appeared to have embarked on, with significant assistance from the Soviet Union. Aiken elaborated:

> It is difficult for us, as it must be for others, to understand the reasons which led the Soviet Government, given the present state of tension existing throughout the world, to take a step which has the effect of upsetting the existing delicate balance of world security, the stability of which it is in the interest of all of us to maintain.

As to Cuba, it was:

> ... a great disappointment ... that ... any small nation, no matter from what motives or under what provocation, should willingly become a new strategic base for the prosecution of the Cold War or a spearhead in a nuclear conflict.

Aiken then recalled one of the principles underlying Irish neutrality in the Second World War:

> Our neutrality had as one of its fundamental bases a principle enunciated by the then leader of our Government, Mr. de Valera. That principle was that under no circumstances would we allow our country to be used as a base for attack against our neighbour, Great Britain. The principle is relevant to the case of all small countries threatened with involvement in conflicts or rivalries in which their powerful neighbours are engaged. It has special validity in the case of small countries placed beside powerful neighbours with whom they may have disputes or disagreements, as at the time of the Second World War we had – and indeed still have – with our neighbour, Great Britain, in regard to the partition of our country, but it is we believe, a principle worthy of the consideration of the Government of Cuba.

He developed the point further later in his speech:

> ... all Governments are bound to use the powers they derive from their national sovereignty not only in the best interests of their own peoples, but with due regard for the preservation of good relations with their neighbours and for the peace of the world.

He concluded by finding some indications of willingness to seek a peaceful solution in the approach of both the US and the Soviet Union:

> ...the danger to peace with which we are faced will not brook delay. Moreover, it can only be dispelled by agreement, and agreement cannot be achieved without discussions and negotiations. Let us hope, therefore, that negotiations will be entered into while there is still time.[39]

Aiken's approach was interesting and sensible. There was of course no question but that in a world crisis of this magnitude Ireland would vote with the United States, particularly since the US President who had laid down the gauntlet to Khrushchev, John F. Kennedy, was Irish-American.

The Irish government also agreed on 1 November, in response to an American request, that planes from Czechoslovakia, which regularly stopped at Shannon on their way to Cuba, would be searched in order to ensure that they were not carrying arms. These searches went on for several weeks thereafter. It is interesting that Sweden took a different line. As U Thant recalls in his memoirs:

> The Swedish government protested the US naval blockade and in fact successfully tested it on October 26 by sending a ship, reportedly with a cargo from the USSR, through the interception zone to Havana.[40]

In the event, the issue did not come to a vote in the UN Security Council. U Thant's messages to both Kennedy and Khrushchev seeking a moratorium had the effect, at least, of averting further escalation of the crisis. The eventual outcome was that Khrushchev, facing the enormity of the threat of possible nuclear war, backed down. He agreed to remove the missiles from Cuba and expressed a willingness to discuss verification by UN representatives. Cuba's Castro initially baulked at this, but U Thant visited Cuba and helped to mediate on the issue. Kennedy for his part agreed to remove certain US missiles that had been stationed in Turkey; a concession that was not reported at the time, but has since come to light.[41] The Cuban missile crisis, the most dangerous event since the Second World War, was effectively over, but the shudder of fear it engendered in the world continued for long after.

Ireland was not centrally involved in the issue, but as one of the eleven members of the Security Council for that year it was much more than a mere observer. Aiken had shown courage and independence five years earlier when the position he took on discussion of the representation of China put him – and Ireland – at odds with the US. It was never likely – indeed, in retrospect probably never even thinkable – that Ireland would put itself at odds with the US in October 1962. John F. Kennedy was President, Lemass had replaced de Valera as Taoiseach, and he was at just that moment negotiating to gain Ireland entry to the EEC. These points were no doubt all relevant in their way to the position that Ireland took on the Cuban issue. The primary reason, however, was the enormity of the danger – the serious possibility, as it seemed at the time, that the world, poised on a knife-edge, would topple over into nuclear war. In abstract argument it might perhaps be possible to stand on the point that Cuba had both a right to defend itself and a right to be concerned about its security, and that, if the Soviet Union wanted to place its missiles in Cuba, it was doing no more than the US had already done by placing its missiles in Turkey and elsewhere within easy reach of Russia. But this was not abstract argument but a world crisis precipitated by a rash act by a nuclear superpower.

Aiken, speaking for Ireland in the Security Council at the high point of the drama, was clear on where it stood fundamentally, but was still able to show some understanding of – even sympathy for – the security concerns of the Cuban government. More than that, he drew on Ireland's own historic experience to suggest a prudent principle that small states situated beside powerful neighbours would do well to follow.

Conclusion

I have served under a variety of ministers – nine in all – during my career in the Department of Foreign Affairs. I would not presume to rate them one against another, but I do feel that Frank Aiken was quite distinctive.

Born in the nineteenth century; a youthful revolutionary as far back as 1913; a veteran of the Civil War who may, perhaps to his later regret, have had some blood on his hands; a man who could recall the struggle of the Irish state to emerge to independence and its effort to have that independence recognised internationally – in all these ways he was a link with an older world. He had been a teenager during the First World War; a minister in the 1930s at the time when the League of Nations, the organisation that was supposed to avert war, faltered and collapsed; and a minister still in the Irish government that steered a neutral Ireland through the Second World War. All of this experience informed his approach to his years as Ireland's voice at the UN.

For each of the ministers I have known, the annual address to the UN General Assembly has been important. The speech nowadays is largely drafted by officials, subject of course to the minister's broad policy preferences. On either side of the speech, the minister spends a week or two at the UN in New York in early September each year, networking and meeting with EU colleagues and with foreign ministers from a variety of other countries, before leaving to deal with many other pressing priorities in Europe and elsewhere. Aiken, as I remember him, was different: the UN *was* his priority – an organisation the very existence of which was of existential importance for small states like Ireland seeking to assert and to maintain their independence. As a result, he stayed in New York for lengthy periods. He was his own person, and though he might take advice he was never dependent on it. I do not say that he wrote all his own speeches – I would think that Conor Cruise O'Brien and Freddie Boland had significant roles in the late 1950s – but in later years he sometimes prepared a first draft and discussed it with his officials, a reversal of the usual roles.

Aiken had an inventive cast of mind, whether dealing with international affairs or in more mundane matters. The ideas that he came up with, more often than not, were his own. Some were ingenious, often a bit quirky, somehow slightly detached from, or at an angle to, the hard-nosed security concerns of other larger Member States. It could be argued that Irish foreign policy as reflected in the approach taken at the UN General Assembly in those years was largely declaratory and expressed in speeches rather than in the more concrete and often difficult policy choices – economic as well as political – that face many small countries today. It is also likely that larger states, particularly those in the rival alliances, probably saw Aiken's speeches as well-meaning, but essentially those of someone outside the 'real' foreign policy arena in which they were engaged. But his ideas and proposals were always conceived with integrity and pursued with stubborn persistence. He was someone who was genuinely concerned to support international cooperation, to support the UN and to make it work. Some of his ideas made his officials a bit nervous, at least initially, and some of his initiatives fell on stony ground. One or two – most notably his concern to achieve a treaty to stop the spread of nuclear weapons – were of real importance and deserve to be remembered.

All in all, he was a distinctive figure in my memory. To paraphrase something said in Irish about another time and place – we shall not see his like again.

Notes

1   Issues not dealt with here include Ireland's role in the Congo crisis; China and Tibet; Southern Africa and colonialism; UN peacekeeping and the financing of peacekeeping; the formal raising of Irish partition; and the outbreak of the Troubles in Northern Ireland. For an account of these and other topics during the 1960s, see Noel Dorr, *Ireland at the United Nations: Memories of the Early Years* (Dublin: Institute of Public Administration).

2   In 1957, Aiken did deliver the annual Estimates speech in the Dáil entirely in Irish. Joseph Morrison Skelly *Irish Diplomacy at the United Nations 1945–1965: National Interests and the International Order* (Dublin: Irish Academic Press, 1997), 89.

3   'Oisín, [lonely] after the Fianna'. According to the Irish storytellers, the legendary hero, Oisín, survived into early Christian times and told stories of the heroic age to St Patrick.

4   Speech by Aiken, 6 Oct. 1960. *Ireland at the United Nations 1960, speeches by Mr. Frank Aiken* (Dublin: Brún agus Ó Nulláin Teo, 1961), 15.

5   Speech by Aiken, 6 Oct. 1960. *Ireland at the United Nations 1960, speeches by Mr. Frank Aiken*, 14. Aiken was mistaken about the date, which was 1919 and not 1921.

6   Speech by Aiken, 10 Sept. 1957. *Ireland at the United Nations 1957, speeches by Mr. Frank Aiken* (Dublin: Brún agus Ó Nulláin Teo, 1958), 6.

7   Speech by Aiken, 10 Sept. 1957. *Ireland at the United Nations 1957, speeches by Mr. Frank Aiken*, 8.

8   Speech by Aiken, 10 Sept. 1957. *Ireland at the United Nations 1957, speeches by Mr. Frank Aiken*, 9.

9   Speech by Aiken, 23 Sept. 1959. *Ireland at the United Nations 1959, speeches by Mr. Frank Aiken* (Dublin: Brún agus Ó Nulláin Teo, 1960), 9.

10   He spoke about the idea of 'Areas of Law' in greater or lesser detail in speeches in 1958, 1959, 1960, 1962, 1963, 1964, 1965, 1966 and 1967 – that is every year except 1961 and 1968. See references in index, *Ireland at the United Nations 1967, speeches by Mr. Frank Aiken* (Dublin: Brún agus Ó Nulláin Teo, 1968), 94.

11   See speech of 23 Sept. 1959, *Ireland at the United Nations 1959, speeches by Mr. Frank Aiken*, 9–10.

12   Skelly, *Irish Diplomacy at the United Nations 1945–1965*, 111–112.

13   George Kennan, *Reith Lectures 1957; Lecture 3 The Problem of Eastern and Central Europe*, transmitted on the BBC Home Service on 24 Nov. 1957, available at downloads.bbc.co.uk/rmhttp/radio4/transcripts/1957_reith3.pdf (accessed 08/07/13).

14   Grant Stockdale served as Ambassador from March 1961 to July 1962. The two diplomats from the Embassy were Messrs. O'Connor and Prince. Seán Morrissey, Seán Ronan and I accompanied the Minister.

15   Skelly, *Irish Diplomacy at the United Nations 1945–1965*, 250.

16   Skelly, *Irish Diplomacy at the United Nations 1945–1965*, 255.

17   For the text of the resolution see *Ireland at the United Nations 1959, speeches by Mr. Frank Aiken*, 77.

18   Speech by Aiken, 13 Nov. 1959. *Ireland at the United Nations 1959, speeches by Mr. Frank Aiken*, 64.

19   For the text of the resolution, see *Ireland at the United Nations 1960, speeches by Mr. Frank Aiken*, 65–66.

20   Speech by Aiken, 30 Nov. 1961. *Ireland at the United Nations 1961, speeches by Mr. Frank Aiken* (Dublin: Brún agus Ó Nulláin Teo, 1962), 13–18.

21   For the text of the resolution, see *Ireland at the United Nations 1960, speeches by Mr. Frank Aiken*, 37.

22   Evgency M. Chossudovsky, 'The Origins of the Treaty on the Non-Proliferation of Nuclear Weapons: Ireland's Initiative in the United Nations, 1958–61', *Irish Studies in International Affairs*, Vol. 3, No. 2 (1990), 129–130.

23 Internal report of the Department of External Affairs on the 1965 session of the General Assembly 25–31. A copy of the report is in my possession. Similar reports were prepared annually during most of the 1960s. I myself contributed to a number of them.

24 In one of his later books, Conor Cruise O'Brien says that Aiken's decision followed a discussion in which the minister asked him how best to be seen to take an independent line at the UN. See Conor Cruise O'Brien, *Memoir: My Life and Themes* (Dublin: Poolbeg Press, 1998), 186–187.

25 See *Ireland at the United Nations 1957, speeches by Mr. Frank Aiken*, 28.

26 Speech by Aiken, 23 Sept. 1957. *Ireland at the United Nations 1957, speeches by Mr. Frank Aiken*, 22–28.

27 Skelly, *Irish Diplomacy at the United Nations 1945–1965*, 226–235.

28 Speech by Aiken, 21 Sept. 1959. *Ireland at the United Nations 1959, speeches by Mr. Frank Aiken*, 6.

29 Article 2.7

30 In my book, *Ireland at the United Nations: Memories of the Early Years*, 126, I wrongly gave the vote as forty-eight votes to thirty-six, with twenty abstentions. The correct totals are as above.

31 Speech by Aiken, 8 Dec. 1964. Aiken, *Ireland at the United Nations 1964*, 14.

32 Speech by Aiken, 30 Sept. 1965 (Department of External Affairs internal report on the 1965 Assembly session 27). A copy is in the possession of the author.

33 Department of External Affairs internal report on the 1966 and 1967 Assembly sessions, 37. A copy is in the possession of the author.

34 John F. Kennedy, *Cuban Missile Crisis Address to the Nation*, available on www.americanrhetoric.com/speeches (accessed on 06/05/13).

35 Stevenson's statement to the Council on 25 Oct. 1962 can be found in US Department of State *Bulletin* Vol. XLVII, No. 1220, 737–740. Available at https://www.mtholyoke.edu/acad/intrel/adlai.htm (accessed on 15/07/13).

36 Skelly, *Irish Diplomacy at the United Nations 1945–1965*, 241.

37 Denis Maher, *The Tortuous Path: The Course of Ireland's Entry into the EEC 1948–73* (Dublin: Institute of Public Administration, 1986), 156–157. On 22 Oct., while Lemass was on his way to Bonn, the Council of the Community 'decided in favour of the opening of negotiations on Ireland's application for membership on a date to be agreed' (Ibid. 160).

38 Address by Aiken to the UN Security Council, 24 Oct. 1962. *Ireland at the United Nations 1962, speeches by Mr. Frank Aiken*, 23–30.

39 Address by Aiken to the UN Security Council, 24 Oct. 1962. *Ireland at the United Nations 1962, speeches by Mr. Frank Aiken*, 23–30.

40 U Thant, *View from the UN* (London: Newton Abbot, David and Charles, 1978), 169.

41 Thant, *View from the UN*, 191.

CHAPTER NINE

'Personally I think it would be positively hilarious': The European Convention, the Cyprus Question and Frank Aiken's state of exception

HELEN O'SHEA

Introduction

Despite the later ubiquity of his name with Irish foreign policy at the United Nations, in the late 1950s, Minister for External Affairs Frank Aiken would surprise many of his critics, who had thought of him only as 'de Valera's bodyguard and shadow', with his grasp of international issues.[1] Indeed, his dedication to the UN was such that he has been recalled fondly as the 'Minister for the United Nations' by one former Irish Ambassador to the UN under his early tutelage,[2] with a more abrasive depiction of the UN as Aiken's 'playpen' allegedly made by former Taoiseach Seán Lemass.[3] Existing accounts of Aiken's thirteen-year UN contribution, based on Irish archival sources, often relay his activist foreign policy, emphasising his instinctive sympathy, not least because of his own revolutionary past, for countries fighting to end British colonial rule

233

such as Cyprus.[4] However, if one looks from a different vantage point, namely that of British government officials at Whitehall, Strasbourg and New York in the late 1950s, a more nuanced account of Aiken's foreign policy manoeuvrings at this time is revealed.

Ireland's foreign modus operandi, with a Minister for External Affairs with a relentless antipathy British imperial rule and Irish partition, was perceived with anxiety by British officials. Between the Twelfth and Fourteenth Sessions at the United Nations in the late 1950s, Aiken's views were often made manifest by his most trusted civil servant in the Irish UN delegation in New York, Conor Cruise O'Brien.[5] Examination of Aiken's stance from the British perspective also reveals contingent factors, namely of an independent Ireland legally *comparable* to British Cyprus during the period in question, which suggest that Aiken's political nous, if not sheer boldness, has been underestimated in the existing Irish diplomatic historiography.[6]

By the time Aiken took up office as Minister for External Affairs for the second time in 1957, the National Organization of Cypriot Fighters (EOKA) was in the midst of fighting a guerrilla campaign against British forces on an island that, until British governance in 1878, had been conquered by Assyrians, Phoenicians, Greeks, Persians, Macedonians, Romans, Byzantines, Franks, Venetians and the Ottomans. While their aim was not simply independence, but rather *enosis* or union with Greece, the psychology of denial in relation to the strength of Irish separatist nationalism prior to independence – regularly stigmatised as artificially created, unreasonable and existent only on the fringes of society – was closely paralleled in the British administration's assessment of the strength of Hellenic irredentism. Britain and the US, despite being at loggerheads after the Suez Crisis, were driven by their strategic Cold War interests and determined to solve the Cyprus Question with quiet diplomacy rather than on the UN stage. Nonetheless, the Cyprus Question was a useful yardstick by which to measure potential attitudes towards the raising of Irish partition at the UN, which, as will be shown, Aiken seriously considered in 1957. However, the eventual decision not to pursue this course of action at the Thirteenth Session of the General Assembly in 1958 did not necessarily mark a private realisation that Irish partition was, in all likelihood, permanent. Instead, it may have been due to the largely obscured, but potentially explosive, factor that a state of emergency was in place on both islands, and perhaps illegally so in the case of Ireland.

Due to the escalation of violence by EOKA from 1 April 1955, Governor John Harding proclaimed a state of emergency in Cyprus on 26 November 1955. Against the background of the Cypriot Emergency, Greece formally lodged the first of its two inter-state cases to the European Commission of Human Rights

(ECmHR), with Britain as the respondent state, on 7 May 1956. Frustrated by his failed attempts to place Cyprus on the UN agenda in 1954 and 1955, Greek Prime Minister Kostas Karamanlis issued instructions to Foreign Minister Evangelos Averoff that the allegations of British atrocities in Cyprus – including internment without trial – should be taken to Strasbourg. Case 176/56, as it became known, was declared admissible on 2 June 1956. The following year, on 5 July 1957, the Irish government reintroduced internment without trial under the Offences against the State Act, ostensibly to deal with the IRA's border campaign in 1956. Subsequently, Aiken, along with the Irish government's legal team, watched Cypriot events, and the Greek case, closely.

The British Official Mind on Frank Aiken's Early Days at the UN

Despite Aiken's need to appease the Irish electorate with sound bites from New York, his support for Greek-Cypriot self-determination is hardly surprising. Along with the majority of the Irish populace, for whom the Irish War of Independence was still a living memory, he saw events in Cyprus as analogous to those in Ireland during the turbulent years from 1919 to 1921, more so than any other insurgency campaign in the history of the British Empire. Its subjects were white, mostly Christian and European, and viewed as part of an ancient and cultured civilization fighting against the same colonial yoke as Ireland had. Because the perceived wholeness of islands was axiomatic for the majority of the Irish populace, the Greek-Cypriot opposition to the possible partition of Cyprus during the late 1950s was implicitly understood. Thus, the Cyprus Emergency had a greater emotional resonance in the Irish imagination than similar events in more distant, non-island colonial outposts.

That the majority of Irish public opinion was against British policy in Cyprus was clearly recognised by British officials. The British Ambassador in Dublin, Sir Alexander Clutterbuck, regarded it as 'virtually inevitable'.[7] In 1958, Arthur Wendell Snelling, Assistant Undersecretary of State at the Commonwealth Relations Office, expanded on the reasons behind Clutterbuck's assessment: 'Cyprus raises issues which have 100 years of emotional overtones in Irish history: the principle of self-determination, partition, the use of troops from another country to maintain law and order'.[8] Notwithstanding the robustness of this assessment, much of British public and political opinion was also opposed to British policy in Cyprus and, admittedly, the Irish public response lay ambiguously on the spectrum between latent anti-Britishness and genuine anti-imperialism. Although largely sympathetic, Irish support for Cypriot self-determination was not necessarily an expression of a wider Irish anti-colonial sensibility. For some, Cyprus merely served as an extended metaphor for Ireland, a suitable peg upon which to hang past Irish grievances. For those of the *Hibernia irredenta* mentality, the Cyprus conflict was significant in terms of the opportunities that it offered to address continued Irish nationalist grievances, primarily partition.

Inevitably, British officialdom was concerned at how the Irish delegation would behave if the Cyprus Question arose during Ireland's first performance on the UN stage. Ronald Stratford Scrivener of the Foreign Office (FO) admitted that 'few people anywhere are likely to see no parallel between Cyprus and the Ireland of the 1920s. Plenty of London newspapers have'.[9] The choice of the Irish Ambassador in London, Frederick Boland, as Ireland's Permanent Representative was a consoling one given that he was, as Scrivener accurately described him, 'exceptionally anglophile'.[10] At the Eleventh UN General Assembly, which convened on 12 November 1956, and to the relief of the British UK delegation, the Fine Gael Minister for External Affairs, Liam Cosgrave, advised by the more experienced Boland, gave a very moderate speech with little reference made to Cyprus.

Ironically, the FO had been unduly anxious before Ireland's first UN session in light of the cautiousness of the second inter-party government delegation. Conversely, with de Valera back in power in 1957, they were therefore overly optimistic that the Irish delegation would adopt a similar line at the next session. Reassurance given by Boland to UK officials was a strong factor in their relaxed assessment. They clearly trusted him – not a particularly large leap of faith to make given how frequently he aired his pro-British leanings. Despite the fact that the idea of the partition of Cyprus was now being bandied about so frequently, particularly by the increasingly intransigent Turkish government, Boland remained, to all appearances, confident that the Irish delegation's line would be moderate. According to Ivor Pink at the FO, Boland had 'expressed indignation about the nonsense talked by the anti-colonials'.[11] 'This was particularly unfair in the case of the United Kingdom', Boland told Pink, 'which had given freedom to many millions of people at a time when the Soviet Union was busy adding to its Empire'. [12] In what would prove to be a stark contrast to the Irish UN agenda as Aiken foresaw it, Pink reported Boland's sentiments:

> He recognised that it was difficult for the U.K. or the other colonial powers to defend themselves on this issue, but thought that something could be done by smaller countries and in particular by Ireland. He recognised that there were certain unresolved political issues between his Government and Her Majesty's Government; nevertheless he did not see why the Irish Delegation should not bring a little realism into

the 'colonial debates' by drawing attention to the United Kingdom record since the war. I naturally welcomed this suggestion.[13]

While Boland's statements were not necessarily disingenuous – and may very well have expressed his personal view – he already knew that other members of the Irish team were anxious to press the issue of Irish partition. Conor Cruise O'Brien, who shared and arguably influenced Aiken's outlook, assumed a more visible role at the UN with the return of Fianna Fáil. He also had greater authority as he was now in charge of the Political Section of the Department of External Affairs, which assumed responsibility for matters pertaining to the UN. While Cosgrave had turned largely to the Anglophile Irish UN ambassador Frederick Boland for advice on how to translate his views into effective action, Aiken now turned to O'Brien.

In response to O'Brien's requests for advice on how they should best bring up Irish partition, Boland had stressed that 'Whatever we do, we must afford our own people the assurance that in shaping our attitude at the United Nations, we have our own national problem constantly in mind'.[14] To this end, he thought that the Cyprus case would again be a convenient peg upon which to hang the speech. It does seem, however, that this advice was given in an effort to dissuade O'Brien and Aiken from taking 'an abrupt or sudden change of policy', which Boland thought 'should be avoided at all costs'.[15] A formal attempt to raise Irish partition at the UN might have been anathema to Boland, but he was only too aware of Aiken's politics. The previous month, Aiken had instructed Con Cremin, the Irish Ambassador in London, to open discussions on partition with the Dublin-born Catholic Sir Gilbert Laithwaite, now Permanent Undersecretary of the Commonwealth Relations Office (CRO). So why, in his interactions with British officials, did Boland offer an overly sanguine analysis? The short answer is that Boland needed to impress. Although he denied it to British officials, J.M.C. James of the CRO had received word from G.E. Cox of the Canadian High Commission in London that 'Boland might be standing for the one of the three Vice-Presidencies of the Assembly this year'.[16]

Notwithstanding the almost obligatory hyperbole employed by any newly independent state like Ireland, it was also in the newly elected government's interests not to appear to lag behind, or ignore, public opinion, as was recognised by some British officials. James claimed that at the next Assembly session, 'they will no doubt have to make at least the usual routine references to it [partition] in the General Debate'.[17] He recognised that 'we obviously cannot rely on their maintaining indefinitely the remarkably high standard of objectivity and responsibility which they achieved at the Eleventh Session … to which Boland's own presence no doubt contributed a good deal'.[18] While the Anglo-Irish relationship remained paramount, the Fianna Fáil government was arguably under more pressure than its predecessors to appease Irish public opinion at the UN. Cosgrave had escaped unscathed after his moderate speech in November 1956. Since then, the Suez and Hungary crises between October and November had overshadowed the Cyprus dispute, and allowances were always going to be made for Ireland's introductory UN session. But after the Eleventh General Assembly, the Irish public was now much more aware of Irish UN participation, sympathy for Cyprus was ever increasing, and the border campaign had reawakened some latent republican sentiments.

Rather than the close alliance with western groups for which Boland had hoped, an independent, activist stance was made apparent from the beginning of the Twelfth Session. Much to Boland's chagrin, this change of agenda, which often saw Ireland in alliance with anti-colonial and, on occasion, Communist groupings, was made undeniably clear when Ireland voted for the inclusion of a discussion on the question of Chinese representation at the UN in September 1957. The Irish delegates were now labelled 'bloody mavericks' by their American counterparts as, much to their annoyance, the Irish delegation could no longer be depended upon to align themselves with the US.[19] Boland was not only worried about the delegation's international standing, but also his own UN career. As O'Brien put it, writing after his embittered exit from the UN and the Irish civil service, the obvious jobs in the 'gift' of the UN – chairmanships of committees, rapporteurships, the Presidency of the General Assembly itself – 'always went to Permanent Mission members': they were 'always in practice the gift of the Americans, who dominated all aspects of the workings of the UN'.[20]

If anyone had been in doubt over Ireland's reduced dependency on the British UN delegation, O'Brien made it clear during his speech on Cyprus in the First Committee on 11 December 1957. 'Ireland feared', he said, that instead of a just solution for Cyprus, 'what is being prepared was that last expedient of tired statesmen: the solution of partition'.[21] Despite O'Brien's best efforts, the Greek resolution failed to get the simple majority it needed to be passed and was, according to Sir Pierson Dixon's Private Secretary, Douglas Hurd, largely down to 'emergency telegrams to capitals of the waverers to get their instructions changed and intensive arm-twisting in the corridors'.[22] While Irish national interests framed what O'Brien included, they also determined what O'Brien omitted from his Cyprus speech. No remarks were made by him on the British emergency measures in Cyprus, in particular internment without trial and the alleged human rights abuses of political detainees there. Any speech that 'twisted the lion's tail' by indicating sympathy for the political detainees in Cyprus could be used damagingly in respect of the Curragh internees, and potentially by the British delegation to point out the inherent hypocrisy to fellow UN Member States. One of the Curragh internees, Gerard Lawless, had brought his case to the ECtHR a month before O'Brien's address. Lawless, a suspected IRA member who had been arrested on 11 July 1957, had his application to the ECmHR transmitted on 18 November 1957. The case before the ECtHR centred on Lawless' claim that the Irish government, by detaining him without trial, had breached Articles 5, 6 and 7 of the ECHR, providing rights to liberty and security, fair trial and the principle of 'no punishment without law' respectively. The British were already in the dock in Strasbourg with two Greek applications – cases 176/56 and 299/57 – and now Ireland was too. Owing to the Lawless case, the Irish delegation was hardly in a position to comment on the alleged maltreatment of detainees in Cyprus.

The UK delegation was bitterly disappointed by the Irish contribution. For them, O'Brien 'had approached the problem from an entirely parochial point of view'.[23] The British UN Ambassador, Sir Pierson Dixon, reported that 'one of the most regrettable features of the proceedings has been the performance of the Irish Republican Delegation'.[24] In this, he was referring to O'Brien, of course. Boland remained, as ever, the consummate diplomat. Dixon stressed that Boland 'made a moderate speech' and 'appealed for moderation, which he said alone could achieve a settlement'.[25] This contrasted with O'Brien's statement. Dixon claimed that it was 'a disquisition on partition', noting that he voted for the extremist Greek draft both in the Committee and in the Plenary.[26] Although Dixon was certain that O'Brien's speech was not an indication that the Irish government was planning to raise the issue of Northern Ireland, he questioned 'whether it is prudent [of them] to allow their representatives here to take a line which might encourage agitation in Ireland for action at the United Nations'.[27] He claimed that:

An examination of the voting list on the Cyprus issue should prove to the Irish government that they have got into strange company: in particular the Communists and the wilder anti-colonialists. This supping with the devil is incongruous for a country which can play a constructive and rather special part in the general defence of democracy … Hopefully some opportunity can be taken of having all this out with the Irish government. I do not think that Mr. Boland here needs much persuasion.[28]

On 1 January, H.G.M. Bass of the CRO wrote to Gurth Kimber of the British Embassy in Dublin, forwarding Dixon's request that representations be made to the Irish government regarding the Irish delegation's actions. Bass, who attached O'Brien's speech, informed Kimber: 'you will see that O'Brien concerned himself very largely with the "partition" aspect of the question and its supposed analogy with partition in Ireland'.[29] In his view, it was 'hard to believe that any legitimate objective of Irish foreign policy could have been achieved by such behaviour, which contrasts with last year's much more reasonable behaviour'.[30] Bass considered it 'particularly unfortunate' that certain members of the Irish delegation took such 'an irresponsible line' after 'the very promising start they made last year under Cosgrave's leadership'.[31] He added:

> We feel sure that Dixon is right in suggesting that Boland is unhappy at these developments. Part of the trouble may be due to the fact that I understand O'Brien has strong personal feelings on the subject of partition, but even so it is strange that he should have been allowed so much latitude, unless with official blessing.[32]

The UN Irish Partition Proposal and Irish–Cypriot Comparisons

At home, Aiken was criticised, particularly by Fine Gael deputies, for two reasons. Firstly, for his proposal, made when speaking on Hungary on 10 September, of the military disengagement of non-national armies on the Continent. Secondly, for his support on 23 September for the Indian amendment proposing that the question of the representation of China should be discussed. Aiken was seen as dabbling in matters that were of little concern to Ireland. His proposals were considered offensive to Ireland's 'friends' abroad, namely Cardinal Francis Spellman of New York, the wider Catholic Irish-American community and the US government. On 28 November, an Opposition Motion, proposed by Fine Gael's Declan Costello, moved that 'Dáil Éireann disapproves of recent developments in the foreign policy of the Government as represented by certain statements and actions of the Minister for External Affairs at the General Assembly of the U.N.O.'[33] Aiken was charged with acting 'against the true interests' of Ireland.[34]

In what can only be interpreted as a tacit approval, the deputies were notably silent on O'Brien's speech on Cyprus. Despite Dixon's pleas, no representations were made in Dublin; it was thought that they would have little effect. Instead, O'Brien simply remained the object of much criticism. An extract from a British official report summarising the Twelfth Session of the General Assembly claimed that 'Mr. Boland's interventions were as witty and competent as ever', while O'Brien's speech was considered 'obnoxious'.[35] The British Embassy in Dublin also continued to express their disappointment. O'Brien was well aware of how he was perceived: 'I was regarded as the "radical" member of the Irish delegation, wearing my mandatory anti-colonialism rather more aggressively than was prudent'.[36]

By the autumn of 1957, from behind the scenes, de Valera, now aged 75 and almost totally blind, was beginning to realise that it was, in all likelihood, his last ever Cabinet. However platitudinous his nationalist rhetoric may have been – and it often was – he was now feeling the 'chill wind of political mortality'.[37] Although strongly denied, there were rumours that he would resign at the Fianna Fáil Árd Fheis in November 1957. Would he realise his dream of ending partition before he was guided – if not pushed – out of Irish politics? De Valera and Aiken had pursued the possibility of a united, federal Ireland rejoining the Commonwealth since their return to power in March 1957. The initiative had first been raised that month by Cardinal John D'Alton, Roman Catholic Primate of All Ireland. But the diplomatic offensive with Sir Gilbert Laithwaite, Permanent Undersecretary of the CRO, and the Earl of Home, CRO's Permanent Secretary and Leader of the House of Lords, had achieved little.[38] With Aiken's approval, O'Brien now pushed the matter with an urgency that was never to be repeated. He may have discovered the 'cavernous inanities' of anti-partition while working under the mercurial Seán MacBride between 1947 and 1951, but he was willing to explore fully the possibility of raising a UN draft resolution on Irish partition in January and February of 1958.[39]

On 24 January 1958, O'Brien set down a memorandum on the question of raising the partition issue formally in the UN. He had discussed the matter with Aiken the week before. The memorandum as it stood represented 'only the views of the Political Section' of the Department of External Affairs.[40] As mentioned earlier, O'Brien was the head of this section, which assumed responsibility for UN affairs. He tabled the memorandum officially through John Belton, Assistant Secretary of the Department of External Affairs. O'Brien stressed that the 'best guide' on the chances of success, assuming that the question was placed on the UN agenda, was the voting on the Cyprus resolution that had taken place in the Assembly before the Christmas recess. He noted that the abstainers were 'no doubt' following the example of the US delegation. The 'solidest support' for the Greek position came from the 'Communist and Arab countries'; the strongest support for the British position came from Western-European countries and the 'white Commonwealth'.[41] He elaborated on why the case of Cyprus at the UN, rather than any other territorial dispute, was the litmus test for the Irish delegation:

Broadly speaking the Cyprus case is the most similar to ours of all the major political claims because Greece and ourselves are European nations with territorial claims. Both, in the measure that the claims are regarded as 'anti-colonial,' can expect support from the more militant among the Afro-Asians but we cannot count, as say Indonesia or Algeria can do, on the very strong and general Afro-Asian support which is generated by any struggle between white and coloured people.[42]

O'Brien felt that an Irish proposal would get a slightly greater degree of support than a Cypriot one for two reasons. Firstly, given that Ireland's record of resistance was well known to most of the Afro-Asian countries, they would find it more embarrassing to fail to support Ireland's claim than that of Greece. Secondly, the Irish case would not have to face the extra opposition of Turkey. Turkey was still likely to vote against them because of the Irish delegation's attitude to Cyprus. All the NATO countries, apart from the US and Iceland, who both abstained, voted against the Greek position. Thus, the fact that Ireland was not a NATO member would mean that they would not be any worse off in votes by reason of Ireland's non-membership of NATO. O'Brien assumed that the US abstention was motivated less by any consideration for Greece as a member of NATO than by the considerable Greek vote in certain key US states. This same consideration would *a fortiori* apply to Ireland. 'All in all', he felt, 'we should do a little better than Greece but not much'.[43] He advised that if the Irish delegation were to make such a move in the next Assembly, and make it effectively, the decision needed to be taken before the end of February.

The new Secretary of the Department of the External Affairs replacing Seán Murphy was the former Ambassador to London, Con Cremin. Both he and Boland were sent copies of the memorandum. While O'Brien waited for their replies, he pressed ahead with the issue. By 7 February 1958, after discussions with Aiken, O'Brien asked Eoin MacWhite, First Secretary of the Political Section, to prepare a memorandum covering the technical steps that they would need to take to press ahead with the formal UN request. It seems at this stage that O'Brien felt it was a real possibility. He wrote to Cremin informing him of the steps MacWhite was preparing, which he claimed 'we will need to take once we decide to go ahead with this'.[44] It was the Cyprus case at the UN that MacWhite examined more closely than any other to find pertinent precedents for the Irish resolution.[45] For him, the most important lesson to be learned from it was the argument that the British initially used to prevent its discussion:

The argument against inclusion of Partition in any shape or form will certainly be based on Article 2 (7) (domestic jurisdiction) and we should have to prepare a very complete brief on all relevant 2 (7) decisions in the Assembly. Another point which the Cyprus case indicates may be a possible British counter if they decide they are beaten on the agenda [*sic*] inclusion is the possibility that they might come back with a counter item, e.g. on IRA attacks.[46]

On 17 February, Boland sent Cremin, MacWhite and O'Brien copies of a memorandum containing his objections against bringing up the question formally at the UN. By this stage, there had been several months of tension – enmity even – between Boland and the Aiken–O'Brien camp. The previous September, O'Brien had advised Aiken to support the Indian amendment proposing that the question of the representation of China should be discussed. The motivation for doing so was to make it clear from the outset of Aiken's first UN session that a more independent line would be taken by an Irish delegation during his watch. In doing so, O'Brien had permanently alienated Boland, who strongly favoured siding with the US on the China issue, and their friendship quickly disintegrated. For Boland, who was more reflexively pro-British than he was pro-American, it was out of the question that the issue should be formally raised.

Boland's memorandum was 'at variance not only with Dr. O'Brien's conclusions but also with some of the arguments on which they are based'.[47] He used the Cyprus case 'as a good case in point' to refute O'Brien's estimation that Ireland would have the support of the Afro-Asian bloc.[48] He protested that 'after years of effort and solicitous support of Afro-Asian causes, Greece couldn't even rally half of the votes!'[49] Instead, Boland stressed the cooperative approach, ostensibly endorsed by de Valera at the previous Árd Fheis in November 1957, as the only possible way to end partition. He concluded by leaving O'Brien in no doubt as to how he felt on the matter:

The idea that the United Nations is a tribunal to which nations can resort in the confidence of obtaining justice is a pure illusion. The UN is simply a den of power-politics in which small, independent countries such as ours are at a complete disadvantage in conflict with countries like Britain … Members of the UN don't judge questions on their merits. They vote purely in accordance with their own interests … The idea, therefore, that by going to the UN, we can get an expression of world moral opinion on the justice or injustice of Partition is a complete illusion.[50]

On 21 February, Cremin forwarded Boland's memorandum to Aiken. He asked that Aiken examine it carefully in light of the strong objections advanced by

Boland.[51] Aiken decided that it was in Ireland's best interests not to put forward a request to place it on the forthcoming UN agenda. Was this attitude due to Boland's advice, or were there other contingent factors in play?

For all the analogies drawn in the Irish newspapers between revolutionary Ireland and late 1950s Emergency Cyprus, the fact remained that, legally, a state of emergency also existed in Ireland from 5 July 1957 until 14 March 1959. As the IRA border campaign had been in operation for four months by the time Aiken returned as Minister for External Affairs, he was now in no position to use inflammatory rhetoric indicating sympathy for the political detainees in Cyprus that would consequently be available to the IRA as propaganda, for use by Sinn Féin in the *United Irishman,* or by the pro-republican Irish-American newspapers. In order to deal with the border campaign, Fianna Fáil brought back into force special powers of indefinite detention without trial under the Offences against the State (Amendment) Act 1940. Yet it could only do so legally under the European Convention of Human Rights (ECHR) by claiming there was an emergency threatening the life of the nation.

This state of emergency was later confirmed by the ECHR in its verdict on the Gerard Lawless case. However, on no occasion was an emergency declared in public by Taoiseach Éamon de Valera, Aiken, or any other member of the government. Given that the government had declared a state of emergency during the Second World War, any announcement that it now existed would have enhanced the prominence of the border campaign. De Valera wanted to give the IRA as little oxygen as possible. Although the Act's reintroduction led to the arrest and detention without trial of over 200 suspected members of the IRA in the Curragh, County Kildare, this hardly indicated the existence of a public emergency threatening the life of the country – after all, the IRA was carrying out operations *across* the border. On 27 June 1957, the UK lodged its notice of derogation in respect of internment in Northern Ireland. Because of the IRA raids in Northern Ireland, it was arguably far more justified in doing so.

Now, not only was Ireland of the past being compared to Cyprus, but Ireland at that time, in light of the emergency legislation on detention, was now seen by some as carrying out the same measures that the British were applying in Cyprus. On 19 July 1957, at a meeting of the Congress of Irish Unions (CIU) in Tramore, County Waterford, Mr J. Hennigan of the Engineering, Industrial and Electrical Union drew on the Ireland–Cyprus comparison. He claimed that 'Outside the Iron Curtain countries and the British in Cyprus, this was the only country in the world at the moment where men could be sentenced without trial, interned and put under such economic duress that they could no longer keep their families'.[52] Mary Caughey, a close friend of the artist Jack B. Yeats, and the subject for his charcoal drawing, *The Cavalier's Wife*, complained to de Valera that the presence of internment camps in the Republic 'makes one feel that Ireland is going to be a second Cyprus'.[53] With the risk of de Valera's internment policy now being compared to British policy in Cyprus, Aiken's foreign policy response to the Cyprus Question became markedly circumspect.

On 1 December 1958, at the Thirteenth General Assembly in New York, the First Committee began its discussions on the Cyprus Question. Again, it was O'Brien who would speak for the Irish delegation. It was easily his most judicious exposition on the Cyprus issue and, notably, it contained no reference to Irish partition. He did make it clear that Ireland would vote against the British draft resolution, which, according to him, appeared to be tantamount to a request for the Assembly to support current British policy on Cyprus.[54] He stated that Ireland would also vote against the Turkish resolution and, as expected, in favour of the Greek resolution, which called for UN endorsement of eventual independence for Cyprus and a special UN committee to work towards this goal. He criticised the complex British arrangements for the future of the island, which he said unintentionally leant towards a partition in which, understandably, as he saw it, the Greeks and Greek-Cypriots had refused to participate.[55] Because of this, he asserted that 'the experiment dwindles to a simple partnership between the United Kingdom, Turkey and the Cypriot minority – a partnership in frustration of the aspirations of the majority of the Cypriot people'.[56]

O'Brien believed that the minority interests should be looked after by the UN, but should not be taken into account in such a way as to negate the wishes of the majority. In a surprise turnaround – though not perhaps without a touch of irony – he gave credit to the British government: 'I find it hard to believe that a partnership of that kind will take place in the pages of history besides those wise and generous examples of partnership in which Britain has, in many other parts of the world, played so creative a part'.[57]

Despite being critical of British plans for Cyprus, his language on the whole was measured, and certainly less confrontational than his previous performance. O'Brien's moderation was noted by *The Irish Times*. Its editorial claimed: 'This country's main contributor to the UN debate on Cyprus was sane and practical'.[58] On 4 December, O'Brien urged the committee, made up of eighty-one nations, to approve a ten-power resolution that called for respect for the 'integrity' of Cyprus, and dismissed as 'utterly destructive' any proposal that would tend towards a division of the island.[59] With the proposed UN resolution on Irish partition now shelved, O'Brien refrained from mentioning

Irish partition when discussing Cyprus. It may have been in the interests of the newly elected Fianna Fáil party to raise Irish partition explicitly at the Twelfth Session, but in the pursuit of the government's national interests it was not considered necessary or wise to do so again. Furthermore, to protest against the same British emergency measure in Cyprus would have left the Irish delegation open to charges of hypocrisy. This change of approach due to the above factors underscores how Irish political expediency, in the pursuit of national interests, was the driving force behind the Irish UN response to the Cyprus Question at all times.

Conclusion

In anticipating Ireland's UN policy, Sir Alexander Clutterbuck accurately predicted that 'a long course of eating its cake and having it has developed a taste for this attractive and nutritious diet, and we must expect that the Republic will do all in its power to maintain the regimen'.[60] Aiken's Irish UN response to Cyprus was, in essence, a precarious balancing act. It had avoided any brandishing of the 'sore-thumb' policy, yet the Irish electorate seemed sufficiently appeased by the statements on partition in the Irish UN speeches on Cyprus. Although aspects of the Irish UN contributions most certainly annoyed the British government on occasion, it did not jeopardise the Anglo-Irish relationship. In fact, the evidence shows that British officials clearly recognised that the Irish UN delegation would, at times, feel compelled to make reference to Irish partition in the context of Cyprus. Of course, they also knew better than to alienate the pro-British Boland. For de Valera's party, anti-partitionist utterances in New York served as a social palliative for a domestic polity experiencing republican resurgence, internment, high unemployment and persistent emigration. Although Aiken was criticised by Fine Gael for several of his initiatives at the UN, it is significant that there was no protest in the Dáil over the stance taken by O'Brien on the Cyprus Question at the Twelfth Assembly. This gives an indication of the strength of Irish public support for Aiken's foreign policy stance in relation to partition, and hints at the private sentiments of many Irish politicians across the political divide.

Aiken could hardly have been unaware of the British capacity to highlight, with damaging effect, the similarities between Irish and British emergency measures, and consequently the inherent hypocrisy in the Irish diplomatic habit of twisting the lion's tail, even if it was largely only to appeal to the Irish electorate. If so, the exact extent to which this was the overriding, rather than a contingent, factor in the return to a more cautious, pro-western UN policy agenda in 1958 remains hard to ascertain. Reports by some British officials indicate, however, that it was a significant, and potentially debilitating, factor in Irish foreign policy considerations. On 3 January 1957, John Hope of the CRO wrote to the Secretary of State for Commonwealth Relations, Alec Douglas-Home, explaining that the Irish government was highly anxious, 'lest the adoption of stronger measures by them' in their containment of IRA activity 'should lead to difficulty in the Council of Europe'.[61] His *schadenfreude* was obvious:

> Having had considerable experience of the Council of Europe I cannot help observing how extremely funny it would be if the Éire Government had to announce its suspension of certain provisions of the Human Rights Convention. Year after year their delegates to the General Assembly have attacked partition in terms of human rights. I would go a long way to see the same delegates having to explain their Government's latest conduct in protecting the rights of citizens north of the border. H. M. Ambassador reports that Mr. Murphy expressed anxiety about the possibility of a 'public and controversial debate.' Personally I think it would be positively hilarious.[62]

On 30 August 1958, the Lawless case was declared admissible by the ECtHR. Given the Irish government's decision to reintroduce emergency measures without an actual formal notice of derogation under the ECHR by Aiken, in his capacity as Minister for External Affairs, the stakes were incredibly high. Coupled with no official public acknowledgement of the existence of an emergency, in light of the Lawless case, Ireland could have been found guilty of two violations by the European Court. Coupled with potential charges of hypocrisy by British UN delegates if diplomatic relations turned sour, in light of this contextual evidence it appears that Aiken's principled, but certainly not disinterested, foreign policy agenda towards the Cyprus Question was sidelined for a far more pragmatic one.[63]

The very feasibility of a negative verdict in Strasbourg indicates that Aiken's role as Minister for External Affairs during this period was potentially far more challenging, and by consequence, ultimately all the more successful, than hitherto assumed. Despite the several contradictory and competing challenges he faced while increasing Ireland's presence on the world stage, Aiken managed, under considerable and competing pressures, to walk a political tightrope in reconciling Ireland's national interests and maintain Ireland's moralistic 'good international citizen' image on the world stage. His fudging of the derogation requirements to the Secretary-General of the European Commission could have irreparably tarnished his diplomatic integrity, making his future role emphasising the primacy of international law untenable.

Exactly how close he came to that, we may never know.

Notes

1   Brian Inglis, *West Briton* (London: *Faber and Faber*, 1962), 166.

2   Noel Dorr, *Ireland at the United Nations: Memories of the Early Years* (Dublin: IPA, 2010), 187.

3   Michael Lillis, 'Aiken's Playpen,' *Dublin Review of Books*, Issue 30, 11 March 2013. The full review is available at http://www.drb.ie/essays/aiken-s-playpen (accessed 12/03/12).

4   Aoife Bhreatnach, 'Frank Aiken and the Formulation of Foreign Policy, 1951–1954; 1957–1969' (M.Phil thesis, National University of Ireland, Cork, 1999), *passim.*

5   Trevor C. Salmon, *Unneutral Ireland: An Ambivalent and Unique Security Policy* (Oxford: OUP, 1989), 229.

6   Despite this particular niche in Irish foreign policy studies, there has been much invaluable work published and edited in recent years by Michael Kennedy, Deirdre McMahon and Joseph Morrison Skelly. See Michael Kennedy and Deirdre McMahon (eds), *Obligations and Responsibilities: Ireland and the United Nations 1955–2005: Essays Marking Fifty Years of Ireland's United Nations Membership* (Dublin: IPA, 2006); Michael Kennedy and Joseph Morrison Skelly (eds), *Irish Foreign Policy 1916–1966: From Independence to Internationalism* (Dublin: Four Courts Press, 2000).

7   Quoted in A. W. Snelling to J. R. Banks, 22 April 1958. National Archives of the United Kingdom (NAUK), Dominions Office (DO) 35/10772.

8   Snelling to Banks, 22 April 1958. NAUK, DO 35/10772.

9   Minutes by Ronald Stratford Scrivener, 17 April 1956, NAUK, Foreign Office (FO) 371/123880.

10   FO Minutes, 17 April 1956. NAUK, FO 371/123880.

11   Ivor Pink to P. M. Crosthwaite, 24 July 1957. NAUK, DO 35/10625.

12   Pink to Crosthwaite, 24 July 1957. NAUK, DO 35/10625.

13   Pink to Crosthwaite, 24 July 1957. NAUK, DO 35/10625.

14   Frederick Boland to Conor Cruise O'Brien, 28 May 1957. National Archives of Ireland (NAI) Department of Foreign Affairs (DFA) 313/36.

15   Boland to O'Brien, 28 May 1957. NAI, DFA, 313/36.

16   J. M. C. James to Gurth Kimber, 27 Aug. 1957. NAUK, DO 35/10625.

17   James to Kimber, 27 Aug. 1957. NAUK, DO 35/10625.

18   James to Kimber, 27 Aug. 1957. NAUK, DO 35/10625.

19   Conor Cruise O'Brien, *To Katanga and Back: A UN Case History* (London: Hutchinson, 1962), 36.

20   Conor Cruise O'Brien, *Memoir: My Life and Themes* (Dublin: Poolbeg Press, 1998), 180–181.

21   *The Irish Times*, 12 December 1957.

22   Douglas Hurd, *Memoirs* (London: Abacus, 2004), 160.

23   UK delegation Report to FO, Unsigned, 14 Dec. 1957. NAUK, FO 371/130136.

24   Telegram from Sir Pierson Dixon to FO, 18 Dec. 1957. NAUK, FO 371/130136.

25   Dixon to FO, 18 Dec. 1957. NAUK, FO 371/130136.

26   Dixon to FO, 18 Dec. 1957. NAUK, FO 371/130136.

27   Dixon to FO, 18 Dec. 1957. NAUK, FO 371/130136.

28   Dixon to FO, 18 Dec. 1957. NAUK, FO 371/130136.

29   H. G. M. Bass to Gurth Kimber, 1 Jan. 1958. NAUK, DO 35/10625.

30   Bass to Kimber, 1 Jan. 1958. NAUK, DO 35/10625.

31   Bass to Kimber, 1 Jan. 1958. NAUK, DO 35/10625.

32   Bass to Kimber, 1 Jan. 1958. NAUK, DO 35/10625.

33   Speech by Costello, 28 Nov. 1957. Dáil Éireann Debates (DE), Vol. 1165, col. 164.

34   Speech by Costello, 28 Nov. 1957. Dáil Éireann Debates (DE), Vol. 1165, col. 164.

35   Report on Commonwealth delegations at Twelfth Session of the General Assembly, 6 February 1958. NAUK, DO 35/10625.

36   O'Brien, *To Katanga and Back*, 44.

37   Bhreatnach, 'Frank Aiken and the Formulation of Foreign Policy, 1951–1954; 1957–1969', 29.

38   For further reading on this subject, see Stephen Kelly, *Fianna Fáil, Partition and Northern Ireland, 1926–1971* (Dublin: Irish Academic Press), 211–217.

39   Conor Cruise O'Brien, 'The Embers of Easter,' in Owen Dudley Edwards and Fergus Pyle (eds), *1916: The Easter Rising* (London: MacGibbon & Kee, 1968), 233.

40   Political Section Memorandum by Conor Cruise O'Brien, 24 Jan. 1958. University College Dublin Archives (UCDA) Frank Aiken Papers (P104)/6115.

41   Memorandum by O'Brien, 24 Jan. 1958. UCDA, P104/6115.

42   Memorandum by O'Brien, 24 Jan. 1958. UCDA, P104/6115.

43   Memorandum by O'Brien, 24 Jan. 1958. UCDA, P104/6115.

44   Conor Cruise O'Brien to Con Cremin, 7 Feb. 1958. UCDA, P104/6116.

45   'Notes on Rules of Procedure of the General Assembly Concerning Placing an Item on the Agenda' by Eoin MacWhite, undated. UCDA, P104/6116.

46   'Notes on Rules of Procedure' by MacWhite. UCDA, P104/6116.

47   Memorandum by Frederick Boland, 17 Feb. 1958. UCDA, P104/6117.

48   Memorandum by Boland, 17 Feb. 1958. UCDA, P104/6117.

49   Memorandum by Boland, 17 Feb. 1958. UCDA, P104/6117.

50   Memorandum by Boland, 17 Feb. 1958. At the 1957 Fianna Fáil Ard Fheis, de Valera vigorously opposed a resolution proposing that a partition resolution be formally raised at the UN. He explained that it was an 'impossible request', and asked supporters not to allow themselves to become 'foolish'. See copy of speech delivered by de Valera at the 1957 Fianna Fáil Ard Fheis, 19 Nov. 1957.UCDA, Éamon de Valera Papers, P150/2075.

51   Con Cremin to Frank Aiken, 21 Feb. 1958. UCDA, P104/6117.

52   *The Irish Times*, 19 July 1957.

53   Mary Caughey to Éamon de Valera, 6 Oct. 1958, NAI, Department of the Taoiseach (DT) S16057C.

54   *The Irish Times*, 2 Dec. 1958.

55   *Éire-Ireland: Weekly Bulletin of Dept. External Affairs*, 15 Dec. 1958, 5.

56   *Éire-Ireland*, 15 Dec. 1958.

57   *Éire-Ireland*, 15 Dec. 1958.

58   *The Irish Times*, 3 Dec. 1958.

59   *The Irish Times*, 5 Dec. 1958.

60   Sir Alexander Clutterbuck to Lord Home, 26 July 1956. NAUK, DO 35/10772.

61   Telegram from John Hope to Lord Home, 3 Jan. 1957. NAUK, DO 35/10625.
62   Hope to Home, 3 Jan. 1957. NAUK, DO 35/10625.
63   It was found that Ireland had not breached its obligations under the European Convention, a judgment passed because the European Court held that there was a state of emergency in Ireland under Article 15 of the Convention, despite no formal derogation or public confirmation to this effect at the time.

CHAPTER TEN

'Initiative and courage': Frank Aiken and the Congo crisis, 1960–1961[1]

MICHAEL KENNEDY

Frank Aiken's mastery over Ireland's United Nations policy in its 'golden years' during the late 1950s and the early 1960s is an established theme in post-war Irish foreign relations.[2] Taoiseach Seán Lemass, the argument goes, gave Aiken, his Minister for External Affairs, free reign in handling Ireland's independent position at the General Assembly as one of the 'fire brigade' states, the middle-powers who proposed compromises to ever-present Cold War tensions. As a result, Aiken spent months at a time in New York, allowing, the argument continues, Lemass to take control of the serious business of Ireland's foreign relations, in particular seeking entry to the European Economic Community (EEC), membership of which was Lemass's ultimate goal for Ireland.

This argument is compelling because it is straightforward. The image of an immaculate Aiken busy in New York surrounded by senior diplomats, including the suave Irish Ambassador to the United Nations Frederick Boland and the cunning intellectual Conor Cruise O'Brien, holds water. Aiken's General Assembly speeches and photocalls with the great statesmen of the 1950s and 1960s show the veteran minister doing his part to ensure that Ireland bestrode the world stage like a colossus, as the over-quoted contemporary phrase from *The Economist* newspaper cast Ireland.[3]

Aiken certainly looked the part, and passionately believed in the UN as an instrument of world peace. Yet in New York he was arguably doing little more than participating in what O'Brien later called the 'sacred drama' of the United Nations.[4] Aiken was top class on the declaratory rhetoric of the General Assembly; more than adequate when coming up with ambitious plans for superpower disengagement and decolonisation; and he came up trumps with the initiative that led to the Nuclear Non-Proliferation Treaty of 1968. However, as this chapter argues, he never had full control over Ireland's United Nations policy when it came to a crisis, or when Ireland's core national interests were at stake. Aiken remained the public face of Irish United Nations policy at such times, but Lemass took ultimate control.

Having been 'Mr de Valera's closest associate for nearly forty years', and appointed as his successor in the External Affairs portfolio by Éamon de Valera in 1951, Aiken saw himself as the natural inheritor of de Valera's foreign policy mantle.[5] Lemass had little time for Aiken, the 'sitting tenant in Iveagh House'; but after succeeding de Valera as Taoiseach in 1959, Lemass 'never felt strong enough to evict him'.[6] The antipathy between the two men was 'mutual but suppressed'.[7] They generally avoided conflict, particularly over UN policy. When Ireland's fundamental interests were affected at the UN, however, Lemass instructed and Aiken followed the Taoiseach's line.[8] In a letter to Aiken in the run-up to the Sixteenth Assembly of the United Nations in September 1961, sent after he had read through Aiken's Cabinet memorandum on Irish policy at the Assembly, Lemass asked Aiken 'to give some further consideration' to the policy.[9] Displaying a more strategic approach than Aiken to overall foreign policy, Lemass explained that when it came to the South Tyrol dispute: 'having regard to our vital interests in retaining Italian goodwill during the EEC negotiations, it is very important that we should not come into conflict with them on the Tyrol question at this time'. He made similar strategic comments concerning Ireland's participation in the UN's peacekeeping operation in Congo.

At the centre of this chapter is a series of events concerning Congo when the core concerns of Irish foreign policy were affected. From 1960 to 1964, Ireland became involved with the United Nations peacekeeping force in Congo, known by its French acronym 'ONUC'.[10] Here, Irish rhetoric at the General Assembly supporting decolonisation was overtaken by pure national interest; Irish soldiers operating under a UN mandate went into action in September 1961 during Operation Morthor in the secessionist Congolese province of Katanga. This United Nations attempt to end Katanga's secession was the Irish Defence Forces' first experience of combat since 1923. They suffered casualties and fatalities, including men missing in action; others were taken hostage and used as pawns in international propaganda.

The military action in Katanga occurred at the instigation of a senior Irish diplomat seconded to United Nations service as the Secretary General's special representative in Katanga, Aiken's former UN strategist and close confidant Conor Cruise O'Brien, and under an Irish Force Commander, Lieutenant General Seán MacEoin, who was in overall military command of ONUC. It took place as Ireland faced into a general election in October 1961; Lemass's first since taking over from de Valera. The Katanga crisis threatened to become a general election issue; it was already a major foreign policy concern, not simply over the Congo and in the context of Ireland's election as a non-permanent member of the Security Council in October 1961, but also regarding the much more important question of Irish participation in European integration, coming as it did shortly after Ireland applied for membership of the European Economic Community in August of that year. Therefore, because of its timing, and the direct involvement of Irish soldiers and diplomats, even if under UN auspices, the September 1961 Katanga fighting and its aftermath was the most critical foreign policy crisis Ireland had faced since 1945. With serious domestic and international interests at stake it was a 'perfect storm' for Irish makers of foreign policy, and shows the Lemass–Aiken relationship in operation, with Lemass in the driving seat of Ireland's United Nations policy, and Aiken very much his dutiful lieutenant, carrying out the Taoiseach's orders.

Aiken's role in the dispatch of Irish troops to Congo

Congo gained independence from Belgium in July 1960, and almost immediately the post-independence government fell apart as the country began to collapse. Rich in minerals, including those required for nuclear weapons, a potential Cold War flashpoint and still within the grasp of Belgian control, it was essential that Congo be stabilised before it became a Cold War proxy conflict or a contagious post-colonial struggle leading to the collapse of other newly independent states in sub-Saharan Africa. Supported by a Security Council resolution, visionary United Nations Secretary General Dag Hammarskjöld brought together a group of African, neutral and non-aligned states to form the core of *Organisation des Nations Unies au Congo*, or ONUC, the UN's largest peacekeeping mission to that date, which swiftly departed for Congo in an attempt to shore up the failing state.

Shortly after the first ONUC contingents deployed, Ireland, which had only previously sent a handful of officers on UN observer missions in the Middle East, was asked to contribute a battalion of troops, approximately 650 of all ranks, to the ONUC. It was a very substantial request, representing close to 10 per cent of the Defence Forces being sent on overseas service. Deployment was a huge task for the Irish military establishment, which was run down following progressive cutbacks since 1945.

Aiken, who had been present at the Congolese independence celebrations in its capital, Leopoldville, brought Hammarskjöld's request for troops to the Cabinet. He explained that Congo faced 'a state of near anarchy', and that the UN was dispatching ONUC to restore order.[11] Under the UN Charter, it was 'incumbent' on Ireland to comply with the request. Aiken felt that it was:

> desirable in the interests of the development along peaceful lines of the emerging states of Africa and the preservation of good relations between Europe and that continent that European countries should be associated with this effort to maintain peace and stability in the Congo.

He emphasised 'the danger of Africa falling more and more into the Communist sphere of influence'. The choice of European states that could serve in Congo was limited, and it was 'most desirable that Ireland should play as active a role in the force as its resources allow'. The Cabinet agreed to Hammarskjöld's request.[12]

In the Dáil it was Lemass, not Aiken, who dealt with the proposed Congo deployment. There was serious business to be undertaken as the Defence Acts had to be amended to allow the Defence Forces to undertake overseas service. Lemass explained that Hammarskjöld had requested Irish involvement in the ONUC because Ireland occupied a 'special position' in world affairs due to her impartial stance at the UN, 'national traditions and outlook'.[13] Irish troops would 'command the confidence of all parties' to the conflict. Lemass stressed that Irish troops would not be under Irish control on UN deployment. He also emphasised that the force would 'have no role to play in any problem of a political nature in the Congo, existing or future'.[14] He added that if the force were used for actions not covered by its mandate, it would be withdrawn.

The 689 Irish soldiers chosen for ONUC service were grouped into a new battalion, the 32nd Infantry Battalion. Watched by emotional crowds, they paraded through Dublin on 27 July 1960. Lemass took the salute as the battalion passed the General Post Office, the centre of Ireland's 1916 uprising against British rule. The battalion then deployed to Kivu Province in north-east Congo, and later to central Katanga.

In late July, Hammarskjöld requested a second Irish battalion to ensure greater balance in the ONUC between African and non-African elements. The Secretary General explained to Lemass that the Taoiseach would realise that in its choice of troops from Europe the UN was limited by political and technical considerations to Swedish and Irish troops, and Hammarskjöld hoped that Dublin would agree to his request. The Department of External Affairs wanted to accept the offer. The Department of Defence wanted to wait until the experience of the 32nd Battalion became clearer. Resources were strained by the deployment and, given the numbers involved, two battalions was all the Defence Forces could hope to send to Congo.

Aiken again took Hammarskjöld's request to the Cabinet, explaining that due to Cold War alliances and the colonial past of many European states, the choice facing the UN was very limited. He added that if the UN failed in Congo there would be 'disastrous consequences for the Congo and Africa', and 'the value of the organisation as a mediator may be compromised and the danger to world peace correspondingly increased'.[15] On 4 August, the Cabinet agreed to provide a second battalion. Lemass told Hammarskjöld that Ireland 'keenly appreciate[d] your difficulties and [was] anxious to cooperate to the utmost in helping you meet them'.[16] The new battalion, the 33rd Infantry Battalion, would deploy to Congo as quickly as possible.

Nine soldiers from the 33rd Battalion were killed in an ambush at Niemba in northern Katanga in November 1960, but Ireland remained committed to the ONUC, and only a matter of days after the ambush the UN requested the replacement of the 32nd and 33rd battalions with one battalion when their tours of duty ended in January 1961. The Cabinet again agreed, but the implementation of the decision would depend on the circumstances in Congo, which were 'so fluid as to counsel prudence in definitively committing ourselves to send a new contingent'.[17] In early December, Dublin informed the United Nations that the 34th Battalion would deploy to Congo. Lemass took charge, telegramming Aiken, who was in New York, that the battalion would go, 'unless, between now and date of departure, conditions so change as to require consideration'.[18]

From July to November 1960, Aiken brought Hammarskjöld's requests for Irish participation in the ONUC through the Cabinet, and his department liaised with the United Nations to ensure that Irish ONUC forces deployed correctly. Aiken laid the moral groundwork for Irish participation in the ONUC, helped greatly by O'Brien, who drafted Aiken's memoranda for the Cabinet supporting his case. But it was Lemass who brought the changes to legislation required for Irish soldiers to deploy overseas through the Dáil. Aiken had a certain freedom of action and certain tasks to undertake, but Lemass remained in overall charge. This was again the case when Hammarskjöld sought the release of the Chief of Staff of the Irish Defence Forces, the then Major General Seán MacEoin, to take over from the unpopular Swedish General Carl von Horn as ONUC Force Commander.

Aiken's ideas on the United Nations, Congo and the ONUC

MacEoin had visited Irish ONUC units in December 1960, and during the visit he came to the notice of Hammarskjöld's personal representative in Congo, Rajeshwar Dayal. Dayal felt that MacEoin had the toughness to organise the ONUC that von Horn lacked. MacEoin informally told Dayal that he would be prepared to succeed von Horn. A formal approach to Aiken was required, however, as there could be constitutional difficulties for the Irish government. Hammarskjöld approached Dublin to release MacEoin for a year's duties as ONUC Force Commander. Aiken was willing, but Lemass again took charge and personally sought MacEoin's view. Having received a report from Lemass, the Cabinet agreed to MacEoin's ONUC appointment. There was no public announcement, but, to ensure cross-party support, Lemass confidentially informed Fine Gael leader James Dillon and Labour leader Brendan Corish, asking them to keep the appointment secret until it was announced formally.

MacEoin's appointment was confirmed by the United Nations on 21 December 1960. From January 1961, he would command 20,000 soldiers from eighteen nations. Civil war in Congo was looming; the possibility of outside intervention was never far away. Aiken thought the situation 'menacing'.[19] The Irish Ambassador to Britain, Hugh McCann, assumed that Dublin would 'obtain private reports' from MacEoin on Congo.[20] The punctilious Secretary General of the Department of External Affairs, Con Cremin, replied that McCann was mistaken. It was Irish policy, he explained, that when governments placed themselves in the hands of the UN, 'they should act solely through the UN', and this precluded Dublin from 'taking action independently from the Secretary General'.[21] This meant that any Irish soldiers in Congo were 'detached entirely from our control'. Dublin knew that other countries ignored this, but Ireland would not do so. It was an honourable attitude, but it left the Irish authorities in the dark about Congolese affairs, culpable of wilful ignorance because of an idealistic desire to follow principle.

Ireland had no diplomatic representation in Congo, and no information on what was occurring there other than guarded reports from the UN. Though there is considerable evidence of officers serving with the ONUC reporting to Army Headquarters, and of these reports then filtering through to Lemass in Government Buildings, they did not filter through to External Affairs, and Aiken remained 'inclined not to depart from our existing practice of not seeking reports from our officers in the Congo'.[22] However correct, it was a lost opportunity. Former Irish Ambassador to the United Nations, Noel Dorr, accurately described Aiken as 'a man of great and gritty integrity, conviction and stubbornness; somewhat puritan in outlook'.[23] This had a positive side in much of Aiken's approach to the UN, but here it had its downside. It led Aiken actively to limit Dublin's understanding from Irish ONUC contingents of how events in Congo were developing, because he felt that to ask them directly about UN operations would be disloyal to the UN. Such idealism was commendable, but naïve and counterproductive, since the difficulty and unreliability of communications with Congo left the Irish authorities largely in the dark on the operation of the ONUC, and reliant on second-hand and often inaccurate information coming direct from the United Nations Secretariat.

Often, Aiken's views on Congo could be downright peculiar. When United States Ambassador to Ireland, Scott McLeod, informed Aiken of the Congo policy being developed by the Kennedy administration, Aiken made an unusual suggestion. To remove the motivation for international intervention in Congo, he suggested the formation of a United Nations corporation to buy out foreign, particularly Belgian, interests in the country. Naively, Aiken then wanted Belgium to use its knowledge of Congo to assist the United Nations. The plan was forwarded to United States Secretary of State, Dean Rusk, and to Boland, who tactfully suggested to Dublin that it was 'rather far out of the range of present thinking' about Congo.[24] Boland felt that Aiken's plans did not deal with Katanga's secession, and that the proposed purchase of foreign investments would be seen as neo-colonialism. Hammarskjöld politely replied that he also 'read the memorandum with interest and would keep it in mind'.[25]

Aiken remained convinced that his ideas on Congo could provide a way forward for the rapidly failing state. Boland had to say to Cremin carefully that 'the thinking at present in UN circles is not such as to provide a good context in which to urge the proposals made' by the minister.[26] He added that, in Hammarskjöld's view, Aiken's proposals 'do not bear closely on the immediate problems', of which the most significant was the likelihood of Congolese civil war and the linked 'danger of an East-West clash'. Covering for his minister, Cremin told Ambassador McLeod that Ireland endorsed the American viewpoint on 'the importance of standing behind the United Nations, both generally and in regard to the Congo'.[27]

Aiken remained concerned about Congo, and asked Boland to provide him with daily reports on developments. By early 1961, the ONUC had been reduced by 6,000 to 14,000 men, and was dangerously thin on the ground. Hammarskjöld was worried about finding replacement troops. Senior UN Secretariat official Ralph Bunche informally asked Boland whether, in addition to the 34th Battalion, a reinforced infantry company could be deployed to replace the contingents being withdrawn. Cremin discussed this with Lemass and Aiken. Within the Cabinet, Minister for Defence Kevin Boland 'was quite sympathetic'.[28] Lemass was 'definitely opposed'.[29] The feeling around the Cabinet table was that Ireland could not undertake this request because of the tense situation on the Northern Ireland border following the murder of a Northern Irish policeman by the IRA. Aiken was 'personally sorry that we could not meet a further request now',[30] and the Cabinet followed Lemass. Dispatching another battalion to Congo would be 'unwise and impolitic' considering domestic security requirements.[31] Again it was Lemass, not Aiken, who took the critical decisions.

An appointment with far-reaching consequences for Aiken was the secondment of one of his senior United Nations advisers, Conor Cruise O'Brien, to the UN Secretariat in mid-May 1961, and O'Brien's ultimate appointment as Hammarskjöld's personal representative in Katanga.[32] The 'charming, slightly pugnacious, black-suited diplomat' knew that his task was to implement Hammarskjöld's wishes in Congo, and that this ultimately meant ending Katanga's secession.[33] Aiken and O'Brien had a close personal friendship, and Aiken looked on O'Brien in an almost fatherly way. Aiken took personal responsibility for O'Brien's secondment, and did not even bring it formally to the Cabinet for discussion. After O'Brien departed for United Nations service, however, External Affairs did not seek information from him, and he did not keep in touch with Iveagh House. British diplomats concluded that Aiken and Cremin were not 'very closely in touch with the changes in the political situation' in Congo.[34] The British Ambassador in Dublin, Sir Ian Maclennan, felt that both were 'content to think of MacEoin and Cruise O'Brien as UN representatives who happened only incidentally to be from the Irish Republic'.[35] It was a harsh judgement, but a fair one; it was Aiken's policy that, once Irish soldiers and diplomats were seconded to UN service, they were of no concern to Dublin.

The background to Aiken's mission to Congo

Following the 34th Battalion, the 1st Irish Infantry Group, the 35th and the 36th Battalions served with the ONUC through 1961. They would play a central role in United Nations' attempt to end Katanga's secession. What no one pointed out to them was that 'in the collective UN view, ONUC was in Congo to settle issues, not to be the spectator of or mediator in them'.[36] This perspective was increasingly taken by O'Brien through the summer of 1961 as the UN moved to end Katanga's secession through the terms of Security Council Resolution 161 of February 1961. Tensions rose in Elisabethville, Katanga's capital city, during the summer, as the UN took steps to remove the European mercenaries who provided the backbone of the Katangese armed forces: the Gendarmerie. External Affairs had a general idea of what was occurring in Katanga, but with no one on the ground upon whom they could rely for accurate information, and the nearest Irish embassy in Lagos, Nigeria, Dublin's understanding of Congolese affairs remained limited.

In late August 1961, the ONUC moved forcefully against the Katangese mercenaries in Operation Rumpunch, a roundup to arrest and repatriate foreigners in Katangese military service. Rumpunch was only partially successful, many mercenaries evading capture. From Dublin, Aiken watched events in Katanga anxiously; he sought any information from Boland indicating that the ONUC was widening its operations. There was no expectation that Rumpunch would lead to any further use of force by the ONUC. O'Brien had other ideas and, in conjunction with Brigadier K. A. S. Raja, the Indian commander of ONUC forces in Katanga, he planned an operation to swoop again, this time with the objective of ending Katanga's secession.

Aiken asked Boland, who was in New York, 'to find out what are the specific objectives of the UN in Katanga ... and how far it is considered by UN authorities that use of force is permissible'.[37] Aiken viewed what seemed to be happening in Katanga negatively, and saw 'danger in stating the general obligation of UN forces to be "to preserve unity and territorial integrity"'.[38] He was 'anxious lest the understandable desire to complete the Congo operation quickly should lead the UN forces to exceed the peace and order role outlined by Taoiseach when our troops were being dispatched'. Unaware of the tensions and conflicts taking place in Congo, he advised using 'the utmost patience'. Patience was in short supply in Katanga.

On 13 September, Irish, Indian and Swedish UN forces struck again against Katanga in Operation Morthor. It was to be a simple two-hour operation to take over communications facilities in Elisabethville, arrest a number of Katangese ministers who had been inciting inter-tribal violence, and ultimately force the Katangese government of Moise Tshombe to bow down to the central Congolese government in Leopoldville, ending Katanga's secession. In the widespread fighting that followed, the UN plan collapsed as Katangese forces fought back aggressively and Tshombe stood his ground.

Irish 35th Battalion infantry and armoured units in Elisabethville were in the thick of the fighting.

However, A-Company, 35th Battalion, had some days previously moved from Elisabethville 125 kilometres north-west to the mining town of Jadotville, where they were to take surrendering mercenaries into custody and protect the European population. This turned out to be a trap; as their colleagues in Elisabethville went into action, A-Company in Jadotville was surrounded, and soon came under attack from the Gendarmerie.

As news of Operation Morthor arrived in Ireland, rumours spread around Dublin newspaper offices of large Irish losses at Jadotville. Katangese propaganda carried high-profile stories of massacres of Irish soldiers in the town, with those remaining held as hostages, ten being shot for every Katangese death. The Dáil had been dissolved that day in the run-up to the 1961 general election, the absence of news in Dublin about the fate of A-Company was disturbing relatives of its members, and there was growing resentment at the inability of the army authorities to keep up with events in Congo. External Affairs also lacked solid information on the developing situation. It all reflected badly on Lemass and his government, and was unwanted negative publicity with the election on the horizon.

On the morning of 15 September, the Defence Forces learned from ONUC Headquarters in Leopoldville that reports of attacks on A-Company had been exaggerated. The casualty report from Elisabethville, however, was unclear. There were 'no reports of any Irish killed in Elisabethville'.[39] A note by Cabinet Secretary Nicholas Nolan stressed that Dublin had received no official reports of any fatalities among Irish troops. News of the deaths of three Irish soldiers in Elisabethville was leaking out. A Rhodesian intelligence report noted that 'UN casualties which they have not announced include at least one Swedish soldier killed and the crew of an [Irish] armoured car killed'.[40]

The *Evening Herald* of 15 September carried the headline: 'Grim News from Katanga. Irish at Jadotville said to have surrendered. Katanga Radio claims 57 killed'. External Affairs learned that the UN Secretariat was 'obviously taken unawares and [is] disconcerted by developments in Katanga'.[41] It was little better for External Affairs, which relied on press reports for news from Katanga. The lack of information was beginning to cause problems on the domestic front, and the pressure of events in Katanga was building on the Irish government. Senator Patrick Quinlan called for O'Brien to be withdrawn because the 'Black and Tan methods of the UN under his leadership are fast putting Katanga – the Catholic part of the Congo – under the heel of the pink regime in Leopoldville'.[42]

News of the three dead in Elisabethville – Corporal Michael Nolan, Trooper Patrick Mullins and Trooper Edward Gaffney – arrived in Dublin from Leopoldville on 15 September, but was not included in Lemass's press statement that evening. Lemass expressed 'profound shock and sorrow' at the recent 'tragic events' in Congo 'involving serious casualties to an extent not yet ascertained amongst Irish soldiers serving with the U.N. Force'. Aiken had sought full information from the UN about the circumstances that led to the fighting in Katanga, but for 'the purpose of getting reliable information about the situation', Lemass announced that he had asked Aiken 'to proceed as soon as possible to the Congo for discussions with UN officials on the spot'.[43]

This was an unprecedented move, showing how worried Lemass was about the position of Irish forces in Jadotville and Elisabethville. He personally ordered Aiken to Congo because 'the position in Katanga is so fluid and liable to sudden change', and the reports coming in 'were so alarming', that Aiken's presence was required 'to secure reliable information on the situation'.[44] The Cabinet in Dublin would then consider Ireland's continued participation in the ONUC. Lemass had instructed Aiken a couple of days earlier that, at the upcoming General Assembly, Ireland, because of increasing international tension, 'should not take a line which would commit us to continue to contribute to the UN force in the Congo as this may not be possible'.[45] Lemass again showed that he was more pragmatic than Aiken when it came to Irish policy at the United Nations.

Following Lemass's instructions, Aiken was about to leave for one of the strangest missions of his long political career. His nine-day visit to Congo was an unusually hands-on approach to the United Nations for a minister who preferred the General Assembly to front-line peacekeeping.

Aiken's nine days in Congo

Aiken stayed in Iveagh House in conference with his senior advisers late into the night of 15 September. No advance details were released about his Congo trip. 'Grim-faced and determined', he flew alone from Dublin airport at 02.00 p.m. on 16 September, telling waiting journalists that there would be no withdrawal of Irish troops from Congo. Asked about O'Brien's position, he cryptically responded in support of O'Brien, saying that 'all UN officials from the beginning have acted in good faith but, as you know, they did not get co-operation from a lot of people they should have got it from'.[46] Aiken's immediate departure was 'an indication of the government's deep anxiety at the grave turn of events in the Congo'.[47] It was an extremely unusual step for an Irish foreign minister to take, as Aiken, unaccompanied by his Iveagh House advisers, had single-handedly to find out what was happening in Katanga and 'confront UN officials on command decisions committing Irish [troops] to battle'.[48]

With a general election only weeks away, Aiken's sudden departure to Congo amidst the bleak newspaper headlines of Irish casualties could be seen as electioneering to make it look like the government in Dublin was following a decisive Congo policy, and thus quell voices like Senator Quinlan's. The *Washington Evening Star* reported: 'word of the bloodshed came as a general election campaign began. Feelings ran high in the capital, but few voices were raised to demand the recall of Irish troops from the United Nations forces'.[49] Lemass was worried; Aiken's trip was no stunt. A sign of Lemass's concern was his cancellation of election meetings in Galway and Athlone, the main towns in the Defence Forces' Western Command, the Command from which A-Company was drawn. News reports explained that many Irish politicians had 'decided to wait for Mr Aiken's report before raising the Katanga fighting as a full-scale election issue'.[50] Discussing Aiken's departure with Hammarskjöld, a senior UN official put it bluntly: 'purpose is to get direct report developments Katanga. Election will take place Ireland in a few weeks'.[51]

Dublin was concerned that Irish troops were being deployed in Katanga for purposes that they had not been sent to Congo to undertake. The *Sunday Express*, under the headline 'Premier briefs Aiken to fly on find-the-truth mission', explained that Lemass was on the verge of withdrawing Ireland from the ONUC unless Aiken got satisfactory answers as to why A-Company was left in Jadotville without support or relief, and to whether or not Irish troops in Katanga had been deployed in accordance with the February resolution.

Aiken arrived in the tropical heat of Leopoldville at 5.00 a.m. on 17 September. Journalists in London had been interested in talking to him as he passed through, but an unusually reticent Aiken 'would not encourage interviews' with journalists, though 'he would not refuse to see them'.[52] He planned to have discussions in Leopoldville with UN officials to get reliable information about what was happening in Katanga. The UN authorities saw his task as being 'to investigate stories of severe Irish losses in Katanga and to confer with UN leaders on the Katanga operation'.[53] The *Connaught Sentinel*, perhaps over-emotionalizing Aiken's mission, considered that 'the sending of Mr Aiken was a good decision but it is a pity Mr Lemass should appear to panic'.[54] It was not panic, rather worry at news reports from Congo. Sir Ian Maclennan informed London that:

> ... the Government must indeed be exceedingly anxious that there should be a cease-fire in Katanga and that the Irish prisoners should be restored to a place of safety, because if any further misfortunes should

befall the Irish contingent the reactions on the electoral prospects of the Fianna Fáil Government are likely to be serious.[55]

In a telex message for the Taoiseach and the Minister for Defence, Aiken explained from Leopoldville that he 'found morale very high'.[56] As he arrived, the 35th Battalion informed ONUC HQ: 'Three other ranks killed. Some wounded. Morale tip-top'.[57] Aiken was silent on these fatalities in his report to Dublin. He was to meet Hammarskjöld on 18 September, and told a journalist that he had 'no immediate plans – I shall not rush out of here tonight, not to Dublin anyway'.[58] He then had long meetings with Congolese Prime Minister Cyrille Adoula, and with Foreign Minister Justin Bomboko, finding them 'extremely cordial'. They asked Aiken to 'convey to [the Irish] Government their gratitude for Irish help and admiration for gallantry of Irish troops and sorrow for casualties'.[59] No other information emerged about these conversations, which seemed to amount to little more than polite pleasantries, but Aiken's presence in the Congo conveyed the desired information back to Ireland and provided calming news in a volatile period.

The *Guardian* felt that the abuse handed out, both to O'Brien for undertaking Morthor and to A-Company at Jadotville, had not shaken Aiken's faith in the UN.[60] Aiken praised A-Company's conduct, and the morale of the 35th Battalion was buoyed by Aiken's arrival; its commanding officer radioed a beleaguered A-Company that 'we place great trust in Aiken'.[61] The minister's main message for Dublin was about the proposed ceasefire in Katanga. After speaking with O'Brien, and with Irish officers at UN Headquarters, he also informed the Department of Defence 'that early reports of Irish casualties in Katanga had been grossly exaggerated'.[62] This was an important achievement because Army Headquarters in Dublin now began to disregard reports from Katangese sources of casualties because they knew 'how unreliable such attributions are'.[63] Aiken's soothing messages were soon reported in Dublin. The situation in Katanga was not at all rosy, but it 'had never been as desperate as was reported'.[64] From what he had 'seen and heard', reports had been 'deliberately written for the purpose of deceiving people'.[65] Aiken was sorry for the trauma this had caused to families in Ireland; his mission had scored a major success.

Aiken's arrival in Leopoldville occurred as A-Company's position in Jadotville worsened, and after bitter fighting the unit was forced to down arms and become Katangese prisoners. Late on the night of 17 September, Lemass instructed Nolan to inform the leaders of the main opposition parties in the Dáil 'that the latest news we had – from General MacEoin … about the situation in Jadotville was bad, that the recent truce there was merely a ruse and that resistance by the Irish Company there had come to an end'.[66] Conscious of public opinion, Lemass instructed Aiken that 'anxiety about [the] Jadotville prisoners' was rising in Ireland, and he was to 'get all possible information, including additional casualties if any, treatment and intentions regarding them'.[67] Dublin learned that A-Company was being well treated. They were allowed to maintain their light arms, though without ammunition. Casualties remained at five, 'but many of the men show signs of the strain that they have been through since they went to Jadotville'.[68] This news arrived in Dublin at 1.20 p.m. on 18 September, and was circulated to Dillon and Corish by 3.00 p.m. This was quite a change from the position before Aiken's departure. There were good diplomatic and political reasons to have Aiken on the ground in the Congo. 'They have the right man out there', a Dublin housewife told the press.[69]

Accompanied by Aide de Camp Commandant Tony Conroy and intelligence officer Captain Basil Greer, Aiken visited Irish casualties in Leopoldville and 'found all well'.[70] He learned first-hand from Sergeant P. J. Gallagher, B-Company, 35th Battalion, of the Katangese attack on the Irish column trying to relieve A-Company in Jadotville, and from Sergeant Tim Carey about the fighting in Elisabethville. Aiken also had 'a full and satisfactory talk' with the UN Chief in Congo, Sture Linner.[71] There was, Aiken thought, 'a general easement in the situation and there seems to be a fair prospect of a truce'. Aiken had in fact telexed Cremin in Dublin that he had held 'completely satisfactory and reassuring talks' with Linner.[72] In Leopoldville, Aiken also learned that, close to midnight on 18 Septermber, Hammarskjöld had been killed when his aircraft crashed approaching Ndola airfield in Northern Rhodesia as he was en route for ceasefire talks with Tshombe. Aiken had the sombre task of paying tribute to Hammarskjöld, whom he described as 'wonderfully calm, very wise and very reasonable'.[73]

Quite what Aiken was now up to was unclear to the Irish diplomatic service. The Irish Permanent Mission to the United Nations inquired of Dublin, 'is Minister still in Congo?'[74] The British Ambassador to Ireland concluded, after meeting with Cremin, that 'even now with Aiken in Leopoldville the Government here are as much in the dark as anyone, both about what is going on and about how the existing situation in Katanga was brought about'.[75]

Having spent five days in Leopoldville, Aiken next set off for Elisabethville. He had been trying to arrange transport to the Katangese capital since he arrived in Leopoldville. The UN was anxious that he would not undertake the journey while the city remained volatile and as aircraft flying into the city were liable to be attacked. They refused to put an aircraft at Aiken's disposal. Commercial air services to Elisabethville were suspended, and Lemass cautioned Aiken that he 'should not proceed [to] Elisabethville if [there was] any considerable risk although in the event of a reliable truce would like you to do so'.[76] But the headstrong Aiken ignored Lemass, and finally set off for Elisabethville in a UN transport aircraft on 22 September. En route, he touched down at the enormous airbase at Kamina in central Katanga, which was being defended against Katangese attack by the 1st Irish Infantry Group, commanded by Colonel J. C. Donovan, and a Swedish force; a total of some 700 ONUC soldiers facing an estimated 1,000 Katangese troops. Aiken's aircraft overshot the runway at Kamina, part of the undercarriage collapsed and a propeller sheared off. Aiken is reported as having coolly remarked: 'we were lucky it did not turn turtle'.[77]

Late on the evening of 22 September, Aiken finally touched down in Elisabethville. He was met by General MacEoin, Commandant Kevin O'Brien, Colonel James Quinn and Captain Greer, and visited Irish troops, in particular the wounded, saw where the fighting had taken place, and met O'Brien, who 'was looking very well after a tough experience'.[78] News agency reports said that O'Brien had dissuaded Aiken from withdrawing Irish forces from Katanga.[79] *The Irish Times* included the telling line in a recent editorial that it hoped that Aiken 'will continue to give the UN the support he has so nobly given it up to the present, and that he will carry his Cabinet colleagues with him'.[80] He also visited the camp near the Irish headquarters in Elisabethville, where 35,000 refugees were living in basic unsanitary conditions on UN food aid. Aiken praised the members of the 35th Battalion he met in Elisabethville, and wanted to continue to Jadotville to meet A-Company in captivity, but was unable to do so.

Not everyone in the 35th Battalion was to meet Aiken. As Aiken's arrival neared, two officers who had served with the Indian ONUC contingent in Elisabethville during Operation Morthor, Captain Art Magennis and Lieutenant Michael Considine, were suddenly told to take leave in Leopoldville. Three of Considine's armoured car crew, Troopers Boyce, Sheedy and Flynn, were also prevented from meeting the minister. Magennis was acting commander of the 35th Battalion Armoured Car Group, and the four men under his command had personally witnessed Indian troops barbarically killing Katangese prisoners.[81] These Indian atrocities were spoken about in Elisabethville, and made international news, but the UN could not criticise India in case it withdrew its significant contribution from the ONUC when its troops were the subject of negative publicity. Aiken was prevented from meeting those who knew too much about the fighting in Elisabethville, and was instead given good public relations opportunities, which would meet with approval in Ireland. He never had to face the hard realities of the fighting in Elisabethville.

Aiken spent fewer than twenty-four hours in Elisabethville; long enough to get the results required for Lemass, but not long enough to see that which the UN did not want him to see. He returned to Leopoldville on 23 September, where he was again met by General MacEoin. 'The firing has ceased and I hope it will continue like that', Aiken told Raymond Smith of the *Irish Independent*.[82] His return flight had its moment of anxiety when Aiken's DC-4 lost power in one engine over central Katanga, and carried on with three engines to Leopoldville. In Leopoldville, Aiken planned to meet Congolese President Joseph Kasavubu, and to have lunch with Congolese Army Chief General Joseph Mobutu, before leaving for Dublin on 25 September via the midnight flight to Brussels.

Lemass instructed Aiken that, if he were to give press interviews on the return trip, he should 'avoid comment on UN purpose in Congo', and was 'to take on this subject the line "no comment pending report to my government".'[83] Aiken sent a general message to Dublin to say that he had visited all Irish posts in the Congo; that he had found all troops in good health and spirits; that the wounded were out of danger and improving; and that he had heard from those who had met Irish prisoners that they were well treated. Before leaving Congo he told Raymond Smith that 'the principal purpose of my visit was to meet the Irish soldiers in the field – and this I have done'.[84] He added that he was 'glad to see our boys. Their morale is high and they are cheerful, I have nothing but praise for them'. It was good general election talk; if Aiken had picked up anything that implicated the UN forces in atrocities, he did not hint at it.

Aiken arrived back in Dublin on the afternoon of 26 September 'looking fresh and fit, despite his gruelling nine-day mission'.[85] The pro-Fianna Fáil *Irish Press* carried a large photograph on its front page of Aiken being greeted by his wife, Maud, at Dublin airport. The returning minister was met by Tánaiste Seán MacEntee; not by Lemass. Aiken spoke of his hopes for peace across Congo, and 'painted a hopeful picture of the situation generally' to journalists on his arrival, explaining that 'my journey to the Congo was to see for myself, so that I could reassure the parents of the men who are prisoners'.[86] The UN, Aiken explained, had acted within the Charter in its actions, and he 'had every hope that there will be no further bloodshed in Katanga'.[87] This was for immediate consumption; Aiken never submitted a written report on his Congo trip to Lemass, to the Cabinet, or to the Department of External Affairs. There is no substantial record of the trip in his personal papers.[88] It had been an unusual piece of diplomacy and electioneering. Beside the *Irish Press* photograph of the Aikens embracing at Dublin airport, and the headline story that 'Irish troops in good spirits, prisoners well cared for – Aiken', was the story that '301 to seek election to 17th Dáil'. It added that, in the forthcoming election, Irish troops in Congo would have a postal ballot.[89]

The following day, Alderman J. W. Reidy attempted to introduce a motion at a meeting of Cork Corporation to ask the government 'to take immediate steps to "bring our boys home from the Congo".[90] Reidy's action was met with cries of 'withdraw', and he could find no one to second his motion. Perhaps Aiken's mission had succeeded? The Congo did not ultimately feature as an election issue, and the October 1961 poll returned Lemass to power, but with a minority government following a lacklustre campaign. Aiken remained at External Affairs, and now had to deal with the fallout from the failure of Operation Morthor. The Irish soldiers taken prisoner in Elisabethville and Jadotville during the fighting were eventually released, and the wounded received hospital treatment before returning to Ireland. MacEoin was blamed for failing to prevent Morthor from taking place, and O'Brien was under increasing international criticism for having exceeded his authority in commencing Morthor in the first place. In fact, Morthor had been undertaken by O'Brien, Linner and Raja with Hammarskjöld's authorization, and MacEoin knew that the operation was imminent. With Hammarskjöld dead, and Morthor a failure, this was covered up for almost half a century.[91]

Aiken's part in Conor Cruise O'Brien's resignation

By autumn 1961, O'Brien had become a figure of international hatred amongst Katanga's powerful supporters, including the British press, for his attempts to end the province's secession. He had outlived his usefulness in Katanga, and concerted moves were underway to remove him from Congo. The biggest obstacle to O'Brien's removal was his main supporter: Frank Aiken. Aiken's 'sense of obligation' to O'Brien was such that he 'did not want him to be transferred in circumstances which might look like a slight'.[92] Aiken remained steadfastly loyal to O'Brien and to the UN; between October and O'Brien's resignation from the UN and the Department of External Affairs in December, a complex strategy was undertaken by the United Nations, the British Foreign Office and even Ireland's Ambassador to the UN, Frederick Boland, to get around Aiken to remove O'Brien. Boland advised the British Foreign Office to have the British Ambassador in Dublin contact Lemass directly to seek O'Brien's recall from UN service. This was a step too far for Ambassador Maclennan, who refused to meddle in the Aiken–Lemass relationship.

Following newly appointed Secretary General U Thant's failure to support him in the face of Belgian criticism, O'Brien wrote to Aiken that he wished to be recalled from UN service. Aiken hesitated in responding, and before he could reply news broke that with O'Brien in Elisabethville was his External Affairs colleague, Máire MacEntee, daughter of Tánaiste Seán MacEntee. It was common knowledge that O'Brien and MacEntee were in a relationship and that O'Brien, whilst separated from his wife, was not yet divorced. The breaking news gave U Thant his opportunity, however, and he asked Aiken to recall O'Brien, saying that if he did not do so the UN would ask for O'Brien's resignation. Aiken used the excuse of shortages in top-ranking personnel at External Affairs to request O'Brien's release.

This annoyed Lemass, who instructed Boland that in Irish statements issued in New York about O'Brien's resignation, 'the maximum responsibility for the charge should be placed elsewhere – and not here, where it does not belong'.[93] Lemass would not allow Ireland's international reputation to be damaged by making it look as if Aiken were responsible for O'Brien's recall due to a human resources issue at Iveagh House. O'Brien's removal was a UN responsibility.

Aiken remained personally loyal to O'Brien to the last. Somewhat naïvely, he did not see that the UN had in fact run rings around him to make him appear responsible for recalling O'Brien. He was simply carrying out their wishes, and their wishes became Aiken's responsibility, neatly deflecting criticism away from the Secretariat. They also deflected attention from London, and in getting O'Brien out of the United Nations Aiken had achieved the outcome the Foreign Office most favoured. It was not that the Great Powers had acted in concert to force Aiken to reign in O'Brien; the UN itself, under pressure from its membership, had done so. This included but was not limited to the Great Powers.

Aiken still maintained his support for O'Brien. In a press statement he explained that, though he no longer had any responsibility for O'Brien's views and that O'Brien's views were not his views, he felt that in Katanga O'Brien had been 'the object of many bitter attacks in some European papers because of the action ONUC took to get rid of the mercenaries in accord with the UN resolutions, and to protect the UN forces'. These personal attacks were, in Aiken's view, 'unfair and unjustified', and did not 'carry conviction to anyone in a responsible position'.[94] Lemass was anxious to dampen down any potential rift in British–Irish relations over Katanga as a result of O'Brien's criticisms. With Irish entry into the Common Market in mind, Lemass specifically told Aiken that 'it must be [our] primary objective at present to avoid indisposing Britain, Belgium [and] France'.[95] Lemass therefore deliberately distanced himself from O'Brien at the time, insisting that he was a UN (rather than an *Irish*) representative. He later told British Commonwealth Secretary, Duncan Sandys, that he had 'great respect' for O'Brien's 'intellectual qualities', but 'doubted whether he was well suited for a practical operation like that undertaken in Katanga'.[96]

Meanwhile, in Dublin on 4 December, the 650 officers and men of the 36th Battalion assembled at McKee Barracks under the command of Lieutenant

Colonel Michael Hogan to be reviewed by Lemass. The request to send a battalion to succeed the 35th had arrived in Dublin in October, and saw Lemass again take a strong line with Aiken. Lemass told Aiken that Ireland could not take any course 'which could be represented as implying a change of mind, or lessening of enthusiasm on our part, about the UN's Congo operation'.[97] But since the fighting in Katanga in September, Irish public opinion had become 'very sensitive about this whole Congo business, and any further fighting there would certainly lead to more vocal demands for our withdrawal, which would be very damaging to national prestige and morale'. It was an unusually strong line for Lemass on a foreign policy issue, and indicates his input into United Nations policymaking at critical moments, as well as the presence of a greater than usual level of concern for the impact of public opinion on foreign policy. Lemass's suggested alternatives ranged between replacing the 35th Battalion without making comment; sending a further battalion, plus specialist contingents; limiting future ONUC contributions to specialist personnel only; and sending a further battalion, but telling the UN that it would not be replaced. Lemass asked Aiken to give these options 'very careful consideration', and left Aiken in no doubt that his preferred option was 'to continue to show our full support by contributing to the UN force but not sending a full battalion of line troops to replace the 35th'.[98]

The Cabinet decision on the 36th Battalion was surprising. This time, Lemass did not get his way. The Cabinet agreed to send a full replacement battalion, and make immediately available eight light anti-aircraft guns plus crews and ammunition. In addition, and here the real surprise lay, the replacement battalion 'should be equipped with such support weapons as the Supreme Commander of the United Nations' Force might consider necessary for their own defence'.[99] MacEoin was, by Cabinet decision, being given control over the armament of the 36th Battalion. Aiken felt that it would be best not to tell the UN that Ireland was willing to deploy a further battalion until the men captured during the September fighting were released. Only on their release would Dublin inform New York that the 36th Battalion would be available to the ONUC.

ONUC commanders sought a second round to get their own back on the Katangese for the UN's failure in September. Following Katangese provocation, including their sealing off of a section of Elisabethville to prevent UN freedom of movement, the ONUC took decisive action on 14 December in Operation Unokat. As the 36th Battalion arrived in Elisabethville, Unokat commenced. The operation had decisive effect, and ultimately began the process that led to the end of Katanga's secession. With O'Brien gone, and MacEoin on the verge of stepping down as Force Commander, Aiken's concerns centred around the ONUC's general intentions following a return to military measures. UN military and civilian figures in Katanga paid little heed to Aiken's conviction that 'force was no solution for the Katanga problem'.[100] He unsuccessfully pressed U Thant for 'vigorous conciliatory efforts and for negotiations to prevent major fighting in Katanga'.[101] Backing the now predominantly Indian ONUC contingents in Elisabethville, Indian Prime Minister Jawaharlal Nehru explained that India considered Tshombe to be 'a rebel who should speedily be brought to book', and that 'swift and effective action' needed to be taken to end the secession of Katanga for the good of Congo.[102] Certain of Washington's support, U Thant followed the same line.

Conclusion

Aiken's actions during 1960 and 1961 over Ireland's response to United Nations' involvement in Congo and Katanga are much more complex than allowed for by the existing historiography. He did not have free reign over Ireland's actions, and had to work with Lemass, and at times work to Lemass's orders, particularly where Ireland's Congo and UN policies had to fit into the wider schema of Ireland's overall international interests. Whatever each man may have thought about the other, there was no sign of rancour between them over Congo, except for Lemass's very evident annoyance at Aiken's handling of O'Brien's resignation. Nevertheless, it is clear from the circumstances surrounding Aiken's Congo trip in September 1961 that Lemass sent him there to be seen to be doing something, and to keep Aiken busy during a period of crisis.[103] Aiken could remain the public face of Ireland's UN policy, photographed in his tropical suit shaking hands and meeting the great and good in Katanga, while in Dublin Lemass took strategic control of Ireland's Congo policy.

Perhaps because de Valera held the External Relations portfolio whilst Taoiseach from 1932 to 1948, the relationship between the Minister for External Affairs and the Taoiseach/President of the Executive Council has received little examination. Adding the peculiarities of the John A. Costello–Seán MacBride relationship during the 1948 to 1951 inter-party government to de Valera's sixteen years at External Affairs mean that, for nineteen of the twenty-nine years from 1922 to 1951, there is little with which to compare the Aiken–Lemass relationship.[104] It seems that, whatever the differences in their personal outlooks, they managed to develop a working relationship over the Congo crisis under the ultimate control of Lemass.

Always the idealist, Aiken sought peaceful solutions to the breakdown of government in Congo and the secession of Katanga. Yet the resulting policies seemed unable to take into account Irish national interests in addition. Lemass had a much greater awareness of what mattered strategically to Ireland. The two men did not overtly clash over Congo and Katanga, but they had differing viewpoints and different priorities. To a fault, Aiken remained loyal to the United Nations, whereas Lemass was conscious of the need to see Ireland's international interests in their totality. Lemass prioritised good relations with London, Paris and Brussels because he prioritised Ireland's EEC application over Ireland's support for the UN's actions in central Africa. Aiken remained resolute in his support for the UN and its Charter, but when it came to the ONUC, Congo and Katanga, Lemass took a wider perspective, and his strategy included keeping Aiken in his place.

Notes

1   Lemass to Aiken, 23 Sept. 1961. University College Dublin Archives (UCDA), Frank Aiken Papers P104/6391.

2   See, for example, Joseph Morrison Skelly, *Irish Diplomacy at the United Nations 1945–1965* (Dublin: Irish Academic Press, 1997) and earlier, Conor Cruise O'Brien, 'Ireland in international affairs', in Owen Dudley Edwards (ed.), *Conor Cruise O'Brien Introduces Ireland* (New York: McGraw Hill, 1969). Similar themes regarding Aiken are made in O'Brien's *To Katanga and Back: A UN Case History* (London: Hutchinson, 1962) and throughout Michael Kennedy and Deirdre McMahon (eds), *Obligations and Responsibilities: Essays Marking Fifty Years of Ireland's Membership of the United Nations* (Dublin: Institute of Public Administration, 2005).

3   Aiken's speeches at the General Assembly were packaged together and published annually under the title *Éire ag na Naisiúin Aontaithe – Ireland at the United Nations*. See also Noel Dorr, *Ireland at the United Nations: Memories of the Early Years* (Dublin: Institute of Public Administration, 2010), 48–61, for a first-hand description of Aiken, Boland and O'Brien.

4   Conor Cruise O'Brien, *The United Nations: Sacred Drama* (London: Hutchinson, 1968). O'Brien, however, remained noticeably uncritical of Aiken in his accounts of the UN and Ireland's role in the organization. One of the most severe was that Aiken 'made some mistakes, but he was a very serious and thoughtful man' (*Memoir: My Life and Themes* (Dublin: Poolbeg Press, 1998), 165).

5   O'Brien, *To Katanga and Back*, 35.

6   For the development of this point, see Ronan Fanning, 'Frank Aiken', *Dictionary of Irish Biography*, available at http://dib.cambridge.org (accessed 08/08/13).

7   Fanning, 'Frank Aiken', *Dictionary of Irish Biography*.

8   Aoife Breathnach argues this point with reference to decolonization in her chapter 'A friend of the colonial powers? Frank Aiken, Ireland's United Nations Alignment and Decolonisation', in Kennedy and McMahon, *Obligations and Responsibilities*, 182–200.

9   Lemass to Aiken, 13 Sept. 1961. UCDA, P104/6328.

10   See Michael Kennedy and Art Magennis, *Ireland, the United Nations and Congo* (Dublin: Four Courts Press, 2014) for more details.

11   Request for Irish assistance for UN military force in the Congo, 18 July 1960. National

Archives of Ireland (NAI), Department of Foreign Affairs (DFA), 305/384/2 Pt 1.

12   For a concise account of Irish policies and views on sub-Saharan Africa since the 1950s, see Kevin O'Sullivan, *Ireland, Africa and the End of Empire: Small State Identity in the Cold War, 1955–75* (Manchester: Manchester University Press, 2013).

13   Speech by Aiken, 20 July 1960. Dáil Éireann (DE), Vol. 183, col. 1882.

14   Speech by Aiken, 20 July 1960. DE, Vol. 183, Col. 1881.

15   Request from UN for second Irish battalion for Congo, 2 Aug. 1961. NAI, DFA 305/384/2 Pt 1.

16   (No. 99) External Affairs (Estero) to Permanent Mission to the United Nations (PMUN), 5 Aug. 1960. NAI, DFA 305/384/2 Pt 1.

17   Cremin to Aiken, 28 Nov. 1960. NAI, DFA 305/384/2/II.

18   Estero to PMUN for Aiken, 10 Dec. 1960. NAI, DFA 305/384/2/III.

19   *Irish Press*, 22 Dec. 1960.

20   McCann to Cremin, 10 Jan. 1961. NAI, DFA PMUN 387.

21   Cremin to McCann, 16 Jan. 1961. NAI, DFA PMUN 387.

22   Minute, Cremin to Ronan, 16 Mar 1961. NAI, DFA PMUN 387.

23   Dorr, *Ireland at the United Nations*, 48.

24   Boland to Cremin, 14 Feb. 1961. NAI, DFA 305/384/III.

25   Boland to Cremin, 14 Feb. 1961. NAI, DFA 305/384/III.

26   Confidential note by Cremin, 17 Feb. 1961. NAI, DFA 305/384/III.

27   Confidential note by Cremin, 17 Feb. 1961. NAI, DFA 305/384/III. See also Dorr, *Ireland at the United Nations*, 54, for a revealing take on Cremin's view of Aiken.

28   Cremin to Boland, 2 Feb. 1961. NAI, DFA PMUN 387.

29   Cremin to Boland, 2 Feb. 1961. NAI, DFA PMUN 387.

30   Cremin to Boland, 2 Feb. 1961. NAI, DFA PMUN 387.

31   Estero to Uneireann, 31 Jan. 1961. NAI, DFA 305/384/2/III. Going some way to meet Hammarskjöld's request, the 1st Irish Infantry Group, roughly a 'half-battalion', served in Katanga from May to Nov. 1961.

32   In contrast to MacEoin's appointment, it does not appear from Cabinet or government minutes that O'Brien's secondment was brought to either body for agreement by Aiken.

33   *Observer*, 17 Sept. 1961.

34   Maclennan to Chadwick, 19 Sept. 1961. The National Archives of the United Kingdom (NAUK), Foreign Office (FO) 371/154957.

35   Maclennan to Chadwick, 19 Sept. 1961. NAUK, FO 371/154957.

36   Anthony Verrier, *International peacekeeping. United Nations Forces in a Troubled World* (Harmondsworth, Penguin, 1981), 41.

37   Estero to Uneireann, 4 Sept. 1961. NAI, DFA PMUN 387.

38   Estero to Uneireann, 6 Sept. 1961. NAI, DFA 305/384/31.

39   Memorandum marked seen by Aiken, 15 Sept. 1961. NAI, Department of the Taoiseach (D/T) S16137I/61.

40   Katanga situation, 15 Sept. 1961. Rhodes House Library, Oxford, Sir Roy Welensky Papers, 261/5.

41   Uneireann to Estero, 15 Sept. 1961. NAI, DFA 305/384/31.

42   *Evening Mail*, 15 Sept. 1961.

43   Press statement by Lemass, 9.45 p.m., 15 Sept. 1961. NAI, DT S16137I/61.

44 Lemass to Macmillan, 19 Sept. 1961. NAUK, FO 371/154989, government and Cabinet minutes suggest that there were no meetings of either body between 12 and 29 September 1961. While informal meetings may have occurred, it could be argued that, with Aiken out of the country, Lemass had a perfect excuse to use Aiken's absence to avoid calling a meeting regarding the fighting in Katanga.

45 Lemass to Aiken, 13 Sept. 1961. UCDA, P104/6328.

46 *The Irish Times*, 18 Sept. 1961.

47 *Irish Independent*, 16 Sept. 1961.

48 *Chicago Sun-Times*, 16 Sept. 1961.

49 *Evening Star*, 16 Sept. 1961.

50 *Evening Star*, 16 Sept. 1961.

51 Cordier to Hammarskjöld, 15 Sept. 1961. National Library of Sweden (NLS), Dag Hammarskjöld Papers, L179/160.

52 Note by Paul Keating on London–Dublin teleprinter message, 1115, 16 Sept. 1961. NAI, DFA 305/384/31.

53 Daily summary of events. United Nations Archives, New York (UNA), S/213/3/4.

54 *Connaught Sentinel*, 19 Sept. 1961.

55 Maclennan to Chadwick, 20 Sept. 1961. NAUK, FO 371/154932.

56 Aiken to External Affairs, 0652, 17 Sept. 1961. NAI, DFA 305/384/31/1.

57 Teleprinter message, 35th Battalion to Liaison Officer, Leopoldville, 17 Sept. 1961. UNA, S/840/2/5.

58 *The Irish Times*, 18 Sept. 1961.

59 *The Irish Times*, 18 Sept. 1961.

60 *Guardian*, 18 Sept. 1961.

61 McNamee to Quinlan, 16 Sept 1961, quoted in Rose Doyle, *Heroes of Jadotville* (Dublin: New Island, 2006), 127.

62 Daily summary of events. UNA, S/213/3/4.

63 Defence Forces Plans and Operations to Liaison Officer, Leopoldville, 16 Sept. 1961. UNA, S/791/43/4.

64 *The Irish Times*, 17 Sept. 1961.

65 *The Irish Times*, 17 Sept. 1961.

66 Note by Nolan, 18 Sept. 1961. NAI, D/T S161371/I/61.

67 Lemass to Nolan, 18 Sept. 1961. NAI, D/T S161371/I/61.

68 Message from ONUC HQ, Leopoldville to Department of Defence, 1133, 18 Sept. 1961. NAI, D/T S161371/I/61.

69 *Guardian*, 19 Sept. 1961.

70 Minute by Nolan, 19 Sept. 1961. NAI, D/T S16137J/61.

71 Government Information Bureau statement, 2000, 19 Sept. 1961. NAI, D/T S16137J/61.

72 Minute by Nolan, 19 Sept. 1961. NAI, D/T S16137J/61.

73 *Irish Press*, 20 Sept. 1961.

74 Uneireann to Estero, 20 Sept. 1961. NAI, DFA PMUN 387.

75 Maclennan to Chadwick, 20 Sept. 1961. NAUK, FO 371/154932.

76 Memorandum, 20 Sept. 1961. NAI, DFA PMUN 433.

77 *Irish Independent*, 25 Sept. 1961.

78 *Irish Independent*, 25 Sept. 1961.

79 *Irish Press*, 25 Sept. 1961.

80 *The Irish Times*, 23 Sept. 1961.

81 See Kennedy and Magennis, *Deliver us from evil*, chapter 8, for further details.

82 *Irish Independent*, 25 Sept. 1961.

83 Lemass to Nolan, 23 Sept. 1961. NAI, D/T S 16137J/61.

84 *Irish Independent*, 26 Sept. 1961.

85 *Irish Press*, 27 Sept. 1961.

86 *Irish Press*, 27 Sept. 1961.

87 *Irish Press*, 27 Sept. 1961.

88 UCDA, P104/542 contains Aiken's appointments diary for 1961. Most of the days of his Congo trip are blank.

89 *Irish Press*, 27 Sept. 1961.

90 *Irish Press*, 28 Sept. 1961.

91 See Alan James, *Britain and the Congo Crisis, 1960–63* (London: St Martin's Press, 1996); O'Brien, *Memoir* and Kennedy and Magennis, *Ireland, the United Nations and Congo*, for an account of the covering up by the United Nations of Operation Morthor.

92 Dean to Foreign Office, 1 Nov. 1961. NAUK, FO 371/154957.

93 Nolan to Lemass, 4 Dec. 1961. NAI, D/T S16137I/61.

94 Press statement issued by Aiken in New York, 4 Dec. 1961. NAI, D/T S16137I/61.

95 Cremin to Aiken, 20 Dec. 1961. NAI, DFA PMUN 450 (M/13/6/12).

96 Bryce Evans, *Seán Lemass: Democratic Dictator* (Cork: Collins Press, 2011), 224.

97 Lemass to Aiken, 13 Oct. 1961. NAI, D/T S16137J/61.

98 Lemass to Aiken, 13 Oct. 1961. NAI, D/T S16137J/61.

99 Draft Cabinet minute (GC 10/1), 17 Oct. 1961. NAI, D/T S16137J/61.

100 Boland to Cremin, 13 Dec. 1961. NAI, DFA 305/384/31/III.

101 Boland to Cremin, 13 Dec. 1961. NAI, DFA 305/384/31/III.

102 Nehru to Macmillan, 8 Dec. 1961. NAUK, FO 371/154961.

103 The obvious comparison is to de Valera's dispatch of Aiken to the United States in 1941 on an ill-fated arms-purchasing and propaganda mission.

104 For Cumann na nGaedheal from 1922 to 1932, President of the Executive Council W. T. Cosgrave got involved in foreign policy issues on a few significant occasions as required; most significantly, in Ireland's joining of the League of Nations in 1923 and visiting the United States in 1928. The relationship between Costello and Liam Cosgrave in the second inter-party government of 1954 to 1957 is perhaps the only other relevant comparison to the Lemass–Aiken relationship.

CHAPTER ELEVEN

'China is more important to you than Armagh':[1] Frank Aiken and Tibet

KATE O'MALLEY

It is clear that China's claim to Tibet is not going to be resisted by any outside States. It could be argued that it is only because Tibet, unlike Korea, Malaya and Indo-China, has no great significance politically, commercially, industrially, or even strategically [except to India] that nobody is prepared to take up the cudgels on her behalf.

– D. P. Waldron, 24 January 1951[2]

This note, accompanied by a few press clippings, amounts to all there is in the Irish Department of External Affairs' headquarters' files on the taking over of Tibet by the People's Liberation Army (PLA) of the People's Republic of China (PRC) in 1950. This is hardly surprising. The quotation itself illustrates well Ireland's geographical and political remoteness from Tibet at this time.[3] What was to come as a surprise, not least to the writer of this short note, was that, less than ten years later, one of the few people to take up the diplomatic cudgels on Tibet's behalf at the United Nations (UN) was his own minister, Frank Aiken.

Much has been written about Aiken's tenure at the UN, and in particular on his infamous and unexpected stance in relation to 'the China vote'.[4] This chapter will revisit the 'China vote' episode only briefly insofar as it helps to contextualise the author's main focus, which is to offer an analysis of Aiken's later attitude towards Tibet and his sustained efforts to provide assistance and advice to Tibetan leaders in exile, including the Dalai Lama, throughout the 1960s.

The long Chinese Civil War came to an end in 1949, with the Communist victors under Mao Zedong keen to move on to unite the region's 'five races' into one motherland. This objective included the Tibetans, who had *de facto* independence since the fall of the Qing Dynasty in 1912. Despite Tibet's claims to independence, the Seventeen-Point Agreement between the Tibetan leaders and the PRC was signed under duress in May 1951, and was finally accepted by the Fourteenth Dalai Lama the following October. Shortly thereafter, the PLA peacefully entered Lhasa. The government of Tibet was to remain in existence, but under the authority of the People's Republic of China, until the Tibetan uprising in the spring of 1959, when the Dalai Lama famously fled into exile.[5]

Until the Dalai Lama's dramatic flight to India, little interest was shown by the international community towards the plight of Tibet. In July 1951, the Irish chargé d'affaires at Canberra, Brendan O'Riordan, sent a piece he had written about developments in Tibet to Dublin. Its dispiriting cover note reveals a tone not unlike the prevailing mood of indifference towards Tibet among the diplomatic corps in the years immediately following the Chinese invasion. The Tibetan government had little contact with other countries, and as a result was diplomatically isolated. 'The enclosed article on Tibet based on material received in the Embassy from time to time, may be of possible background interest. I wrote it some months ago and am tired of finding it in my tray when I reach the bottom'.[6] The short piece was entitled 'Tibet the Ireland of Asia'. Although somewhat naïve in his observations (he began: 'Although not a Christian country, Tibet like Ireland is one of the most religious countries in the world ...') O'Riordan's overview of Tibet and its history drew basic comparisons with Ireland that Aiken would no doubt also recognise a few years later. Whilst acknowledging the vast geographical differences between the two lands, Tibet, sitting some 11,000 to 15,000 feet above sea level, resembled Ireland in its agricultural economy and in its high standards of education, a result of its monasteries housing one-third of the male population. O'Riordan thought it doubtful on this account whether Communism would ever have any permanent or substantial influence on Tibetan culture, 'even should it be temporarily enforced at the point of the gun'. More significantly, Tibet resembled Ireland because 'for several centuries [it had] been the victim of invaders; and in that the invaders whether Russian, Chinese or British have endeavoured to play on the religious feelings of the people'. No action was taken in the wake of O'Riordan's report, the only substantial review of the situation by an Irish diplomat at the time. There it stayed, much like it had sat on his 'in' tray in Canberra.

The year 1956 saw the PRC attempt to initiate mass land reforms in Tibet, which resulted in violent opposition in the Kham and Amdo regions; this action marked the beginning of a large-scale Tibetan uprising. There ensued a brief flurry of activity in the Irish Department of External Affairs, with an internal summary document drawn up by Bob McDonagh.[7] The department received a letter from the Irish scientist and well-known mountaineer Frank Winder. His was a somewhat prophetic communication. Whilst expressing his concern for the people of Tibet, he also suggested that the situation offered:

... an admirable opportunity for Ireland to use her newly found voice in the United Nations Organisation, and play the Communist powers at their own game of colonial power-baiting by raising this matter at the appropriate time ... it would be a tragedy if the struggle of this tiny, but independently minded nation ... were to be ended without a word being said in her support by a western country – and we are one of the few western nations who are sufficiently far from the glass-house to be able to throw stones.[8]

As indicated in Winder's letter, Ireland had been finally admitted to the UN in 1955 after a period of international isolation in the wake of the Second World War; an enforced seclusion generally believed to have been a rebuke to Ireland's neutrality during that conflict. Frank Aiken, as Minister for External Affairs from 1957 to 1969, was one of the chief architects of Ireland's early UN policy. His was a radical tenure, with neither the international community nor those at home able to predict the positive impact that he would have at the UN. In particular, Ireland's stance on non-proliferation paved the way for the 1968 Nuclear Non-Proliferation Treaty; in honour of his contribution, Aiken was one of the first signatories. There is general consensus among historians that at the heart of his UN policymaking lay an 'anti-imperialist instinct'; one that coincided well with the great wave of decolonisation that was spreading like wildfire throughout Africa and Asia in the 1950s and 1960s.

Patrick Keatinge argues that Aiken was keen to voice Ireland's strong support of the break-up of the European maritime empires. In addressing the General Assembly in 1960, Aiken assured his listeners:

We know what imperialism is and what resistance to it involves. We do not hear with indifference the voices of those spokesmen of African and

Asian countries who passionately champion the right to independence of the millions who are still, unfortunately, under foreign rule. On the contrary, those voices strike an answering chord in every Irish heart.[9]

This chord was particularly melodious in Aiken's heart, and ran through his UN speeches. His appearances at the UN were often eagerly anticipated and well received, in great contrast to his Dáil performances over the years, where he was often criticised for a defensive, even aggressive, style, and where he discouraged public discussion of international affairs.[10] But Irish UN policy during this 'Golden Age' was not simply one-dimensional. While an anti-colonial and gradually acquired pacifist stance suited Aiken well, and was indeed his default position on many issues that came before the UN, other Department of External Affairs policymakers took a much more nuanced approach behind the scenes.

The annual 'China vote' had become something of a Cold War ritual at the UN by 1957. The United States was unyielding in its insistence that the PRC continue to be excluded from the 'China' seat held by Formosa/Taiwan (the refuge of the defeated forces in the Chinese Civil War, also known as the Republic of China (ROC)) to such an extent that it had in fact condensed the recurrent 'China vote' from a straightforward PRC versus ROC vote to a vote on whether the assembly should even *discuss* the problem. Conor Cruise O'Brien, who headed the UN division of the Department of External Affairs at the time, has credited himself with coming up with the idea of using the annual 'China vote' at the UN as a means to getting attention for Aiken's debut. Aiken, upon taking up the reins at External Affairs, seemingly asked him for the best tactic in taking an independent line. Cruise O'Brien told him that 'the test', especially for a presumed pro-American safe bet like Ireland, would be the annual vote on the representation of China.[11]

Aiken shocked the UN by voting in favour of discussion in 1957. Condemnation was rife in Ireland, from the Catholic Church, as well as in the United States, with many commentators incorrectly interpreting Aiken's position as equating to some form of support for the PRC from Ireland. But Aiken was ultimately a pragmatist, and one cannot help but conclude, as indeed Noel Dorr has done, that this is exactly the stance he would have taken anyway, irrespective of the backlash or of Cruise O'Brien's well-intentioned advice.[12] His view was that a vote for discussion was clearly the correct approach, but this candid argument did not hold water with his many detractors. The intricacies of the annual China vote have been thumbed over many times already, and need not be discussed in detail here. What is important, however, is to acknowledge that the vote received a lot of negative reaction at home and abroad, and it clearly had an impact on Aiken and others working on Irish UN policy. Although this was a factor in relation to the Irish Tibet policy adopted at the UN, it had less impact than might initially appear.

On 6 April 1959, First Secretary Eoin MacWhite submitted a brief on the situation in Tibet to his superiors. The previous week saw news that the Dalai Lama had entered India after a gruelling two-week journey across the Himalayas. Filling the three-year lacuna of information on Tibet was as difficult for MacWhite as it was for the rest of the international community. Although it was generally accepted that the PRC had been repressing a Tibetan rebellion that had grown in strength since 1956, precise details were obscure and contradictory. In considering the UN's perspective, MacWhite stated that 'Formosa China is studying the possibility of bringing the matter to the UN ... [but is] unlikely to get very far ...'.[13] On the same day that MacWhite submitted his report, the Secretary of the Department, Con Cremin, received a confidential report from Freddie Boland, Ireland's Ambassador to the UN, detailing his views on the Tibetan situation as he had already outlined to Aiken:

> As I told the Minister before he left, I am convinced that it would be an excellent thing, from every point of view, if he would make an early public statement condemning Red China's attack on the autonomy of Tibet. A clear and positive reference to it in his constituency or elsewhere would be enough ... the constitutional niceties of the question are of secondary importance ... Tibetan internal autonomy is an old tradition and the people of the country have always fought hard to assert and defend it.[14]

Boland was extremely forthright in expressing his opinions on Tibet, and on the likely consequences for Ireland of speaking out against Chinese aggression. His analysis, encapsulating Ireland's views on international law and the role of small nations, was one that Cruise O'Brien appropriated and used in a draft of the speech he would write for Aiken that week.[15] Boland continued to argue that:

> The policies we have always stood for in the past indicate the broad lines which any statement we make should follow. We have always held that without due respect by powerful states for the rights of her weaker neighbours, there can be no rule of law in world affairs, and without a rule of law in world affairs, there can be no peace and security.[16]

He followed this, in a pressing tone not often evident in Boland's correspondence, with:

> It is immaterial that Tibet is very remote from Ireland; that her system of Government is very different from ours; and that her people are devotees of religious beliefs and practices which defeat our understanding. What matters is the principle involved.[17]

In his concluding paragraph, Boland went further than merely suggesting that Aiken speak out publicly about the recent events in Tibet; he planted the seed for a UN initiative by reporting that:

> Some delegations here … are examining the possibility of trying to get the question of Tibet before the United Nations in some way. It is generally thought that they are unlikely to succeed. On the question of timing, I don't think we should wait for these developments. In my view, we have nothing to lose and much to gain by speaking out now and it seems to me entirely right and consistent with our general policy at the United Nations.

Aiken expressed his views on the PRC's actions in Tibet for the first time on a Sunday afternoon in County Louth. At first, the chosen location might seem incongruous, but it was there, some thirty or so years earlier, that Aiken had fought his own war of independence and attempted to avert a civil war. He told his listeners at the Dundalk Fianna Fáil convention that this unprovoked aggression had 'shocked the conscience of the world, particularly that of small nations like our own which knew the evils of foreign rule'.[18] In his speech he invoked the words of Terence MacSwiney in the hope that they would sustain Tibetans in their suffering: 'It is not they who can inflict most but they who can endure most, will conquer'. It was what he said in relation to Tibet and the UN, however, that would garner this Dundalk speech worldwide press coverage. He told his listeners that:

> … so far it had not been possible to have the Tibetan case considered by the United Nations, as were the cases of Korea, Hungary and Suez, but we could record our condemnation of acts of oppression wherever and by whomsoever they are perpetrated. In doing so we are asserting a principle of the United Nations Charter which is not only vital to ourselves but is vital for world peace.[19]

Boland, and the other staff at the Irish Permanent Representative to the UN Headquarters in New York, widely circulated the text of the speech, and reported back on 13 April that 'reactions so far [are] excellent'.[20] Aiken's words received worldwide coverage, and the text was included on the Voice of America, the US overseas radio station. Henry Cabot Lodge, the US Representative to the UN, wrote to Boland that Aiken had 'spoken out with courage and forthrightness, and his statement made a very good impression here'.[21] Boland also saw to it that one of the harshest critics on the 'China vote' two years earlier, Cardinal Spellman of New York, received the text of the speech, which was duly acknowledged, although without comment. In this, there is a point worth drawing out. Great care was taken by Boland and his staff, as well as by the other Irish representatives in the United States, to ensure that the Catholic press in the US received the text of the speech. There was a keen desire to use the opportunity of Tibet to balance the Red scales in Ireland's favour after the negative coverage of the 'China vote' affair.[22]

It seems that Aiken's speech came as a welcome surprise in the United States. The following autumn, the US Ambassador to the UN and some of his staff met with Aiken not long after he arrived in New York. They were keen to encourage Ireland to sponsor a resolution on Tibet. Although Aoife Bhreatnach argues that 'the suggestion for inscription by Ireland of the Tibetan question originated with the Americans', they were pushing an already open door.[23] As seen above, Boland had been considering such a possibility, if not explicitly expressing as much, from as early as April 1959. Nonetheless, Aiken and Boland were happy to show the Americans a draft of their proposed resolution in advance. Boland was well aware that US support did not make things cut and dried, and the UN Secretary General, Dag Hammarskjöld, told him that 'he was opposed to the inscription of a special item, his main fear being that, if an item were inscribed it would inevitably lead to a profitless "cold-war" discussion'.[24] Despite Aiken and Boland courting the Americans,[25] Boland concluded that it did not mean that a special resolution on Tibet was guaranteed. What it meant was that Ireland had 'taken the lead in publicly expressing the view that it would be appropriate that there should be a special item on Tibet on the Assembly agenda'.[26]

The newly instated Taoiseach, Seán Lemass, was not enamoured of Aiken's record at the UN to date, nor was he impressed with using the UN as an arena in which the new Afro-Asian states, concerned as they were with colonialism, could 'propose unrealistic resolutions calling for types of action which the General Assembly could not possibly implement'.[27] As Cathal Dowling notes, Lemass looked on Aiken's activities in the UN as idealistic, and not in the best sense of the word, and the two men shared a mutual antipathy.[28] But Lemass was happy with Ireland's stance on Tibet, albeit for different reasons to Aiken's and Boland's. Cremin subtly passed this on to the delegation in New York:

> I might mention that when I was speaking to [the Taoiseach] this morning, he expressed his keen satisfaction at the Minister's intention to sponsor a resolution on Tibet – on the ground that this would dispose effectively of certain of the charges directed against us because of our attitude on the question of Chinese representation.[29]

This was an early rebuke for Aiken's 'independent line' from Lemass, a mere three months after his taking office as Taoiseach.

In the end Ireland found a co-sponsor in Malaya, and together they put forward a resolution on Tibet, which was adopted during the Fourteenth Session in October 1959. It was moderate in scope, confined to the human rights aspects of the situation with no explicit reference to Tibetan independence. When news of the Irish resolution reached the Tibetan leaders in exile, an initial sense of surprise at its origins (their expectation was that any Tibetan initiative would have been sponsored entirely by the Afro-Asian states) was quickly replaced with a keen desire to express their gratitude to Ireland. On 1 October, Irish Ambassador in London, Hugh McCann, had a surprise visit from the Dalai Lama's brother, Gyalo Thondup. While the Dalai Lama had judiciously avoided any contact with the more radical Tibetan activists, who throughout the 1950s received the support of the CIA, his brother Thondup had enthusiastically taken charge of this side of the movement.[30] McCann reported to Dublin how Thondup and his colleagues 'expressed deep appreciation of our initiative at the United Nations'. Thondup moreover grasped at the opportunity that this glimmer of support from the international community gave his nation, and tried to maximise it. Aiken's Louth speech provided them with ample comfort, but also with a bargaining tool:

> They are anxious however that the Tibetan question should be raised in the United Nations not only from the human rights point of view but also from the point of view of the independence of the country. Mr Tondup [sic] referred to the Minister's speech in Dundalk ... where he condemns 'aggression' against Tibet. They fasten on this reference to aggression in the Minister's speech and say that it gives them great heart.[31]

Thondup went on to New York from London in an effort to lobby for further support. The Irish delegation was keen to meet him, but also to make sure that any press coverage he might receive would not have a negative impact on the resolution, and to that end cables were exchanged between New York and London via Dublin until the parties met in person in early October.[32]

The proposal to include a Tibet resolution was presented by Ireland and Malaya on 9 October 1959, and it was accepted and debated the following week. In his concluding remarks, Aiken's argument was forceful and pragmatic:

> This organisation represents the experience of our evolving world society. It cannot escape its responsibilities. We know what has happened in Tibet. The People's Republic of China has not denied it. That government and its friends in this assembly have tried to justify it. The question is: do the delegates here interpret our charter as permitting China to overrun Tibet, to impose its will by force upon the Tibetan people, and do they wish such conduct of the powerful against the weak to become generalised? ... [T]he Assembly ... must be just, impartial, and consistent in the application of the laws of our Charter or we dishearten those who would uphold them and encourage those who would violate them. We must seize this opportunity to give them life.[33]

The resolution was adopted by forty-five votes to nine, with twenty-six abstentions, on 21 October 1959. News of its success was extremely well received, in Ireland, abroad and by the international press. Cremin conveyed to Aiken any positive feedback the department in Dublin had received, including a softening on the part of Lemass towards Aiken's UN performance, at least in relation to this issue. 'The Taoiseach has now expressed his great pleasure at the result of the vote and his satisfaction with the nature and quality of the Minister's interventions'. Cremin continued:

> The Taoiseach's satisfaction about the Tibet affair is shared by everybody I have met... [A]t dinner ... in the Aras in honour of the Papal Nuncio, the President also told me how happy he was that the Minister had raised the question, had dealt with it in such a comprehensive and able manner and had secured such a striking vote in favour of our Resolution. It is of course recognised that many of the abstentions were due to special and understandable causes.[34]

The success of the vote buoyed the Tibetan community, especially those in the West working for further recognition. Hugh McCann in London began to receive letters about Ireland's stance in relation to Tibet, and requests for audiences with

London-based Tibetan sympathisers. Many of these activists and politicians were members of the Tibet Society of Britain, such as Francis Beaufort-Palmer,[35] Marco Pallis[36] and Sir Olaf Caroe.[37] Lord Birdwood contacted the Irish Embassy in London in advance of tabling a motion on Tibet in the House of Lords. He had been a member of the UK delegation at the UN during the previous year, and took a keen interest in Aiken's speeches during the debate.[38] The Department of External Affairs in Dublin also began to receive an increase in correspondence in relation to Tibet and Asia in general from the likes of the Afro-Asian Council based in Delhi, and letters from the heads of government of some of the resolution's co-sponsors and supporters.[39]

Two more resolutions on Tibet were adopted at the UN, in 1961 and 1965. By 1961, as Noel Dorr has recently recounted, Aiken (with co-sponsors Malaya, El Salvador and Thailand) changed the terminology of the discourse and included the idea that the Tibetan people had a right to self-determination for the first time. Despite concerns that this may have been a step too far, the resolution was adopted: fifty-six votes in favour to eleven against, with twenty-nine abstentions.[40] This was a significant development, and one for which the Tibetan government in exile had been lobbying numerous countries. The Dalai Lama was fulsome in his thanks to Aiken, telling him how he read the resolution 'with great pleasure' and that he was:

> ... grateful to [Aiken] personally, for I fully appreciate the keen and abiding interest which you have shown in the matter from the very beginning ... I fully realise that the cause of Tibetan freedom would not have received recognition from the World Assembly without [your] painstaking and persistent efforts.[41]

His brother Thondup, having met Aiken in New York, also wrote to him with thanks. In his reply, Aiken told him:

> I am glad that the representatives of Tibet should have found it useful even though, like you, I realise that it cannot bring any immediate results. I hope, however, that it may be one of a series of events that will eventually lead to the restoration of the fundamental human rights and freedoms of the Tibetan people, including self-determination.[42]

Throughout the 1960s, Aiken continued to engage in a sustained correspondence with the Dalai Lama and Thondup. They took great solace in Aiken's support, and regularly asked his advice on how best to keep Tibet to the fore in international affairs. These letters were initially very formal. For example, on behalf of Aiken, External Affairs wrote to the Dalai Lama in 1960:

> Mr Aiken understands that your esteemed brother, His Excellency Gyalo Thondup, will probably be in New York when the question of Tibet is due to be considered by the General Assembly. In renewing his pleasant acquaintanceship with your Excellency's brother the Minister will look forward to discussing in detail with him the course of events affecting Tibet since the last General Assembly debate and the most useful action which the Assembly can now effectively take in the interests of the Tibetan people.[43]

Two years later, their correspondence was less stilted, and there emerged a regular exchange of ideas between Aiken and Tibetans in New York while he was there for the General Assembly sittings. In true Aiken style, there was a practical aspect to their networking:

> I need not assure Your Excellency of our unwavering support for any course of action calculated to secure the triumph of the Tibetan cause and we shall continue to do what we can within the UN to this end. It would perhaps be premature to consider now what further action can be taken at the next Session of the General Assembly. However my delegation will keep in touch with our friends in New York to see what can be done.[44]

There was an upsurge in expectations on the part of Tibetans in the wake of the Sino–Indian Border Conflict in 1964.[45] However, their hope that India would come to the aid of Tibet at the UN were dashed when, in 1965, a final resolution was co-sponsored by Ireland and six other countries, India not among them. Crucially, the 'self-determination' wording had been dropped. This represented a fear, which Aiken had regularly expressed to the Dalai Lama, that any further initiative at the UN had to be as forthright and successful as the 1961 Resolution had been, both in wording and support. Ever the pragmatist, Aiken felt that any further move had to be a step forward and not a step back for the Tibetans. He told the US Ambassador to the UN in 1963 that:

> Ireland would not be willing to support any resolution the provisions of which were not at least as strong as the terms of the resolution of 20th December 1961. If therefore the Indian Government proposed to

inscribe a resolution which excluded any reference to the principle of, and the right to, self-determination, Ireland would not 'go along with it'.[46]

Aiken's concern was proving all too valid, and by 1965 interest in Tibet at the UN was beginning to wane.[47] The situation in Tibet had not changed materially, and there was no indication that the PRC had paid any attention to the previous UN resolutions.

Conclusion

Aiken's support of Tibet at the UN has been viewed as a political move 'to right the wrong' that his 'China vote' had on perceptions of Ireland in the eyes of the Catholic Church and the wider world. As seen above, this was indeed the reason behind Lemass's support of Aiken's actions. For Aiken, however, this was merely a useful sideshow as opposed to the main attraction. There is no evidence to support the supposition that his were the manoeuvrings of a cynical minister navigating the realpolitik of conference diplomacy. On the contrary, his continued support of the Tibetan cause throughout the 1960s in the face of its declining prospects proves that his motivations were sincere. It must also be acknowledged that the issue of Tibet struck a chord with Aiken's revolutionary past. His support of a country whose people, then and since, have been held up as bastions of peace and non-violence provides a counterpoint to his own past as an IRA Commandant. If Aiken 'owed his early success to military rather than political leadership',[48] this was reversed during his time at the UN, thanks in part to his championing of the right of the Tibetan people to self-determination.

In the wake of Aiken's death, *The Irish Times* aptly described the unexpected success of his later years. 'The man who had been regarded by so many of his political opponents at home as dour, even narrow, showed a remarkable breadth and depth of feeling and an acute understanding of world politics'.[49] At the height of Aiken's activities at the UN, and during his very public move towards pacifism, he received a bullet in the post. It was contained in a letter from an Irishman living in the Bronx, clearly enraged over Aiken's 'China vote'. He threatened him with more bullets in recognition of 'twelve years of nothing at the UN'. It was his parting shot that explains his venom: 'China is more important to you than Armagh', he wrote. However, it was Tibet and not China that was personally important to Aiken, for in Tibet he saw the shadows of Armagh and Louth, and in supporting the Tibetan struggle for self-determination, he tried to reconcile his violent past with his role as constitutional politician and international statesman.

Notes

1   Letter from unnamed Irishman in the Bronx, New York City, enclosing a bullet, Nov. 1966. University College Dublin Archives (UCDA), Frank Aiken Papers, P104/6658.

2   Minute by D. P. Waldron, 24 Jan. 1951. National Archives of Ireland (NAI), Department of External Affairs (DEA), 305/134/2.

3   Ireland did not establish bilateral relations with China until 1979, although the department was kept informed of events during and after the civil war through Irish missionary channels. Likewise, Ireland had no Ambassador to India until 1964. After the Dalai Lama fled Tibet, Conor Cruise O'Brien noted on file how 'we should, no doubt, know more about it if we were represented in India'. Note from O'Brien to John A. Belton, 6 April 1959. NAI, DFA, 304/134/2.

4   See Aoife Bhreatnach, 'Frank Aiken: Federation and United Nations Internationalism', *Irish Studies in International Affairs*, Vol. 13 (2002); Cathal Dowling, 'Irish Policy on the Representation of China at the United Nations, 1957–9', *Irish Studies in International Affairs*, Vol. 7 (1996), 87–91; and Norman Macqueen, 'Frank Aiken and Irish Activism at the United Nations, 1957–61', in *The International History Review*, Vol. 6, No. 2 (Abingdon: Taylor & Francis, 1984).

5   For further and more detailed reading of this period, and Tibetan history in general, see M. C. Goldstein, *A History of Modern Tibet, Volume 2: The Calm Before the Storm: 1951–1955*, (Berkeley: University of California Press, 2007); P. French, *Tibet, Tibet: A Personal History of a Lost Land* (London: Harper Collins, 2003); S. van Schaik, *Tibet: a History* (New Haven and London: Yale University Press, 2011); and J. Ardley, *The Tibetan Independence Movement: Political, Religious and Gandhian Perspectives* (London: Routledge Curzon, 2002).

6   O'Riordan to William Fay, 9 July 1951. NAI, DEA, 305/134/2.

7   Summary document titled 'Situation in Tibet', initialed 'R. McD.', 31 July 1956. NAI, DEA, 305/134/2.

8   Winder to Seán Murphy, Secretary, Department of External Affairs, 26 July 1956. NAI, DEA, 305/134/2.

9   P. Keatinge, *A Place Among Nations. Issues of Irish Foreign Policy* (Dublin: Institute of Public Administration, 1978), 173–4.

10   Ronan Fanning, 'Frank Aiken', *Dictionary of Irish Biography*, available at http://dib. cambridge.org (accessed 18/04/13) and Macqueen, 'Frank Aiken', 227.

11   Conor Cruise O'Brien, *Memoir: My Life and Themes* (Dublin: Poolbeg, 1999), 186–187.

12   Noel Dorr, *Ireland at the United Nations. Memories of the early years* (Dublin: Institute of Public Administration, 2010), 115–116.

13   Memo titled 'Situation in Tibet' by Eoin MacWhite. NAI, DEA, 305/134/2.

14   F. H. Boland to Con Cremin, 2 April 1959. NAI, DEA, 305/134/2. This report was received in Dublin on 9 April, and seen by Aiken. For a further examination of this Confidential Report, see Joseph Morrison Skelly, *Irish Diplomacy at the United Nations, 1945–1965, National Interests and the International Order* (Dublin: Irish Academic Press, 1997), 172–174. Skelly focuses on other aspects of this report, such as a difference in opinion between Cruise O'Brien and Boland over Ireland's China policy. He also suggests that Aiken was ambivalent about whether to refer to Tibet in his Dundalk speech of

some days later, only deciding to do so at the last minute. Boland's letter is as solid a policy document as exists in relation to Aiken's attitude towards Tibet. Aiken's personal papers contain speech drafts and news clippings on Tibet, as well as telegrams and correspondence, but little in the way of policy formulation is evident from these.

15 Skelly, *Irish Diplomacy*, 174.

16 Boland to Cremin, 2 April 1959. NAI, DEA, 305/134/2.

17 Boland to Cremin, 2 April 1959. NAI, DEA, 305/134/2.

18 *Irish Press,* 13 April 1959.

19 *Irish Press,* 13 April 1959.

20 Uneireann to Estero, 13 April 1959. NAI, DEA, 305/134/2.

21 Cabot Lodge to Boland, 16 April 1959. NAI, DEA, 305/134/2.

22 See various correspondence and telegrams in the wake of Aiken's Dundalk speech in mid-April 1959 on file NAI, DEA, 305/134/2. There is a large batch of correspondence from members of the public in both Ireland and the United States addressed to Aiken criticizing his China policy in his personal papers in UCD archives. There is also evidence to support Noel Dorr's recollection that reaction to the China vote from the Catholic Church was not 'a damp squib' (as described by Cruise O'Brien, see Dorr, *Ireland at the United Nations,* 116–118). Great efforts were made by DEA officials in both New York and Dublin to document this criticism, whatever their opinions of it.

23 Memorandum on meeting with US delegation by Boland, 15 Sept. 1959. NAI, DEA, 410/15. Aoife Bhreatnach covers this meeting in some detail. See Aoife Bhreatnach, 'A friend of the colonial powers? Frank Aiken, Ireland's United Nations alignment and decolonisation', in Michael Kennedy and Deirdre McMahon (eds), *Obligations and Responsibilities: Ireland and the United Nations, 1955–2005* (Dublin: Institute of Public Administration, 2005), 183–184.

24 Secret Report, Boland to Cremin, 18 Sept. 1959. NAI, DEA, 410/15.

25 There is a subplot worth noting here: Ireland was simultaneously seeking US support of Boland's candidature for the Presidency of the 15th Session of the General Assembly. See Michael Kennedy, '"Persuade an alternative European candidate to stand": why Ireland was elected to the United Nations Council in 1961', in Kennedy and McMahon, *Obligations,* 160–167.

26 Kennedy and McMahon, *Obligations,* 160–167.

27 Keatinge, *A Place Among Nations,* 175.

28 C. Dowling, 'Irish Policy', 95.

29 Very Confidential Report, Cremin to Boland, 29 Sept. 1959. NAI, DEA, 410/15.

30 S. van Schaik, *Tibet,* 239.

31 Telegram No. 2900, London to Dublin, 1 Oct. 1959. NAI, DEA, 410/15.

32 See various telegrams on file dating from the first week of Oct. 1959. NAI, DEA, 410/15.

33 Typed copy with handwritten note 'Min's reply to debate on Tibet 21/10/59'. NAI, DEA, 410/15.

34 Cremin to Boland, Confidential, 24 Oct. 1959. NAI, DEA, 410/15. India had abstained because, although they had granted asylum to the Dalai Lama, they had signed the Panchsheel Treaty with the PRC in April 1954.

35 Sir Francis Beaufort-Palmer was a writer, the great-grandson of Admiral Sir Francis Beaufort, and a distant relative of Seán MacBride.

36 Marco Pallis was a Greek-British mountaineer, Tibetan scholar and musician. He was a friend of Lord Christopher Birdwood, a British hereditary peer, author and soldier who had served in India. They, along with Sir Olaf Caroe, were all founders of the Tibet Society of Great Britain.

37 Sir Olaf Caroe was an Indian civil servant who became Governor of the North-West Frontier Province in 1946. After Indian independence, he returned to Britain and became a Middle East and Asia specialist.

38 Birdwood to McCann, 21 March 1960. NAI, DEA, 410/15.

39 See, for example, Tanku Abdul Rahman to Seán Lemass, 12 Aug. 1960. NAI, DEA, 410/15.

40 Dorr, *Ireland and the United Nations*, 122.

41 Dalai Lama to Aiken, 17 Jan. 1962. NAI, DEA, 410/15.

42 Aiken to Thondup, 26 Jan. 1962. NAI, DEA, 410/15. Aiken and Thondup would meet again when Thondup paid a visit to Dublin in July 1964; he was the guest of the government for two days en route to New York. He met de Valera, and the Aikens entertained the Thondup party at the Russell Hotel.

43 Jack Molloy to the Dalai Lama, 24 Sept. 1960. NAI, DEA, 410/15. External Affairs was liaising with the Department of Taoiseach, in particular Nicholas Nolan, Assistant Secretary, on a draft of their first reply to the Dalai Lama. Nolan took exception to their use of the term 'His Holiness', and, in his characteristically meticulous style, returned the draft with clear instructions: 'You will note that apart from the substitution of "Excellency" for "Your Holiness" in the salutation, "your" for "Your Holiness's" in the first line and "Excellency" for "Holiness" elsewhere in the text, the reply is in the terms of the draft that accompanied your letter of the 8th'. Nolan to Cremin, 12 Feb. 1960. NAI, DEA, 410/15.

44 Aiken to the Dalai Lama, 26 Feb. 1962. NAI, DEA, 410/15.

45 See report of meeting between Boland and Thondup, Boland to MacCann (seen by Aiken), 5 Dec. 1963, NAI, DEA, 410/10. Thondup told Boland: 'Mr Nehru was becoming more and more receptive to supporting a resolution at the UN'. Nehru was not, however, in favour of supporting 'self-determination'. He died the following year.

46 Note by Seán Ronan, 22 Aug. 1963. NAI, DEA, 410/15.

47 Dorr, *Ireland at the United Nations*, 123.

48 Fanning, 'Frank Aiken', *Dictionary of Irish Biography*.

49 *The Irish Times*, 21 May 1983.

CHAPTER TWELVE

A man with a cause: Frank Aiken, the Palestine refugee issue and the evolution of Ireland's Middle East policy, 1957–1969

RORY MILLER

From Politician to Statesman

In March 1957, following the Fianna Fáil victory in national elections, Frank Aiken replaced Liam Cosgrave as Ireland's Minister for External Affairs. He would hold this post until his retirement in 1969. During these years, Aiken was responsible for entrenching Ireland's policy of neutrality in international affairs.[1] Central to this strategy was his belief in the need to adopt an independent stance at the United Nations; a body that Ireland had only joined in 1955.

As discussed in the Introduction to this edited collection, from Aiken's earliest speeches before the United Nations General Assembly it was clear that Ireland's new foreign minister was determined to play a formative role at the international body in a number of major areas, ranging from decolonization to nuclear non-proliferation and peacekeeping.[2] Within one year of taking office, he became the first Irish foreign minister to commit troops to serve in a UN peacekeeping mission, and he quickly developed a reputation, in the words of

US Secretary of State Dean Rusk, as one of the 'great champions' of 'effective peace-keeping operations at the UN'.[3]

What is much less well known is the extent of the involvement of Aiken, and the Irish delegation, in the diplomacy, politics and economics of the Middle East in general, and the Israel–Palestine conflict in particular, during the late 1950s and throughout the 1960s. In fact, with the exception of my own research,[4] there is a dearth of scholarship on Ireland and the Middle East across the entire twentieth century. The exceptions are Patrick Keatinge's chapter-length examination of Ireland and the Arab–Israeli conflict published in 1984, and Ben Tonra's brief examination of the same in the context of Ireland's involvement in EU foreign policymaking published in 2001. Otherwise, the main contribution to the subject area is a number of books and articles (some more scholarly than others) dealing with the experience of Irish soldiers stationed with the UN force in Lebanon between 1978 and 2001.[5]

Aiken was particularly concerned with the fate of the Palestinian refugees made homeless in the 1948 Arab–Israeli war. In fact, his entire engagement with the Middle East conflict, including his role during the UN diplomatic efforts in the summer of 1967, evolved out of his interest in, and concern about, this issue. This chapter will examine Aiken's preoccupation with the matter, and will show how this had a profound influence over Ireland's evolving Middle East policy during his tenure as the country's senior foreign policymaker.

Peacemaker in the Middle East

It is estimated that, by April 1948 (the month prior to the Arab invasion of Israel in May 1948), over 100,000 Palestinian Arabs, mostly from the main urban centres of Jerusalem, Jaffa and Haifa, and from villages along the coastal plain of Palestine, had fled to the surrounding Arab states. By the time that fighting had ceased in early 1949, the total number of Palestinian Arab refugees was estimated to be between 538,000 (Israeli sources), 720,000 (UN estimates) and 850,000 (Palestinian sources).[6]

In both 1957 and 1958, in speeches at the UNGA, Aiken addressed the problem of the Palestinian refugees, which he described as the 'greatest single obstacle' to a lasting peace in the Middle East. In his 1958 speech before the Emergency Special Session he had called on the UN to 'guarantee full compensation' for the refugees, for both property lost and damage suffered as a 'result of their exile'. Though he accepted that Israel was not exclusively responsible for the tragedy, he did call on it to state how many refugees it was prepared to accept, and argued that the UN should 'arrange for repatriation for the maximum possible number of those who would rather return than receive full compensation'.[7]

Aiken's 'concrete proposals'[8] on the refugee crisis, as Conor Cruise O'Brien, then a junior Irish diplomat in New York, described them, were welcomed back home as 'both wise and practicable'.[9] They also set the standard for the contribution of members of successive Irish UN delegations in discussions at the UNGA Special Political and Ad Hoc Committees.[10]

This sympathy for the plight of the Palestinian refugees at UN forums was the result of Aiken's sincerely held belief that, while Ireland lacked political and diplomatic influence over the parties to the conflict, it did have an important, if not unique, moral contribution to make. This belief was backed up by the first Irish financial donations to the United Nations Relief and Works Agency (UNRWA) in his first full year as foreign minister.

This UN body had been founded as a temporary measure by UNGA Resolution 302 (IV) of 8 December 1949, with the mandate to carry out aid programmes to alleviate the suffering of Arab refugees who, as a result of the hostilities in Palestine in 1948, had fled to Jordan, Lebanon, Syria and the Gaza Strip. However, it quickly evolved into the main provider of basic services to the refugees, regardless of whether they were registered as refugees or not. It also became a unique body in the realm of international aid by entrenching itself as a permanent organization dedicated to the relief of one particular national group: Palestinian Arabs.

In October 1958, Paul Keating, Ireland's Representative on the UNGA Ad Hoc Committee, announced that although up to this point Ireland's 'own domestic economic problems' had prevented her from contributing to UNRWA, the Irish had been 'very conscious of the very great problem and the great source of anguish' engendered by the Palestinian refugee crisis, and thus pledged a 'purely token' £1,000 to the organization.[11] In the following year this contribution was raised to the sterling equivalent of US$2,800, and from this time until the end of the financial year 1966, Irish donations to the organization totalled US$126,800.[12]

This financial support for UNRWA underlined Ireland's 'serious concern' over the Palestinian refugee problem, as well as its 'appreciation' of UNRWA's role.[13] Financially, Ireland's commitment also exceeded that of most other nations during these years. With its first contribution to UNRWA in 1958, Ireland became only the thirty-first nation (plus the Vatican) to support UNRWA financially. By 1966 it was still one of only forty-three of the UN's 121 members to donate funds. According to official figures, Ireland ranked eleventh in Western Europe, ahead of Austria, Finland, Greece, Luxemburg and Turkey, and sixth overall, in terms of its contribution as a proportion of Gross National Product.[14]

There is little doubt that this commitment to UNRWA was a direct consequence of a developing Irish foreign policy that viewed humanitarian crises with the utmost concern. But it was also directly related to Aiken's belief in the centrality of the Palestine refugee problem to the ongoing conflict in the Middle East.

In August 1958, Aiken had referred to the deadlock between Israel and the Arabs over the refugee problem as perhaps the greatest single obstacle to the establishment of peace in the region.[15] In his sporadic meetings with Israeli diplomats, Aiken, in the words of his own officials, 'made much of the problem of the Arab refugees'.[16] During a 1962 meeting with an Israeli diplomat, Aiken noted that, as far as the Middle East was concerned, Ireland's 'main pre-occupation' was the Arab refugees, and he favoured compensation coupled with the repatriation of some of the refugees back to Israel.[17]

Although the early years of Aiken's foreign policy reign marked a new beginning in Ireland's practical involvement in humanitarian aspects of the Palestine problem, there was little appetite for engagement in the politics or diplomacy of the Arab–Israeli conflict. At the time of its entry into the UN in 1955, Ireland only had *de facto* diplomatic relations with the two Middle Eastern States of Egypt and Israel. Prior to delivering his 1958 UN statement on the refugee issue, Aiken had been counselled by his influential Ambassador at the UN, Frederick Boland, to delete a call for Arab recognition of Israel in its existing borders on the grounds that it would alienate the Arab world, thus making it harder for Ireland to pursue an independent policy at the UN.[18] Following Aiken's speech, Conor Cruise O'Brien presented Irish support for UNRWA in terms of the necessity for members of the international community to tackle the humanitarian crisis without regard to the 'political aspects of the situation'.[19]

As such, Ireland refrained from using its two-year temporary membership of the UN Security Council (UNSC) in 1960–1962 to engage in Middle East diplomacy. As Aiken informed an Israeli foreign ministry official, the Irish position on the conflict was discreet, and limited to private suggestions to the parties involved.[20] This view was reiterated by Irish UN diplomat Brendan Nolan on the eve of the 1967 Arab–Israeli War at a meeting of the UN Special Political Committee. No one, Nolan explained, denied the 'political significance' of the problem, but Ireland viewed the crisis in non-political terms and urged the UN to increase its 'moral and material' support for UNRWA.[21] In the same month, Nolan's colleague in New York, Noel Dorr, voted against an amendment to a draft resolution on UNRWA funding that attempted to politicise the issue by calling on Israel specifically, rather than on all countries, to cooperate with UNRWA on the grounds that Ireland solely 'tried to address itself to humanitarian aspects'.[22]

This apolitical approach would change fundamentally in the months and years that followed the June 1967 Arab–Israeli War. The summer of 1967 saw the displacement of a further 200,000 Palestinians, which exacerbated the existing problem. This deeply affected Aiken, who had been in New York on a prearranged visit at this time of heightened tension on the eve of the June conflict. On 18 May, President Gamal Abdel Nasser of Egypt had requested the immediate withdrawal of the decade-old United Nations Expeditionary Force (UNEF) from Egyptian territory. Four days later, on the same day that Aiken had a pre-scheduled lunch meeting with UN Secretary-General, U Thant, Nasser went further and reconstituted the blockade of the Straits of Tiran. This prevented Israeli vessels from accessing the international shipping lanes of the Middle East, and was viewed by Jerusalem as a *casus belli*.

Prior to this meeting, two former senior members of the US mission, Charles Yost and Ernest Gross, sought Aiken out, and 'very anxious to have a chat with him', broached the subject of the UNEF expulsion in the hope that he would convey, to Thant, American dissatisfaction with his decision to remove UNEF forces without consultation, and solely on the basis of Nasser's demands.[23]

Aiken was sympathetic to the Secretary General's view that the UN could not keep troops in Egypt once they were unwelcome, and, rather than add his own backing to the American position, his preferred solution to the crisis, at this point, was for Israel, which had refused to accept UNEF troops on its own territory since 1956, to agree to allow UNEF forces to patrol the armistice lines from the Israeli side.[24]

However, in attempting to use Aiken as a go-between with the UN Secretary General, American officials were acknowledging his status as a veteran UN operator, whose devotion to the institutions of the UN, and whose belief in the necessity for Ireland to take an independent position, had earned him much regard among UN delegations and within officialdom in the decade since Irish entry.

At times, Aiken's independent outlook had caused Washington some concern, most notably in 1957, when he unexpectedly decided to support discussions over Communist China's entry into the UN.[25] However, Aiken's stature within the body was also an asset to the United States in a crisis such as this, in which one of the parties to the conflict (the Arabs) was highly suspicious of the American position (indeed, once hostilities began in early June, Arab radio began to claim, incorrectly, that American fighter planes were participating in the bombing of targets in Egypt). Thus, it is not surprising that, over the following days, members of the American UN delegation approached their Irish counterparts with a view to securing support for a joint declaration by maritime powers on freedom of passage through the Straits of Tiran and the Gulf of Aqaba.[26]

Even if the Americans had not involved Aiken directly in these early deliberations on how to limit the crisis and prevent the outbreak of war, it is probable that the specific nature of the crisis, in particular the issue of UNEF withdrawal, would have attracted his interest.

More generally, Aiken had long been aware of the potential seriousness of any Middle East conflagration. This had been a key issue in his 1958 UNGA speech when he warned against the 'progress towards disaster'[27] facing the Middle East. In 1962 he had told one Israeli official that he viewed the region as 'one of the potential trouble spots in the world'.[28] By January 1967, Cornelius (Con) Cremin, the senior Irish diplomat in New York, was reporting back to Dublin on the 'continuing anxiety' over the situation on Israel's borders and, on returning home from New York in late May, Aiken himself expressed 'anxiety' and pessimism over the fate of 'a very important strategic area'.[29]

Aside from such discussions and public calls for a peaceful settlement, between 5 and 14 June there was little that the foreign minister of a small, neutral, European nation without a seat on the UNSC could do, as diplomatic deliberations during these ten days centred on the UNSC. Indeed, it is likely that Aiken's contribution to the diplomatic negotiations at the UN would have been confined to his various meetings while in New York in late May if it were not for the Soviet determination to redeem itself in the face of the humiliating military defeat of its Arab clients and its own failure to get a strongly worded anti-Israeli draft resolution passed at the UNSC before the body adjourned on 14 June.[30]

Reeling from this failure on two fronts, Soviet Foreign Minister, Andrei Gromyko, had written to Secretary General Thant on 13 June to request the 'immediate convening of an emergency special session of the UNGA'. There was no provision for such an emergency special session in UN procedures and, according to Cremin (one of the first permanent representatives to be informed by Thant of the Soviet request) the move 'evoked astonishment' in all quarters.[31]

Nevertheless, the Secretary General's Office set about contacting the permanent missions of all 122 Member States to ask if they supported the Soviet request because, under General Assembly rules of procedure, a majority of members needed to favour the convening of a special session. Within a week, ninety-eight Member States had responded positively, three (Israel, the United

States and Botswana) rejected it, and eighteen countries did not reply either way. Interestingly, and in stark contrast to Aiken's involvement once the session was under way, Ireland was among this final group of nations.

Despite this apparent indifference, and the fact that the New York discussions would coincide with a visit to Ireland by Jacqueline Kennedy, once the special session convened on 17 June, there was general agreement within the Department of External Affairs in Dublin and the Irish UN delegation that Aiken would participate in the substantive discussions set to commence on 19 June. This view was fuelled by the statement of US Secretary of State, Dean Rusk ,who, during a stopover in Shannon on the way to a NATO meeting in Luxembourg on 15 June, had praised Aiken as a leading statesman at the UN 'for many years', to whom he looked for 'counsel and wisdom' at this time of crisis.[32]

Aiken arrived in New York on 19 June at the beginning of a period of intense diplomatic effort that saw thirty-three meetings of the UNGA special session (between 17 June and 21 July), seventeen of which were devoted to a general debate on the crisis. Even before he had arrived in New York, the Irish press recorded that Aiken would take the opportunity of his speech to the fifth emergency special session of the UNGA on 27 June to put forward 'definite views on the Middle East'.[33] His presence in New York gave new momentum to Ireland's permanent mission staff, who had 'no precise instructions' on what to do or say up until this time.[34]

Aiken made the speech at a time of deep concern over the fate, not just of the Middle East, but of the world at large. He began by expressing his conviction 'that if a stable peace cannot be secured the race for the bomb is bound to begin in real earnest, particularly if the great powers do not agree without delay upon a treaty to prevent the spread of nuclear weapons'.[35] As such, he described the war of June 1967 as part of a 'continuing' problem that had to be dealt with decisively, rather than one that could be isolated, bandaged over and forgotten.[36]

Apart from his predictions of nuclear catastrophe and his statement of confidence in the UN Secretary General, his address touched on three issues at the heart of the Arab–Israeli conflict. Israeli withdrawal from territory occupied in the course of war; the status of the holy places of Jerusalem; and, most importantly, the plight of the Palestinian refugees.

Prior to his departure for New York, Aiken told the press that the Arab refugee crisis was the major problem requiring 'foremost attention', and that 'it would pay the world to contribute to the settlement of the refugee problem'.[37] Following his arrival in New York, the Irish UN delegation reported home that the 'Minister is strongly in favour of something being done by the Assembly' on the refugee issue, and favoured 'a fairly substantial contribution by us for the emergency relief for Arab refugees'.[38]

In his speech before the special session, Aiken began his discussion on the refugees by first acknowledging the ill treatment meted out to the Jews in Europe on grounds of race and religion. But he continued:

> ... it would however be altogether unacceptable that a restitution for European injustice and barbarous persecution should be at the expense of under-privileged Arab families who have been deprived of their homes and lands and are living in miserable refugee camps.[39]

He then called for increased funding of UNRWA to give 'immediate assistance to the people displaced and rendered destitute by the recent hostilities'. Finally, he explained that he still believed that his 1958 proposals put before the UN, for either the restoration of Arab lands, or for full compensation and an opportunity to settle elsewhere with a capital amount of US$1000 per family member, should form the basis of a permanent solution to the Middle East problem.[40]

Aiken's speech was immediately recognised as a major contribution to the UN debate on the conflict. It gained international press coverage,[41] and received praise and notice from politicians and notable international figures. The world-renowned historian Arnold Toynbee wrote a long letter to Aiken full of praise for his statements at the UN in 1958 and 1967, which together he held to be 'historic documents'.[42] A more dispassionate assessment came from Arthur Lall, India's former ambassador to the UN, and the author of a 1968 scholarly analysis of the UN's role in the Six Day war (to this day one of the most fluid and authoritative works on the subject) that highlighted for special attention Aiken's 'distinctive and important statement' of 27 June, which Lall viewed as 'perhaps the most far reaching of all those made in the Assembly's debate'.[43]

Aiken's reputation at this time was further evidenced by the fact that the Danish President of the Security Council, Hans Tabor, and Britain's UN Ambassador, Lord Caradon, with the backing of both the Canadian and Dutch representatives, wanted Ireland to 'go it alone' and be the sole sponsor of a UNGA draft resolution put forward by the western block of UN Member States. The Norwegian and Italian representatives, however, made the case for Ireland to be one of the co-sponsors representing the western nations if they decided to support a Latin American draft instead of putting forward their own.[44]

Aiken declined both these offers, but in the wake of his speech he continued to raise the refugee issue in meetings in New York with senior figures such as Rusk, to whom he stressed the importance of a solution to the refugee crisis, 'which has too long been neglected'.[45] He also instructed the Irish delegation in New York to involve itself in a Swedish initiative to present the emergency special session with a draft resolution calling on increased support for UNRWA. This resulted in Ireland's co-sponsorship of the 4 July 1967 UNGA resolution on the refugee crisis that urged the international community to make special contributions to UNRWA.[46]

Unsurprisingly, UNRWA leadership was highly grateful for Aiken's efforts. In mid-July 1967, John Reddaway, Deputy Commissioner General of UNRWA, visited Dublin in order to brief Aiken and senior Department of External Affairs officials H. J. McCann and Seán G. Ronan (respectively Secretary and Assistant Secretary of the Department for External Affairs) on the 'plight of the refugees in the Middle East'. Reddaway's decision to visit Ireland at 'such a busy time' was 'much appreciated' by those he met, and is evidence of the high esteem in which Aiken was held. Indeed, Reddaway believed that Aiken's June 1967 UNGA speech was 'excellent' and that it 'exactly fits the situation in the Middle East'.[47]

The fifth emergency special session of the UNGA adjourned on 21 July 1967. Despite a proviso that the session could be reconvened if necessary,[48] from this point on, responsibility for the ongoing conflict once again reverted to the UNSC. On his return to Dublin, Aiken lobbied hard for the Irish government to make a 'special contribution' of around US$100,000 for the relief of victims of the recent hostilities, although, according to Con Cremin, he was flexible as to whether these special funds should go in their entirety to UNRWA, and was willing for some to be distributed through other agencies such as the Red Cross. Rather, for Aiken, 'the important point … is that we should be able to announce a special contribution at an early date'.[49]

The figure of US$100,000 that Aiken proposed was far greater than Ireland's previous donations to UNRWA (which totalled US$126,800 for the years 1959–1966 inclusive), and though the Department for External Affairs admitted in early July that previous contributions to UNRWA had been 'too small', there was reluctance within the department to support an emergency grant of US$100,000 as Aiken desired. One official, for example, believed that the 'evidence for [Aiken's] higher figure is inadequate'.[50] Instead, the Department of External Affairs proposed that UNRWA should now receive an annual sum equivalent to 0.17 per cent of Ireland's annual contribution to the UN budget (which was itself 0.17 per cent of the total UN budget). On this basis, the Department of External Affairs estimated that Ireland should contribute US$68,000 to UNRWA.[51]

Thus, in July the Department of External Affairs settled on a compromise formula proposed by Brendan Nolan, whereby in addition to the US$25,000 for UNRWA and US$15,000 for UNICEF that had already been budgeted for the financial year 1967, Ireland would also donate a once-off emergency contribution of US$50,000 (US$40,000 to UNRWA and US$10,000 in cash to UNICEF), and from 1968 onwards the annual UNRWA contribution would increase to US$50,000 per annum.[52]

The Irish government's contribution was accompanied by a IR£14,000 contribution from the Irish Red Cross Society, a joint sponsor of a resolution on the refugee crisis at a meeting of the International Red Cross in September 1967, to the International Committee of the Red Cross for Refugee Relief in the Middle East. In addition, the society forwarded approximately US$335 of voluntary personal contributions to the League of Red Cross Societies for Jordan Refugees.[53]

Aiken announced this in the Dáil in late July 1967.[54] Once his department had managed to stave off an attempt by the Minister of Industry and Commerce, George Colley, to tie the emergency aid to the purchase of Irish goods by promising that if such donations were 'repeated or made regularly' the policy would be reconsidered,[55] Con Cremin officially informed the UN Secretary General of Ireland's 'special contribution'.[56]

In August, after Ireland had decided on its emergency contribution to UNRWA, Reddaway wrote to the Department of External Affairs to thank it for Ireland's 'most generous response' and 'continued support'.[57] His superior, Lawrence Michelmore, UNRWA's chief, also contacted Aiken to thank him for the 'most generous expression of concern on the part of the people of Ireland'.[58]

The Irish contribution, though worthy, was by no means exceptional, and was part of an enormous worldwide humanitarian effort (the Pope himself personally donated £18,000) on behalf of the Palestinian refugees, coordinated by UNRWA, UNICEF and the International Committee of the Red Cross.[59] As Reddaway acknowledged, however, the real value of Aiken's efforts were that they kept up the international profile of UNRWA's cause and 'heartened' his organization 'during this critical period'.[60]

By the winter of 1967, reports emanating from UNRWA sources painted a bleak picture for the refugees. On 14 December 1967, Aiken took to the floor at UNRWA debate of the UNGA special political committee to address what he viewed to be the 'critically important' subject of the Palestine refugees. He praised UNRWA's 'splendid record in alleviating the lot of the refugees, in diminishing their sufferings, and in giving them that minimum sense of self-respect which is essential if the concept of the dignity of man is not to be entirely denied'. But he reminded those delegates present that the UN had a responsibility, not simply to debate how to help UNRWA, but also to resolve the problem.

He therefore called on the UN to make 'a really extraordinary effort to break the deadlock by guaranteeing full compensation to the refugees' and to ensure that 'all refugees not repatriated should get full compensation for the property they had lost and the damage they had suffered'. He then restated his belief that the proposal he had first put forward in 1958 'still represents the best way to tackle the problem and that best calculated to give a comprehensive and final solution'. Finally, he urged the UN to 'arrange for the repatriation of the maximum possible number of refugees and for full compensation, not merely resettlement for the remainder'.[61]

He followed up this speech with instructions to the Department of External Affairs to draft a letter to the UN Secretary General regarding the UN's sponsorship of a refugee fund along the lines outlined in his proposals. Department of External Affairs officials were also instructed to discuss the plan with their counterparts in the Departments of the Taoiseach and Finance, and to get an indication as to whether he was free to give an Irish financial commitment to the fund if it was endorsed by the Secretary General.[62]

By March 1968, the Department of External Affairs estimated that, if the UN established such a fund, and if Ireland contributed to it on the basis of its annual percentage contribution to the UN (of 0.17 per cent of the total UN budget), it would cost it US$2,295,000 (IR£956,000) if it only covered registered UNRWA refugees (those made refugees in the 1948 war); and would cost it US$2,669,000 (IR£1,112,000) if the 1967 refugees were also included.[63]

Such a potential drain on financial resources was not popular within the departments of the Taoiseach or Finance. Indeed, by December 1967 they had even managed to convince Aiken to remove a paragraph from his UNRWA speech that would have committed the Irish government to a financial contribution to any UNRWA fund for compensating or settling refugees.[64] This caution proved unnecessary. Although Aiken's proposals coincided with an appeal by the UN Secretary General for all governments to contribute to the 'emergency refugee situation',[65] the UN leadership never endorsed his proposals. As Ambassador Gunner Jarring, the UN's Special Envoy to the Middle East, told Con Cremin in 1969, Aiken's plans 'had not [been] forgotten', but 'the propitious moment to give them detailed consideration has not yet arrived'.[66]

Despite the fact that Aiken's proposals for a refugee fund had, in the words of the Department of External Affairs' Brendan Nolan, 'fallen on deaf ears'[67] at the highest levels of the UN, Ireland's Middle East policy following the June 1967 war was preoccupied with the search for a settlement of the Palestinian refugee crisis through financial support of UNRWA and international diplomacy via the UN, to the exclusion of other international forums or bilateral involvement.

Contributions to this body took up an increasingly large share of the foreign aid budget. In December 1967, the Department of Finance gave clearance for contributions of US$40,000 to UNRWA, US$15,000 to UNICEF and US$7,500 to the United Nations Higher Committee for Refugees (hereafter, the UNHCR) for the financial year 1968–1969.[68] This was a most welcome development given the fact that UNRWA faced an estimated deficit of US$4 million for 1968–69.[69]

Moreover, one should compare the increasingly generous funding of UNRWA with Ireland's parallel contributions to other multilateral aid agencies in the same years. For example, the UNHCR had responsibility for 3.5 million refugees in Europe, Cuba, Africa and Asia, and though most of the European refugees were settled, and thus primarily required legal and political protection, many of those in Asia and Africa were in need of practical assistance. Indeed, the Department of External Affairs estimated that the year 1967–1968 saw the number of refugees under UNHCR care rise by 200,000.

The UNHCR, however, only received Irish aid of US$5,000 per annum between 1959 and 1967, and US$7,500 in 1968. The Department of External Affairs estimated that this 'token contribution' was four-and-a-half times less than that of Denmark; five times less than that of the Netherlands; and ten times less than the Swedish, Belgian and Norwegian contributions to the organisation. Thus, not surprisingly, whereas between 1959 and 1968 inclusive Ireland had contributed US$56,459 to the UNHCR,[70] in the same years she had donated (including the special 1967 contribution of US$40,000) US$238,800 to UNRWA.[71]

In late 1968, the head of the UNHCR, Sadruddin Aga Khan, had written to Aiken asking for a special contribution to his organization to meet emergency needs. Though Aiken was 'anxious' to help, and favoured increasing Ireland's annual contribution to the UNHCR to US$10,000, the Department of External Affairs ultimately refused the Aga Khan's appeal.[72] However, in the same month (December 1968), following intense negotiations with the Department of Finance, the Department of External Affairs instructed the Irish representative at the UN Special Political Committee to pledge US$50,000 to UNRWA for the financial year 1969–1970 (an increase of 25 per cent over the previous year).[73]

By late 1970, though the Department of External Affairs viewed Ireland's annual contribution to UNRWA as 'reasonably adequate' compared with that to the UNHCR of US$10,000 (which was characterised as 'very poor') and to UNICEF of US$50,000 (which was characterised as 'well out of line' with the contributions of similar sized countries), the Department of External Affairs once more granted an increase of US$10,000 for UNRWA.[74]

In November 1967, the UNSC unanimously adopted the hugely significant UNSC Resolution 242, whose basic premise of 'land for peace', though subject to widely differing interpretations, has provided the framework for a negotiated settlement up to the present day. Apart from sanctioning the creation of a UN Middle East envoy, UNSC Resolution 242 raised two issues central to any settlement of the Arab–Israeli conflict: the final status of territories occupied in the course of the 1967 war, and the fate of those made refugees since the founding of Israel in the late 1940s. On the question of territory, Resolution 242 called for Israeli withdrawal 'from territories occupied in the recent conflict', while in relation to the refugee problem it simply (and vaguely) called for 'a just settlement of the refugee problem'.[75]

Israel welcomed the resolution's clause on the refugees because it did not propose any specific solution to the problem, and did not exclusively refer to Arab refugees. As such, it did not contradict the UNSC's post-war position that the refugee issue could only be solved as part of a general peace between Israel and the Arab states. As Michael Comay, Israel's Ambassador at the UN, explained in the first UN statement on refugees in the wake of the war, there would only be a solution to the refugee problem 'in the broad context of peacemaking'.[76]

The Arab response was completely different. In New York, the Palestinian Arab delegation rejected UNSC Resolution 242 in total as a 'treasonable act that vitiates the United Nations Charter and the principles of international law and justice', and provides the 'Zionist racist colonial illegal occupation' recognition of sovereignty and secured borders.[77]

Such a response was hardly surprising given the fact that since 1949 the Arab world had demanded the absolute right of the refugees to return to their former homes, or the right to free choice between repatriation or compensation on the basis of paragraph eleven of UNGA Resolution 194 (111) of 11 December 1948. This UN resolution stated that those refugees 'wishing to return to their homes and live at peace with their Israeli neighbours should be permitted to do so at the earliest practicable date'. As such, the Arabs rejected any UN initiatives, such as those proposed by the Netherlands and the United States in 1961, 1962 and 1963, calling on the Arabs and Israel to enter into direct negotiations on the refugee issue.

Noting that the Arab world had voted against UNGA Resolution 194 in December 1948, Israel rejected the Arab interpretation of the resolution, and argued that it related only to those Arab refugees who wanted 'to live at peace' with the Jewish state, and only to such a time as Israel believed 'practicable'. It also criticised the Arab position of demanding complete repatriation to the exclusion of any other solution. Or, as Abba Eban put it, the 'aim of wrecking any alternative to repatriation has been pursued … with an ingenuity worthy of a better cause'.[78]

Instead, Israel argued that the original refugee crisis was the consequence of the Arab rejection of the UN's November 1947 call for a two-state solution, and that the 'misery and deadlock' had been created by the 'brutal Arab invasion'.[79] Secondly, given the fact that defeat in 1948 had not inclined the Arabs, in particular the Palestinian Arabs, to accept the legitimacy of Israel, it was not possible for security reasons to repatriate vast numbers of Arabs into the Jewish state. As Foreign Minister Moshe Sharett noted in 1949, the return of large numbers of Arab refugees who refused to recognise Israel was 'liable to blow up our state from within'.[80]

Moreover, Israel also argued that, in the wake of the 1948 war, it had absorbed significant numbers of Jews (estimated at 250,000 between 1949 and 1951, and around 700,000 by the end of the 1950s) who had been forced out of the Arab world due to anti-Jewish sentiment aroused by its establishment.[81] As such, there was a limit to the number of Arab refugees who could be absorbed. For all these reasons, the Israeli position between 1948 and 1967 was that the only way to solve the Arab refugee crisis was for the resettlement of the vast majority of refugees in the Arab states, though it was prepared to compensate refugees for real property left behind and to assist the resettlement programme.[82]

Ireland, in line with the vast majority of UN Member States, endorsed UNSC Resolution 242 as an important contribution to a lasting peace, and also supported the resolution's creation of a special UN envoy to the region. But over the next two years, as the political aspect of the Israeli–Palestinian conflict came increasingly to the fore, fundamental differences emerged between Ireland and Israel on the issue of the refugees as set out in UNSC Resolution 242.

As noted earlier, despite its deep commitment to the Palestinian refugees prior to the 1967 war, Ireland had looked to avoid entanglement in the politics of the Arab–Israeli conflict. As the Arab and Israeli negotiating positions crystallised in the wake of the June 1967 war, however, it became increasingly difficult to separate the humanitarian issue relating to the fate of the Palestine Arab refugees from the political issues concerning the Israeli occupation of the West Bank and Gaza and, more generally, the relationship between a solution of the Palestinian refugee problem and a settlement of the Arab–Israeli dispute.

Until June 1967, the international community, including Ireland, viewed the Palestinian issue overwhelmingly in humanitarian terms, and there was little support for the political aspirations of the Palestinian people, who for the most part lived as refugees in Arab states, or under Egyptian and Jordanian control in

Gaza and the West Bank respectively. Following the 1967 war, the Arab–Israeli military conflict entered a new phase, characterised by an upsurge in Palestinian guerrilla warfare and terrorist operations. This enhanced the belief that Zionism was an anachronistic, even illegitimate, ideology, while the Palestinian struggle was one of liberation.

In 1964, the Palestine Liberation Organization (PLO) was founded under Egyptian auspices, in part because of President Nasser's belief that Israel had successfully marginalised the Palestine issue in the West.[83] In the same year, Fatah, Yasser Arafat's power base in the Palestinian movement, began organised guerrilla operations against Israel from its base in Ba'athist Syria.

Since its founding in the late 1950s, Fatah had compared itself to the *Front de Libération Nationale* (FLN) in Algeria and the National Front for the Liberation of Southern Vietnam (NLF), better known as the Viet Cong.[84] Over the next decade, the period of time that Aiken was at the helm of Irish foreign policy, Arab regimes and their media organs began playing up to the anti-colonial feelings in the western world by hailing the Vietnamese offensive against US-backed forces as a precedent for the Palestinians, and by promoting an Algerian or a North-Vietnamese model of liberation against Israel. As Israel's Foreign Minister, Abba Eban, confided to Nicholas Katzenbach, the acting US Secretary of State, this new approach of mimicking what had been 'practiced in Algeria, Vietnam' had 'created a major problem' for Israel, both on and off the battlefield.[85] Fawaz Turki subsequently captured this evolving reality. 'Suddenly', he recalled, 'Palestine became the Palestinians, the Palestinians became the PLO, and the PLO became in an age that looked romantically at such things, a national liberation movement'.[86]

It is possible to explain Aiken's (and Ireland's) own evolving attitude to the Palestine question in terms of this politicization of the Palestine issue combined with a deep frustration over the failure of the international community to find a viable solution to the Palestinian refugee problem. Indeed, the most notable aspect of Ireland's Middle East policy from the time of Aiken's diplomatic involvement at the UN in the summer of 1967 was how the matter of the Palestinian refugees was increasingly coming to transcend mere financial relief. As one member of the Department of External Affairs noted in the summer of 1967:

[Aiken] regards the present situation in the Middle East, and especially the plight of the refugees, as a major crisis with the gravest implications for world peace and he feels that Ireland should make as generous contribution as possible, not only for humanitarian reasons but also in the interest of peace in the Middle East and the world in general.[87]

In March 1968, Aiken told the Dáil that the existence of the Arab refugees was 'one of the great humanitarian problems of our time [and] … must be settled *before* there can be any hope of lasting peace in the Middle East'.[88] By the end of 1968, the Irish position was that 'a permanent solution of the refugee problem is a *main factor* in the establishment of a durable peace in the Middle East'.[89] In early 1969, Aiken was again informing the Dáil that the '*main* and *most pressing* objective' in relation to the Middle East crisis was 'settling the refugee problem and negotiating a stable peace in the area' (my italics).[90]

The importance attached by Aiken and his officials to the issue of Palestinian Arab refugees had a profound impact on Ireland's Middle East priorities. In the immediate wake of the June 1967 war, the Department of External Affairs did not list the refugee issue as one of its main strategic concerns in the Middle East (these were the freedom of oil supplies; the free navigation of the Suez Canal; the prevention of the spread of nuclear weapons in the area; and a peaceful solution of the Arab–Israeli conflict).[91] By 1969, however, a settlement of the refugee problem was one of three 'essential points' (together with the guaranteed freedom of communication and travel, and the guarantee by the UN and the Great Powers against future aggression) set out in a Department of External Affairs memorandum on the Middle East.[92]

This in turn set the context for bilateral Irish–Israeli diplomatic relations over subsequent decades. Israeli leaders found little to disagree with in Aiken's proposals for the establishment of an international fund to aid in the resettlement of the refugees along the lines proposed by the Irish minister. In September 1967, Israel's Foreign Minister, Abba Eban, told Aiken that Israel was willing to consider a 'regional and international solution of population problems created by the wars of 1948 and 1967'.

However, Eban had stipulated that this would only have Israeli support 'in the context of a formal peace settlement with each of the Arab states'.[93] This caveat was to become the major point of disagreement between Israel and Ireland, as Aiken increasingly came to believe that a solution to the refugee crisis was a necessary prerequisite to (rather than a welcome consequence of) a general solution to the conflict.

In his December 1967 speech, Aiken had called for the repatriation of the 'maximum possible number of refugees and for full compensation – and not merely resettlement for the remainder'.[94] This was completely unacceptable to Israel. As the Irish ambassador in Berne reported home, though his Israeli counterpart in Switzerland was 'obviously aware' of Aiken's proposals, he preferred to talk in terms of resettlement of Arabs outside of Israel.[95]

A second issue of disagreement related to the Israeli claim that the international community was paying insufficient attention to the plight of Jewish victims of the Arab–Israeli conflict, especially those Jewish refugees from Arab states. One of the main reasons that Israel had welcomed the statement on the refugees contained in UNSC Resolution 242 was because it did not explicitly mention Arab refugees, thus enabling Israel to interpret the clause as calling for a 'just settlement' of the Jewish refugee claims against Arab states as part of a solution to the Arab–Israeli conflict.

There was, however, little interest on the Irish side for this aspect of the Middle East refugee problem. In particular, Con Cremin in New York was sceptical on this issue, and he discounted Israel's 'able, but perhaps rather clever' claim that UN refugee resolutions drawn up after the war concerned Jewish, as much as Arab, suffering. Indeed, Cremin was of the view that the 'principle, I would say sole, preoccupation' of the co-sponsors of resolution 2252 (ES-V), of whom Ireland was one, was with 'Arab inhabitants displaced by hostilities of June 1967'.[96]

Thus, by the end of Aiken's decade as Minister for External Affairs in 1969, the gulf between the Irish and Israeli positions on how to address the Palestinian refugee issue was wide. Successive Irish governments embraced Aiken's legacy by prioritizing the refugee issue, and viewing aid to UNRWA as a political act linked to a final settlement of the conflict. As Patrick Hillery, Aiken's successor as Minister for Foreign Affairs, acknowledged privately, Irish funding to UNRWA could be explained 'on political grounds [as a way of] demonstrating in a practical manner the government's wish to assist in alleviating the cause of tension in the Middle East'.[97] It is a testament to Aiken's influence over Ireland's Middle East policy over the last forty years that up to the present day the approach he set out in his last years as minister has continued to dominate Irish thinking on the Palestine issue. In doing so, it has particularly defined Irish–Israeli bilateral political and diplomatic relations to an extent that could not have been predicted when the humanitarian aspect of the conflict was paramount in Irish thinking in his early years in office.

Notes

1   On Aiken's contribution to the development of Irish foreign policy, see 'Frank Aiken – A Tribute', in *Ireland Today, Bulletin of the Department of Foreign Affairs*, 999 (June, 1983), 7. For an informative case study on how Aiken's commitment to the UN and his independent stance gave Ireland a significant role in international crises in these years, see Joseph Skelly's, 'National Interests and International Mediation: Ireland's South Tyrol Initiative at the United Nations, 1960–1961', in Michael Kennedy & Joseph Skelly (eds), *Irish Foreign Policy 1919–1966* (Dublin: Four Courts Press, 2000), 286–307.

2   See, for example, Aiken's speech at the 13th Session of the UNGA, 19 Sept. 1958, in *Official Records of the General Assembly 13th Session, Plenary Meetings, Verbatim Records of Meetings*, 16 Sept.–13 Dec. 1958, 39–45.

3   *Irish Press*, 15 June 1967.

4   For my writings on the subject area, see Rory Miller, *Ireland and the Palestine Question, 1948–2004* (Dublin: Irish Academic Press, 2005); 'Ireland and the Israeli–Palestinian Conflict: A Case Study in European–Israeli Relations', *Yale Israel Journal*, No. 8 (Winter, 2006), 18–29; 'Ireland and Israel', in Manfred Gerstenfeld (ed.), *European–Israeli Relations: Between Confusion and Change* (Jerusalem: Jerusalem Centre for Public Affairs, 2007), 181–194; *Ireland and the Middle East: Trade, Society and Peace* (Dublin: Irish Academic Press, 2007); 'Ireland and the Middle East at the United Nations, 1955–2005', in Michael Kennedy & Deirdre McMahon (eds), *Obligations and Responsibilities: Ireland and the United Nations, 1955–2005* (Dublin: Institute of Public Administration, 2005), 54–78; 'Frank Aiken, the UN and the Six Day War, June 1967', *Irish Studies in International Affairs*, Vol. 14 (2003), 57–74; 'Public Tensions, Private Ties: Ireland, Israel and the Politics of Mutual Misunderstanding', in Clive Jones and Tore T. Petersen (eds), *Israel's Secret Diplomacies* (London and New York: Hurst/Oxford University Press, 2013), 189–208.

5   See Patrick Keatinge, 'Ireland', in David Allen & Alfred Pijpers (eds), *European Foreign Policy Making and the Arab–Israeli Conflict* (The Hague, Boston, Lancaster: Martinus Nijhoff Publishers, 1984), 18–30; Ben Tonra, *The Europeanisation of National Foreign Policy: Dutch, Danish and Irish Foreign Policy in the European Union* (Aldershot: Ashgate Publishing, 2001). On Ireland's role in Lebanon, see James Parker, 'UNIFIL and Peacekeeping: the Defence Forces Experience', *Irish Studies in International Affairs*, Vol. 2, No. 2 (1986), 63–77; Comdt Brendan O'Shea (ed.), *In the Service of Peace: Memories of Lebanon, From the Pages of An Cosantoir* (Cork: Mercier Press, 2001).

6   Ruth Lapidoth, 'Legal Aspects of the Palestinian Refugee Question', *Jerusalem Viewpoints*, 485, 1 (Jerusalem, Jerusalem Centre for Public Affairs, Sept., 2002), 1–2.

7   See Aiken's speech before the UNGA, 19 Sept. 1958, in *Official Records of the General Assembly, 13th Session*, 39–42.

8   See meeting 159, UNGA Special Political Committee, 26 Nov. 1959, *Official Records of the General Assembly, 14th Session*, 150.

9   *Leader*, 28 Sept. 1957, 4.

10 See meeting 105, UNGA Special Political Committee, 13 Nov.1958, *Official Records of the General Assembly, 13th Session*, 77–78. See also meeting 159, UNGA Special Political Committee, 26 Nov. 1959, *Official Records of the General Assembly, 14th Session*, 150–151.

11 See meeting of the UNGA Ad Hoc Committee, 27 Oct. 1958, *Official Records of the General Assembly, 13th Session*, 9.

12 With US$2,800 being contributed in 1959, US$7,000 in 1960, US$14,000 in 1961; US$20,000 in 1962, 1963 and 1964 and US$25,000 in 1965 and 1966). The Irish financial contribution to UNRWA in these years can be found in the *Official Records of the General Assembly*, 14th Session 1959 to 22nd Session 1967.

13 See meeting of the UNGA Ad Hoc Committee, 20 Oct. 1960, *Official Records of the General Assembly, 15th Session*, 3.

14 See Brendan Nolan to Tadhg O'Sullivan, 10 July 1967. National Archives of Ireland (NAI), Department of Foreign Affairs (DFA), 2001/43/871.

15 See Meeting 105, UNGA Special Political Committee, 13 Nov. 1958, *Official Records of the General Assembly, 13th Session,* 77–78.

16 Cremin to Boland, 17 June 1961. NAI, DFA, PS35/1.

17 See minutes of a meeting between Max Nurock, Israeli Foreign Ministry and Aiken, Dublin 24 Jan. 1962, 31 Jan. 1962, NAI, DFA 2001/43/119.

18 For Boland's views on this matter see Skelly, *Ireland at the UN,* 157–159.

19 For O'Brien's statement at meeting 105 of the special political committee, 13 Nov. 1958, see *Official Records of the General Assembly, 13th Session,* 77–78. See also his similar argument at meeting 159 of the special political committee, 26 Nov. 1959, *Official Records of the General Assembly, 14th Session,* 150.

20 See minutes of Nurock's meeting with Aiken, 31 Jan. 1962. NAI, DFA 2001/43/119.

21 Statement of Brendan T. Nolan, in the special political committee on the report of the commissioner-general of UNRWA for Palestine Refugees in the Near East, 4 Nov. 1966. NAI, DFA 2001/43/871. See also the letters from Nolan to the Secretary and Assistant Secretary of the DEA, 2 Nov. 1966 and 7 Nov. 1966. NAI, DFA 2001/43/871. See also *Irish Press,* 5 Nov. 1966.

22 See vote on four-power draft resolution A/SPC/L.120, meeting 515 of the Special Political Committee, 14 Nov. 1966, *Official Records of General Assembly, 21st Session,* 98–99. See also Noel Dorr's explanation of vote in special political committee, 14 Nov. 1966. NAI, DFA 2001/43/871 and Dorr's report on special political committee UNRWA Debate, 17 Nov. 1966. NAI, DFA 2001/43/871.

23 Cremin to McCann, 26 May 1967. NAI, DFA 98/6/401.

24 Cremin to McCann, 26 May 1967. NAI, DFA 98/3/86.

25 For a general description of Aiken's independent stance at the UN, see Dermot Keogh, *Twentieth Century Ireland: Nation and State* (Dublin: Gill & Macmillan, 1994), 234–236.

26 See memorandum on fifth emergency session of the UN, 1967. NAI, DFA 2001/43/99.

27 See statement by Aiken, UNGA Plenary Meeting 682, 20 Sept. 1957, *Official Records of the General Assembly, 12th Session,* 46. See also his speech before the UNGA, 19 Sept. 1958, in *Official Records of the General Assembly, 13th Session,* 39–42.

28 See minutes of Nurock's meeting with Aiken, 31 Jan. 1962. NAI, DFA 2001/43/119.

29 See Permanent Representative, UN, to McCann, DEA, 19 Jan. 1967. NAI, DFA 2001/43/120. See also *Irish Press,* 27 May 1967.

30 Five previous UNSC resolutions – S/Res/233 to S/Res/237 – had been adopted by the UNSC prior to the Soviet draft resolution. These resolutions had, between them, expressed concern at the outbreak of fighting and called for a cessation of all military activities and an immediate ceasefire. There was also a call for Secretary General, U Thant to make immediate contact with Syria and Israel; a condemnation of all violations of the ceasefires; and finally a call on the Israeli government to ensure the welfare of inhabitants in areas that it controlled and to allow for those who had fled since the outbreak of hostilities to return.

31 Cremin to McCann, 14 June 1967. NAI, DFA 98/3/86.

32 *Irish Press,* 15 June 1967.

33 *Irish Independent,* 17 June 1967.

34 Cremin to McCann, 20 June 1967. NAI, DFA 98/3/86.

35 Statement by Mr Frank Aiken, T.D, Tánaiste and Minister for External Affairs of Ireland on the Middle East Question, at the Emergency Special Session of the General Assembly of the

United Nations, 27 June 1967 (hereafter, Statement by Aiken before UNGA, 27 June 1967). NAI, DFA 2001/43/98.

36   Fifth emergency special session on the Middle East: Notes on telephone message from the PMUN, 19 June 1967. NAI, DFA 2001/43/98.

37   *Irish Press*, 20 June 1967; *Irish Independent,* 20 June 1967.

38   Irish UN mission, New York, to Brendan Nolan, DEA, 26 June 1967. NAI, DFA 2001/43/871. See also Cremin to McCann, 30 June 1967. NAI DFA 2001/43/871.

39   See statement by Aiken before UNGA, 27 June 1967. NAI, DFA 2001/43/98.

40   See statement by Aiken before UNGA, 27 June 1967. NAI, DFA 2001/43/98.

41   See, for example, *The New York Times*, 28 June 1967; *Indian Express*, 29 June 1967; and lastly, *Melbourne Herald*, 28 June 1967.

42   Toynbee to Cremin, 11 Sept. 1967. NAI, DFA 98/6/401.

43   Arthur Lall, *The UN and the Middle East Crisis* (New York: Columbia University Press, 1967), 151–152.

44   Cremin to McCann, 11 July 1967. NAI, DFA 2001/43/99.

45   DEA memorandum on fifth emergency session, 10 July 1967. NAI, DFA 2001/43/99.

46   UNGA Resolution 2252 (ES-V). Apart from Ireland, this resolution was co-sponsored by 25 other nations and was adopted by 116 votes to 0 with 2 abstentions. See letter from PMUN to Secretary, DEA, 6 July 1967. NAI, DFA 2001/43/871.

47   See J. D. R. Kelly, UNHCR representative to Ireland and the United Kingdom to Brian Durnin, DEA, 20 July 19678. NAI, DFA 2001/43/871.

48   See draft resolution A/L529 adopted as resolution 2256 (ES-V), 21 July 1967, *Official Records of the General Asssembly, 5*th *Emergency Special Session*, 2930.

49   See memorandum from Cremin, to McCann, Secretary, DEA, 30 June 1967. NAI, DFA 2001/43/871.

50   See minutes attached to Nolan's memorandum on UNRWA contributions, 10 July 1967. NAI, DFA 2001/43/871.

51   See DEA minutes on UNRWA contributions, 10 July 1967. NAI, DFA 2001/43/871.

52   See memorandum on emergency aid for Arab refugees in the Middle East, 13 July 1967. NAI, DFA 2001/43/871. See also speech by Aiken, 25 July 1967. Dáil Éireann (DE), Vol. 230, cols. 708–709; Cremin to UN Secretary General, 15 Aug. 1967. NAI, DFA 2001/43/872; Nolan to O'Sullivan, 10 July 1967. NAI, DFA 2001/43/871.

53   See letter from Irish Red Cross Society to Aiken, 5 Oct. 1967. NAI, DFA 2001/43/872.

54   Speech by Aiken, 25 July 1967. DE, Vol. 230, col. 709.

55   See Department of Industry and Commerce to DEA, 2 June 1967. NAI, DFA 2001/43/871. See also memorandum drawn up by DEA official Dr Donal O'Sullivan on the possibility of attaching spending conditions to UNRWA emergency contributions, 21 July 1967. NAI, DFAC2001/43/871; Sean Ronan, Assistant Secretary, DEA, to John Reddaway, Deputy Commissioner General, UNRWA, 16 Aug. 1967; Reddaway to Ronan, 21 Sept. 1967 and O'Sullivan to Reddaway, 4 Dec. 1967. NAI, DFA 2001/43/872.

56   See Cremin to UN Secretary General, U Thant, 15 Aug. 1967. NAI, DFA 2001/43/872.

57   Reddaway to Ronan, 31 Aug. 1967. NAI, DFA 2001/43/872.

58   See telegram from Lawrence Michelmore to Frank Aiken, n.d. Aug. 1967. NAI, DFA 2001/43872.

59   *Irish Press*, 17 July 1967.

60 Reddaway to Aiken, 12 Dec. 1967 & 28 Dec. 1967. NAI, DFA 2001/43/872. See also Aiken's reply to Reddaway, 3 Jan. 1968. NAI, DFA 2001/43/872. In mid-1968, Reddaway resigned and was replaced as Acting Deputy Commissioner General by Lloyd Callow.

61 See Statement by Mr Frank Aiken, T.D., Tánaiste and Minister for External Affairs of Ireland on the Question of Palestine Arab Refugees, in the Special Political Committee of the 22nd Session of the General Assembly of the United Nations, 14 Dec. 1967. NAI, DFA 2001/43/872.

62 See minutes attached to minister's memorandum, 4 Jan. 1968. NAI DFA 2001/43/872.

63 See the government's memorandum on the question of the Palestine Arab Refugees, March 1968. NAI, DFA 2001/43/872. This was based on a UNRWA estimate that the total number of pre-1967 refugees amounted to 1,350,000 and that the total number of post-1967 refugees was 1,570,000.

64 See Aiken's speech on Palestinian Refugees before the special political committee, 14 Dec. 1967. See also DEA to DT, 14 Dec. 1967. NAI, DFA 98/6/401.

65 *The Irish Times*, 16 March 1968.

66 Cremin to McCann, 8 Oct. 1968 & 19 Feb. 1969. NAI, DFA 2001/43/101.

67 See Brendan Nolan, Irish UN delegation, Geneva, to DEA, 25 Nov. 1969. NAI, DFA 2001/43/102.

68 See Irish delegation, New York, to Secretary, DEA, 1 Dec. 1967. NAI, DFA 2001/43/872.

69 *The Irish Times*, 16 March 1968.

70 See DEA memorandum on the UNHCR, 19 July 1967. NAI, DFA 2001/43/880. See also draft paragraphs for insertion into minutes financial sanctions for 1968–9 voluntary contributions, Aug. 1968. NAI DFA 2001/43/872.

71 See minister's briefing note for Dáil questions, n.d. 1969–70. NAI, DFA 2001/43/102.

72 See Sadruddin Aga Khan to Aiken, 7 Nov. 1968 and DEA to UNHCR, 30 Dec.1968. NAI, DFA 2001/43/880.

73 See Noel Dorr's statement before meeting 629 of the special political committee, 6 Dec. 1968, *Official Records of the General Assembly, 23rd Session*, 4. See also memorandum on total contributions of US$35,750,474 to UNRWA for 1969 pledged by 38 governments, *UN Press Service*, 6 Dec. 1968. See also the *Evening Herald*, 7 Dec. 1968.

74 See memorandum on proposed contributions to International Aid Agencies, 5 Dec. 1970. NAI, DFA 2002/19/243.

75 See meeting 1382 of UNSC, 22 Nov. 1967, *UN Security Council Official Records, 22nd Year*, 1–8.

76 See statement by Michael Comay, Israel's ambassador to the UN, at meeting 150 of the special political committee, 12 Nov. 1959, *Official Records of the General Assembly, 14th Session*, 109–110.

77 See for example, *Justice Will Triumph, The Palestine Arab Delegation* (New York, June, 1968), 4.

78 Statement by Michael Comay, meeting 150 of the special political committee, 12 Nov. 1959, *Official Records of the General Assembly, 14th Session*, 110 .

79 Statement of Foreign Minister Abba Eban's, *Israel Documents*, 1, 18 Nov. 1955, 398.

80 Statement of Foreign Minister Moshe Sharett's, *Israel Documents*, 1, 15 June 1949, 373.

81 See statement by Ambassador Arthur Lourie, meeting 250 of the special political committee, 14 April 1961, *Official Records of the General Assembly 15th Session* (Part II), 110.

82 See statement of Ambassador Comay, at meeting 128 of the special political committee, 19 Feb. 1957, *Official Records of the General* Assembly, 11th *Session*, 128.

83 Moshe Shemesh, 'The Founding of the PLO 1964', *Middle Eastern Studies*, 20 4 (Oct., 1984), 105–141, l08.

84 Eric Rouleau, 'The Palestinian Quest', *Foreign Affairs*, 53, 2 (Jan., 1975), 264–283, 273.

85 See telegram from Department of State to US embassy in Israel, 14 Dec. 1966, document 366, *Foreign Relations of the United States, 1964–1968*, XVIII, Arab–Israeli Dispute 1964–1967 (Washington, DC, 2000), 715.

86 Turki Fawaz, *Exile's Return: The Making of a Palestinian-American* (New York; The Free Press, 1994), 189.

87 See minutes attached to Nolan's memorandum on UNRWA contributions, 10 July 1967. NAI, DFA 2001/43/871.

88 Speech by Aiken, 28 March 1968. DE, Vol. 233, col. 1363.

89 See telegram from DEA to PMUN, 6 Dec. 1968. NAI, DFA 2001/43/872.

90 DE, 4 Feb. 1969. Vol. 238, col. 42.

91 Note for Aiken, n.d. July. NAI, DFA 2001/43/99.

92 See memorandum on Irish policy in regard to the Middle East Situation, 16 May 1969. NAI, DFA 2001/43/102.

93 Eban to Aiken, Sept. 1967. NAI, DFA 2001/43/100.

94 See Aiken's statement on the Question of Palestine Arab Refugees, special political committee, 14 Dec. 1967. NAI, DFA 2001/43/872.

95 See report on Mid East by Irish Ambassador at Berne, 29 Aug. 1967. NAI, DFA 2001/43/99.

96 Cremin to McCann, 9 Aug. 1968. NAI, DFA 2001/43/101.

97 See memorandum on proposed contributions to International Aid Agencies, 5 Dec. 1970. NAI, DFA 2002/19/243.

Conclusion

BRYCE EVANS AND STEPHEN KELLY

'The nation has lost a very gallant gentleman'.
  – *The Irish Times*, 21 May 1983[1]

Frank Aiken's death on 18 May 1983, at the age of eighty-five, marked the end of a glittering and controversial political career. From his teenage years in Armagh, through his lifelong dedication to the Fianna Fáil party and the Irish state, Aiken's life was consumed by what contemporary British policymakers dubbed the 'Irish Question'. A proud Ulsterman, he played a prominent role in Ireland's struggle for independence from the British Empire, culminating in his appointment as Chief of Staff of the anti-Treaty IRA forces in 1923. He simultaneously opposed partition and worked within its confines, serving as a deputy of Dáil Éireann for fifty years. For thirty-three of those fifty years he was a government minister, and finally Tánaiste. From 1969 until his death he served as a member of the Council of State under four consecutive Irish Presidents.[2] In the course of a very active public life he was decorated and honoured by many countries, receiving the Grand Cross of the Pian Order, the Grand Cross of the Order of Merit of the Federal Republic of Germany, and the Grand Cross of the Belgian Order of the Crown.[3]

Aiken belonged to the first generation of post-independence Irish politicians, the majority of whom placed political principles before material benefits. He was a man of integrity and sternness, driven by the conviction of his beliefs. As such, he was the ostensible antithesis to one of the leading members of the second generation of mainstream Irish republicans, Charles J. Haughey. If Haughey – power-hungry, ruthless and ostentatious – epitomised the 'ambition' that his father-in-law and Aiken's long-time colleague Seán Lemass sought to inculcate into 1960s Ireland, then Aiken's outlook remained relatively puritan. In the words of his protégé, George Colley, Aiken was 'one of the giants' of Irish parliamentary politics, a man of 'rock-like integrity and dedication to principle'.[4]

This unbending aspect to his character ensured that Aiken was hardly a popular public figure for much of his lifetime. His 'iron man' anti-liberal image during the Emergency is a case in point. Francis Carty of the *Irish Press* recalled interviewing Aiken shortly before his retirement. Carty wrote that 'One senses a lack of warmth, a reluctance to keep flowing the flotsam and jetsam of casual conversation …'.[5] James Kelly, Northern Irish nationalist and journalist, wrote of his disappointment on finally coming face-to-face with the great republican of South Armagh: 'I found him dry and taciturn, with little to say beyond an occasional "yes, yes, yes", one of the most ill-at-ease politicians I have ever met …'.[6]

Aiken never took much time (or indeed interest) in grooming his public image, and this directly impacted upon how others perceived him. His direct and at times abrasive style was ill-suited to the television era. Whether he was speaking in Dáil Éireann, addressing a gathering of the UN General Assembly or giving a rare television interview, he never looked entirely comfortable. *The Irish Times* once described his parliamentary manner as 'brusque and uncompromising'.[7] Aiken's long-serving fellow Fianna Fáil Cabinet minister Seán MacEntee once criticised his colleague for his 'lack of lightness or sparkle' in his after-dinner speeches, adding 'God forgive him who inflicts them on his audience'.[8] David Andrews, a second-generation Fianna Fáiler, recalled that Aiken 'wasn't a very articulate man …', he could come across as a 'dour Northerner … sometimes he could be embarrassingly silent. He was a shy man'.[9]

Aiken disliked giving interviews, and his reluctance to court the media compounded an image of aloofness. In this respect, he differed from his close friend and political colleague, Éamon de Valera. The latter routinely used the press as a means of publicising his political initiatives, periodically testing public opinion on particular policies. Aiken, it seems, was happy to follow his chief's lead, and was personally shy of publicity and dismissive of the need for a more favourable 'public image of himself'.[10] And yet his outward appearance masked the warmth and sociability emphasised by family and friends and displayed in numerous informal photographs. He was a fiercely loyal colleague and a proud family man. Despite his somewhat austere public image, in private he could be funny and quick-witted. To his detractors, Aiken's lack of public panache connoted a lack of intelligence, rationalism and culture. But behind the austere persona lay a clever man, eager to learn. Senior civil servant T. K. Whitaker recalled with fondness that Aiken was a 'ceaselessly inquisitive minister'.[11] His mind was constantly busy, and he enjoyed a wide range of personal interests, cultivated a curious fascination with inventions and scientific progress and displayed acumen in his business dealings.

Realist and idealist

Frank Aiken was, then, simultaneously a realist and an idealist. He was a man for whom ideas mattered deeply rather than a simple ideologue. At the same time, his principles were buffeted by the major tempests in world affairs during the twentieth century.

His at-times authoritarian reflexes were derived from his sometimes idiosyncratic conception of modern nationalism and civic republicanism. Aiken's particular version of republicanism was full of totalising assumptions that left little room for independent thought if it went against the mainstream nationalist grain. There was also, though, a constant vein of liberty and universalism flowing through his ideology. This militated against the global trend towards racial and ethnic essentialism in vogue at the outset of his political career. Clearly, his advocacy of revolutionary violence encompassed a degree of barbarism. It is important, nonetheless, to view his alleged incitement of sectarian violence against the situation in post-war Europe where – following the defeat and break-up of the Habsburg, Ottoman and Russian Empires – violence against, and the transfer of, ethnic and religious minority populations was the norm.

The genesis of his much-derided, anti-intellectual and sometimes farcical domestic censorship policy during the Second World War was his commitment to hard-line neutrality if the circumstances demanded it. This, in itself, had its origins in Ireland's Civil War, when, even after the republican break with Dáil Éireann and the occupation of the Four Courts in March–April 1922, Aiken was still to be found encouraging the IRA to wait for the publication of the Free State Constitution.

Yet the occupation of the rhetorical middle ground was no comfortable furrow for Aiken. His was a rough-hewn political pragmatism borne of the Civil War years, when he upset republican colleagues by repeatedly admitting that the majority of the people were pro-Treaty, even if they disagreed with them. Despite his pragmatism, Aiken did not believe, to use a popular political phrase, in changing horses mid-stream, and often found himself written off as a republican ideologue as a result. Actions such as the public snubbing in 1932 of the Governor General of the Irish Free State, James McNeill, did little to dispel this impression. But while Aiken harboured many long-held visions of his own, the intensity of his personal loyalty to de Valera raises questions about his political far-sightedness. Aiken's labours for his 'Chief' in America from 1928 to 1929, for example, comprised a demanding tour to raise subscriptions for the *Irish Press* newspaper. De Valera instructed him to 'move heaven and earth' to raise the funds.[12] Aiken dutifully obeyed, to the detriment of his health. It is hard to conceive of him undertaking such exertions for anyone else.

When it came to the economy, Aiken possessed a revolutionary belief in the social role of finance and economic planning. Looking to the French Popular Front governments, Aiken asserted that 'banks should not exist to amass profits but should perform such functions as they were performing in France where they managed credit and issued money for the benefit of ordinary people'.[13] Such left-leaning was, naturally, accompanied by the caveats of a quasi-authoritarianism typical of the interwar period. A mass road concreting scheme to alleviate unemployment, which Aiken proposed in the mid-1930s, was to be financed by paying workers less than what they would receive in unemployment assistance.[14] Faith in the redistributive power of state interventionism was mitigated somewhat by a thorough conditioning by Department of Finance mandarins during his two-and-a-half-year stint as Minister for Finance between 1945 and 1948.

Shortly after the advent of the Cold War, Aiken moved from Finance to External Affairs. As a scientist, he was aware of the frighteningly swift advances in scientific understanding that the twentieth century had witnessed. Such advances hastened the prospect of great salvation, but also terrible destruction, and Aiken agonised about a world in which the great power blocs of Allied and Axis, of East and West, threatened to undermine the small nation sovereignty for which he had fought. Aiken's uninspiring first term as Minister for External Affairs (1951–1954) aside, in his remaining years in the Foreign Affairs portfolio (1957–1969) he helped to forge Ireland's reputation on the world stage. His determination to establish a distinctive and independent Irish identity at the UN, chiefly from 1957 to 1961, merits particular attention.

Aiken on the world stage

Between 1957 and 1969, Aiken strove to pursue a non-aligned stance on an array of issues, including troop withdrawal from central Europe; decolonisation in Africa and Asia; the Algerian war; UN peacekeeping in the Congo; the representation in the UN of the Peoples' Republic of China; and nuclear non-proliferation. That such activism often upset and at times infuriated the sensibilities and strategic interests of the West's great power – the United States of America – never seemed to bother Aiken.

The plight of small nations and their struggles for independence were at the heart of his mission at the UN. Due to Ireland's success in throwing off the yoke of British rule, he believed that the country had a responsibility to champion the policy of self-determination. He regularly spoke of 'the emergence to independence of subject races and people', describing this ongoing process as a 'heartily' welcome development. 'Ireland, as a small and experienced nation', he explained, supports 'the rights of small nations to self-determination and national unity and the rights of the individual to enjoy his basic human rights and freedoms'.[15] He remained convinced that, since there was now an organisation such as the UN to support African and Asian calls for self-determination, it was no longer necessary for national liberation movements to resort to the use of physical force, a course he had taken in an era when no such organisation existed.

Viewed critically, there was a degree of condescension implicit in this attitude. Aiken, like many a mellowed revolutionary before and since, held a very selective opinion on when violence was legitimate: one that coincided all too neatly with the stages of his own political journey to power. This was bound up with a sometimes misplaced faith in the ability of the UN to confront economic and political imperialism meaningfully.

Throughout his seventeen years as Minister for Foreign Affairs, he publicly espoused pacifism. That Aiken had made the transition from a revolutionary in his youth to an elder statesman convinced of the futility of violence ensured that he acquired a particular aura in the UN General Assembly, particularly among the newly admitted African delegations. Ralph Bunche, Undersecretary General of the United Nations and Nobel Peace Prize-winner, recalled with fondness Aiken's 'towering (literally and figuratively) presence' at the UN.[16]

As Ireland entered the 1960s, with Seán Lemass replacing de Valera as Fianna Fáil leader and Taoiseach, Aiken's freedom at the UN was gradually curtailed. The arrival of a host of African and Asian countries, together with Lemass's pursuit of a 'pro-western' policy, inhibited the ability of Ireland to punch above its weight in the UN. Nonetheless, he still managed to fly the Irish flag. When the Non-Proliferation Treaty was signed in Moscow in July 1968, his steadfast commitment to international peace was recognised: he was invited to be its first signatory. This occasion marked a milestone in Aiken's stance on foreign affairs, signalling his transition from an Irish politician preoccupied with Irish national self-interest to an international statesman committed to the imperatives of world peace and security. Even the British government, wary of Aiken's perceived Anglophobia, recognised his 'considerable interest in the working of the United Nations' and his 'special interest in disarmament, non-dissemination of nuclear weapons and peace-keeping'.[17] Similarly, despite his unwillingness to entertain American imperialism, Aiken developed a warm personal relationship with Jackie Kennedy following her husband's assassination.[18]

Retirement

Under Lemass's premiership, the link between Fianna Fáil and business was institutionalised through the establishment of Taca, a fundraising organization of 500 businessmen who paid £100 per year and in return obtained privileged access to ministers and exclusive dinners in the Gresham Hotel, Dublin.[19] In Aiken's eyes, Taca was indicative of the party's moral collapse. He was gravely concerned by accusations that some senior Fianna Fáil figures had abused planning laws, with inside information easing the accumulation of substantial private fortunes.

Aiken's concerns over the direction that the Fianna Fáil organisation was taking came to a head when Lemass announced his decision to retire as Taoiseach in November 1966. He was caught off guard by Lemass's decision, and was fearful for the future of Fianna Fáil if Charles J. Haughey secured the party leadership. Aiken made it be known that he was in favour of rival candidate George Colley, and he tried his 'upmost to persuade' Lemass to carry on for another few years in order to allow Colley sufficient time to gain further ministerial experience and to raise his national profile.[20] At a gathering of the Fianna Fáil parliamentary party, on 9 November 1966, a vote was taken on Lemass's successor in order to avoid 'acrimonious discussions and intemperate statements that could cause unnecessary division in the party'.[21] Aiken 'spoke at length', and said that 'the decision they were to make that day would be a momentous one'. Having groomed George Colley as Lemass's successor, Aiken objected to what he called the 'tyranny of consensus' through which Cork TD Jack Lynch was elected as a candidate for Taoiseach, and formally proposed Colley as the new leader of the party.[22] He told party members that he was 'firmly convinced that George Colley had something to give the nation'.[23] Although initially disappointed by Colley's failure to secure the Fianna Fáil leadership, Aiken offered his unconditional support during Lynch's premiership thereafter.

Following Fianna Fáil's general election victory in June 1969, however, Lynch effectively sacked a surprised Aiken from the government, and in his place appointed Patrick Hillery as Minister for External Affairs. Aiken's steadying presence at the Irish Cabinet table was acutely missed during the turbulent outbreak of the Troubles, particularly during mid-August 1969, when some Fianna Fáil ministers advocated sending the Irish Army into Northern Ireland, chiefly Neil Blaney, Kevin Boland and the hawkish Haughey. Despite his absence from Lynch's Cabinet, behind the scenes Aiken acted as a voice of moderation, categorically objecting to the argument that the use of physical force represented government policy. As mentioned in the Introduction when the Arms Crisis erupted in May 1970, Aiken strongly advised Lynch to sack ministers Haughey and Blaney and throw them out of the Fianna Fáil organisation. In a meeting with the Taoiseach at government buildings, at which Lynch supplied him with 'files on the two' ministers, Aiken demanded that the whip be withdrawn from both men, instructing Lynch 'you are the leader of the Irish people – not just the Fianna Fáil Party'.[24]

As noted previously Aiken's mistrust of Haughey remained so intense that he informed Lynch that he would not stand at the 1973 general election if Haughey were ratified as a Fianna Fáil candidate. Aiken made it clear that, if Haughey were ratified, he would write a letter to the newspapers explaining his reasons for resigning. On 12 February, Aiken learned that Haughey had been ratified, and immediately withdrew his nomination. It was only after Lynch mobilised the services of Seán MacEntee, George Colley, Paddy Smith and his close friend Joe Farrell, that Aiken agreed not to record publicly his reasons for retiring from mainstream politics. He would not, though, waver from his decision to bow out of Irish public life. The following day, 13 February, at a meeting in Dundalk Town Hall to mark Aiken's seventy-fifth birthday, Lynch announced the former's retirement from politics on 'doctors' orders'.[25] Further outraged and bemused by Lynch bringing Haughey back to the opposition front bench in January 1975, in the last ten years of his life Aiken never attended a Fianna Fáil Ard Fheis, or any other party event. These last years pained him greatly as he watched from afar as the Fianna Fáil organisation almost tore itself apart under Haughey's leadership. It was a sad end to Aiken's lifelong commitment to the Fianna Fáil party. He spent the last years of his retirement at his home in Sandyford, County Dublin.

Notes

1   *The Irish Times*, 21 May 1983.

2   Aiken was a member of the Council of Ireland during the consecutive Irish Presidencies of Éamon de Valera, Erskine Childers, Cearbhall Ó Dálaigh and Patrick Hillery.

3   Aiken also received the following honours: the Grand Officer with the plaque of the Order of St Charles LL. D (*Honoris Causa*), National University of Ireland; St John's Universities, Jamaica; and LL. D (*Honoris Causa*) Dublin University. See *The Irish Times*, 19 May 1983.

4   *Irish Press*, 20 May, 1983.

5   *Irish Press*, 9 July 1969.

6   James Kelly, *Bonfires on the Hillside: an Eyewitness Account of the Political Upheaval in Northern Ireland* (Belfast: Fountain Publishing, 1995), 179.

7   *The Irish Times*, 30 Aug. 1958.

8   Seán MacEntee to Frank Aiken, 10 March 1959. University College Dublin Archives (UCDA), Frank Aiken Papers, P104/6126.

9   *The Irish Times*, 19 May and 21 May 1983.

10   *Irish Press*, 9 July 1969.

11   On the subject of Aiken's decision-making process, Whitaker recalled that 'It was best to acknowledge first the good points of any idea he put forward and introduce the caveats only tentatively and gradually. He pondered those in silence for extended period trying to neutralise them ...'. T. K. Whitaker, 'An able minister and a kind friend', *Irish Press*, 20 May 1983.

12   Mark O'Brien, *De Valera, Fianna Fáil and the Irish Press* (Dublin: Irish Academic Press, 2001), 20.

13   Kieran Allen, *Fianna Fáil and Irish Labour: 1926 to the Present* (London: Pluto, 1997), 85.

14   Allen, *Fianna Fáil and Irish Labour*, 22.

15   Address by Aiken, 'International Affairs – an Irish View', 5 June 1961. National Archives of Ireland (NAI), Department of Taoiseach (D/T)/GIS/1/3.

16   Bunche to Aiken, 1 Oct. 1969. UCDA, P104/6990.

17   Character profile of Frank Aiken, 1968. National Archives of the United Kingdom (NAUK), Dominions Office (DO) 182/149.

18   See UCDA, P104/8450 and P104/896.

19   Dick Walsh, *The Party, Inside Fianna Fáil* (Dublin: Gill and Macmillan, 1986), 83–84.

20   Handwritten drafts of telegram and copy of letter from Aiken to Lemass, 28 Oct.–3 Nov. 1965. UCDA, P104/2044.

21   Meeting of Fianna Fáil parliamentary party, 9 Nov. 1966. UCDA,Fianna Fáil Party Papers (P176)/448.

22   Meeting of Fianna Fáil parliamentary party, 9 Nov. 1966.UCDA, P176/448.

23   Meeting of Fianna Fáil parliamentary party, 9 Nov. 1966.UCDA, P176/448.

24   For further reading into Aiken's stance on Northern Ireland during the emotive years from 1969 to 1971, see Stephen Kelly, *Fianna Fáil, Partition and Northern Ireland, 1926–1971* (Dublin: Irish Academic Press, 2013), 301–322, 352.

25   Typescript copy of an article by Geraldine Kennedy, 'Frank Aiken: the story that was never told', as related by Francis Aiken (Frank Aiken's son), June 1983. UCDA, P104/2341.

Bibliography

Primary Sources

Archival institutions

Republic of Ireland

Kilmainham Gaol Archive, Dublin

- Pádraig Quinn's diary/memoir

Military Archives, Cathal Brugha Barracks, Dublin

- Irish Free State Army Volunteer Force (reserve), 3. File A.C.S G2/0044

Military Service Pensions Collection (MSPC)

- Frank Aiken (34REF59339)
- Tom Barry (34REF57456)
- James Daly (Con.Ran.23 (DP17))
- John McCoy (34REF16473)
- 4th Northern Division GHQ (RO/403)

Bureau of Military History (BMH), Witness Statements (WS)[1]

- Patrick Casey (WS 1148)
- John T. Connolly (WS 598)
- Sean Corr (WS 458)
- John Cosgrave (WS 605)
- Edward Fullerton (WS 890)
- John Grant (WS 658)
- Hugh Gribben (WS 640)
- Robert Kelly (WS 378)
- Peadar McCann (WS 171)

---

1 Apart from the hard copies houses at the Military Archives PDF searchable versions of the Witness Statements and Military Pensions Service Collection are available from www. bureauofmilitaryhistory.ie.

- John McCoy (WS 492)
- Jack McElhaw (WS 634)
- Seamus McGuill (WS 353)
- Paddy McHugh (WS 664)
- Paddy Rankin (WS 163)

National Archives of Ireland (NAI)

- Cabinet Minutes
- Department of Foreign Affairs (DFA)
- Department of Industry and Commerce (IND)
- Department of the Taoiseach (DT)
- Government Cabinet Minutes
- Jack Lynch Papers

National Library of Ireland (NLI)

- Joseph Brennan Papers (MS 26,172)
- Frank Gallagher Papers (MS 18,375)
- Thomas Johnson Papers (MS 17, 143)
- Joseph McGarrity Papers (MS 17,456)
- Florence O'Donoghue Papers (MS 31,421)
- Seán T. O'Kelly Papers (MS 8469)

University College Dublin Archives (UCDA)

- Frank Aiken Papers (P104)
- Todd Andrew Papers (P91)
- Ernest Blythe Papers (P24)
- Éamon de Valera Papers (P150)
- Fianna Fáil Party Papers (P176)
- Desmond FitzGerald Papers (P80)
- Patrick Hillery Papers (P205)
- Seán MacEntee Papers (P67)
- Richard Mulcahy Papers (P7)
- Donnchadh Ó Briain Papers (P83)
- Ernie O'Malley Papers (P17)
- Desmond Ryan Papers (LA10)
- Moss Twomey Papers (P69)
- Kenneth Whitaker Papers (P175)

Northern Ireland

Cardinal Ó Fiaich Memorial Library and Archive (COFLA), Armagh

- John McCoy Tapes

Public Records Office of Northern Ireland (PRONI)

- Cabinet Papers (Cab)
- Cahir Healy Papers (D2991)
- Ministry of Home Affairs (HA)
- Prime Minister's Office (PREM)
- Ellison Spence Papers (D2481)

Great Britain

Rhodes House Library, Oxford

- Sir Roy Welensky Papers, 261/5

National Archives of the United Kingdom (NAUK)

- Cabinet Minutes (CAB)
- Dominion's Office (DO)
- Foreign and Commonwealth Office (FCO)
- Northern Ireland Office (CJ)
- Prime Minister's Office (PREM)
- Security Service Files (KV)
- War Office (WO)

University of Birmingham Special Collections (UBSC)

- Neville Chamberlain Papers (NCP) 18/1

University of Oxford (UO), Bodleian Library (BO)

- Clement Attlee Papers (MS. Dep. 83)

Sweden

National Library of Sweden (NLS)

- Dag Hammarskjöld Papers, L179/160

America

Franklin D. Roosevelt Library[2]

- David Gray Papers

---

2 Available from http://www.fdrlibrary.marist.edu.

United Nations Archives, New York (UNA)

- File S/213/3/4; File S/791/43/4; and File S/840/2/5

Private Papers

- Gerald Boland unpublished handwritten memoirs (copy in possession of Dr Stephen Kelly).

Interviews and Correspondence

- Frank Aiken Jnr, 23 March 2013
- David Andrews, 20 Feb. 2013
- Pádraig Faulkner, 10 July 2006
- Dr Rory O'Hanlon, March and July 2013

Published Primary Sources

- *Documents on Irish Foreign Policy* (Vol. IV 1937–1939 and Vol. V 1939–1941), Royal Irish Academy (Dublin), (eds) Catriona Crowe, Ronan Fanning, Michael Kennedy, Dermot Keogh, Eunan O'Halpin.
- *Ireland at the United Nations 1957, speeches by Mr. Frank Aiken* (Dublin: Brún agus Ó Nulláin Teo, 1958); *Ireland at the United Nations 1959, speeches by Mr. Frank Aiken* (Dublin: Brún agus Ó Nulláin Teo, 1960); *Ireland at the United Nations 1960, speeches by Mr. Frank Aiken* (Dublin: Brún agus Ó Nulláin Teo, 1961); *Ireland at the United Nations 1961, speeches by Mr. Frank Aiken* (Dublin: Brún agus Ó Nulláin Teo, 1962); *Ireland at the United Nations 1962, speeches by Mr. Frank Aiken* (Dublin: Brún agus Ó Nulláin Teo, 1963); and *Ireland at the United Nations 1967, speeches by Mr. Frank Aiken* (Dublin: Brún agus Ó Nulláin Teo, 1968).
- Moynihan, Maurice (ed.), *Speeches and Statements by Eamon de Valera 1917–1973* (Dublin, 1980).
- *Official Records of the United Nations General Assembly 14th Session, 1959 to 22nd Session 1967.*

Parliamentary Sources

Dáil Éireann debates (DE)
Seanad Éireann debates (SE)

Newspapers, periodicals, magazines, etc.

An Phoblacht	*The Irish Times*
Armagh Guardian	*Newry Reporter*
Chicago Sun-Times	the *Evening Star*

Diplomatic History   the *Guardian*
Dundalk Democrat   *Tuairim*
Frontier Sentinel
History Ireland
Irish Independent
Irish News
Irish Press

Secondary Sources

Works of Reference

Dictionary of Irish Biography (Dublin: Cambridge University Press, 2010).
Oxford Dictionary of National Biography (Oxford: Oxford University Press, 2004).

Works of History and Politics (selected)

Adams, T. Ian, *The Sabotage Plan: The IRA Bombing Campaign in England, 1939–1940* (Titchfield: Lulu, 2010)

Aiken, Frank, *A Call to Unity* (Dublin, June, 1926).

Allen, David & Pijpers, Alfred (eds), *European Foreign Policy Making and the Arab– Israeli Conflict* (The Hague, Boston, Lancaster: Martinus Nijhoff Publishers, 1984).

Allen, Kieran, *Fianna Fáil and Irish Labour, 1926 to the Present* (London: Pluto Press, 1997).

Allen, Trevor, *The Storm Passed By: Ireland and the Battle of the Atlantic, 1940–41* (Dublin: Irish Academic Press, 1996).

Anderson, Brendan, *Joe Cahill: A Life in the IRA* (Dublin: O'Brien Press, 2002).

Andrews, C.S., *Dublin Made Me* (Dublin: Lilliput Press, 2001).

– *Man of No Property* (Cork: Mercier Press, 2001).

Andrews, David, *Kingstown Republican* (Dublin: New Island, 2007).

Arnold, Bruce, *Haughey, his Life and Unlucky Deeds* (London: HarperCollins, 1993).

Augusteijn, Joost, *From Public Defiance to Guerrilla Warfare* (Dublin: Irish Academic Press, 1996).

– (ed.), *Ireland in the 1930s, New Perspectives* (Dublin: Four Courts Press, 1999).

Bew, Paul (ed.), *A Yankee in De Valera's Ireland: the Memoir of David Gray* (Dublin: Royal Irish Academy: 2012).

– *Ideology and the Irish Question* (Oxford: Oxford University Press, 1994).

– *The Politics of Enmity, 1789–2006* (Oxford: Oxford University Press, 2007).

– and Henry Patterson, *Seán Lemass and the Making of Modern Ireland 1945–66* (Dublin: Gill and Macmillan, 1982).

Boland, Kevin, *The Rise and Decline of Fianna Fáil* (Dublin: Mercer Press, 1982).

– *Under Contract with the Enemy* (Dublin: Mercer Press, 1988).

Boot, Max, *Invisible Armies: An Epic History of Guerrilla Warfare from Ancient Times to the Present* (New York: W. W. Norton, 2013).

Boyce D. George, *Nationalism in Ireland* (London: Gill and Macmillan, 1991).

Bowman, John, *De Valera and The Ulster Question, 1917–1973* (Oxford: Oxford University Press, 1982).

Bhreatnach, Aoife, 'Frank Aiken and the Formulation of Foreign Policy, 1951–1954; 1957–1969' (M.Phil thesis, National University of Ireland, Cork, 1999).

Carroll, Joseph, *Ireland in the War Years* (New York: David and Charles, 1975).

Cole, Robert, *Propaganda, Censorship and Irish Neutrality in the Second World War* (Edinburgh: Edinburgh University Press, 2006).

Collins, Stephen, *The Power Game, Fianna Fáil Since Lemass* (Dublin: O'Brien Press, 2000).

Cousins, M., *The Birth of Social Welfare in Ireland 1922–52* (Dublin: Four Courts Press, 2003).

Cronin, Seán, *Washington's Irish Policy 1916–1986* (Dublin: Anvil Books, 1987).

Daly, E. Mary, *Social and Economic History of Ireland* (Dublin: The Educational Company, 1981).

Davis, D. Troy, *Dublin's America Policy, Irish–American Diplomatic Relations 1945–1952* (Washington D.C: Catholic University of America Press, 1998).

De Valera, Terry, *A Memoir, Terry de Valera* (Dublin: Currach Press, 2005).

Dorr, Noel, *A Small State at the Top Table, Memories of Ireland on the UN Security Council, 1981–82* (Dublin: IPA, 2011).

– *Ireland at the United Nations: Memories of the Early Years* (Dublin: IPA, 2010).

Duggan, P. John, *A History of the Irish Army* (Dublin: Gill and Macmillan, 1991).

Dunphy, Richard, *The Making of Fianna Fáil Power in Ireland* (Oxford: Oxford University Press, 1995).

Dwyer, T. Ryle, *De Valera's Finest Hour: In Search of National Independence 1932–1959* (Cork: Mercier Press, 1982).

– *Nice Fellow, Jack Lynch* (Cork: Mercier Press, 2001).

Edwards, Dudley, Owen (ed.), *Conor Cruise O'Brien Introduces Ireland* (New York: McGraw Hill, 1969).

English, Richard, *Armed Struggle, A History of the IRA* (London: Pan Macmillan, 2003).

– *Irish Freedom, the History of Irish Nationalism* (London: Pan Macmillan, 2006).

– *Radicals and the Republic: Socialist Republicanism in the Irish Free State 1925–1937* (Oxford: Oxford University Press, 1994).

– and Cormac O'Malley (eds), *Prisoners: The Civil War Letters of Ernie O'Malley* (Dublin: Poolbeg Press, 1991).

Evans, Bryce, *Ireland during the Second World War: Farewell to Plato's Cave* (Manchester: Manchester University Press, 2014).

– *Seán Lemass, Democratic Dictator* (Cork: Collins Press, 2011).

Fanning, Ronan, *Fatal Path, British Government and Irish Revolution, 1910–1922* (London: Faber and Faber, 2013).

– *Independent Ireland* (Dublin: Helicon, 1983).

Farrell, Brian, *Seán Lemass* (Dublin: Gill and Macmillan, 1983).

– *The Foundation of Dáil Eireann, Parliament and National Building* (Dublin: Gill and Macmillan, 1971).

Faulkner, Pádraig, *As I saw It, Reviewing over 30 years of Fianna Fáil and Irish Politics* (Dublin: Wolfhound, 2005).

Feeney, Tom, *Seán MacEntee, A Political Life* (Dublin: Irish Academic Press, 2009).

Ferriter, Diarmaid, *The Transformation of Ireland, 1900–2000* (London: Profile Books, 2005).

Fisk, Robert, *In Time of War, Ireland, Ulster and the Price of Neutrality, 1939–45* (Dublin: Gill and Macmillan, 1983).

FitzGerald, Garret, *All in a Life, Garret FitzGerald, An Autobiography* (Dublin: Gill and Macmillan, 1991).

Fitzpatrick, David, *Harry Boland's Irish Revolution* (Cork: Cork University Press, 2003).

Foley, Conor, *Legion of the Reargurd: the IRA and the Modern Irish State* (London: Pluto, 1992).

French, F. *Tibet, Tibet: A Personal History of a Lost Land* (London: Harper Collins, 2003).

Garvin, Tom, *Judging Lemass, The Measure of the Man* (Dublin: Royal Irish Academy, 2009).

– *Preventing the Future, Why was Ireland so Poor for so Long?* (Dublin: Gill and MacMillan, 2004).

Geiger, Till, 'Trading with the Enemy: Ireland, the Cold War and East–West Trade, 1945–1955', *Irish Studies in International Affairs*, Vol. 19 (2008).

Gerstenfeld, Manfred (ed.), *European-Israeli Relations: Between Confusion and Change* (Jerusalem: Jerusalem Centre for Public Affairs, 2007),

Girvin, Brian, *The Emergency: Neutral Ireland 1939–45* (London: Macmillan, 2006).

– and Geoffrey Roberts (eds), *Ireland during the Second World War: Politics, Society, Remembrance* (Dublin: Four Courts, 2000).

Goldstein, C. M., *A History of Modern Tibet, Volume 2: The Calm Before the Storm: 1951–1955*, (Berkley: University of California Press, 2007).

Gray, Tony, *The Lost Years: The Emergency in Ireland, 1939–45* (London: Sphere, 1997).

Hanley, Brian, 'Irish Republicans in Inter-War New York', *Irish Journal of American Studies*, *IJASonline*, 1 (June, 2009) at http://www.ijasonline.com/BRIAN-HANLEY.html.

– *The IRA: a Documentary History, 1916–2005* (Dublin: Gill and Macmillan, 2010).

– *The IRA, 1926–1936* (Dublin: Four Courts Press, 2002).

– 'The Volunteer Reserve and the IRA', *The Irish Sword* 83 (Summer, 1998), 93–104.

Horgan, John, *Seán Lemass, The Enigmatic Patriot* (Dublin: Gill and Macmillan, 1999).

Hopkinson, Michael, *Green against Green: the Irish Civil War* (Dublin: Gill and Macmillan, 1988).

Inglis, Brian, *West Briton* (London: Faber and Faber, 1962).

Jackson, Alvin, *Home Rule, An Irish History, 1800–2000* (London: Phoenix, 2003).

James, Alan, *Britain and the Congo Crisis, 1960–63* (London: St Martin's Press, 1996).

Keatinge, Patrick, *A Place Among the Nations, Issues of Irish Foreign Policy* (Dublin: IPA, 1978).

– *The Formation of Irish Foreign Policy* (Dublin: IPA, 1973).

Kelly, Stephen, *Fianna Fáil, Partition and Northern Ireland, 1926–1971* (Dublin: Irish Academic Press, 2013).

Kennedy, Michael, *Division and Consensus, The Politics of Cross-Border Relations in Ireland, 1925–1969* (Dublin: IPA, 2000).

– *Guarding Neutral Ireland: The Coast Watching Service and Military Intelligence, 1939–1945* (Dublin: Four Courts Press, 2008).

– and Art Magennis, *Ireland, the United Nations and Congo* (Dublin: Four Courts Press, 2014).

– and Joseph Morrison Skelly (eds), *Irish Foreign Policy 1916–1966: From Independence to Internationalism* (Dublin: Four Courts Press, 2000).

– and Deirdre McMahon (eds), *Obligations and Responsibilities: Ireland and the United Nations 1955–2005: Essays Marking Fifty Years of Ireland's United Nations Membership* (Dublin: IPA, 2006).

Keogh, Dermot, *Jack Lynch, a Biography* (Dublin: Gill and Macmillan, 2008).
– *Twentieth Century Ireland, Nation and State* (Dublin: Gill and Macmillan, 1994).
– and Gabriel Doherty (eds), *De Valera's Ireland* (Cork: Cork University Press, 2003).
– and Mervyn O'Driscoll (eds), *Ireland in World War Two: Neutrality and Survival* (Cork: Mercier Press, 2004).
Laffan, Michael, *The Partition of Ireland 1911–1925* (Dundalk: Dundalgan Press, 1983).
Lee, J. J., *Ireland 1912–1985, Politics and Society* (Cambridge: Cambridge University Press, 1989).
– (ed.), *Ireland, 1945–70* (Dublin: Gill and MacMillan, 1979).
Lewis, W.M., 'Frank Aiken and the Fourth Northern Division: a personal and provincial experience of the Irish Revolution, 1916–1923', Ph.D Thesis, Queen's University Belfast (QUB), 2011.
Longford and O'Neill – The Earl of Longford and Thomas P. O'Neill, *Eamon de Valera* (London: Hutchinson, 1970).
Lynch, Robert, *The Northern IRA and the Early Years of Partition, 1920–1922* (Dublin: Irish Academic Press, 2006).
Lynn, Brendan, *Holding the Ground: the Nationalist Party in Northern Ireland, 1945–72* (Aldershot: Ashgate, 1997).
Lysaght, O'Connor, R. D., *The Republic of Ireland* (Dublin: Mercier Press, 1970).
MacEoin, Uinseann, *The IRA in the Twilight Years, 1923–1948* (Dublin: Argenta Publications, 1997).
MacEvilly, Michael, *A Splendid Resistance: the Life of IRA Chief of Staff Dr. Andy Cooney* (Dublin: De Burca, 2011).
MacManus, F., (ed.), *The Years of the Great Test 1926:39* (Cork: Mercier Press, 1967).
Maguire, John, *IRA Internments and the Irish Government: Subversives and the State, 1939–1962* (Dublin: Irish Academic Press, 2008).
Martin Mansergh, *The Legacy of History, For Making Peace in Ireland* (Cork: Mercier Press, 2003).
Manning, Maurice, *James Dillon, A Biography* (Dublin, 1999).
McCullagh, D., *A Makeshift Majority: The First Inter-Party Government 1948–51.* (Dublin: Institute of Public Administration, 1998).
McGarry, Fearghal, *Eoin O'Duffy: Self-Made Hero* (Oxford: Oxford University Press, 2007).
McGee, Owen, *The IRB: The Irish Republican Brotherhood from the Land League to Sinn Féin* (Dublin: Four Courts Press, 2005).
McMahon, Paul, *British Spies and Irish Rebels: British Intelligence and Ireland 1916–1945* (Woodbridge: the Boydell Press, 2008).
Miller, Rory, *Ireland and the Palestine Question: 1948–2004* (Dublin: Irish Academic Press, 2005).
Murphy, Gerard, *The Year of Disappearances: Political Killings in Cork, 1920–1921* (Dublin: Gill and MacMillan, 2010).
Murphy, John A., *Irish Times* supplement 'Fifty Years of Fianna Fáil', 19 May 1976.
Moynihan, Maurice, *Currency and Central Banking in Ireland, 1922–60* (Dublin: Gill and Macmillan, 1975).
Nowlan, K. D. & Williams, D. T. (eds), *Ireland in the War Years and After 1939–51* (Dublin: Gill and Macmillan, 1969).
Ó Beacháin, Donnacha, *Destiny of the Soldiers: Fianna Fáil, Irish Republicanism and the IRA, 1926–1973* (Dublin: Gill and Macmillan, 2011).
O'Brien, Conor Cruise, *Herod: Reflections on Political Violence* (London: Hutchinson, 1978).
– *Memoir my Life my Times* (Dublin: Poolbeg Press, 1999).

– *States of Ireland* (London: Viking, 1972).

– *To Katanga and Back: A UN Case History* (London: Hutchinson, 1962).

– *The United Nations: Sacred Drama* (London: Hutchinson, 1968).

O'Brien, Justin, *The Arms Trial* (Dublin: Gill and Macmillan, 2000).

O'Brien, Máire Cruise, *The Same Age as the State* (Dublin: O'Brien Press, 2003).

Ó Broin, Leon, *No Man's Man: A Biographical Memoir of Joseph Brennan, Civil Servant & First Governor of the Central Bank Dublin* (Dublin: Institute of Public Administration, 1982).

O'Carroll, J.P. and Murphy, John A., *De Valera and his Times* (Cork: Cork University Press, 1986).

O'Donnell, Catherine, *Fianna Fáil, Irish Republicanism and the Northern Ireland Troubles, 1968–2005* (Dublin: Irish Academic Press, 2007).

O'Donoghue, David, *The Devil's Deal: The IRA, Nazi Germany and the double Life of Jim O'Donovan* (Dublin: New Island, 2010).

O'Drisceoil, Donal, *Censorship in Ireland, 1939–1945, Neutrality, Politics and Society* (Cork: Cork University Press, 1996).

Ó Gráda, Cormac, *A Rocky Road: The Irish Economy Since the 1920s* (Manchester: Manchester University Press 1997).

O'Halpin, Eunan, 'British Intelligence, the Republican Movement and the IRA's German Links, 1935–45', in McGarry, Feargal (ed.), *Republicanism in Modern Ireland* (Dublin: UCD Press, 2003), 108–131.

– *Defending Ireland: The Irish State and Its Enemies since 1922* (Oxford: Oxford University Press, 2000).

– 'Long fellow, long story: MI5 and de Valera', *Irish Studies in International Affairs* Vol.14 (2003), 185–203.

– *Spying on Ireland: British Intelligence and Irish Neutrality during the Second World War* (Oxford: Oxford University Press, 2008).

O'Malley, Cormac and Dolan, Ann, (eds), *No Surrender Here! The Civil War papers of Ernie O'Malley, 1922–1924* (Dublin: Lilliput Press, 2012).

O'Malley, Ernie, *The Singing Flame* (Cork: Mercier Press, 1978).

O'Malley, Kate, *Ireland, India and Empire, Indo-Irish Radical Connections, 1919–1964* (Manchester: Manchester University Press, 2008).

O'Sullivan, Kevin, *Ireland, Africa and the End of the Empire: Small State Identity in the Cold War, 1955—75* (Manchester: Manchester University Press, 2012).

Patterson, Henry, *Ireland Since 1939, The Persistence of Conflict* (Dublin: Penguin Ireland, 2006).

– *The Politics of Illusion, Republicanism and Socialism in Modern Ireland* (London: Radius Books, 1989).

Phoenix, Eamon, *Northern Nationalism, Nationalists Politics, Partition and the Catholic Minority in NI, 1890–1940* (Ulster Historical Foundation, 1994).

Puirséil, Niamh, *The Irish Labour Party 1922–1973* (Dublin: UCD Press, 2007).

Regan, M. John, *The Irish Counter-Revolution 1921–1936: Treatyite Politics and Settlement in Independent Ireland* (Dublin: Gill and Macmillan, 1999).

Reynold, Raymond James, 'David Gray, the Aiken Mission, and Irish Neutrality, 1940–41', *Diplomatic History*, Vol. 9, No. 1 (winter, 1985), 55–71.

Salmon C. Trevor, *Unneutral Ireland: An Ambivalent and Unique Security Policy* (Oxford: Oxford University Press, 1989).

Sheehy, Michael, *Divided We Stand, A Study of Partition* (London: Faber and Faber, 1955).

Skelly, Morrison, Joseph, *Irish Diplomacy at the United Nations, 1945–1965, National Interests and the International Order* (Dublin: Irish Academic Press, 1997).

Skinner, Liam, *Politicians by Accident* (Dublin: Metropolitan Publishing, 1946).

Staunton, Enda, *The Nationalists of Northern Ireland, 1918–1973* (Dublin: Columba Press, 2001).

Tonra, Ben, *Global Citizen and European Republic, Irish Foreign Policy in Transition* (Manchester: Manchester University Press, 2006).

– *The Europeanisation of National Foreign Policy: Dutch, Danish and Irish Foreign Policy in the European Union* (Aldershot: Ashgate Publishing, 2001).

Townshend, Charles, *The Republic: The Fight for Irish Independence 1918–1923* (London, Allen Lane, 2013).

Verrier, Anthony, *International Peacekeeping. United Nations Forces in a Troubled World* (Harmondsworth,: Penguin, 1981).

Walker, Brian W., *Parliamentary Election Results in Ireland, 1918–92* (Dublin: Royal Irish Academy, 1992).

Walsh, Dick, *The Party, Inside Fianna Fáil* (Dublin: Gill and Macmillan, 1986).

Walsh, John, *Patrick Hillery, The Official Biography* (Dublin: New Island, 2008).

Whelan, Noel, *Fianna Fáil, A Biography of the Party* (Dublin: Gill and Macmillan, 2011).

Wilson, T. *Frontiers of Violence: Conflict and Identity in Ulster and Upper Silesia, 1918–1922* (Oxford: OUP, 2010).

Index